Reform, Recovery, and Growth

A National Bureau
of Economic Research
Project Report

Reform, Recovery, and Growth

Latin America and
the Middle East

Edited by Rudiger Dornbusch and
Sebastian Edwards

The University of Chicago Press

Chicago and London

RUDIGER DORNBUSCH is the Ford International Professor of Economics at the Massachusetts Institute of Technology and a research associate of the National Bureau of Economic Research. SEBASTIAN EDWARDS is chief economist for Latin America and the Caribbean at the World Bank. He is also the Henry Ford II Professor of International Business Economics at the Anderson Graduate School of Management, University of California, Los Angeles, and a research associate of the National Bureau of Economic Research.

The University of Chicago Press, Chicago 60637
The University of Chicago Press, Ltd., London

Library of Congress Cataloging-in-Publication Data

Reform, recovery, and growth : Latin America and the Middle East /
    edited by Rudiger Dornbusch and Sebastian Edwards.
        p.   cm. — (A National Bureau of Economic Research project
    report)
        Includes bibliographical references and index.
        1. Structural adjustment (Economic policy)—Latin America.
    2. Structural adjustment (Economic policy)—Turkey.   3. Structural
    adjustment (Economic policy)—Israel.   4. Economic stabilization—
    Latin America.   5. Economic stabilization—Turkey.   6. Economic
    stabilization—Israel.   7. Latin America—Economic conditions—
    1982– .
    I. Dornbusch, Rudiger.   II. Edwards, Sebastian, 1953– .
    III. Series.
    HC125.R4127   1995   94-27934
    338.956—dc20   CIP

Relation of the Directors to the
Work and Publications of the
National Bureau of Economic Research

1. The object of the National Bureau of Economic Research is to ascertain and to present to the public important economic facts and their interpretation in a scientific and impartial manner. The Board of Directors is charged with the responsibility of ensuring that the work of the National Bureau is carried on in strict conformity with this object.

2. The President of the National Bureau shall submit to the Board of Directors, or to its Executive Committee, for their formal adoption all specific proposals for research to be instituted.

3. No research report shall be published by the National Bureau until the President has sent each member of the Board a notice that a manuscript is recommended for publication and that in the President's opinion it is suitable for publication in accordance with the principles of the National Bureau. Such notification will include an abstract or summary of the manuscript's content and a response form for use by those Directors who desire a copy of the manuscript for review. Each manuscript shall contain a summary drawing attention to the nature and treatment of the problem studied, the character of the data and their utilization in the report, and the main conclusions reached.

4. For each manuscript so submitted, a special committee of the Directors (including Directors Emeriti) shall be appointed by majority agreement of the President and Vice Presidents (or by the Executive Committee in case of inability to decide on the part of the President and Vice Presidents), consisting of three Directors selected as nearly as may be one from each general division of the Board. The names of the special manuscript committee shall be stated to each Director when notice of the proposed publication is submitted to him. It shall be the duty of each member of the special manuscript committee to read the manuscript. If each member of the manuscript committee signifies his approval within thirty days of the transmittal of the manuscript, the report may be published. If at the end of that period any member of the manuscript committee withholds his approval, the President shall then notify each member of the Board, requesting approval or disapproval of publication, and thirty days additional shall be granted for this purpose. The manuscript shall then not be published unless at least a majority of the entire Board who shall have voted on the proposal within the time fixed for the receipt of votes shall have approved.

5. No manuscript may be published, though approved by each member of the special manuscript committee, until forty-five days have elapsed from the transmittal of the report in manuscript form. The interval is allowed for the receipt of any memorandum of dissent or reservation, together with a brief statement of his reasons, that any member may wish to express; and such memorandum of dissent or reservation shall be published with the manuscript if he so desires. Publication does not, however, imply that each member of the Board has read the manuscript, or that either members of the Board in general or the special committee have passed on its validity in every detail.

6. Publications of the National Bureau issued for informational purposes concerning the work of the Bureau and its staff, or issued to inform the public of activities of Bureau staff, and volumes issued as a result of various conferences involving the National Bureau shall contain a specific disclaimer noting that such publication has not passed through the normal review procedures required in this resolution. The Executive Committee of the Board is charged with review of all such publications from time to time to ensure that they do not take on the character of formal research reports of the National Bureau, requiring formal Board approval.

7. Unless otherwise determined by the Board or exempted by the terms of paragraph 6, a copy of this resolution shall be printed in each National Bureau publication.

(Resolution adopted October 25, 1926, as revised through September 30, 1974)

Contents

Preface

The papers collected in this volume are the final product of a research project jointly organized by the National Bureau of Economic Research and the Inter-American Development Bank. Earlier versions were presented at a conference held at the IDB on December 17–18, 1992. This project was conceived as a follow-up to the program on populism undertaken by the NBER and the IDB during 1990, and whose final output was published as *The Macroeconomics of Populism in Latin America* (Chicago: University of Chicago Press, 1991).

We are indebted to the Rockefeller Foundation for research support. The IDB, once again, provided an exciting environment for the conference. We are especially grateful to Nora Rey de Marulanda and Enrique Iglesias for their enthusiasm. We sincerely thank the NBER, whose staff have made this project possible. We are particularly thankful to Kirsten Foss Davis and Deborah J. Kiernan for their assistance and support.

Any opinions expressed in this volume are those of the authors and do not necessarily represent the views of the NBER, the IDB, or any of the sponsoring organizations.

Introduction

Rudiger Dornbusch and Sebastian Edwards

The debt crisis unleashed in 1982 generated serious dislocations in most developing countries. Balance-of-payments deficits soared, and in most cases the foreign debt almost paralyzed investment. Growth came to a halt and inflation increased dramatically. After some hesitation and in some cases a brief flirtation with heterodoxy, adjustment programs based on fiscal austerity, real exchange rate devaluations, trade liberalization, privatization, and deregulation were implemented in a large number of nations.

In many countries considerable progress has been made in the implementation of structural adjustment reforms. The results, however, have been uneven, with some countries successfully moving toward recovery and growth, while others continue to exhibit a timid performance. Chile is, perhaps, the prime example of a successful adjuster: inflation is moving toward one digit, exports have boomed, wages have grown rapidly, and aggregate growth is solid. Bolivia, on the other hand, is a case where growth has continued to be shy even years after the completion of the basic adjustment program. The experience of a large cross section of countries during the last few years suggests that the connection between structural reforms and economic recovery is not automatic. Even though structural reforms appear to be a *necessary* condition for growth, they are not a *sufficient* one.[1]

A key question, then, is why some countries have succeeded in engineering

Rudiger Dornbusch is the Ford International Professor of Economics at the Massachusetts Institute of Technology and a research associate of the National Bureau of Economic Research. Sebastian Edwards is chief economist for Latin America and the Caribbean at the World Bank. He is also the Henry Ford II Professor of International Business Economics at the Anderson Graduate School of Management, University of California, Los Angeles, and a research associate of the National Bureau of Economic Research.

1. See Dornbusch (1991) for a discussion on the distinction between necessary and sufficient conditions for growth.

a recovery, while elsewhere per capita income stagnates a decade after the eruption of the debt crisis. The papers collected in this volume deal with this issue, and concentrate on aspects of the transition from stabilization and adjustment to growth. In particular they address the following questions:

- What are the requirements for a successful stabilization policy that reduces inflation to *acceptable* levels in a reasonable amount of time, and at a reduced cost?
- What is the effect of structural reforms, and especially trade liberalization, deregulation, and privatization, on growth in the short and long runs?
- How do macroeconomic instability and adjustment policies affect income distribution and poverty in the long run, and in the period immediately following a major stabilization effort?
- What is the role of the external environment in the recovery process that follows major structural reforms?
- In what form, if any, does the specific design of the structural adjustment effort—including its speed, scope, and sequencing—affect its results?

We clearly recognize that *macroeconomic populism*—an approach based on the use of overly expansive macroeconomic policies to achieve distributive goals—has failed again and again throughout the world.[2] Policies that rely on large fiscal deficits, price freezes, and real exchange rate overvaluation generate, at best, short-run economic growth. As history has shown repeatedly, in the medium run they result in serious crises, lower real wages, runaway inflation, and chaos. The question, then, is not whether macroeconomic stability and equilibrium should be sought, but *how* to implement stabilization and structural adjustment policies. We are convinced that the specific design of adjustment policies has important effects on growth and income distribution. In addressing these questions the papers collected in this book deal with broad analytical and theoretical issues and review the recent experiences in a number of countries in Latin America (Argentina, Bolivia, Brazil, Chile, Mexico, and Peru), and the Middle East (Israel and Turkey).

Structural Reforms and Growth

Trade liberalization has probably been the central component of most adjustment programs undertaken in the developing world during the 1980s and 1990s. The main objective of these reforms is to reverse the negative consequences of protectionism and, especially, its antiexport bias. Basic static international trade theory suggests that a trade liberalization process will result in a reallocation of resources according to comparative advantage, in a reduction

---

2. See the collection in Dornbusch and Edwards (1991) for a detailed discussion on the macroeconomics of populism, including a series of case studies based on the Latin American experience.

of waste, and in a decline in imported goods prices.[3] Moreover, to the extent that the new trade regime is more transparent—for example, through a relatively uniform import tariff—it is expected that lobbying activities will be greatly reduced, releasing highly skilled work from "unproductive" jobs. According to traditional international trade theory it is expected that, once negative effective rates of protection and overvalued exchange rates are eliminated, exports will not only grow rapidly but will also become more diversified.

From a growth perspective the fundamental objective of trade reforms is to transform international trade into "the engine of growth." In fact, newly developed models of "endogenous" growth have stressed the role of openness.[4] For example, Romer (1989) has developed a model where by taking advantage of larger markets—"the" world market—an open economy can specialize in the production of a relatively large number of intermediate goods and thus grow faster. Other authors have recently concentrated on the relationship among openness, technological progress, and productivity growth. Grossman and Helpman (1991) and Edwards (1992), for example, have argued that openness affects the speed and efficiency with which small countries can absorb technological innovations developed in the industrial world. This idea, based on an insight first proposed by John Stuart Mill, implies that countries with a lower level of trade distortions will experience faster growth in total factor productivity and, with other things given, will grow faster than countries that inhibit international competition.

In recent papers a number of authors have tried to test the general implications of these theories using cross-country data sets.[5] Although different empirical models have yielded different results, the general thrust of this line of research is that indeed countries with less distorted external sectors appear to grow faster. As Dornbusch (1991) has pointed out, openness affects growth not only through one channel, but through a combination of channels, including the introduction of new goods, the adoption of new methods of production, the new organization of industries, the expansion in the number of intermediate goods available, and the conquest of new markets that permit the expansion of exports.

The importance placed by liberalization strategists on the reduction of the antiexport bias has resulted in significant emphasis on the role of exchange rate

3. Of course, this amounts to the important textbook notion that freer trade increases the level of domestic welfare. However, modern approaches go beyond this goal and also consider the acceleration of growth as a goal of trade policy (see Edwards 1992).

4. Traditional neoclassical growth models concentrated on the effect of national economic policies on the *level* of income per capita. The new generation of endogenous growth models have shifted the attention to relationship between different policies and the rate of growth of the economy. See Lucas (1988).

5. See Tybout (1992) for a general survey on empirical models of the relationship between trade orientation and growth of total factor productivity. See also Edwards (1992) and De Gregorio (1992).

policy during a trade reform effort. A number of authors have argued that a large devaluation should constitute the first step in a trade reform process (Bhagwati 1978; Krueger 1978). It has been pointed out that in the presence of quotas and import licenses a (real) exchange rate depreciation will reduce the rents received by importers, shifting relative prices in favor of export-oriented activities and thus reducing the extent of the antiexport bias.[6]

The papers by Sebastian Edwards, Aaron Tornell, Federico Sturzenegger, and Anne Krueger in this volume address some important issues related to trade liberalization, including the timing of reforms, the appropriate speed and sequencing of trade liberalization, and the consequences of these policies on exports expansion and growth. The chapter by Arnold Harberger, on the other hand, deals with the actual design of trade reform and discusses the merits of alternative tariff structures, including uniform tariffs.

Social Conditions, Stabilization, and Adjustment

The impact of stabilization programs on the poor has been a source of important controversies in recent analyses of adjustment and reform in the developing and east European countries. A rapid rate of economic growth has traditionally been considered the main vehicle for reducing inequalities and poverty. In particular, the multilateral financial institutions, and especially the World Bank, have argued that the "right type" of growth, based on comparative advantages, employment creation, and productivity growth, would generate higher wages and better economic conditions for the poor. Increasingly, however, empirical evidence has indicated that, although crucially important, higher growth is not enough. In general, it takes a long time for the fruits of faster growth to spread to the most vulnerable and poorest segments of society. As a result of this, in the late 1980s and early 1990s an increasing number of authors began to argue in favor of a two-pronged approach toward human resources, where faster growth is supplemented with social programs targeted at providing social services to the neediest (World Bank 1992).

For many years it was thought that income distribution only changed slowly through time. This belief was largely based on data from the advanced nations, which suggests that there is significant persistence in distributional data. Most analysts argued that in the absence of major shocks—such as a revolution or war—the distribution of income would only change gradually, as the result of policies aimed at improving education and other social services. New research based on time series data for some Latin American countries suggests, however, that in some of these countries income distribution can exhibit very large changes in relatively short periods of time. For example, the contribution by Eliana Cardoso, Ricardo Paes de Barros, and Andre Urani to this volume shows that the Gini coefficient in Brazil exhibited large cyclical variations be-

---

6. See Krueger (1978, 1981) and Michaely, Choksi, and Papageorgiou (1991).

tween 1980 and 1991. They show that real exchange rate overvaluation has negatively affected the poor, as have increases in the level and variability of inflation. These results are confirmed by the multicountry study by Mauricio Cárdenas and Miguel Urrutia, also in this volume.

There are two fundamental reasons why macroinstability negatively affects poverty. First, in many poor countries real exchange rate overvaluation hurt labor-intensive exports, and thus employment and wages. Second, the poor are significantly more vulnerable to inflationary forces, as they do not have the ability to protect themselves from the direct and indirect consequences of the inflation tax. These findings support the view that programs aimed at reducing macroeconomic imbalances—particularly programs that reduce inflation— will tend to have a positive effect on income distribution. In fact, there is abundant evidence that ending very rapid inflations tends to reduce poverty, as was the case of Bolivia in 1986.

Historical experiences in Latin America with populist policies have dramatically shown the links between macroeconomic disequilibrium and income distribution. Dornbusch and Edwards (1991) argue that, although populist episodes have had specific and unique characteristics in different nations, they tend to have some fundamental common threads. In particular, populist regimes have historically tried to deal with income inequality problems through the use of overly expansive *macroeconomic* policies. These policies, which have relied on deficit financing, generalized controls, and a disregard for basic economic principles, have almost unavoidably resulted in major macroeconomic crises that ended up hurting the poorer segments of society. At the end of every populist experiment, inflation is out of hand, macroeconomic disequilibria are rampant, and real wages are lower than they were at the beginning of these experiences.

Overview of the Volume

The first part of the volume contains two papers that deal with trade policy, foreign direct investment, and privatization. In chapter 1 Edwards argues that in open economies it is important to distinguish between technological innovations and imitations. He develops a simple model where commercial policies affect a small developing country's ability to absorb technological innovations developed in the more advanced nations. According to this model more open economies will experience faster rates of productivity growth than countries that distort their external sectors. His analysis, based on a broad cross-country data set and on evidence from recent Latin reforms, supports this view. However, a comparison between the Chilean and Mexican cases suggests that, in order for productivity increases to be widespread, it is necessary to first implement broad reforms and deregulation programs that affect a wide range of sectors. The analysis also suggests that maintaining a "competitive" real exchange rate is the most important requirement for successful trade liberalization reforms. In chapter 2 Tornell deals with the timing and scope of structural adjustment reforms. He notes that some developing countries recently have embarked on reform programs, including trade liberalization, in response to economic crises. What is particularly interesting in these cases is that groups that have traditionally lobbied for protectionism—and have strongly opposed any liberalization measures—have tended to *support* the reduction of trade barriers. This has been the case, for example, among powerful industrial groups in Mexico. Tornell develops a game-theoretic model to investigate this apparent puzzle. He argues that in difficult times structural adjustment is like musical chairs: when the music stops, one of the players will have no chair and will be out of the game. In hard times, then, rent-seeking groups will support a reform program if they believe that they will maintain (at least) some of their rents.

Part 2 concentrates on some aspects of the political economy of reform, including the distributive consequences of macroeconomic policies. In chapter 3 Cárdenas and Urrutia argue that macroeconomic stability is necessary for sustained social progress. They use cross-section analysis to investigate whether more stable countries have higher rates of growth in social indicators, including infant mortality, life expectancy, birth rates, school enrollment, and income inequality. They examine eleven social indicators in four coffee-producing countries—Côte d'Ivoire, Kenya, Costa Rica, and Colombia—and conclude that higher government budget deficits and lower social indicators go together. The fastest social progress occurs when the macroeconomy is most stable. Chapter 4, by Raúl Labán and Felipe Larraín, deals with the profound transformation undergone by the Chilean economy since the mid-1970s. From very high levels of protection, with pervasive state intervention, Chile has been transformed into an economy integrated to world markets, with a vigorous private sector. Today Chile seems one of the few Latin American countries where the reform program has entered into a consolidation phase. Since 1990, when democratically elected authorities replaced sixteen years of authoritarian rule, the government has reduced inflation and trade barriers and increased social spending, raising taxes to pay for it. The authors show that the transition from stabilization to growth in Chile took a significant amount of time and was not free of partial setbacks, including a major financial crisis in 1982–83. They argue that, in spite of the progress made in structural reforms during the last few years, there are still a number of areas—especially related to the social sectors—that will require great attention. More specifically, Labán and Larraín argue that in order to achieve sustainable rates of growth there will be a need to improve the coverage and quality of education and to increase the level of investment. Moreover, they point out that the implementation of environmentally sound policies and the reduction of poverty appear to be the major policy challenges facing Chile today.

Part 3 deals with specific country experiences in Brazil, Israel, Argentina, and Bolivia. In chapter 5 Cardoso, Paes de Barros, and Urani deal with the relationship among macroeconomic policy, income distribution, and poverty in Brazil. They estimate that income inequality in Brazil—measured as the ratio of the income of the richest 10% to the poorest 10% of the population—has fluctuated significantly in Brazil in the last three decades; it rose from 22 in 1960 to 40 in 1970, 41 in 1980, and 80 in 1989. The authors argue that rising unemployment increases inequality, because low-skilled, poorly paid workers lose their jobs before other workers do. Very high inflation also increases inequality, because the rich have access to assets that are fully indexed, while the poor hold cash and thus pay the "inflation tax." Wage differentials by education level are responsible for almost half of the inequality in labor incomes in Brazil, the authors report. But they conclude that increased macroeconomic instability during the 1980s was the major cause of rising inequality. Chapter 6 deals with the Israeli experience. Gil Bufman and Leonardo Leiderman reexamine Israel's post-1985 disinflation and concentrate on the transition from stabilization to growth. They argue that economic recovery was delayed in Israel because the government neglected policies aimed at increasing public investment in infrastructure. They also argue that the exchange rate policy followed in the post-1985 period affected economic performance. More specifically, they point out that Israel's exchange rate band from 1989 to 1991 lacked credibility, because it maintained a fixed central parity rate while domestic inflation continued to exceed world inflation. The shift to a crawling band in 1992 played an important role in restoring at least part of the policy's credibility and in generating a policy environment conducive to growth.

In chapter 7 Rudiger Dornbusch discusses the recent Argentine efforts to stabilize the economy. He notes that pervasive reforms in Argentina, ranging from deregulation and privatization to trade opening, have raised productivity and helped reduce budget deficits. In less than two years, inflation has been greatly reduced and growth has returned, and with it a sense of great confidence in the future. However, Dornbusch argues that the recent policies have generated a familiar malaise: overvaluation. He notes that a nominal devaluation is likely to be counterproductive, since it would disturb expectations and would introduce significant uncertainty. According to him an adjustment package based on sharp fiscal controls and a reduction of aggregate demand is more likely to succeed. Chapter 8 is devoted to the Bolivian experience with adjustment and structural reform. Sturzenegger analyzes the sources of growth for the Bolivian economy and investigates why, almost eight years after the defeat of hyperinflation, growth is still so meager. His empirical analysis suggests that historically total factor productivity in Bolivia has been closely related to the price of mineral products. He also finds that macroeconomic instability, and especially inflation, has had a significant negative effect on the level of productivity, while political instability has not. During the hyperinflation, the economy worked at about 80% of its potential productivity, and productivity has not grown since 1985. Stabilization's positive impact on productivity barely compensated for the decline in Bolivia's terms of trade, Sturzenegger concludes.

Part 4 is devoted to the tax reform and deregulation. In chapter 9 Harberger focuses on some lessons from a large number of experiences with tax reform in a number of developing countries. He discusses uniformity of tariffs as a way of improving administration and compliance, and describes "radial reductions of distortions" as the most effective way to implement a tariff reform. He also specifies ways to build a system of value-added taxation that is moderately progressive. Finally, he discusses in some detail the relationship between evasion and coverage, shows how better choices concerning coverage can help control evasion, and comments on the relationship between enforcement and evasion. In chapter 10 Arturo Fernández discusses the role of deregulation in Mexico's structural reforms program. He notes that, before privatization took place, the vast network of regulations was strangling production and productivity. Further, certain workers benefited more than others from labor regulations, and abuses were widespread. He describes in great detail the way in which regulations on Mexico's trucking industry generated large inefficiencies and rents. Deregulation gave a boost to the automobile and telephone industries, in particular. Fernandez argues that an often ignored positive side effect of these reforms is that now Mexicans are becoming more mindful of potential side effects of deregulation, such as pollution.

The last part of the volume contains two papers on economic stabilization. In chapter 11 Krueger deals with the 1980 Turkish stabilization program. She argues that the program had two fundamental objectives: moving to a market-oriented economy integrated with the rest of the world, and lowering the rate of inflation from triple digits. Reforms designed to liberalize the economy—including trade and financial reforms—continued throughout the 1980s. Despite the difficult external environment, exports grew at an average annual rate of over 20%, and GDP growth by the latter half of the 1980s exceeded 7% annually. However, failure to control public finances resulted in resumption of rapid monetary expansion and, with it, inflation. By the early 1990s, inflation was accelerating very fast. At this point there are still questions whether the successful microeconomic reforms were sustainable in the presence of these macroeconomic difficulties. Chapter 12, by Miguel Kiguel and Nissan Liviatan, discusses recent stabilization efforts in Argentina, Brazil, and Peru aimed at eliminating hyperinflations. The authors point out that, in contrast to the European hyperinflations of the 1920s, these more recent inflations were not caused by a sudden, large increase in the budget deficit and seigniorage. Instead, they were the final stage of a long process of high and increasing rates of inflation that lasted for around two decades. In addition, the process of restoring price stability in the recent episodes appears to be longer and more costly than Sargent's evaluation of the end of the European hyperinflation suggested.

References

Bhagwati, Jagdish. 1978. *Anatomy and Consequences of Exchange Control Regimes.* Cambridge, MA: National Bureau of Economic Research.

De Gregorio, José. 1992. Economic Growth in Latin America. *Journal of Development Economics* 39 (1): 59–84.

Dornbusch, Rudiger. 1991. Policies to Move from Stabilization to Growth. In *Proceedings of the World Bank Annual Conference on Development Economics.* Washington, DC: World Bank.

Dornbusch, Rudiger, and Sebastian Edwards, eds. 1991. *The Macroeconomics of Populism in Latin America.* Chicago: University of Chicago Press.

Edwards, Sebastian. 1992. Trade Orientation, Distortions, and Growth in Developing Countries. *Journal of Development Economics* 39 (1): 31–58.

Grossman, Gene, and Elhanan Helpman. 1991. *Innovation and Growth in the Global Economy.* Cambridge: MIT Press.

Krueger, Anne. 1978. *Foreign Trade Regimes and Economic Development: Liberalization Attempts and Consequences.* Cambridge, MA: National Bureau of Economic Research.

———, ed. 1981. *Trade and Employment in Developing Countries.* Chicago: University of Chicago Press.

Lucas, Robert. 1988. On the Mechanics of Economic Development. *Journal of Monetary Economics* 22 (1): 3–42.

Michaely, Michael, Armeane Choksi, and Demetris Papageorgiou, eds. 1991. *Liberalizing Foreign Trade.* Oxford: Blackwell.

Mill, John Stuart. 1848. *Principles of Political Economy.* New York: Appleton and Co.

Romer, Paul. 1989. Capital Accumulation in the Theory of Long-Run Growth. In Robert Barro, ed., *Modern Business Cycle Theory.* Cambridge: Harvard University Press.

Tybout, James. 1992. Linking Trade and Productivity: New Research Directions. *World Bank Economic Review* 6 (2): 189–211.

World Bank. 1992. *Poverty and Income Distribution in Latin America: The Story of the 1980s.* Washington, DC: World Bank.

I Trade Policy, Foreign Investment, and Privatization

1   Trade Policy, Exchange Rates, and Growth

Sebastian Edwards

1.1   Introduction

After decades of protectionist policies, most of Latin America began to open up to the rest of the world in the late 1980s. This process, pioneered by Chile, is perhaps the most impressive achievement of the structural adjustment programs of the last decade. It has effectively put an end to more than four decades of generalized import substitution policies aimed at encouraging an industrial sector, that turned out to be largely inefficient.[1]

The process leading to these trade reforms has not been easy. As recently as in the mid-1980s the protectionist view was still dominant in many parts of Latin America. In fact, the debt crisis of 1982 provided a new impetus to the protectionist paradigm. Initially, many analysts interpreted the crisis as a failure of "the world economic order" and argued that the only way for Latin America to avoid the recurrence of this type of shocks was to further isolate itself from the rest of the world, through selective protectionism and government intervention. This sentiment was compounded by the fact that a number of observers considered the experiences of the Southern Cone countries—Argentina, Chile, and Uruguay—with liberalization reforms during the 1970s as

Sebastian Edwards is chief economist for Latin America and the Caribbean at the World Bank. He is also the Henry Ford II Professor of International Business Economics at the Anderson Graduate School of Management, University of California, Los Angeles, and a research associate of the National Bureau of Economic Research.

The author is grateful to discussants at the conference for helpful comments and to participants at a seminar at the Instituto Tecnológico Autónomo de México (ITAM), Mexico City, for helpful discussions. He thanks Fernando Losada for excellent research assistance.

1. Even though the experiences of the individual Latin American countries varied during 1950–80, in the majority of them some variant of inward-looking development was the dominant policy. Since the early 1960s a number of trade liberalization attempts have taken place in the region. Almost every one of them has ended in frustration. In fact, until the late 1970s–1980s very little progress was made in this area.

a failure. This view has been clearly synthesized by Lance Taylor (1991, 119), who has argued that the "trade liberalization strategy is intellectually moribund" and that there are "no great benefits (plus some costs) in following open trade and capital market strategies" (141). From here he goes on to say that "development strategies oriented internally may be a wise choice towards the century's end" (141).

Immediately following the eruption of the debt crisis, it seemed that increased protectionism was indeed the path that Latin American countries had chosen as a possible way out of their problems. Even Chile, the strongest supporter of free trade, tripled its import tariffs.[2] As a result of this, in the mid-1980s Latin America had one of the most distorted external sectors in the world, with extremely high import tariffs and, in some cases, quantitative restrictions that covered every single import item (see table 1.1).

However, by 1987–88 it became increasingly apparent that a permanent solution to the region's economic problems would require a fundamental change in its development strategy. In particular, policymakers began to realize that the long-standing protectionist trade policy was central to the region's problems. The poor performance of the Latin American countries offered a dramatic contrast to the rapidly growing East Asian countries that had aggressively implemented outward-oriented strategies. With the help of the multilateral institutions, a larger and larger number of countries began to reduce their levels of protection during the late 1980s and early 1990s. This trade reform process has been supplemented with broad deregulation and privatization, and is proceeding at an increasingly rapid pace. Tariffs have been drastically slashed, in many cases import licenses and prohibitions have been completely eliminated, and a number of countries are actively trying to sign free trade agreements with the United States.

Latin America's long tradition with protectionist policies molded the region's economic structure in a fundamental way, creating a largely inefficient manufacturing sector.[3] Tariffs and prohibitions also generated a severe anti-export bias that discouraged both growth and diversification of exports.[4] This process took place through two main channels. First, tariffs and other forms of protection increased the cost of imported intermediate materials and capital goods used in the production of exportable goods, reducing their effective rate of protection. Second, and perhaps more important, the maze of protectionist policies resulted in massive real exchange rate "overvaluation" that reduced

2. However, as I argued in Edwards (1988a), in many countries this increase in protectionism was dictated by necessity.

3. There has long been a literature documenting the consequences of protectionism in the Latin American economies. For recent studies, see the Latin American cases covered in the Michaely, Choski, and Papageorgiou (1991) project.

4. In the 1960s some countries decided to implement export promotion schemes based on government support and adjustable exchange rates. To some extent this was partially successful in Brazil. However, as Fishlow (1991) has pointed out, this development did little to reduce Brazil's vulnerability to foreign shocks.

Table 1.1   **Import Protection in the Developing World, 1985 (%)**

	Total Tariff Protection[a]	Non-tariff Barriers Coverage[b]
South America	51	60
Central America	66	100
Caribbean	17	23
North Africa	39	85
Other Africa	36	86
West Asia	5	11
Other Asia	25	21

Source: Erzan et al. (1989).
Note: The data on both tariffs and NTBs reported here are weighted averages.
[a]Includes tariffs and paratariffs.
[b]Measures as a percentage of import lines covered by NTBs.

the degree of competitiveness of exports.[5] Paradoxically, the policies that were supposed to reduce Latin America's dependency on the worldwide business cycle ended up creating a highly vulnerable economic structure, where the sources of foreign exchange were concentrated on a few products intensive in natural resources (Fishlow 1985).

The trade liberalization programs implemented during the last decade have two basic policy objectives. First, these reforms have sought to reduce the anti-export bias of commercial policies. It is expected that, once negative effective rates of protection and overvalued exchange rates are eliminated, exports will not only grow rapidly but will also become more diversified.

The second fundamental objective of trade reforms is to transform international trade into "the engine of growth." The new literature on "endogenous" growth has stressed the role of openness in explaining cross-country growth differentials over the long run.[6] For example, Romer (1989) has argued that more open economies can take advantage of larger markets, increasing their degree of efficiency and their rate of growth. Other authors, including Grossman and Helpman (1991a, 1991b) and Edwards (1992b), have recently argued that openness affects the speed and efficiency with which small countries can absorb technological innovations developed in the industrial world. This idea, based on an insight first proposed by John Stuart Mill, implies that countries

5. Krueger (1978) documents these developments for a large number of countries. Diaz-Alejandro (1975, 1978) argues that real exchange rate overvaluation was one of the most negative economic developments in Argentina. For an analysis of a large number of Latin countries, see Bianchi (1988). For an early discussion on the Chilean case, see Behrman (1976). Since 1967 Colombia pursued a crawling-peg exchange rate policy explicitly aimed at avoiding overvaluation. The overall degree of protection, however, remained high (Garcia-Garcia 1991).

6. Traditional neoclassical growth models concentrated on the effect of national economic policies on the *level* of income per capita. The new generation of endogenous growth models have shifted attention to the relationship between different policies and the rate of growth of the economy. See Lucas (1988).

with a lower level of trade distortions will experience faster total factor productivity growth and thus will grow faster than countries that inhibit international competition.[7]

The purpose of this paper is to explore, from different perspectives, the relationship between trade liberalization and growth. The analysis deals with both long-run and transitional issues. I first concentrate (section 1.2) on the long-run relation between trade regimes and productivity growth. I use a broad fifty-four-country data set to investigate the way in which trade distortions have affected productivity growth in the 1971–82 period. The results obtained support the view that more open economies tend to have faster rates of productivity growth than countries that have distorted international trade. In sections 1.3 and 1.4, I discuss some of the most important problems faced during the transition by countries engaged in trade liberalization programs. While in section 1.3 I focus on general transitional issues at an analytical level, in section 1.4 I deal with the recent Latin American trade reforms. I first document the extent of trade liberalization. Second, I investigate whether, as predicted by some authors, these reforms have been associated with faster productivity growth. In section 1.5 I discuss the recent behavior of real exchange rates in Latin America, emphasizing the way in which they are likely to affect the sustainability of the trade reforms. Finally, in section 1.6 I present a summary of the paper, and I discuss some of the unresolved issues related to Latin American trade policy.

1.2   Openness and Growth: Cross-Country Evidence

1.2.1   A Simple Model

A number of researchers have found that factor accumulation explains between one-half and two-thirds of long-run growth (Fischer 1988). The large unexplained residual in growth accounting exercises has been attributed to "technological progress" or "productivity gains." From a policy perspective a key question is what determines these productivity improvements. In particular, it is important to understand whether national domestic policies—including financial and trade policies—can affect the pace of productivity growth. If this is the case, policymakers will have additional degrees of freedom to pursue those avenues that will enhance long-run performance.

The recent interest on "endogenous" growth models has generated a revival in applied research on the determinants of growth. Some authors have empha-

---

7. In chapter 17 of his *Principles of Political Economy* (1848) Mill said that "a country that produces for a larger market than its own can introduce a more extended division of labor, can make greater use of machinery, and is more likely to make inventions and improvements in the process of production." Arthur Lewis makes a similar proposition in his 1955 classic book on economic growth. See Tybout (1992) for a survey on the early empirical work in this area.

sized the role of openness in determining the pace at which countries can absorb technological progress originating in the rest of the world.[8] Edwards (1992), for example, has recently assumed that there are two sources of total factor productivity (TFP) growth: (1) a purely domestic source stemming from local technological improvements (innovation); and (2) a foreign source related to the absorption of inventions generated in other nations (imitation). More specifically, assume that the country's ability to appropriate world technical innovations (or to imitate) depends on two factors: positively on the degree of openness of the economy and, also positively, on the gap between the country's level of TFP and "the world's" stock of TFP. The first channel is the "openness effect" discussed by Lewis (1955): more open countries have an advantage in absorbing new ideas generated in the rest of the world. In this context "more open" should be interpreted as referring to a less distorted foreign trade sector. The second channel is a "catch-up" effect, common to growth models based on "convergence" notions.

If the aggregate production function is defined as $y_t = Af(K_t, L_t)$, then TFP is $A_t = y/f(\cdot)$, and total productivity growth is $(\dot{A}/A)$. The role of the two sources of technical progress discussed above—innovation and imitation—can be captured by the following simple expression:

$$(1) \qquad \frac{\dot{A}}{A} = \alpha + \left[\beta\omega + \gamma\left(\frac{A^* - A}{A}\right)\right],$$

where α and γ are positive parameters, A^* is the level of world's (appropriable) TFP, and ω is the rate of growth of world's TFP (that is, $A_t^* = A_0^* e^{\omega t}$). β is a parameter between zero and one that measures the country's ability to absorb productivity improvements originating from the rest of the world, and is assumed to be a negative function of the level of trade distortions in the economy (δ).

$$(2) \qquad \beta = \beta(\delta); \beta' < 0,$$

where δ is an index of trade distortions that takes a higher value when international trade, both in imports and/or exports, becomes more distorted.

Parameter α is the basic rate of domestic productivity growth or innovation, which for simplicity is assumed to be exogenous. On the other hand, $(\gamma(A^* - A)/A)$ is the "catch-up" term that says that domestic productivity growth will be faster in nations whose stock of knowledge lags further behind the world's accumulated stock of appropriable knowledge.[9]

In this setting the path through time of domestic TFP will be given by[10]

---

8. Grossman and Helpman (1991a) provide a series of elegant models along these lines.

9. I assume that not all inventions generated in the world can be freely appropriated. In that sense, A^* could be interpreted as the accumulated stock of innovations in the more advanced countries that have spilled over to the rest of the world.

10. This, of course, is the solution to differential equation (1).

(3)
$$A_t = \left[A_0 - \left(\frac{\gamma}{\gamma + \omega(1 - \beta) - \alpha}\right)A_0^*\right]e^{-(\gamma - \alpha - \beta\omega)t}$$
$$+ \left(\frac{\gamma}{\gamma + \omega(1 - \beta) - \alpha}\right)A_0^* e^{\omega t}.$$

It follows from equation (3) that the long-run rate of growth of domestic TFP will depend on whether $(\gamma - \alpha - \beta\omega) \lessgtr 0$. If $(\gamma - \alpha - \beta\omega) > 0$, in the steady-state TFP will grow at the rate of world's productivity ω. This means that the level of domestic TFP (and of GDP) will be a function of the degree of trade intervention, with higher trade distortions resulting in a lower level of real income. A key implication of this result is that countries that engage in trade liberalization programs will be characterized, during the transition between two steady states, by higher rates of productivity growth and thus by faster rates of GDP growth.

A second case appears when $(\gamma - \alpha - \beta\omega) < 0$. Long-run TFP growth $(\dot{A}/A)$ will depend on how large the world's rate of growth of TFP (ω) is relative to the domestic rate of productivity improvement. If $\omega > (\alpha - \delta)/(1 - \beta)$, domestic TFP will grow in the steady state at the world rate ω. If $\omega < (\alpha - \gamma)/(1 - \beta)$, and $(\gamma - \alpha - \beta\omega) < 0$, however, the long-run equilibrium rate of TFP growth will be equal to $(\alpha + \beta\omega - \delta)$[11] and will depend negatively on δ, the country's level of trade distortions. That is, in this case more open countries (those with low δ) will grow faster during steady-state equilibrium. This is because in this case the domestic source of technological inventions is strong enough to drive, even in the steady state, the aggregate rate of technological innovations.[12]

The model developed above suggests that TFP growth will depend on the degree of trade distortions in the economy, and on a catch-up term that measures the gap between the country's and "the world's" level of productivity. I constructed a cross-country data set to test these implications of the model. More specifically, I estimated equations of the following type:

(4)
$$\rho_n = b_0 + b_1\delta_n + b_2g_n + \sum a_i x_{in} + \mu_n,$$

where ρ_n is the average rate of growth of TFP in country n; δ_n is, as before, an index of trade distortions; g_n is the catch-up term; the x_i are other possible determinants of TFP growth; and μ is an error term.

Recently, Barro (1991), Edwards (1992), and Roubini and Sala-i-Martin (1992), among others, have suggested that, in addition to the degree of openness, productivity growth will also be affected by the following factors: (1) human capital, usually measured by schooling attainment; (2) the importance of government in the economy measured by schooling attainment; (2) the im-

---

11. Of course, in this case, $(\alpha + \beta\omega - \delta) > \omega$.

12. In Grossman and Helpman's (1991a) micromodel of technological progress, it is also possible that, under some circumstances, more open economics will exhibit higher long-run growth.

portance of government in the economy measured by the ratio of government expenditure to GDP; (3) the degree of political instability; and (4) the inflation rate.[13] In the estimation of equation (4) reported below, I have incorporated these variables as possible determinants of productivity growth.

1.2.2   Data Definitions and Sources

TFP growth. A problem faced in the estimation of equations of the type of (4) refers to the measurement of TFP growth. In particular, it is difficult to obtain long time series of capital stocks for a large number of countries. In this paper I deal with this problem by constructing three measures of TFP growth from the residuals of country-specific GDP growth regressions. These indices are denoted TFP1, TFP2, and TFP3. The specific methodology used in constructing each of these indices is presented in appendix A.[14]

Trade distortions. Traditionally, studies that have investigated the relationship between trade policy and economic performance have had difficulties measuring the extent of trade distortions. In this paper I tackle this problem by using two variables. In most of the basic estimates I use the ratio of total revenue from taxes on foreign trade—import tariffs plus export taxes—over total trade as a proxy for trade distortions. This variable is measured as an average for 1971–82. Since this variable, denoted TRADETAX, measures the "true" extent of trade distortions with error, in the estimation of the TFP growth equation I also use an instrumental variable technique that tries to correct for measurement error. The second proxy I use is the 1971–82 average trade dependency ratio—imports plus exports as a percentage of GDP. These two indices of trade distortions were constructed with raw data obtained from the International Monetary Fund (IMF).

Catch-up term. Following the recent literature on endogenous growth (Barro 1991; Edwards 1992), I use initial GDP per capita—for year 1971 in this case—as a measure of the gap between a particular country's level of productivity and that of the world. This variable is denoted as GDP71; the data were obtained from Summers and Heston (1988). The coefficient of this variable is expected to be negative, indicating that countries with a lower initial per capita GDP have more "catching up" to do and thus will grow faster.

Human capital. I use two indices. The first one is the attainment of secondary education in 1981. The second one is the increase in secondary education coverage between 1961 and 1981. When alternative indices, such as secondary and higher education, were used, the results obtained were not altered. The

13. See, for example, Barro (1991).
14. Naturally, these indices are at best proxies for TFP growth. formally, we can think that they measure TFP growth with error. To the extent that this measurement error term is additive, it can be collapsed into disturbance μ in equation (4).

data were obtained from the World Bank's *World Development Report*. The coefficient of this variable is expected to be positive.

Role of government. This index is defined as the share of government over GDP and is taken from Summers and Heston (1988). Barro (1991) has argued that this coefficient should be negative, capturing the effect that greater government activities tend, in general, to crowd out the private sector.

Political instability. This variable is defined as the average perceived probability of government change and is obtained from Cukierman, Edwards, and Tabellini (1992).[15] Its coefficient in the TFP growth equations is expected to be negative, reflecting the fact that in politically unstable situations economic agents do not devote their full energies to pursue economic objectives.

Inflation tax. This variable is defined as the average collection of inflation tax for 1971–82 and is computed as πm, where π is the rate of inflation and m is the ratio of M1 to GDP. The coefficient of this variable is expected to be negative, reflecting the effects of higher inflation on uncertainty and economic activity.

1.2.3   Econometric Results

Tables 1.2 and 1.3 summarize the results obtained from the estimation of several versions of equation (4). Table 1.2 contains weighted least squares estimates—with population in 1971 as weight—for all three measures of TFP growth;[16] table 1.3 presents instrumental variables regressions for the TFP1 definition of productivity growth. (When the other two indices were used, the results were not altered significantly.)

As can be seen from these tables, the results are highly satisfactory. Almost every coefficient has the expected sign and is significant at conventional levels. Particularly important for the discussion pursued in this paper is that in every regression the proxies for trade distortions and openness are highly significant. Moreover, the computation of standardized beta coefficients indicate that trade impediments are the second most important explanatory variable of TFP growth, after the catch-up term.[17]

As pointed out above, both the TRADETAX coefficient and the trade dependency ratio are imperfect proxies of trade distortions. In particular, they do not capture directly the role of quantitative restrictions on trade. In order to deal with this measurement error problem I estimated instrumental-variables ver-

15. These authors computed this index from a probit analysis on government change using pooled data for 1948–81.
16. In simple ordinary estimates, least squares heteroskedasticity was detected. Barro (1911) and Edwards (1992), among others, also used weighted least squares in equations of this type.
17. In equation (4.1) the standardized beta coefficient of TRADETAX is -0.75; that of GDP71 is -0.78.

Table 1.2   **Total Factor Productivity Growth Regressions: Cross-Country Results (weighted least squares)**

	Eq. 4.1	Eq. 4.2	Eq. 4.3	Eq. 4.4	Eq. 4.5	Eq. 4.6
Definition of TFP growth[a]	TFP1	TFP1	TFP2	TFP2	TFP3	TFP3
Constant	−0.013	−0.012	−0.018	−0.005	0.074	0.030
	(−1.041)	(−1.326)	(−1.418)	(−0.439)	(6.163)	(1.772)
GDP71	−1.9E−06	−7.3E−07	−1.8E−06	−1.1E−06	−3.7E−06	−1.5E−06
	(−3.433)	(−1.929)	(−2.960)	(−2.451)	(−3.673)	(−2.187)
TRADETAX	−0.076	—	−0.074	—	−0.199	—
	(−3.033)		(−2.620)		(−4.902)	
Trade dependency	—	0.017	—	0.025	—	0.025
		(3.147)		(3.910)		(2.480)
Government	−6.1E−04	−4.2E−04	−6.5E−04	−4.1E−04	−2.0E−03	−2.0E−03
	(−2.429)	(−1.708)	(−2.292)	(−1.433)	(−5.157)	(−4.827)
Education	1.19E−04	1.56E−07	5.90E−05	1.30E−04	—	1.20E−04
	(1.536)	(2.130)	(0.675)	(1.560)		(0.895)
Δ Education	—	—	—	—	1.60E−04	—
					(1.453)	
Political instability	−0.017	−0.017	−0.026	−0.043	−0.014	−0.023
	(−2.117)	(−2.480)	(−2.846)	(−5.253)	(−1.607)	(−1.802)
Inflation tax	—	8.3E−05	—	8.8E−05	—	−2.7E−05
		(0.540)		(0.487)		(−0.921)
R^2	0.400	0.351	0.492	0.487	0.598	0.416
N	54	52	54	52	52	52

Notes: t-statistics in parentheses. N is the number of observations; R^2 is the coefficient of determination. See appendix B for a list of the countries considered in this regression.

[a]For exact explanations on how TFP1, TFP2, and TFP3 were constructed, see appendix A.

sions of some of these equations. In reestimating equation (4) I used the trade penetration ratio of imports to GDP as instruments for TRADETAX.[18] The results obtained are presented in table 1.3. As can be seen, they confirm those discussed previously and provide additional support to the view that, after controlling for other factors, countries with more open and less distorted foreign trade sectors have tended to exhibit a faster rate of growth of TFP, over the *long run,* than those nations with a more distorted external sector. The results presented in tables 1.2 and 1.3, however, provide no information on the transition from a closed economy to one that is more open and integrated to the rest of the world. I turn to those issues in sections 1.3–1.5.

18. The instruments themselves don't have to be measured free of error. Of course, the use of instrumental variables is not the only way of dealing with measurement error. In Edwards (1992) I use reversed regressions to construct intervals for a different proxy of openness in standard growth equations for a group of thirty countries.

Table 1.3   Total Factor Productivity Growth Regressions: Instrumental Variables (dependent variable TFP1)

	Eq. 4.7	Eq. 4.8
Constant	0.036	0.050
	(1.689)	(2.037)
GDP71	−3.4E−06	−3.7E−06
	(−2.766)	(−2.677)
TRADETAX	−0.171	−0.185
	(−2.432)	(−2.314)
Government	−4.9E−04	−5.5E−04
	(−1.708)	(−2.292)
Education	3.00E−05	4.80E−05
	(2.130)	(0.675)
Political instability	−0.029	−0.040
	(−2.333)	(−2.823)
Inflation tax	−8.1E−05	−2.5E−05
	(−0.776)	(−0.939)
R^2	0.248	0.392
N	52	52

Notes: t-statistics in parentheses. N is the number of observations; R^2 is the coefficient of determination. The following instruments were used: a constant, GDP71, government, education, trade dependency, imports/GDP ratio, political instability, and inflation tax. These equations were weighted by population in 1971.

1.3   Policy Issues during a Trade Liberalization Transition

The analysis presented in section 1.2 provides support for the hypothesis that in the *long run* more open economies have experienced faster productivity growth than countries that distort international trade. However, as the former communist countries have recently found out, designing a strategy for moving from a controlled to a liberalized economy is not an easy task.

Two fundamental problems have to be addressed in the transition toward freer trade. First, it is important to determine what is the adequate speed of reform. For a long time analysts argued for gradual liberalization programs (Little, Scitovsky, and Scott 1970; Michaely 1985). According to these authors gradual reforms would give firms time for restructuring their productive processes and thus would result in low dislocation costs in the form of unemployment and bankruptcies. These reduced adjustment costs would, in turn, provide the needed political support for the liberalization program. Recently, however, the gradualist position has been under attack. There is increasing agreement that slower reforms tend to lack credibility, inhibiting firms from actually engaging in serious restructuring. Moreover, the experience of Argentina in the 1970s has shown that a gradual (and preannounced) reform allows those firms negatively affected by it to (successfully) lobby against the reduction in tariffs. According to this line of reasoning, faster reforms are more credible and thus tend to be sustained through time (Stockman 1982).

The thinking on the speed of reform has also been influenced by recent empirical work on the short-run unemployment consequences of trade liberalization. Contrary to traditional conventional wisdom, a study directed by Michaely, Choski, and Papageorgiou (1991) on liberalization episodes in nineteen countries strongly suggests that, even in the short run, the costs of reform can be small. Although contracting industries will release workers, those expanding sectors positively affected by the reform process will tend to create a large number of employment positions. The Michaely, Choski and Papageorgiou study shows that in sustainable and successful reforms the *net* effect—that is, the effect that nets out contracting and expanding sectors—on short-run employment has been negligible. A key question, then, is what determines a successful reform? Most historical studies on the subject have shown that maintaining a "competitive" real exchange rate during the transition is one of the most, if not the most, important determinants of successful trade reforms. A competitive, that is depreciated, real exchange rate encourages exports, and helps maintain external equilibrium at the time the reduction in tariffs has made imports cheaper.

The second problem that has to be addressed when designing a liberalization strategy refers to the sequencing of reform (Edwards 1984). This issue was first addressed in the 1980s in discussions dealing with the Southern Cone experiences, and emphasized the macroeconomic consequences of alternative sequences. It was generally agreed that resolving the fiscal imbalance and attaining some degree of macroeconomic reform should constitute the first stage of a structural reform. On subsequent steps, most agreed that the trade liberalization reform should precede the liberalization of the capital account, and that financial reform should be implemented simultaneously with trade reform.

The behavior of the real exchange rate is at the heart of this policy prescription. The central issue is that liberalizing the capital account would, under most conditions, result in large capital inflows and in an appreciation of the real exchange rate (McKinnon 1982; Edwards 1984; Harberger 1985). The problem with an appreciation of the real exchange rate is that it will send the "wrong" signal to the real sector, frustrating the reallocation of resources called for by the trade reform. The effects of this real exchange rate appreciation will be particularly serious if, as argued by Edwards (1984), the transitional period is characterized by "abnormally" high capital inflows, and the economy is characterized by high adjustment costs. If the opening of the capital account is postponed, however, the real sector will be able to adjust, and the new allocation of resources will be consolidated. According to this view, only at this time should the capital account be liberalized.

More recent discussions on the sequencing of reform have expanded the analysis and have included other markets. An increasing number of authors have argued that reform of the labor market—particularly removal of distortions that discourage labor mobility—should precede trade reform, as well as relaxation of capital controls. It is even possible that liberalization of trade in the presence of highly distorted labor markets will be counterproductive, generating overall welfare losses in the country in question (Edwards 1992b).

As the preceding discussion has suggested, there is little doubt that the behavior of the real exchange rate is a key element during a trade liberalization transition. According to traditional manuals on "how to liberalize," a large devaluation should constitute the first step in a trade reform profess. Bhagwati (1978) and Krueger (1978) have pointed out that in the presence of quotas and import licenses a (real) exchange rate depreciation will reduce the rents received by importers, shifting relative prices in favor of export-oriented activities and thus reducing the extent of the antiexport bias.[19]

Maintaining a depreciated and competitive real exchange rate during a trade liberalization process is also important in order to avoid an explosion in imports growth and a balance-of-payments crisis. Under most circumstances a reduction in the extent of protection will tend to generate a rapid and immediate surge in imports. On the other hand, the expansion of exports usually takes some time. Consequently, there is a danger that a trade liberalization reform will generate a large trade balance disequilibrium in the short run. This will not happen, however, if there is a depreciated real exchange rate that encourages exports and helps maintain imports in check. However, many countries have historically failed to sustain a depreciated real exchange rate during the transition. This failure has mainly been the result of expansionary macroeconomic policies, and has resulted in speculation, international reserves losses, and, in many cases, the reversal of the reform effort. In the conclusions to the massive World Bank project on trade reform, Michaely, Choski, and Papageorgiou (1991) succinctly summarize the key role of the real exchange rate in determining the success of liberalization programs: "The long term performance of the real exchange rate clearly differentiates 'liberalizers' from 'nonliberalizers'" (119). Edwards (1989) used data on thirty-nine exchange rate crises and found that in almost every case real exchange rate overvaluation gave rise to drastic increases in the degree of protectionism.

1.4   Recent Trade Liberalization Reforms in Latin America

During the last few years trade liberalization reforms have swept through Latin America; every country in the region has today a significantly more open trade sector than in the early and mid-1980s. The pioneer in the liberalization process was Chile, which between 1975 and 1979 unilaterally eliminated quantitative restrictions and reduced import tariffs to a uniform level of 10%. After a brief interlude with higher tariffs (at the uniform level of 30%) Chile currently has a uniform tariff of 11% and no licenses or other forms of quantitative controls. Uruguay implemented a reform in 1978 and, after a brief reversal, pushed forward once again in 1986. Bolivia and Mexico embarked on their

---

19. See Krueger (1978, 1981) and Michaely, Choski, and Papageorgiou (1991).

reforms in 1985–86, followed by a series of countries in the late 1980s. At the current time a number of countries, including Brazil, are proceeding steadily with scheduled rounds of tariff reduction and the dismantling of quantitative restrictions. However, it is still unclear whether all these reforms will be sustained, becoming a permanent feature of the Latin economies, or whether some of them will be reversed. Developments in Argentina in October 1992 indeed suggest that in some countries higher tariffs may be implemented, once again, in the near future.

The Latin American trade reforms have been characterized by four basic elements: (1) the reduction of the coverage of nontariff barriers (NTBs), including quotas and prohibitions; (2) the reduction of the average level of import tariffs; (3) the reduction of the degree of dispersion of the tariff structure; and (4) the reduction or elimination of export taxes. In this section I document the extent of the recent liberalization programs, and I provide a preliminary evaluation of the effects of these reforms on productivity growth and exports expansion.

1.4.1   The Policies

Nontariff Barriers

A fundamental component of the trade reform programs has been the elimination, or at least the severe reduction, of NTBs coverage. During the early and mid-1980s in some countries, such as Colombia and Peru, more than 50% of import positions were subject to licenses or outright prohibitions. In Mexico NTBs coverage reached almost 100% of import categories in 1984, as was the case in most of Central America in 1984 (table 1.1).

Table 1.4 contains data on protectionism in 1985–87 and 1991–92, and shows that in almost every country the coverage of NTBs has been dramatically reduced.[20] In a number of cases NTBs have been fully eliminated. The process through which NTBs have been eased has varied from country to country. In some cases, such as Honduras, they were initially replaced by (quasi) equivalent import tariffs and then slowly phased out. In other countries, like Chile, NTBs were rapidly eliminated without a compensating hike in tariffs.

As table 1.4 shows, in spite of the progress experienced in the last few years, significant NTBs coverage remains in a number of countries. In most cases these NTBs correspond to agricultural products. For example, in Mexico approximately 60% of the agriculture's sector tariff positions were subject to im-

---

20. These are *unweighted* averages and thus are not comparable to those presented in table 1.1. There has been a long discussion in applied international trade theory on whether tariffs and NTBs should be measured as weighted or unweighted averages. Both views have some merits and some limitations. An obvious problem of the weighted average approach (where the weights are the import shares) is that more restrictive distortions will tend to have a very small weight. In the extreme case, prohibitive tariffs that effectively ban the importation of a particular item will have a zero weight! Corden (1969) provides an early and still highly relevant discussion on these issues.

Table 1.4   The Opening of Latin America: Selected Countries

Country	Tariff Protection (tariffs plus paratariffs, unweighted averages)		Coverage of Nontariff Barriers (unweighted averages)		Range of Import Tariffs					
					1980s			Current		
	1985	1991–92	1985–87	1991–92	Year	Min. (%)	Max. (%)	Year	Min. (%)	Max. (%)
Argentina	28.0	15.0	31.9	8.0	1987	0.0	55.0	1991	0.0	22.0
Bolivia	20.0	8.0	25.0	0.0	1985	0.0	20.0	1991	5.0	10.0
Brazil	80.0	21.1	35.3	10.0	1987	0.0	105.0	1992	0.0	65.0
Chile	36.0	11.0	10.1	0.0	1987	0.0	20.0	1992	11.0	11.0
Colombia	83.0	6.7	73.2	1.0	1986	0.0	200.0	1991	0.0	15.0
Costa Rica	92.0	16.0	0.8	0.0	1986	1.0	100.0	1992	5.0	20.0
Ecuador	50.0	18.0	59.3	n.a.	1986	0.0	290.0	1991	2.0	40.0
Guatemala	50.0	19.0	7.4	6.0	1986	1.0	100.0	1992	5.0	20.0
Mexico	34.0	4.0	12.7	20.0	1985	0.0	100.0	1992	0.0	20.0
Nicaragua	54.0	n.a.	27.8	n.a.	1986	1.0	100.0	1990	0.0	10.0
Paraguay	71.7	16.0	9.9	0.0	1984	0.0	44.0	1991	3.0	86.0
Peru	64.0	15.0	53.4	0.0	1987	0.0	120.0	1992	5.0	15.0
Uruguay	32.0	12.0	14.1	0.0	1986	10.0	45.0	1992	10.0	30.0
Venezuela	30.0	17.0	44.1	5.0	1987	0.0	135.0	1991	0.0	50.0

Source: World Bank, International Economics Department database; UNCTAD (1987); Erzan et al. (1989).

port licenses in mid-1992. In fact, an important feature of the region's liberalization programs is that they have proceeded much more slowly in agriculture than in industry. This has largely been the result of the authorities' desire to isolate agriculture from fluctuations in world prices and of unfair trade practices by foreign countries.[21] However, as a recent study by Valdes has shown (1992), this approach based on NTBs entails serious efficiency costs. Slowly, however, more and more countries are addressing these concerns by replacing these quantitative restrictions by variable levies (see Valdes 1992).

Tariff Dispersion

The import substitution development strategy pursued for decades in Latin America created highly dispersed protective structures. According to the *World Development Report* (1987), Brazil, Chile, and Colombia had some of the broadest ranges of effective rates of protection in the world during the 1960s. Also, Heitger (1987) shows that during the 1960s Chile had the highest rate of tariff dispersion in the world—with a standard deviation of 634%—closely followed by Colombia and Uruguay. Cardoso and Helwege (1992) have pointed out that highly dispersed protective structures generate high welfare costs, by increasing uncertainty and negatively affecting the investment process. These highly dispersed tariffs and NTBs were the result of decades of lobbying by different sectors to obtain preferential treatment. As the relative power of the different lobbies changed, so did their tariff concessions and the protective landscape.

An important goal of the Latin trade reforms has been the reduction of the degree of dispersion of import tariffs. Table 1.4 contains data on the tariff range for a group of countries for two points in time—mid-1980s (1985–87) and 1991–92—and clearly documents the fact that the reforms have indeed reduced the degree of tariff dispersion.

In many cases reducing tariff dispersion has meant *increasing* tariffs on goods that were originally exempted from import duties. In fact, table 1.4 shows that in many countries the minimum tariff was 0% in the mid-1980s. Generally, zero tariffs have been applied to intermediate inputs used in the manufacturing process.[22] From a political economy perspective the process of raising some tariffs, while maintaining a proliberalization rhetoric, has not al-

21. The issue of protecting local producers from dumping is important in the design of the new liberalized trade regimes. The crucial problem is to enact legislation that is able to distinguish true cases of unfair trade practices from simple cases of increased foreign competition stemming from more efficient productive processes. At this time the approval of a dynamic and flexible antidumping legislation should be high in the region's agenda for legal and institutional reform.

22. This system with very low (or zero) tariffs on intermediate inputs and high tariffs on final goods generated very high rates of effective protection or protection to domestic value added. In recent years a number of authors have argued that the use of effective protection is misleading. The reason for this is that effective rates of protection (ERPs) are unable to provide much information on the general equilibrium consequences of tariff changes (Dixit 1986). In spite of this, ERP measures are still useful, since they provide an indication on the degree of "inefficiency" a country is willing to accept for a particular sector.

ways been easy. Those sectors that had traditionally benefited from the exemptions suddenly saw their privileged situation come to an end and tried to oppose them strongly.

An important question addressed by policymakers throughout the region is, by how much should tariff dispersion be reduced? Should the reforms implement a *uniform* tariff, or is some (small) degree of dispersion desirable? From a strict welfare perspective uniform tariffs are only advisable under very special cases. However, they have a political economy appeal. More specifically, a uniform tariff system is very transparent, making it difficult for the authorities to grant special treatments to particular firms or sectors (Harberger 1990).

Average Tariffs

Reducing the average degree of protections is, perhaps, the fundamental policy goal of trade liberalization reforms. Traditional policy manuals on the subject suggest that once the exchange rate has been devalued and quantitative restrictions have been reduced or eliminated, tariffs should be slashed in a way such that both their range and average is reduced.[23] Table 1.4 contains data on average total tariffs (tariffs plus paratariffs) in 1985 and 1991–92. As can be seen, the extent of tariff reduction has been significant in almost every country. Even those nations that have acted somewhat cautiously in the reform front, such as Brazil and Ecuador, have experienced important cuts in import tariffs, allowing a more competitive environment and reducing the degree of anti-export bias of the trade regime.

Countries that have embarked on trade liberalization in recent years have moved much faster than those nations that decided to open up earlier. There has been a clear change in what is perceived to be our *abrupt* and *rapid* removal of imports impediments. What only fifteen years ago were seen as brutally fast reforms are now looked at as mild and gradual liberalizations. When Chile initiated the trade reform in 1975, most analysts thought that the announced tariff reduction from an average of 52% to 10% in four and a half years was an extremely aggressive move that would cause major dislocations, including large increases in unemployment. The view on the speed of reform has become very different in the early 1990s, when an increasing number of countries have been opening up their external sectors very rapidly. For instance, Colombia slashed (total) import tariffs by 65% *in one year,* reducing them from 34% in 1990 to 12% in 1991. This fast approach to liberalization has also been followed by Argentina and Nicaragua, who eliminated quantitative restrictions in one bold move and slashed import tariffs from an average of 110% in 1990 to 15% in March of 1992. As suggested previously, the speed of trade reforms has been directly related to the belief that faster reforms are more credible and thus more likely to be sustained through time.

23. However, "tariffs" is sometimes a misleading term, since many countries have traditionally relied on both import duties (that is, tariffs proper) and import duty surcharges, or paratariffs.

Exchange Rate Policy

In the vast majority of the countries the first step in the trade reform process was the implementation of large (nominal) devaluations. In many cases this measure represented a unification of the exchange rate market. Most countries implemented large exchange rate adjustments as early as 1982 in order to face the urgencies of the adjustment process. The purpose of these policies was to generate *real* exchange rate devaluations, as a way to reduce the degree of antiexport bias of incentives systems.

Many countries adopted crawling-peg regimes to protect the real exchange rate from the effects of inflation. Although these systems helped avoid the erosion of competitiveness, they also added fuel to the inflationary process. They introduced a certain degree of inflationary inertia, and have contributed in many countries to the slow reduction of the rate of inflation. More recently, a number of countries have begun to use the exchange rate as an anchor in order to bring down inflation. This has resulted in the slowing down of the rate of crawl below inflation differentials or, in some cases, in the fixing of the exchange rate, as in Argentina.

Table 1.5 contains data on real exchange rates for a group of Latin American countries for 1970, 1980, 1987, and 1991. As is customary in Latin America, an increase in the index represents a real exchange rate *depreciation* and thus an improvement in the degree of competitiveness. As can be seen between 1980 and 1987 almost every country in the sample experienced very large real depreciations. In many cases, however, these have been partially reversed in the last few years. This has been the consequence of a combination of factors, including the inflow of large volumes of foreign capital into these countries since 1990, and the use of the exchange rate as the cornerstone of the disinflation policies. This issue is addressed in greater detail in section 1.5.

Table 1.5	Real Exchange Rates in Selected Latin American Countries (1985 = 100)			
Country	1970	1980	1987	1991
Argentina	78.7	35.8	80.7	44.0
Bolivia	98.3	88.1	107.9	112.1
Brazil	51.9	70.7	78.0	51.4
Chile	29.4	55.3	94.8	83.0
Colombia	86.1	79.2	115.9	126.3
Costa Rica	58.4	65.8	94.9	97.2
Ecuador	118.6	105.6	153.3	173.7
Mexico	86.1	83.3	123.9	77.0
Paraguay	104.6	74.4	111.4	114.3
Peru	59.3	77.1	46.1	23.1
Uruguay	73.0	49.7	77.2	62.0
Venezuela	80.3	84.2	134.8	132.8

Source: International Financial Statistics, International Monetary Fund.

1.4.2   Adjustment and Productivity

The relaxation of trade impediments has had a fundamental impact on the region's economies. Suddenly, Latin America's industry, which to a large extent had developed and grown behind protective walls, was forced to compete. Many firms have not been able to survive this shock and have become bankrupt. Others, however, have faced the challenge of lower protection by embarking on major restructuring and by increasing their level of productivity.

The ability (and willingness) of firms to implement significant adjustment depends on two main factors: the degree of credibility of the reform, and the level of distortions in the labor market. If entrepreneurs believe that the reform will not persist through time, there will be no incentives to incur the costs of adjusting the product mix and of increasing the degree of productive efficiency. In fact, if the reform is perceived as temporary, the optimal behavior is not to adjust; instead it is profitable to speculate through the accumulation of imported durable goods. This was, as Rodriguez (1982) has documented, the case in Argentina during the failed Martinez de Hoz reforms.[24]

Labor market conditions affect the adjustment process in several ways. First, in order to survive, firms facing stiffer foreign competition have to increase labor productivity, which in many cases means reducing the number of workers. This reduction in employment will tend to be offset by new hires in expanding firms in the sectors with comparative advantage. Many times, however, existing labor market regulations are extremely cumbersome, inhibiting the adjustment process and forcing out of business firms that are structurally viable in the long run. Additionally, labor market distortions negatively affect the investment process, including direct foreign investment (see Cox-Edwards 1992).

In their studies on the interaction between labor markets and structural reforms, Krueger (1980) and Michaely, Choski, and Papageorgiou (1991) found that most successful trade reforms have indeed resulted in major increases in labor productivity. This has been the case in some of the early Latin American reforms for which there are data. For example, according to Edwards and Cox-Edwards (1991) labor productivity in the Chilean manufacturing sector increased at an average annual rate of 13.4% between 1978 and 1981. On the other hand, the available evidence suggests that the increases in labor productivity in the Mexican manufacturing sector in the postreform period have been moderate. According to World Bank (1992) data, labor productivity in Mexico barely increased between 1988 and 1991—the index went from 92.7 to 105.1. In a recent study Ibarra (1992) has calculated that labor productivity in the Mexican manufacturing sector—excluding the *maquiladora* sector—has increased at an average rate of 2.3% per annum.

---

24. See Corbo, Condon, and de Melo (1985) for a detailed microeconomic account of the process of adjustment in a large group of Chilean manufacturing firms.

As discussed in section 1.2, recent models of growth have suggested that countries that are more open to the rest of the world will exhibit a faster rate of technological improvement. From an empirical point of view this means that countries that open up their external sectors and engage in trade liberalization reforms, will experience an *increase* in TFP growth relative to the prereform period. Table 1.6 contains data on the change in TFP growth in the period following the implementation of trade liberalization reform in six Latin countries.[25] As can be seen, Chile and Costa Rica, two of the earlier reformers, experienced very large increases in TFP growth in the postreform period. The results for Chile coincide with those obtained by Edwards (1985), who found that in the late 1970s, after the trade reforms had been completed, TFP growth was approximately three times higher than the historical average.[26] Although the outcome has been less spectacular, Argentina and Uruguay still exhibit substantial improvements in productivity growth in the period following the opening up. Bolivia, on the other hand, presents a flat profile of TFP growth. Sturzenegger (1992) argues that the very slow improvement in Bolivian productivity growth has been, to a large extent, the result of negative terms of trade shocks and, in particular of the collapse of the tin market.

Perhaps the most interesting and puzzling result in table 1.6 is the slight decline in aggregate TFP growth in Mexico after the reforms. Martin (1992) shows that this finding is robust to alternative methods of measuring TFP growth, including different procedures for correcting for capacity utilization. Also, Harberger (1992) finds a slowing down of TFP growth in Mexico in 1986–90 relative to 1975–82. However, the aggregate nature of the TFP growth data in table 1.6 tends to obscure the actual sectoral response to the trade reform. According to new theories on endogenous growth, faster productivity will be observed in those sectors where protectionism has been *reduced,* and not in those still subject to trade barriers or other forms of regulations.

A distinctive characteristic of the Mexican reform is that, contrary to the Chilean case, it has been uneven. In particular, while most of the manufacturing sector—with the exception of automobiles—has experienced a significant reduction in protection, agriculture continues to be subject to relatively high tariffs and substantial NTBs. Moreover, until very recently the Mexican land tenure system was subject to substantial distortions that, among other things,

---

25. The original TFP growth data comes from Martin's (1992) study on sources of growth in Latin America. The countries in table 1.6 are those that initiated the reform before 1988. In order to compute series on TFP growth, Martin (1992) analyzed the contributions of capital and labor and explicitly incorporated the role of changes in the degree of capital utilization. The countries considered in this study are Argentina, Bolivia, Chile, Colombia, Costa Rica, Dominican Republic, El Salvador, Guatemala, Honduras, Mexico, Nicaragua, Panama, Peru, Uruguay, and Venezuela. Harberger (1992) presents data on TFP growth before and after a series of historical trade reform episodes. He finds that in the majority of the cases productivity growth increased after the liberalization process.

26. It may be argued, however, that the major increase in TFP growth in Chile has been the result of the *complete* structural reform package implemented in that country.

Table 1.6   Changes in Total Factor Productivity Growth

Argentina	1.91	Costa Rica	3.25
Bolivia	0.11	Mexico	−0.32
Chile	4.96	Uruguay	2.02

Source: Martin (1992).

Note: For all countries but Chile, computed as the difference of TFP growth for 1987–91 and 1978–82. For Chile the prereform period is 1972–78.

severely restricted the market for land—the *ejido* system. Additionally, during much of the post–debt crisis period large fragments of services sector—including telecommunications and financial services—were under direct government control and subject to distortions.

Table 1.7 contains data on TFP growth in Mexico's manufacturing sector for 1940–89.[27] Interestingly enough, these figures indicate that in the post–trade reform period the rate of productivity growth in the Mexican manufacturing sector has exceeded every subperiod since 1940 for which there are data. This provides some evidence in favor of the view that, once the sectors actually subject to increased competition are considered, Mexican productivity growth has indeed improved after the trade reform. It should be noted, however, that recent TFP growth in manufacturing in Mexico (see table 1.8 for disaggregated data) has not been as large as in Chile's postreform period, where some sectors experienced growth in TFP of the order of 15% in 1978–82 (Fuentes 1992). There are a number of possible explanations for this marked difference in behavior, including the uncertainties about North American Free Trade Agreement approval, which resulted in the postponement of investment in some of the key manufacturing sectors subject to increased foreign exposure.

By and large, however, the data analyzed in this subsection provides broad support to the position that TFP growth has tended to increase in the period following major trade reforms in Latin America.

1.4.3   Trade Reforms and Exports

An important goal of the reforms has been to reduce the traditional degree of antiexport bias of Latin American trade regimes, and to generate a surge in exports. This reduction of the bias is expected to take place through three channels: a more competitive—that is more devalued—real exchange rate; a reduction in the cost of imported capital goods and intermediate inputs used in the production of exportable goods; and a direct shift in relative prices in favor of exports.

The volume of international trade in Latin America, and in particular of

27. Since these figures come from two different sources, they may not be fully comparable and thus should be interpreted with care.

Table 1.7   **Total Factor Productivity Growth in Manufacturing in Mexico, 1940–90 (%)**

1940–50	0.46
1950–60	0.53
1960–70	3.00
1970–80	N.A.
1985–89	3.40

Sources: The data for 1940–80 are from Elias (1992). The figure for 1985–89 is from Ibarra (1992).

Table 1.8   **Disaggregated Productivity Growth, in Mexico's Manufacturing Sector, 1985–90 (%)**

Division	Labor Productivity	Total Factor Productivity
Food, beverages, and tobacco	1.7	3.4
Textiles and apparel	0.7	0.4
Wood products	0.2	3.4
Paper and printing	2.3	4.8
Chemicals, rubber, and plastics	2.3	2.3
Nonmetallic products	1.1	3.5
Metal products	7.5	3.5
Machinery	4.4	4.7
Other manufacturing	−4.8	N.A.
Total manufacturing	2.3	3.4

Source: Ibarra (1992).

exports, increased significantly after the reforms were initiated.[28] For example, while for the region as a whole the *volume* of exports grew at an annual rate of only 2.0% between 1970 and 1980, it grew at a rate of 5.5% between 1980 and 1985, and at a rate of 6.7% between 1986 and 1990.[29] Although, strictly speaking, it is not possible to fully attribute this export surge to the opening-up reforms, there is significant country-specific evidence suggesting that a more open economy, and in particular a more depreciated real exchange rate, has positively affected exports growth.[30] Some countries, especially Costa Rica, have accompanied the opening-up process with the implementation of a bat-

28. Trade liberalization aims at increasing a country's total volume of trade. Under textbook conditions it is expected that at the end of the reform trade will be balanced. However, there are a number of circumstances, including the need to pay the country's foreign debt, under which trade will not grow in a balanced way after a reform. This has been the case in the majority of the Latin American countries.

29. The real *value* of exports, however, has evolved at a somewhat slower pace. The reason for this is that terms of trade have experienced, in every subgroup of countries, a significant deterioration during 1980–91 (see CEPAL 1991). These data are from CEPAL (1991).

30. See, for example, Nogues and Gulati (1992).

tery of export promotion schemes, including tax credits—through the Certificado de Abono Tributario—duty-free imports, and income tax exemptions. However, some authors, including Nogues and Gulati (1992), have argued that these systems have not been an effective way of encouraging exports.

Table 1.9 presents detailed country-level data on the rate of growth of the total value of exports (in constant dollars) for three periods. Table 1.10, on the other hand, contains information on the evolution of exports volume throughout the period. A number of facts emerge from these tables. First, while there has been a rapid growth in exports for the region as a whole, there are nontrivial variations across countries; in some cases there has even been a decline in the real value of exports—this is the case, for example, of Peru. Second, exports performance during two of the subperiods (1982–87 and 1987–91) has not been homogeneous. In the majority of the countries exports performed significantly better during 1987–91, than in the previous five years, reflecting, among other things, the fact that it takes some time for exports to actually respond to greater incentives.

An interesting fact that emerges from these tables is that in the country that has lagged behind in terms of trade reform—Ecuador—the performance of exports volume has been in recent years below the 1970–80 historical average. On the other hand, in two of the early reformers—Bolivia and Chile—exports had a very strong behavior in the 1987–91 subperiod.

The case of Chile is particularly interesting. Since most of its liberalization effort was undertaken prior to 1980, there are enough data points to provide a

Table 1.9   **Value of Exports of Goods and Nonfactor Services: Annual Growth Rates (%)**

Country	1972–80	1982–87	1987–91
Argentina	7.1	2.6	10.3
Bolivia	−1.8	0.6	11.4
Brazil	8.8	9.7	3.4
Chile	15.2	6.5	10.5
Colombia	4.9	10.2	6.6
Costa Rica	4.3	3.8[a]	9.1
Ecuador	6.7	3.3	9.2
Mexico	7.9	6.0	5.1
Paraguay	6.7	4.8	20.2
Peru	2.6	−3.7	0.9
Uruguay	10.0	4.2	7.1
Venezuela	−7.3	3.6	5.6

Sources: World Bank, International Economics Department database; ECLAC, *Statistical Yearbook for Latin America,* several issues.

Note: Based on constant 1990 prices (U.S. dollars).

[a]Changes over the period 1981–87.

Table 1.10   Volume of Exports: Annual Growth Rates (%)

Country	1972–80	1982–87	1987–91
Argentina	2.1	0.8	15.2
Bolivia	−1.7	−5.2	16.5
Brazil	8.2	8.0	2.4
Chile	7.4	7.6	7.5
Colombia	3.6	14.8	6.3
Costa Rica	3.8	6.2[a]	8.6
Ecuador	14.6	6.8	7.6
Mexico	10.2	6.1	5.2
Paraguay	7.3	9.2	27.1
Peru	2.3	−4.0	1.3
Uruguay	5.4	−0.5	8.1
Venezuela	−5.8	2.1	8.3

Sources: World Bank. International Economics Department database; ECLAC, *Statistical Yearbook for Latin America,* several issues.
[a]Changes over the period 1981–87.

more detailed evaluation of export response to the new regime. Between 1975 and 1980—when tariffs were reduced to a uniform 10% and NTBs were completely eliminated—the behavior of Chilean exports was spectacular, growing (in volume terms) at an average of 12% per year—many times higher than the historical average of 1960–70 of only 2.6% per annum. What is particularly impressive is that most of the exports surge has taken place in the nontraditional sector, including manufacturing, agriculture, and fishing products (CEPAL 1991).

Among the early reformers, Mexico exhibits a rather slower rate of growth of total exports in the postreform period than during 1970–80. This, however, is largely an illusion stemming from the fact that during the 1970s Mexico's oil production increased substantially—at a rate exceeding 18% per year. When nontraditional exports are considered, the postreform performance is remarkable, with an annual average rate of growth for 1985–91 exceeding 25%.[31]

A stated objective of trade reforms has been to increase the degree of diversification of exports. Tables 1.11 and 1.12 contain data on the share of nontraditional exports and manufacturing exports for a large number of countries, and show that in the period following the trade reforms their importance has increased steadily. Also, in the majority of the countries the share of the ten most important export goods in total exports has declined significantly in the last few years (CEPAL 1991).

A critical question is whether the rapid growth and diversification of exports in Latin America will be sustained, or whether it will be a temporary phenome-

31. A large percentage of this growth, however, has been in the *maquiladora,* or in-bond sector.

Table 1.11   **Composition of Exports of Goods: Nontraditional Exports/Total Exports**

Country	1980	1982	1985	1987	1990
Argentina	0.27	0.31	0.28	0.31	0.39
Bolivia	0.15	0.09	0.05	0.19	0.47
Brazil	0.57	0.59	0.66	0.69	0.70
Chile	0.38	0.22	0.35	0.39	N.A.
Colombia	0.41	0.42	0.41	0.55	0.64
Costa Rica	0.36	0.38	0.37	0.42	0.54
Ecuador	0.24	0.09	0.12	0.14	0.10
Mexico	0.13	0.20	0.18	0.38	0.43
Paraguay	0.58	0.71	0.82	0.68	0.65
Peru	0.21	0.23	0.24	0.27	0.29
Uruguay	0.61	0.58	0.66	0.67	0.63
Venezuela	0.04	0.07	0.09	0.13	0.19

Source: ECLAC, *Economic Survey of Latin America,* several issues.

Table 1.12   **Composition of Exports of Goods: Exports of Manufactures/Total Exports**

Country	1970	1980	1982	1985	1987	1990
Argentina	0.14	0.23	0.24	0.21	0.31	0.29
Bolivia	0.03	0.02	0.03	0.01	0.03	0.05
Brazil	0.15	0.37	0.38	0.44	0.50	0.52
Chile	0.04	0.09	0.07	0.11	0.09	0.10
Colombia	0.11	0.20	0.24	0.17	0.19	0.25
Costa Rica	0.19	0.28	0.25	0.22	0.24	N.A.
Ecuador	0.02	0.03	0.03	0.01	0.02	0.02
Mexico	0.33	0.11	0.10	0.21	0.38	0.43
Paraguay	0.08	0.04	0.09	0.06	0.10	0.10
Peru	0.01	0.17	0.16	0.13	0.17	N.A.
Uruguay	0.15	0.38	0.32	0.35	0.55	0.50
Venezuela	0.01	0.02	0.02	0.10	0.06	0.15

Source: ECLAC, *Statistical Yearbook for Latin America,* several issues.

non. To a large extent this will depend on the policies undertaken, and on the behavior of variables such as the real exchange rate. This is the subject of the next section.

1.5   Recent Real Exchange Rate Behavior in Latin America

In the last years competitive real exchange rates have been at the center of the vigorous performance of most of Latin America's external sectors. Recently, however, in most Latin countries real exchange rates have experienced rapid real appreciations (fig. 1.1). These developments have generated considerable concern among policymakers and political leaders. A number of observers have argued that the reduction in exports competitiveness is negatively affecting the most dynamic sectors in these economies, reducing growth and employment expansion (see Calvo, Leiderman, and Reinhart 1992).

These real appreciations have been the result of two basic factors: first, the use in many countries of the exchange rate policy as an anti-inflationary tool and, second, massive capital inflows into Latin America that have made foreign exchange "overabundant."

In the late 1980s some analysts, including the staff of the IMF, argued that the crawling-peg regimes adopted by most of Latin America after the debt crisis had become excessively inflationary. In particular, it was argued that crawling pegs introduce substantial inflation *inertia*. According to this view exchange rate policy in the developing countries should move toward greater rigidity—and even complete fixity—as a way to introduce financial discipline, provide a nominal anchor, and reduce inflation.[32]

A number of Latin countries have, in fact, decided to use an exchange rate anchor as a way to reduce inflation. In practice they have done this by either slowing down the rate of the crawl—as in Mexico and Chile, to some extent—or by adopting a completely fixed nominal exchange rate—as in Argentina and Nicaragua. Much of the recent enthusiasm for fixed nominal exchange rates is intellectually rooted in the modern credibility and time consistency literature.[33] According to this approach, which was pioneered by Calvo (1978) and Kydland and Prescott (1977), governments that have the *discretion* to alter the nominal exchange rate—as in the crawling-peg system—will tend to abuse their power, introducing an inflationary bias into the economy. The reason for this is that under a set of plausible conditions, such as the existence of labor market rigidities that preclude the economy from reaching full employment, it will be optimal for the government to "surprise" the private sector through unexpected devaluations.[34]

By engineering (unexpected) devaluations the government hopes to induce a reduction in real wages and thus an increase in employment and a boost in output. Naturally, in equilibrium the public will be aware of this incentive faced by the authorities and will react to it by anticipating the devaluation surprises, hence, rendering them ineffective. As a consequence of this strategic interaction between the government and the private sector, the economy will reach a high inflation plateau. What is particularly interesting about this result is that this inflationary bias will be present even if it is explicitly assumed that the

32. For a flavor of the discussion within the IMF, see, for example, Burton and Gillman (1991); Aghevli, Khan, and Montiel (1991); Flood and Marion (1991). In Edwards (1993) I deal with some of these issues.

33. The new impetus for fixed rates has strongly emerged in the IMF. See Aghevli, Khan, and Montiel (1991).

34. This assumes that wages are set before the government implements the exchange rate policy but after it has been announced.

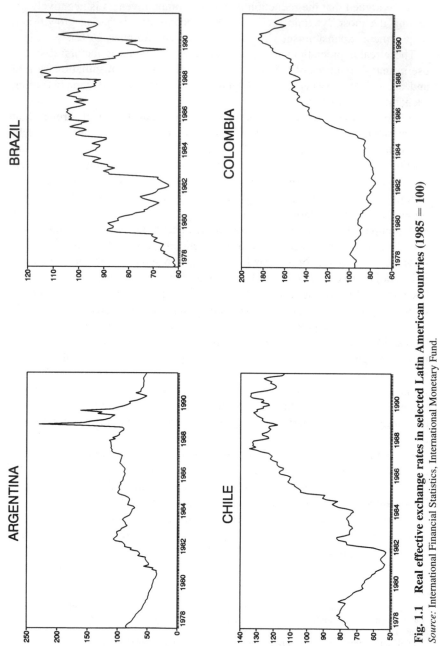

Fig. 1.1 Real effective exchange rates in selected Latin American countries (1985 = 100)

Source: International Financial Statistics, International Monetary Fund.

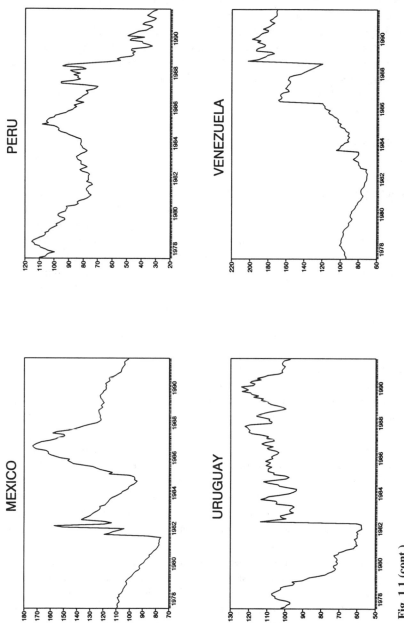

Fig. 1.1 (cont.)

government has an aversion for inflation. This is because the government perceives that the marginal benefits of higher inflation—associated with the increase in employment once nominal wages have been set—outweigh its marginal costs (see Persson and Tabellini 1990).

An important feature of the credibility literature is that under most circumstances policy commitment is welfare-superior to discretionary policy. If the government can credibly commit itself to low (or no) inflation, society will be better off: employment will be the same as in the discretionary policy case, but inflation will be lower. The problem, however, is that governments have a hard time making credible commitments. In the absence of effective constraints that will tie the government's hands, any promise of low inflationary policy will not be credible and thus will be self-defeating.

A key policy implication of this literature is that defining (and implementing) constraints that will make government precommitments *credible* will result in an improvement in society's welfare. Here fixed (or predetermined) exchange rates come into the picture. It has been argued that the adoption of a fixed exchange rate will constrain governments' ability to surprise the private sector through unexpected devaluations. Promises of fiscal discipline will become credible, and private sector actions will not elicit successive rounds of inflationary actions (Aghevli, Khan, and Montiel 1991). In particular, it has been argued that fixed exchange rates provide a *reputational* constraint on government behavior. The authorities know that if they undertake overly expansive credit policy they will be forced to abandon the parity and devalue. As the recent (mid-1992) crisis of the exchange rate mechanism has shown, exchange rate crises can indeed shatter the reputation of politicians.

In spite of its elegant appeal, this view has, in its simplest incarnation, some serious problems. First, in these simple settings exchange rate policy has a very limited role. In fact, in most of these models its only effect is to alter the domestic rate of inflation. That is the channel through which the government alters real wages. However, in most modern exchange rate models, nominal devaluations can also help accommodate shocks to real exchange rate fundamentals—including shocks to the terms of trade—helping to avoid real exchange rate misalignment.[35] Second, in economies with stochastic shocks, contingent exchange rate rules can, at least in principle, be superior to fixed rates (Flood and Isard 1989). Third, it is not clear why a country that can credibly commit itself to unilaterally fixing the exchange rate cannot commit itself to providing a monetary anchor.

However, one of the most serious limitations of the nominal exchange rate anchor policy is that, under almost every circumstance, once the exchange rate is fixed, other prices—including wages—will continue to increase, generating a change in relative prices in favor of nontradables. This has indeed been the case in both Argentina and Nicaragua, the two countries in Latin America that

---

35. See, for example, Edwards (1988c).

in the early 1990s adopted strictly fixed exchange rates as a way to drastically reduce inflation. In both cases the stabilization programs were based on a severe fiscal correction that virtually eliminated the fiscal deficit, on restrictive credit, and on a nominal exchange rate anchor. Although this policy succeeded in both countries in greatly reducing inflation, it has resulted in serious relative price misalignment. In Argentina this has been reflected in the fact that wholesale price inflation, which is heavily influenced by tradables, is only 3% per year, while consumer price inflation—highly dependent on nontradables—exceeds 18% per year. In Nicaragua tradable-related inflation rates have been very low (in the order of 2–3%), while nontradable inflation has exceeded 30% in the last twelve months.

Mexico followed a variant of the exchange rate anchor policy, announcing a predetermined rate of devaluation at a pace deliberately below ongoing inflation. The purpose of this policy has been both to anchor tradables prices and to reduce expectations. However, since domestic inflation has systematically exceeded the predetermined rate of devaluation, Mexico experienced a sizable real appreciation, which exceeded 35% between 1985 and mid-1992.

The second cause behind the generalized real appreciations in Latin America has been the large increase in capital inflows into the region in the last two years. As table 1.13 shows, after eight years of negative resource transfers, 1991–92 saw a significant turnaround (see table 1.14 for more disaggregated data). This increased availability of foreign funds has affected the real exchange rate through increased aggregate expenditure. A proportion of the newly available resources has been spent on nontradables—including in the real estate sector—putting pressure on their relative prices and on domestic inflation. An interesting feature of the recent capital movements is that a large proportion corresponds to portfolio investment and relatively little is direct foreign investment.

Real exchange rate appreciation generated by increased capital inflows is not a completely new phenomenon in Latin America. In the late 1970s most countries in the region, but especially the Southern Cone nations, were flooded with foreign resources that led to large real appreciations. The fact that this

Table 1.13	Capital Inflows and Net Resource Transfers: Latin America, 1981–92		
	Net Capital Inflows	Interest and Profit Income	Net Resource Transfers
1982–85	55.3	−111.7	−56.4
1986–89	33.5	−138.7	−105.2
1990	17.0	−35.7	−18.7
1991	36.3	−31.1	5.2
1992[a]	42.8	−21.2	21.6

Source: Jaspersen (1992).

[a]Projection.

Table 1.14   Net Capital Inflows as Percentage of GDP in Selected Latin American Countries

Country	1982	1983	1984	1985	1986	1987	1988	1989	1990	1991
Argentina	2.4	0.5	3.0	2.9	1.8	2.6	3.9	0.2	1.0	6.3
Brazil	4.2	2.1	1.8	0.1	0.6	1.3	−0.5	0.4	1.3	0.2
Chile	4.4	2.3	8.3	5.0	3.0	3.7	3.7	4.3	7.8	2.5
Colombia	6.5	4.1	2.6	5.9	2.9	0.0	2.1	1.0	0.0	2.8
Mexico	5.6	−1.5	−0.6	−1.2	0.7	−0.7	−0.8	0.8	5.0	10.6
Peru	5.7	2.4	3.4	1.1	2.1	2.3	3.5	1.5	2.4	9.5
Venezuela	−2.5	−6.6	−3.6	−1.8	−1.9	0.8	−1.5	−5.7	−4.1	4.9

Source: Inter-American Development Bank, *Economic and Social Progress in Latin America* (1992).

previous episode ended in the debt crisis has added dramatically to the current concern on the possible negative effects of these capital flows.

Whether these capital movements are temporary—and thus subject to sudden reversals as in 1982—is particularly important in evaluating their possible consequences. In a recent study Calvo, Leiderman, and Reinhart (1992) argue that the most important causes behind the generalized inflow of resources are external. In particular, their empirical analysis suggests that the recession in the industrialized world and the reduction in U.S. interest rates are the two main causes that have triggered these capital movements. These authors suggest that once these world economic conditions change, the volume capital of capital flowing to Latin America will be reduced. This means that at that point the pressure over the real exchange rate will subside and a real exchange rate depreciation will be required.

The countries in the region have tried to cope with the real appreciation pressures in several ways. Colombia, for instance, tried to sterilize the accumulation of reserves by placing domestic bonds (OMAs) in the local market in 1991.[36] However, in order to place these bonds the local interest rate had to increase, making them relatively more attractive. This generated a widening interest rate differential in favor of Colombia, which attracted new capital flows that, in order to be sterilized, required new bond placements. This process generated a vicious cycle that contributed to a very large accumulation of domestic debt, without significantly affecting the real exchange rate. This experience shows vividly the difficulties faced by the authorities wishing to handle real exchange rate movements. In particular, it indicates that real shocks—such as an increase in foreign capital inflows—cannot be tackled successfully using exclusively monetary policy instruments.

Argentina has recently tried to deal with the real appreciation by engineering a "pseudo" devaluation through a simultaneous increase in import tar-

36. An important peculiarity of the Colombia case is that the original inflow of foreign exchange came through the *trade account.*

iffs and export subsidies. Although it is too early to know how this measure will affect the degree of competitiveness in the country, preliminary computations suggest that the magnitude of the adjustment obtained via a tariffs-cum-subsidies package may be rather small. Mexico has followed a different route, and has decided to postpone the adoption of a completely fixed exchange rate. In October 1992 the pace of the daily nominal exchange rate adjustment was doubled to 40 cents. As in the case of Argentina, it is too early to evaluate how effective these measures have been in dealing with the real appreciation trend.

Chile has tackled the real appreciation by implementing a broad set of measures, including conducting exchange rate policy relative to a three-currency basket, imposing reserve requirements on capital inflows, and undertaking limited sterilization operations. In spite of this multifront approach, Chile has not avoided real exchange rate pressures. Between December 1991 and July 1992 the Chilean bilateral real exchange rate appreciated almost 10%. As a result, exporters and agriculture producers have been mounting increasing pressure on the government for special treatment, arguing that by allowing the real exchange rate to appreciate an implicit contract has been broken. This type of political reaction is becoming more and more generalized throughout the region, adding a difficult social dimension to the real exchange rate issue.

Although there is no easy way to handle the real appreciation pressures, historical experience shows that there are at least two possible avenues that the authorities can follow. First, in those countries where the dominant force behind real exchange rate movements is price inertia in the presence of nominal exchange rate anchor policies, the adoption of a pragmatic crawling-peg system will usually help. This means that, to some extent, the inflationary targets will have to be less ambitious, as a periodic exchange rate adjustment will result in some inflation.[37] However, to the extent that this policy is supplemented by tight overall fiscal policy there should be no concern regarding inflationary explosions. Second, the discrimination between short-term (speculative) capital and longer-term capital should go a long way in helping resolve the preoccupations regarding the effects of capital movements on real exchange rates. To the extent that capital inflows are genuinely long term, and especially if they help finance investment projects in the tradables sector, the change in the real exchange rate will be a "true equilibrium" phenomenon and should be recognized as such by implementing the required adjustment resource allocation.

1.6 Concluding Remarks

In this paper I have dealt with trade policy and growth. The analysis has focused on the long-run relationship between trade orientation and productivity improvements, as well as on some of the most important transitional issues.

---

37. More specifically, with this option the *one-digit* inflationary goal will be postponed.

With regard to the latter, the analysis has focused on the recent Latin American experiences.

In section 1.2 I argued that more open economies will experience faster rates of productivity growth than countries that distort their external sectors. A regression analysis based on a broad cross-country data set provided support for this view. The analysis of the recent Latin reforms presented in section 1.4 also supports the hypothesis that those countries that have embarked in trade liberalization programs have experienced an acceleration in the rate of productivity growth. However, the data on Mexico indicate that in order for productivity increases to be widespread it is necessary to implement broad reforms and deregulation programs that affect a wide range of sectors. In section 1.5 I discussed the evolution of real exchange rates in the region, and I pointed out that the recently observed generalized real appreciations have become a cause of concern among policymakers. A key element in determining the effects of these flows, and in designing policy response packages, is whether these movements are temporary or permanent. If the latter, it is difficult to justify an activist stance in economic policy.

Appendix A
TFP Growth Computations

One of the difficulties in computing TFP growth series for a large number of countries is that capital-stock series are rarely available. One way to deal with this problem is to use data on investment-GDP ratios (Harberger 1992). The problem with this approach, however, is that it requires data on the capital-output ratio. Although these are not generally available, they can be obtained using alternative procedures.

TFP growth (ρ) is defined in the following way:

(A1) $\rho = (\dot{y}/y) - \alpha(\dot{K}/K) - (1 - \alpha)(\dot{L}/L),$

where y is real GDP, K is the stock of capital, L is employment, and α is the share of capital in GDP. Since $(\dot{K}/K)$ is equal to gross investment (I), equation (A1) can be rewritten as follows:

(A2) $\rho = (\dot{y}/y) - [\alpha(y/K)(I/y) + (1 - \alpha)(\dot{L}/L)].$

(I/y) is the gross investment to GDP ratio and is readily available. (y/K) on the other hand is the inverse of the capital-output ratio and has to be estimated.

In order to obtain data on ρ, in this paper I have used the following procedure. First, I used specific country time series data for 1950–88 to estimate GDP growth equations with (I/y) and rate of growth of population (a proxy

$\dot{L}/L$) as regressors. From these regressions I obtained estimated values for parameters $[\alpha(y/K)]$ and $[1 - \alpha]$ in equation (A2). In the second stage, I used these coefficients to construct TFP data using equation (A2). In the third stage I averaged the estimated TFPs for 1971–82 for each country. This average corresponds to variable TFP1 used in the regression analysis in section 1.2.

A limitation of the procedure described above is that it assumes a constant capital-output ratio (K/y) in computing $[\alpha(y/K)]$ in (A2). However, it is likely that this ratio will change through time. In particular, we can assume that $(y/K) = (y/K)_0 + \gamma$ time. In this case (A2) can be rewritten as

(A3) $\rho = (\dot{y}/y) - [\alpha(y/K)(I/y) + [\alpha\gamma](I/y) \times \text{time} + (1 - \alpha)(\dot{L}/L)]$.

This equation was estimated for each of the fifty-four countries to compute the TFP2 variable in section 1.2.

Finally, TFP3 was constructed using cross-country estimates of $[\alpha(I/y)]$ in equation (A2). A shortcoming of this approach is that is assumes the same coefficient across countries. In that regard, TFP3 can be considered a less desirable measure of TFP growth.

Appendix B
Countries in Sample

United States	Brazil	Thailand
United Kingdom	Dominican Republic	Burundi
Austria	Honduras	Cameroon
Denmark	Mexico	Central African Republic
France	Nicaragua	Chad
Germany	Paraguay	Congo
Italy	Venezuela	Zaire
Netherlands	Jamaica	Ethiopia
Norway	Trinidad and Tobago	Côte d'Ivoire
Sweden	Iran	Lesotho
Canada	Kuwait	Mauritania
Finland	Oman	Morocco
Greece	Burma	Nigeria
Ireland	Sri Lanka	Zimbabwe
Portugal	India	Rwanda
Spain	Malaysia	Tanzania
Turkey	Pakistan	Togo
Australia	Singapore	Tunisia

References

Aghevli, P., M. Khan, and P. Montiel. 1991. Exchange Rate Policy in Developing Countries: Some Analytical Issues. IMF Occasional Paper 78. Washington, DC.

Barro, R. 1991. Economic Growth in a Cross Section of Countries. *Quarterly Journal of Economics* 106 (2): 407–43.

Barro, R., and X. Sala-i-Martin. 1991. Convergence across States and Regions. *Brookings Papers on Economic Activity* (1): 107–58.

Behrman, J. R. 1976. *Foreign Trade Regimes and Economic Development: Chile.* New York: Columbia University Press.

Bhagwati, J. 1978. *Anatomy and Consequences of Exchange Control Regimes.* Cambridge, MA: Ballinger.

Bianchi, A. 1988. Latin America 1981–1984: Crisis, Adjustment, and Recovery. In M. Urrutia, ed., *Financial Liberalization and the Internal Structure of Capital Markets in Asia and Latin America.* Tokyo: United Nations University, 1988.

Bianchi, A., R. Devlin, and J. Ramos. 1987. The Adjustment Process in Latin America, 1981–1986. In V. Corbo, M. Goldstein, and M. Khan, eds., *Growth-Oriented Adjustment Programs.* Washington, DC: International Monetary Fund and World Bank.

Burton, D., and M. G. Gillman. 1991. Exchange Rate Policy and the IMF. *Finance and Development* 28 (3): 18–21.

Calvo, G. 1978. On the Time Consistency of Optimal Policy in a Monetary Economy. *Econometrica* 46 (6): 1411–28.

Calvo, G., L. Leiderman, and C. Reinhart. 1992. Capital Inflows and Real Exchange Rate Appreciation. IMF Working Paper 92/62. Washington, DC, August.

Cardoso, E., and A. Helwege. 1992. *Latin America's Economy: Diversity Trends and Conflicts.* Cambridge: MIT Press.

Comision Economica para America Latina (CEPAL). 1991. *Equidad y Transformación Productiva: Un Enfoque Integrado.* Santiago: CEPAL.

Corbo, V. 1985. Reforms and Macroeconomic Adjustments in Chile during 1974–1984. *World Development* 13 (8): 893–916.

Corbo, V., T. Condon, and J. de Melo. 1985. Productivity Growth, External Shocks, and Capital Inflows in Chile: A General Equilibrium Analysis. *Journal of Policy Modeling* 7 (3): 379–405.

Corbo, V., and J. de Melo. 1985. Liberalization with Stabilization in the Southern Cone of Latin America: Overview and Summary. *World Development* 13 (8): 863–66.

Corden, W. M. 1969. Effective Protective Rates in the General Equilibrium Model: A Geometric Note. *Oxford Economic Papers,* n.s. (July): 135–41.

Cox-Edwards, A. 1992. Labor Markets and Structural Adjustment. Working paper.

Cukierman, A., S. Edwards, and G. Tabellini. 1992. Seigniorage and Political Instability. *American Economic Review* 82 (3): 537–55.

Diaz-Alejandro, C. 1975. *Essays on the Economic History of the Argentine Republic.* New Haven: Yale University Press.

———. 1978. *Foreign Trade Regimes and Economic Development: Colombia.* New York: Columbia University Press.

Dixit, A. 1985. Tax Policy in Open Economies. In A. Auerbach and M. Feldstein, eds., *Handbook of Public Economics.* New York: North-Holland.

———. 1986. Trade Policy: An Agenda for Research. In P. Krugman, ed., *Strategic Trade Policy and the New International Economics.* Cambridge: MIT Press.

Edwards, S. 1984. *The Order of Liberalization of the External Sector in Developing Countries.* Essays in International Finance 156. Princeton, NJ: Princeton University Press.

————. 1985. Stabilization with Liberalization: An Evaluation of Ten Years of Chile's Experiment with Free-Market Policies, 1973–1983. *Economic Development and Cultural Change* 33 (2): 223–54.

————. 1987. Sequencing Economic Liberalization in Developing Countries. *Finance and Development* 24 (1): 26–29.

————. 1988a. Real and Monetary Determinants of Real Exchange Rate Behavior: Theory and Evidence from Developing Countries. *Journal of Development Economics* 29 (3): 311–41.

————. 1988b. Structural Adjustment Policies in Highly Indebted Countries. In J. Sachs, ed., *The Developing Country Debt Crisis*. Chicago: University of Chicago Press.

————. 1988c. Terms of Trade, Tariffs, and Labor Market Adjustment in Developing Countries. *World Bank Economic Review* 2 (2): 165–85.

————. 1989. *Real Exchange Rates, Devaluation, and Adjustment: Exchange Rate Policy in Developing Countries*. Cambridge: MIT Press.

————. 1992. Trade Orientation, Distortions, and Growth in Developing Countries. *Journal of Development Economics* 39 (1): 31–58.

————. 1993. Exchange Rates as Nominal Anchors. *Weltwirtschaftliches Archiv* 129(2): 1–32.

Edwards, S., and A. Cox-Edwards. 1991. *Monetarism and Liberalization: The Chilean Experiment*. Chicago: University of Chicago Press.

Elias, V. 1992. *Sources of Growth in Latin America*. San Francisco: ICS Press.

Erzan, R., K. Kuwahara, S. Marchese, and R. Vossenar. 1989. The Profile of Protection in Developing Countries. *UNCTAD Review* 1 (1): 3–22.

Fischer, S. 1987. Economic Growth and Economic Policy. In V. Corbo, M. Goldstein, and M. Kahn, eds., *Growth-Oriented Adjustment Programs*. Washington, DC: International Monetary Fund and World Bank.

————. 1988. Symposium on the Slowdown in Productivity Growth. *Journal of Economic Perspectives* 2 (4): 3–7.

Fishlow, A. 1985. Revisiting the Great Debt Crisis of 1982. In K. S. Kim and D. F. Ruccio, eds., *Debt and Development in Latin America*. Notre Dame, IN: University of Notre Dame Press.

————. 1991. Liberalization in Latin America. In T. Banuri, ed., *Economic Liberalization: No Panacea*. Oxford: Oxford University Press.

Flood, R. P., and P. Isard. 1989. Monetary Policy Strategies. *International Monetary Fund Staff Papers* 36 (3): 612–32.

Flood, R., and N. Marion. 1991. The Choice of the Exchange Rate System. IMF Working Paper no. 90. Washington, DC.

Fuentes, J. R. 1992. Economic Policies, Human Capital, and Their Importance in the Process of Growth: Theoretical and Empirical Implications, Ph.D. diss., University of California, Los Angeles.

Garcia-Garcia, J. 1991. Liberalizing Foreign Trade: Colombia. In M. Michaely, A. Choski, and D. Papageorgiou, eds., *Liberalizing Foreign Trade,* vol. 4. Cambridge, MA: Blackwell.

Grossman, G., and E. Helpman. 1991a. *Innovation and Growth in the Global Economy*. Cambridge: MIT Press.

————. 1991b. Trade, Knowledge Spillovers, and Growth. *European Economic Review* 35 (2–3): 517–26.

Harberger, A. 1985. Observations on the Chilean Economy, 1973–1983. *Economic Development and Cultural Change* 33 (3): 451–62.

————. 1990. Towards a Uniform Tariff Structure. University of Chicago. Mimeo.

————. 1992. The Sources of Economic Growth and Economic Liberalization: With

Application to Mexico for the 1990s. University of California, Los Angeles, Nove. Mimeo.

Heitger, B. 1987. Import Protection and Export Performance: Their Impact on Economic Growth. *Weltwirtschaftliches Archiv* 123 (2): 249–61.

Ibarra, L. 1992. Credibility and Trade Reform in Mexico. Ph.D. diss., University of California, Los Angeles.

Jaspersen, F. 1992. External Resource Flows to Latin America: Recent Developments and Prospects. IDB Working Paper.

Krueger, A. 1978. Alternative Trade Strategies and Employment in LDCs. *American Economic Review* 68 (2): 270–74.

———. 1980. Trade Policy as an Input to Development. *American Economic Review* 70 (2): 288–92.

———, ed. 1981. *Trade and Employment in Developing Countries.* Chicago: University of Chicago Press.

Kydland, F., and E. Prescott. 1977. Rules Rather Than Discretion: The Inconsistency of Optimal Plans. *Journal of Political Economy* 85 (3): 473–91.

Lewis, A. W. 1955. *The Theory of Economic Growth.* London: Allen and Unwin.

Little, I., T. Scitovsky, and M. Scott. 1970. *Industry and Trade in Some Developing Countries.* London: Oxford University Press.

Lucas, R. 1988. On the Mechanics of Economic Development. *Journal of Monetary Economics* 22 (1): 3–42.

McKinnon, R. 1982. The Order of Economic Liberalization: Lessons from Chile and Argentina. *Carnegie Rochester Conference Series on Public Policy* 17 (Autumn): 159–86.

Martin, R. 1992. Sources of Growth in Latin America. World Bank. Mimeo.

Michaely, M. 1982. The Sequencing of Liberalization Policies: A Preliminary Statement of the Issues. Manuscript.

———. 1985. The Demand for Protection against Exports of Newly Industrialized Countries. *Journal of Policy Modelling* 7 (2): 123–32.

———. 1988. Liberalizing Foreign Trade: Lessons from Experience. Manuscript.

Michaely, M., A. Choski, and D. Papageorgiou, eds. (1991). *Liberalizing Foreign Trade.* Cambridge, MA: Blackwell.

Mill, J. S. 1848. *Principles of Political Economy.* New York: Appleton and Co.

Nogues, J. 1991. Liberalizing Foreign Trade: Peru. In M. Michaely, A. Choski, and D. Papageorgiou, eds., *Liberalizing Foreign Trade,* vol. 4. Cambridge, MA: Blackwell.

Nogues, J., and S. Gulati. 1992. Economic Policies and Performance under Alternative Trade Regimes: Latin America during the 1980s. LAC Technical Department Report no. 16. World Bank, Latin America and the Caribbean Region, Washington, DC.

Persson, T., and G. Tabellini. 1990. *Macroeconomic Policy, Credibility, and Politics.* Fundamentals of Pure and Applied Economics, vol. 38. Chur, Switzerland: Harwood Academic.

Rodriguez, C. 1982. The Argentine Stabilization Plan of December 20th. *World Development* 10 (2): 801–11.

Romer, P. 1989. Capital Accumulation in the Theory of Long-Run Growth. In R. Barro, ed., *Modern Business-Cycle Theory.* Cambridge: Harvard University Press.

Roubini, N., and X. Sala-i-Martin. 1991. Financial Development, Trade Regime, and Economic Growth. Center Discussion Paper 646. New Haven: Economic Growth Center, Yale University.

———. 1992. A Growth Model of Inflation, Tax Evasion, and Financial Repression. Center Discussion Paper 658. New Haven: Economic Growth Center, Yale University.

Stockman, A. 1982. The Order of Economic Liberalization: Comment. In K. Brunner and A. Meltzer, eds., *Economic Policy in a World of Change.* Carnegie-Rochester Conferences on Public Policy. Amsterdam: North-Holland.

Sturzenegger, F. 1992. Bolivia: Stabilization and Growth. University of California, Los Angeles, October. Mimeo.

Summers, R., and A. Heston. 1988. A New Set of International Comparisons of Real Product and Price Levels Estimates for 130 Countries, 1950–1985. *Review of Income and Wealth* 34 (1): 1–25.

Taylor, L. 1991. *Varieties of Stabilization Experience: Towards Sensible Macroeconomics in the Third World.* World Institute for Development Economics Research, Studies in Development Economics. Oxford: Oxford University Press.

Tybout, J. 1992. The Link between Productivity and Trade Regimes. *World Bank Research Review* 6 (March): 1–32.

United Nations Conference on Trade and Development (UNCTAD). 1987. *Handbook of Trade Control Measures in Developing Countries.* Geneva: UNCTAD.

Valdes, A. 1992. The Performance of the Agricultural Sector in Latin America. World Bank. Mimeo.

World Bank. 1992. *Poverty and Income Distribution in Latin America: The Story of the 1980s.* Washington, DC: World Bank.

Comment   Miguel A. Savastano

Sebastian Edwards has written a concise and informative progress report on trade reforms in Latin America over the past decade. The task was particularly difficult, considering that during that period the countries of the region underwent dramatic changes and were exposed to almost every imaginable shock, domestic and external. The paper addresses most of the issues relevant for understanding the recent evolution of trade policy in Latin America, identifies some common trends, and analyzes their implications for the region's growth prospects. However, even after taking into account space limitations, I feel that some of the important issues raised in the paper may have required a fuller and more comprehensive discussion. My comments will focus on four of these issues.

The first issue has to do with the starting point of the trade liberalization process in Latin America. Edwards places the start of this generalized and renewed impetus with trade reform at the late 1980s, when all the protectionist measures that had been imposed as part of the adjustment to the debt crisis began to be dismantled. Although it is unquestionable that the region as a whole has nowadays a much more open trade regime (especially in terms of the level of imports protection) than six or seven years ago, I find it a little misleading to claim that *it all started then.* In at least one aspect Latin America

Miguel A. Savastano is an economist in the Research Department of the International Monetary Fund. The views expressed in these comments are those of the author and do not necessarily reflect those of the International Monetary Fund.

had become an outward-oriented region long before the late 1980s; this was on recognizing the importance of maintaining a depreciated real exchange rate (RER) and of diversifying its export base. In fact, the data reported in tables 1.5 and 1.12 show clearly that the large RER depreciations and the surge of manufacturing exports occurred in the early 1980s and cannot be attributed to the recent opening up. Admittedly, those features reflect the region's response to the urgent need for effecting a large transfer abroad in the midst of the debt crisis and were far from being part of a liberal strategy aimed at reducing domestic distortions, but they nevertheless went a long way in creating an export mentality and reducing the antiexport bias that had characterized the region in the preceding two decades. Moreover, there is little doubt that the large real depreciations that such a response provoked in most Latin American countries by the mid-1980s exerted a strong influence on the region's developments of the following years, including the particular way in which the recent opening-up has taken place.

The second issue is related to what I consider a striking feature of the recent trade liberalization episodes reviewed in the paper: the fact that they were implemented much faster than in the past and in many cases without conforming with what Edwards calls the "conventional wisdom" on the appropriate sequence of liberalization (wisdom that he himself has contributed to form). Specifically, in the past few years countries like Argentina, Mexico, Nicaragua, and Peru cut drastically the level of import protection *almost at the same time* as they embarked on major stabilization efforts that resulted in a large real appreciation of their currencies. In all these cases the authorities' overriding (and understandable) concern for reducing inflation prevailed in the dispute for *the* crucial instrument (the exchange rate) at the expense of the real depreciation that in theory was required by the tariff reduction. This raises a very important question: to what extent do these attempts at stabilizing and opening-up simultaneously have to be considered the result of a "bad" policy decision that in the end will jeopardize the sustainability of the trade reforms? Clearly, if one were to answer this question following strictly the "conventional wisdom," the reforms would not seem to stand a chance to succeed because of the substantial RER appreciation experienced so far by these countries. However, I think that a closer look at these episodes is somewhat more reassuring, as it reveals at least two elements that distinguish them from the long list of frustrated liberalization attempts in Latin America's recent history: first, that most of the trade reforms started at a point where the RER was highly depreciated (some analysts would even say overdepreciated); and second, that the trade reforms were just one element of a broader package supported by extremely tight financial policies that marked a drastic (and so far credible) change in the "policy regime" of these countries. It would be interesting to know whether Edwards thinks that these two factors will suffice to sustain these countries' trade reforms or whether he feels that a major adjustment of their nominal exchange rates will still be required.

I also had problems with the paper's discussion of the effects on total factor productivity of the recent trade liberalizations. Specifically, I have some reservations regarding *the time* that should be given to a trade reform before one can reasonably expect to observe some improvements in factor productivity. In this regard I wonder whether it is appropriate (or fair, for that matter) to compare the increases in factor productivity in a group of recent liberalizers with those experienced by Chile, where structural reforms have had more than a decade to consolidate (table 1.6). In the context of this comparison, Edwards seems especially concerned about the modest gains in total factor productivity in Mexico following the comprehensive reforms of the trade and investment regimes of the late 1980s. Even after discounting for the relatively short period the reforms have been in place, however, I tend to share Edwards's concern. Mexico's growth performance in the postreform years has been far from spectacular, despite the pronounced increase in foreign capital inflows (most of them in the form of portfolio investment) and the sustained growth of imports of intermediate and capital goods. The sluggish response of output might well be related to the prominence given to the inflation objective and to the major reallocation of factors prompted by the structural reforms. Furthermore, if one follows the implications of Aaron Tornell's model (in chap. 2 of this volume), that sluggishness can even be interpreted as a "blessing in disguise" in the sense that it has prevented the "size of the pie" from increasing before NAFTA locks in the reforms and eliminates the incentives for rent-seeking behavior. Quite independently of the story one wants to believe, however, I agree with Edwards that the actual growth figures suggest very clearly that the transition period is not over and that Mexico has yet to find the path of rapid and sustainable growth that has historically characterized the successful reformers.

Finally, on the issue of how to deal with the real appreciation syndrome that has recently spread throughout Latin America, Edwards outlines two types of responses. In a nutshell, he suggests that in those cases where the appreciation has been driven by the use of the exchange rate as a nominal anchor the authorities should adopt a "pragmatic" crawling peg and accept a less ambitious inflation target; while in those cases where the appreciation is being caused by *genuinely long-term* capital inflows the authorities should refrain from trying to prevent what is basically an equilibrium adjustment of the RER. I think that most analysts will agree with the general thrust of these recommendations; however, I also believe that they are extremely difficult to follow through: first, because in some cases *both* factors are behind the observed appreciation of the currency; second, because it is not at all easy, even after a few months have passed, to distinguish between "genuine" and "volatile" capital inflows; and third, because in some cases political economy considerations have made of the convergence to single-digit inflation rates the primary objective of authorities who feel they have too much to lose if that goal is abandoned. This situation is complicated further by the difficulties in assessing how much of the appreciation would really need to be reversed in each particular case. I do not have any clear-cut answer to the dilemma posed by this situation, and I'm almost certain that there isn't one. However, I wonder whether the current circumstances would justify considering more seriously the possibility once mentioned to me by a policymaker faced with a similar dilemma: "when in doubt about the exchange rate, let it float; at least in that way you can always blame the market."

2 Are Economic Crises Necessary for Trade Liberalization and Fiscal Reform? The Mexican Experience

Aaron Tornell

> The bourgeoisie confesses that . . . in order to save its purse it must forfeit the crown, and the sword that is to safeguard it must at the same time be hung over its own head as a sword of Damocles.
>
> K. Marx, "Eighteenth Brumaire of Louis Bonaparte"

2.1 Introduction

In 1979, one of the oil boom years, President López Portillo announced Mexico's intention to adhere to the General Agreement on Tariffs and Trade (GATT). In 1980, having engaged in consultations with major interest groups, he then reversed this decision. Under President de la Madrid (1982–88), Mexico experienced several negative shocks, namely the collapse of the oil price and the interruption of foreign credit influx at a time when around 5% of the GDP was being used to service foreign debt. To make matters worse, the country suffered one of the severest earthquakes of the century. Still, in 1985, in the midst of this crisis, Mexico finally did accede to GATT. By 1987, it had transformed itself from an extremely closed economy into one of the most open ones in the world. And in 1993, it signed the North American Free Trade Agreement (NAFTA) with Canada and the United States. This transformation occurred notwithstanding the fact that trade liberalization implied significant adjustment costs for the private, import-competing sector, and that the state-owned sector had seen its subsidies vanish. Nonetheless, the import-competing sector, which had opposed trade liberalization in 1979, did not oppose it in 1985. It was curious that it should have been President de la Madrid, typically portrayed as weak and indecisive, who initiated the change, rather than President López Portillo, who tended to be seen as the strong leader.

Following the liberalization of trade, the government implemented a far-reaching fiscal reform. The majority of state-owned companies were privat-

Aaron Tornell is assistant professor of economics at Harvard University and a faculty research fellow of the National Bureau of Economic Research.

The author thanks Carlos Bazdrech, Rudi Dornbusch, Lorenza Martinez, and Andrés Velasco for helpful comments.

ized, bringing their number down from 1,155 in 1982 to less than 220 in 1993; the income tax rate was reduced from 42% to 34% and tax compliance was enforced, resulting in increased tax collection; and government subsidies were significantly reduced. This reform changed the sign of the primary fiscal balance from negative during the period 1970–82 to positive for each year of the period 1983–93. It is worth noting that the reform took place in a context of deteriorating terms of trade. As can be seen in figure 2.1, the index fell around 50% between 1981 and 1986.

The Mexican experience raises the question of why the reforms were implemented at a time of economic crisis rather than at a time of bonanza, when the country might have been able to "afford" the short-term costs more easily. One may look at this puzzle in at least two ways. A first perspective would be that the government has the latitude to act as if it were a central planner who maximizes some objective function and does not face any pressure from interest groups. According to this view, in the Mexican case, Presidents Echeverría (1970–76) and López Portillo (1976–82) either did what they deemed best, or what was in fashion throughout the world at that particular time, while Presidents de la Madrid (1982–88) and Salinas (1988–94) decided to follow the reformist vogue of the eighties. For this perspective, the story ends here.

By contrast, the second view would be that governments do not act in a vacuum, but in a jungle of rent-seeking groups. In this view, economic policy ceases to be the design of a central planner and becomes the result of interaction by rent-seeking groups. Thus in order to understand changes in economic policy, we would have to analyze the gains and losses of each interest group.

In all likelihood, the correct explanation is a combination of both these perspectives. However, for the purpose of shedding some light on the aforementioned puzzle, I will make the extreme contention that only interest-group interaction matters. That is, even if a government is concerned about social welfare, it will be able to implement structural reforms, such as trade liberalization, *only if* it does not encounter opposition from interest groups that have the power to block the reform.

In Mexico, the two major interest groups that blocked trade liberalization during the seventies were the import-competing, private sector elite and the state-owned companies (parastatal elite). Through the political process, these groups had almost unlimited access to fiscal revenue. They enjoyed subsidized inputs and profited from convoluted regulations and high trade barriers, which had the effect of increasing the profitability of the fixed factors in these sectors. Trade liberalization left both groups in a worse situation than the one they enjoyed under the status quo. Why is it, to reiterate the puzzle, that the private elite supported trade liberalization during bad times, even if it preferred the status quo over trade liberalization? And why is it that it would not support trade liberalization during good times?

The first point I make in this paper is that, when fiscal revenue was high in Mexico, subsidies to interest groups were high. Thus a "cohabitation equilibrium" existed between these two groups, and both were unanimously blocking

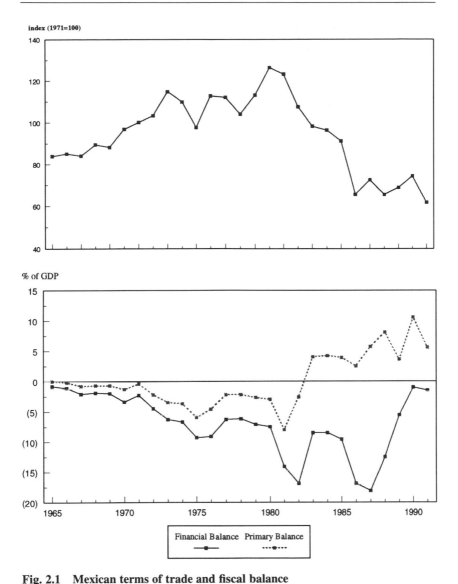

Fig. 2.1   Mexican terms of trade and fiscal balance
Notes: The primary balance includes interest payments, while the financial balance excludes them. In both cases the revenue from privatization is excluded.

trade liberalization. However, when fiscal revenue plummeted, the cohabitation equilibrium broke down, as it became profitable for each group to undertake actions to diminish the power of the other group, and thus secure a greater share of fiscal revenue for itself. In other words, previously friendly rivals switched to an attitude of "if I don't shoot, he will shoot." Support of trade liberalization was one such action.

As fiscal revenue collapsed in the early eighties, the parastatal elite took the first action. It induced the expropriation of all private banks in 1982. This move took everyone by surprise, and it was rumored that more expropriations were to follow. However, to the astonishment of many, the next move was trade liberalization. This time trade liberalization was supported by the private elite even though it faced severe costs in terms of reallocation of factors of production. It supported trade liberalization because *the choice for the private elite was not between the status quo and trade liberalization, as in the seventies, but between more expropriations and trade liberalization.*

Trade liberalization reduces the risk of further expropriation because it entails what one might call a "discipline effect." This effect has two components, foreign and domestic. The foreign component derives from the fact that under free trade it is no longer easy for the government to expropriate, since it has to fear that foreigners will retaliate by withdrawing investment or erecting trade barriers. Moreover, international agreements such as NAFTA penalize the imposition of regulations that protect some sectors. Thus, when seeking protection and subsidies, interest groups have to face the potential retaliation from foreigners. The domestic component in turn has two aspects; first, free trade generates new strong groups, that is, exporters who have an interest in maintaining free trade. Second, under free trade, regulations become simpler and more transparent. The previous involved system of import licensing and multiple tariffs is replaced by a much more straightforward law mandating only one or two rates to be applied across all industries. These new rules expose rent-seeking behavior by individual groups more effectively. As a result, other groups may block it at inception.

The second point of the paper is that, as the major interest groups had been weakened by their internecine struggles (which were reflected in bank expropriation and trade liberalization), the governments of Presidents de la Madrid and Salinas achieved a temporary *autonomy* from the established elites. This enabled them to press on with further reforms that had been deemed impossible just a few years back, such as the privatization of the majority of state-owned companies, including the banks, a radical deregulation process that eliminated monopolistic rents on items ranging from jelly jars to ports, and a major tax reform.

In sum, trade liberalization was supported by the private elite in order to save itself from the parastatal elite. Under free trade, the parastatal elite has to face new interests: exporters and foreigners. However, free trade also limits the ability of the private elite to obtain monopoly rents. Referring to the quote from Marx's "Eighteenth Brumaire of Louis Bonaparte," we might say that in the Mexican case trade liberalization acted as the sword of Damocles.

In order to make these points more precise, I present in section 2.3 a game-theoretic model that analyzes the interaction between the two interest groups. I explain why in good times trade liberalization is blocked unanimously by all powerful interest groups, and why in bad times this unanimity breaks down, with some groups supporting trade liberalization, even if all groups end up worse off than under the status quo.

The model is based on the observation that each group has the potential to reduce the power of the second group by temporarily using part of its fixed factors in activities other than production. This entails a short-run cost in terms of forgone profits, and a long-term gain derived from a weaker second group. For example, consider the case of trade liberalization. When it is implemented, some of the fixed factors remain temporarily idle because they have to be reallocated. Although this involves a short-term loss, the future power of rent-seeking groups to expropriate will be reduced because of the discipline effect of trade liberalization.

The cohabitation equilibrium breaks down when one group finds it profitable to incur the short-run cost and displace the second group. If in addition the payoff of matching is greater than the payoff of staying put, the second group will also incur the short-run cost and eliminate the power of the first group. In these circumstances, both groups lose their power, and reform might take place. I show that this occurs when fiscal revenues, and thus subsidies, are sufficiently small. This is because the profitability of fixed factors goes down, making it less costly to have part of them idle during the short run, and raising the incentives to displace other groups and having access to a greater share of the smaller fiscal revenue. This situation is similar to the game of musical chairs. If there are two chairs for Helen and Mary, they have no reason to fight even when the music stops. If we remove a chair, however, Helen and Mary will scream and fight for that chair even before the music stops.

I would like to point out that this paper *does not* suggest that the reforms that took place in Mexico would have happened regardless of who was the president. The autonomy to act can be used in various ways, and the protagonists as well as fashionable academic ideas will influence the course chosen. It might well be that if the government had been headed by persons other than de la Madrid and Salinas, they would have misused their temporary autonomy. What is clear, however, is that the mutual weakening of the major interest groups gave the government the latitude to implement the reforms.

Finally, a few words about how this paper relates to the literature. The model I present is a two-period version of a preemption game. These games are used in industrial organization to study the adoption of a new technology or the introduction of a new product. Since such a move entails a cost, any firm would prefer to adopt as late as possible, provided the other firms also wait. However, since introducing the product first gives a monopolistic advantage, at some point in time each firm would find it optimal to preempt, if the other firms were waiting to adopt at a later date. Therefore, there might be early adoption even if it is against the interest of the industry as a whole.

Alesina and Drazen (1991) use a war-of-attrition model to analyze delays in stabilizations. In a war of attrition, the game ends when one player concedes, and as long as the war continues both groups incur a cost. In contrast to preemption games, in a war of attrition each player wants the game to end as soon as possible, and prefers the other to concede first. In the model of Alesina and

Drazen, delays occur because players are *uncertain* about the payoffs of the other players. By waiting they induce the weaker players to concede first.

Fernandez and Rodrik (1991) present a model where *uncertainty* regarding the probable winners and losers from reform leads to a bias toward the status quo. Thus reforms that would have been blocked might find support if they could be implemented.

Lastly, Velasco (1993) presents an argument along the same lines as mine to explain the reforms that took place in Chile during the seventies. Unlike Mexico, in Chile it was not a drastic collapse in the terms of trade that induced the breakdown of the status quo, but rather "the arrival of several new guests at the dinner table of the distributive state" in the sixties. Among them were the traditional urban labor movement, the shanty-town dwellers, and rural labor. However, the effect was the same as in Mexico: less available fiscal revenue for each group. This increased the incentives to incur the short-run costs necessary to eliminate the power of the other groups. The results were the wave of expropriations and strikes of 1970–73 and the trade liberalization of 1975. As established interest groups weakened one another, Pinochet acquired autonomy to act as he saw fit.

This paper is structured as follows. In section 2.2 I review the Mexican experience in detail. In section 2.3 I present the model. In section 2.4 I analyze the role of politics. In section 2.5 I address the issue of whether the reforms should outlast the crisis that generated them. Lastly, in section 2.6 I present the conclusions.

2.2   The Mexican Experience

During the fifties and sixties, Mexico followed an import substitution policy and a tight fiscal policy. The economy experienced an extraordinary average GDP growth of almost 7% per year and annual inflation rates of less than 5%. However, industrialization had been attained by way of very protectionist trade policies and heavy regulation.[1] By the end of the sixties, the emerging consensus held that the import substitution strategy had been exhausted and that a reform was needed. At the same time, there was mounting pressure from the left for a reduction in poverty and income inequality.

In order to address these demands, the administration of President Echeverría (1970–76) increased the emphasis on redistributive policies and increased its involvement in production. Thus the administration started an ambitious program of building state-owned enterprises in sectors that had been private in the past, such as steel. Increased government expenditures were not matched by higher taxes because opposition from the private sector did not allow the government to implement a tax increase. As a result, the fiscal deficit

---

1. For an analysis of the "Desarrollo Estabilizador," see Ortiz Mena (1970). For an analysis of the period 1970–82, see Bazdresch and Levy (1991).

increased from 4% of GDP in 1970 to 10% in 1976. This in turn led to higher inflation, higher foreign debt, and higher current account deficits. It is interesting to note that, prior to becoming president, Echeverría was the minister of the interior, and at that time he was considered an economic conservative.

Echeverría's six years ended with a depreciation of the currency of 60%, tense relations between government and private sector, and the emergence of the parastatal elite as a strong new interest group. Indeed, this group had benefited the most from the new investment projects initiated by the government. Unfortunately, contrary to expectations, indicators of income distribution had not improved.[2] It should be emphasized that, despite its antibusiness rhetoric, the Echeverría government did not introduce trade and fiscal reforms, even though these had been deemed necessary since the early seventies.

When President López Portillo took office in 1976, he tried to reestablish cordial relations with the private sector. Although in 1977 the government announced intentions of a structural reform, and a fiscal contraction was begun, these plans were soon abandoned. This was due to the discovery of significant oil reserves and the increase in the price of oil. A free-for-all fiscal policy was implemented, meaning that the increase in the fiscal revenue was matched by a more than proportional increase in government expenditures. The investment program in government-owned enterprises was accelerated; prices of electricity, oil, and gas were heavily subsidized; and a very ambitious program to reduce poverty was implemented. An indicator of the increase in fiscal transfers is the evolution of expenditures of the parastatal sector, which represented 9.8% of GDP in 1970 and reached 22.2% in 1982. An indicator of the transfers to the private sector is the half-billion-dollar bailout in 1981 of Grupo Alfa, one of the biggest private companies in Mexico. As a result of these policies, the fiscal deficit jumped from 10% in GDP in 1977 to 17% in 1982.

Since fiscal revenue was sufficient to give transfers to almost every group—to the parastatal and private elites, to the urban middle class and to the rural poor—it is fair to say that every powerful group was satisfied with the status quo, and no incentive existed to implement the reforms contemplated since 1970. That is, high subsidies led to high profitability of fixed factors owned by powerful groups. Therefore no group found it profitable to incur the short-run cost necessary to weaken the other groups, and secure for itself a greater share of future fiscal revenue. Hence in those years of bonanza, all powerful groups blocked reform. An example, mentioned in the introduction, is the 1979 presidential announcement of Mexico's intentions to adhere to GATT. This plan generated criticism from the private and the parastatal elite, and in 1980 the decision not to accede to GATT was made public. It should be noted that, were one to embrace the central-planner view of policy making, another plausible explanation for this outcome is that the members of the economic cabinet did not consider free trade to be welfare improving.

2. See Aspe and Beristain (1984).

The populist transfer policies had to be halted at the beginning of the eighties due to the fall in the price of oil and the interruption in foreign lending. As a result, fiscal resources were no longer sufficient to satisfy all interest groups. Thus there was an increase in the net payoff that a group could expect from inducing a change in the status quo. The first move was made by the parastatal elite. In September 1982, just three months before he left office, President López Portillo announced the expropriation of all the Mexican private banks during his last and very dramatic address to Congress. The bank owners were considered one of the strongest groups within the private elite, and the banks an important conduit of fiscal revenue to the private sector (through subsidized credit and through implicit guarantees of their borrowings from foreign banks). The expropriation occurred simultaneously with the imposition of capital controls, and with the resignation of the orthodox governor of the Central Bank, Miguel Mancera. He was replaced by Carlos Tello, an economist with interventionist ideas, who was close to José A. de Oteyza, the extremely influential minister of energy, mines, and parastatal industry. The reaction of the private sector representatives was to call a national strike for September 8. However, on September 7, this strike was canceled.

In the midst of this crisis, President de la Madrid took office in December 1982. There were fears that under his tenure expropriations would continue and statism would increase, since after all he had been the minister of budget and planning during the administration of President López Portillo. However, the opposite occurred. During his tenure, three important decisions were made: not to interrupt debt service to foreign banks, to open the economy by joining GATT in 1985, and to privatize the parastatal sector. Confirming the commitment to monetary austerity, Miguel Mancera was reappointed governor of the Central Bank (a position he holds until the present).

Trade liberalization was painful for the private sector. The puzzle is why it did not oppose trade liberalization this time around, given that it had opposed reform in the past. The argument of the paper is the following: The reversion of lending flows from inflows to outflows and the deterioration in the terms of trade resulted in a reduction in the fiscal revenue available for rent-seeking groups. In order to eliminate the access that the private sector had to fiscal revenues via subsidized credit, the parastatal elite decided to induce the expropriation of the banks. The private sector matched this move by incurring the adjustment costs associated with trade liberalization. Adherence to GATT and later to NAFTA had a double effect. First, it blocked the access of the parastatal group to fiscal revenues because these treaties required Mexico to deregulate and to eliminate the bulk of fiscal subsidies. Second, expropriation of private industries was more difficult in an open economy. In other words, the private elite did not oppose trade liberalization because its choice was not between trade liberalization and the status quo, but between trade liberalization and becoming the follower. It chose the first because it thereby could weaken the parastatal elite and stop further expropriations.

The moves undertaken by the parastatal and the private elites were costly to these groups, and reduced their access to fiscal revenue. Indeed, it is very likely that for these groups (not for the economy as a whole) the status quo would have been more advantageous than the free trade regime, deregulation, and reduction in subsidies. The question is why they nonetheless acted the way they did, given that they were rational and had perfect foresight. The answer is simple: As fiscal revenues shrank, the payoff of becoming the "leader" and displacing the other group became greater than the payoff of retaining the status quo. Thus the implicit agreement not to take any action against the other group was not sustainable anymore, and was broken by the parastatal elite with the expropriation of the banks. For the private sector the expected payoff of matching by supporting trade liberalization was greater than the expected value of not liberalizing and becoming the follower (with the risk of being further expropriated by the leader). Therefore, the private elite decided to match the move by the parastatal elite.

The result was that both groups lost their power, giving autonomy to the government to implement further reforms. Thus the de la Madrid administration was able to implement the whole package of reforms that had been considered necessary since the late sixties. Foreign trade liberalization was completed, the privatization and deregulation processes were initiated, and the primary fiscal balance, which had been in deficit during the last decade, was transformed into a surplus. Figures 2.1 and 2.2 show the evolution of the Mexican terms of trade and of the primary fiscal surplus. As can be seen, the reforms of 1983–87 coincided with the sharp decline in the terms of trade. We might also note the sharp swing in the primary fiscal balance, which was transformed into a surplus in 1983 and remains positive.

In the political arena, the private sector reacted to trade liberalization partly by becoming more active in party politics. This broke the pattern of lack of political competition involving private interests noted by Skidmore and Smith (1984). According to Maxfield and Anzaldua (1987), before 1982 an implicit agreement had obliged businessmen to stay out of party politics, while in return the government promised to ensure a profitable investment climate.[3] The bank nationalization of 1982 dealt a blow to this accord and induced a structural shift. Since then some businessmen became involved in electoral politics by supporting Partido Acción Nacional (PAN), an opposition party from the right, and by running as candidates of the Partido Revolucionario Institucional (PRI), the party in power. For example, in the presidential elections of 1988, the candidate of the PAN was Clouthier, a former member of PRI who was the leader of the business association when the banks were expropriated.

Some members of the parastatal sector reacted by splitting from the PRI a few months before the presidential elections of 1988. Combining with leftist parties, a group headed by Cuauhtemoc Cárdenas and Porfirio Munoz Ledo

---

3. For an insightful analysis of the Mexican political system, see Cosio Villegas (1972).

% of GDP

Fig. 2.2   Revenues and expenditures of the Mexican government

formed the Partido de la Revolución Democratica (PRD) and obtained a third of the votes. Cárdenas is the son of the former president who founded the modern PRI, and was the manager of the Sicarsa steel plant (built during the seventies) and a governor of the state of Michoacán. Munoz Ledo was a cabinet minister and head of the PRI.

2.3   The Model

I present a two-period model where, under the status quo, all rent-seeking groups have common access to fiscal revenue. During good times none of the groups has incentives to change the status quo, while during bad times, it is optimal for each group to incur the costs necessary to bar the other groups from access to fiscal revenue. The model contains three ingredients: rent-seeking groups that compete to appropriate fiscal revenue; a sector that is not organized politically, that is the source of fiscal revenue; and a rule describing how one group can bar another group from access to fiscal revenue. There is neither capital accumulation nor depreciation in the model.[4]

The rent-seeking sector is composed of two groups (a and b), which live for two periods and which produce a consumption good that is traded internationally and is the numeraire. This good is produced using capital and a variable input provided by the government at a subsidized price. The objective of each group is to maximize the present value of its profits. For each period the profits of group i are given by

$$(1) \qquad \pi(g_i, z) = g_i^\beta k_i^\gamma - z g_i, \qquad 0 < \beta \le 1, \quad \gamma > 0,$$

where g_i is the amount of government input used by group i, z is the unit price of this input, and k_i is the capital stock of group i. The g's may also have a more indirect interpretation as import tariffs. In this case, z would represent bribes to the bureaucracy that administers trade policy or patronage payments to politicians.

Setting up the problem in this way captures the fact that in many countries fiscal transfers to rent-seeking groups take the form of government inputs, such as electricity, gas, and soft credit, provided at subsidized rates. For instance, in the case of Mexico, transfers from the federal government to the national electric utility (in order to sell cheap electricity) represented 0.3% of GDP in 1971 (when President Echeverría took office), 0.5% in 1977, and 1.7% in 1983, (when President López Portillo left office). At present, following the fiscal reform, these subsidies represent only around 0.1% of GDP.

Next, we will describe the nonorganized sector, which is the source of fiscal revenue. This sector is composed of investors that live for only one period. During each period, the representative investor is born with an endowment of W units of the consumption good. She can invest it abroad and receive a fixed tax-free rate of return r, or she can invest it domestically to produce a good that is not consumed domestically, using a decreasing returns technology. The government cannot tax foreign source income. Thus the investor must pay only taxes equal to a proportion τ of the profits on her domestic investment. The investor spends all of her after-tax income on the importable consumption good.

Since the exportable good is produced using the consumption good as the only input, it follows that the representative investor has an after-tax income equal to

$$(2) \qquad Y = [1 - \tau]pw^\alpha + [1 + r][W - w], \qquad 0 < \alpha < 1,$$

4. In Tornell (1992), I characterize the evolution of a similar economy, in which there is capital accumulation and property rights switch endogenously between private and common access.

where τ is the tax rate, w is the amount of working capital invested domestically, and p represents the terms of trade (i.e., the price of the exportable good produced by the nonorganized sector, in terms of the importable consumption good). If instead the nonorganized sector produced the consumption good, then p would be a shift parameter measuring the profitability of investing domestically.

Lastly, we consider the government. It produces the input used by rent-seeking groups at a cost of one in terms of the consumption good. However, it sells this input at $z < 1$. To cover the costs, the government collects taxes from the nonorganized sector. I assume that the government cannot issue debt, so that the fiscal budget has to be balanced during each period. I also assume that payments made by rent-seeking groups for government inputs are not used to cover the fiscal budget. They are made for purposes of patronage or corruption. It follows then that

$$(3) \qquad\qquad g_a(t) + g_b(t) = T(t),$$

where $T(t)$ is total fiscal revenue during period t.

The objective of the government is to maximize income in the nonorganized sector. Thus, if it were unconstrained, it would set g_a, g_b, and τ equal to zero during each period. However, the government's power is limited by the power of rent-seeking groups. I will consider three possible regimes under which τ is determined:

1. "Common access": under this regime the government is powerless, and both groups have equal power. The tax rate is set equal to the revenue maximizing level ($\hat{\tau}$).[5]

2. "Leader-follower": under this regime all power is concentrated in one group, "the leader." The government and the other group ("the follower") are powerless. As in the previous regime, τ is set equal to $\hat{\tau}$.

3. "Autonomous": under this regime both groups are weak. The only constraint faced by the government is to transfer to the groups a small proportion $\underline{\tau}$ ($< \hat{\tau}$) of the nonorganized sector's domestic income.

Tax rates are derived assuming the following sequence of events. During each period, conditional on $p(t)$ and on the prevalent regime, the government sets $\tau(t)$. Then, conditional on $p(t)$ and $\tau(t)$, investors choose $w(t)$ and each group is allocated its respective share of $T(p(t))$, $g_a(t)$ and $g_b(t)$. Under the leader-follower and common access regimes, the government sets τ so as to maximize tax revenues, taking as given that the representative investor allocates her working capital so as to equalize after-tax rates of return. I show in the appendix that tax revenue is maximized at $\hat{\tau} = 1 - \alpha$. Therefore, under these regimes the tax revenue function is

---

5. Aizenman (1992) and Tornell and Velasco (1992) analyze the common access regime in a dynamic setup.

(4) $\hat{T}(p) = p\hat{w}(\hat{\tau}(p), p)^\alpha \hat{\tau}(p) = Bp^{1/(1-\alpha)},$ $B > 0.$

Under the autonomous regime, the government sets $\tau = \underline{\tau} < 1 - \alpha.$ Thus

(5) $T_{aut}(p) = pw(\underline{\tau}, p)^\alpha \underline{\tau}.$

Since $T(p, \tau)$ is concave in τ (see equation [A3]), and since $\underline{\tau} < 1 - \alpha,$ it follows that $\hat{T}(p) > T_{aut}(p)$ for all p.

Consider the following two-stage game between both rent-seeking groups. In the first stage, both groups have common access to fiscal revenue. At time 0, after $p(0)$ and $p(1)$ are revealed and after $\tau(0), g_a(0),$ and $g_b(0)$ are chosen, each group decides whether or not to lose a proportion q of its profits, in order to eliminate the access to fiscal revenue that the other group will have at time 1. In the second stage, $\tau(1), g_a(1),$ and $g_b(1)$ are chosen.[6]

The preceding sequence of moves is meant to capture the two effects of trade liberalization that I identified in the introduction. To see this, let the two groups be the import-competing elite and the parastatal elite. On the one hand, the efficiency effect of trade liberalization implies that productive factors must be reallocated. This entails a short-run cost to the import-competing elite. On the other hand, the discipline effect of trade liberalization implies a reduction in the ability of the parastatal elite to expropriate the assets of other groups in the future.

There are three possible outcomes in this game.

1. Status quo: neither group incurs the cost $q\pi$, and common access to fiscal revenue prevails.

2. Matching: both groups incur the cost $q\pi$, both lose their power, and a shift to the autonomous regime takes place.

3. Leader-follower: one group incurs the cost $q\pi$ and becomes the leader, while the other group does not and becomes the follower. The leader gets the government input for free, and it can expropriate all the wealth of the follower.

Next, I determine the equilibrium levels of g_a and g_b. To make precise the idea that rent-seeking groups are inefficient in production, and that the government subsidizes them through low input prices, I make two assumptions that hold for all regimes and for all realizations of p. First, neither group finds it profitable to buy an extra unit of the input at a price of one (recall that the inputs' marginal cost of production is one). Second, there exists an excess demand for the government input at the price z. Since p takes values in the interval $[\underline{p}, \bar{p}]$, since the leader gets the government input for free, and since $\beta \leq 1$, these conditions hold if and only if

(6) $\beta[T_{aut}(\underline{p})/2]^{\beta-1}k^\gamma < 1,$ $\beta[\hat{T}(\bar{p})/2]^{\beta-1}k^\gamma \geq z.$

---

6. The same results could be obtained if the cost was a proportion q of revenues, or of the capital stock.

I assume that in the case of the autonomous and the common access regimes half of total fiscal revenue is allocated to each group. Condition (6) implies that it is not optimal for any group to buy the input at its market price. Consequently, we have that the g's are given by

(7) $g_l(p) = \hat{T}(p)$, $g_f(p) = 0$, $g_{ca,i} = \hat{T}(p)/2$, $g_{aut,i} = T_{aut}(p)/2$.

To determine which of the three possible outcomes mentioned above will be equilibrium outcomes, I derive the payoffs associated with each. Using (1) and (7), the payoffs of the follower and the leader are

(8) $$F(p_0) = \pi(\hat{T}(p_0)/2, z),$$

and

(9) $$L(p_0, p_1) = [1 - q]\pi(\hat{T}(p_0)/2, z) + \delta\pi(\hat{T}(p_1), 0),$$

where δ is the discount factor.

Under the status quo, the common access regime prevails in both periods. Thus the payoff of each group is

(10) $$SQ(p_0, p_1) = \pi(\hat{T}(p_0)/2, z) + \delta\pi(\hat{T}(p_1)/2, z).$$

Lastly, in the matching case, both groups incur the short-run cost, and their power to set the tax rate is eliminated. The payoff of each group is

(11) $$M(p_0, p_1) = [1 - q]\pi(\hat{T}(p_0)/2, z) + \delta\pi(T_{aut}(p_1)/2, z).$$

In order to characterize the Nash equilibria of the game, it is useful to represent it in the following strategic form,

		Group a	
		I	*NI*
Group b	*I*	(*M, M*)	(*F, L*)
	NI	(*L, F*)	(*S, S*)

where I stands for incurring the short-run cost, NI for not incurring it, M for matching, S for status quo, F for follower, and L for leader. The first and second terms in parentheses are the payoffs to groups a and b, respectively; they are given by equations (8)–(11).

The size of L relative to S and the size of M relative to F determine which of the three possible outcomes (status quo, leader-follower, or matching) will be an equilibrium outcome. For instance, if $L \geq S$ and $M \geq F$, the unique Nash equilibrium is matching (i.e., that both groups incur the short-run cost q). On the one hand, given that group a incurs the cost, the best response of group b is to match because the payoff of matching is greater than that of becoming the follower. On the other hand, regardless of group b's action, group a finds it profitable to incur the cost. It either gets L, which is greater than S if b does not move, or M, which is greater than F if b moves. For future reference, the equilibrium outcomes are summarized here.

Payoffs		Equilibrium Outcomes
$L \geq S$	$M \geq F$	shift to autonomous regime
	$M < F$	shift to leader-follower regime
$L < S$	$M \geq F$	status quo prevails, or
		shift to autonomous regime
	$M < F$	status quo prevails

As can be seen in equations (8)–(11), the relative sizes of the payoffs depend on the values of p_0 and p_1. In order to address the issue of when trade liberalization will take place, I let p_0 vary while keeping p_1 constant. I will show that for sufficiently small p_0 the only equilibrium outcome is matching (i.e., a shift to the autonomous regime), while for sufficiently high p_0 the only equilibrium outcome is the status quo. That is, trade liberalization is an equilibrium outcome during bad times, but not during good times.

The key to this result is that, as p_0 goes up, the value of remaining in the status quo increases more rapidly than the value of becoming the leader, and the value of following increases more rapidly than the value of matching. To illustrate we use figure 2.3, which depicts the payoffs F, L, M, and S as functions of p_0 (p_1 is held constant). All payoffs are increasing in p_0 because higher terms of trade increase the profitability for the nonorganized sector to invest domestically. This in turn increases total tax collection, and thus increases government subsidies at time 0. The higher the government subsidies are, the higher the profits of rent-seeking groups are under each regime.

To see why the payoff function of leading is flatter than that of the status quo, note that at time 0 the leader loses a share q of its profits (profits are $[1 - q]\pi(0)$), while under the status quo no cost is incurred (profits are $\pi(0)$). Thus an increase in $p(0)$ has a greater impact on the payoff of the status quo than in the payoff of leading, because $\pi(0)$ is increasing in $p(0)$ and because the future reward, in terms of a greater share of government subsidies, remains unchanged ($p(1)$ is fixed). In other words, at very low levels of $p(0)$ it is "cheap" to engage in nonproductive activities in order to induce change.

As can be seen in figure 2.3, during normal times ($p(0) = p$) the status quo is preferred to leading and following is preferred to matching. Thus at p the status quo is the only equilibrium outcome. However, during bad times ($p(0) \leq p'$) the only equilibrium outcome is matching. In this equilibrium, both groups lose πq at $t = 0$ and both lose their access to fiscal revenue. During good times ($p(0) > p''$), the only equilibrium outcome is the status quo. I analyze the case in which $p(0)$ is in $(p', p'']$ in the next section.[7]

7. There is another case in which $p' > p''$. In this case matching is the only equilibrium outcome for $p(0) < p''$, leader-follower is the only equilibrium outcome for $p(0) \in (p'', p']$, and the status quo is the only equilibrium outcome for $p(0) > p'$.

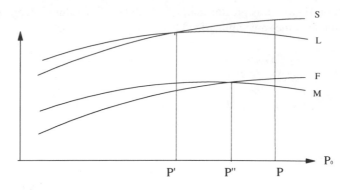

Fig. 2.3   Pair of functions

2.4   Does the Government Matter in This Model?

Up to now we have assumed that under the status quo interest groups can block any government decision. While maintaining this assumption, let us now suppose that the government has the ability to influence a group's expectations concerning the move that the other group will make. Let us define "political manipulation" as the act of influencing these expectations. It follows that political manipulation matters when there are multiple Nash equilibria in the game played by interest groups. In this case there is room for the government to induce interest groups to end up in the Nash equilibrium that is best for the economy as a whole, although it may be bad for the interest groups.

To illustrate this point, suppose that in the status quo both groups have common access to fiscal revenue, and consider the case in which $p(0)$ is between p' and p''. In this case the value of remaining in the status quo is greater than that of becoming the leader, and the value of matching is greater than that of following. Therefore, there are two Nash equilibria: In the first, neither group incurs the short-run cost $q\pi$, and the status quo prevails. In the second, both groups incur the cost, and there is a shift to the autonomous regime. Both groups are better off under the first equilibrium. However, the second equilibrium is sustained by the fear of each group that the other group will make the move. In this case, the role of political manipulation would be to bring about the second equilibrium. That is, the government would induce expectations among groups, that the other group will make the move. This is likely to be a difficult task for the government because the status quo is the Pareto-superior outcome.

The role of political manipulation as defined above is limited to this case. If p_0 were outside the interval (p', p'') or if p' were greater than p'', there would be a unique Nash equilibrium, as is clear from figure 2.3. Therefore, in these cases the outcome is independent of the government's political manipulation.

I should note that in the model we are considering groups that move simultaneously. In the real world, by contrast, groups can move sequentially and can follow more complicated strategies that depend on the history of the game. However, to the extent that there exists an advantage to moving first, the results of this paper should remain valid.

2.5 Reversion of the Reforms and Policy Implications

A question often asked is whether or not trade liberalization and fiscal reform will outlast the crisis that generated them, or whether there will be a reversion to the old ways if good times return.

In the case of Mexico, beginning in 1989, the wind started to blow in a favorable direction. There was a 35% reduction in foreign debt, exports were more diversified than in 1982, and financial capital started to flow in again. The reforms initiated by President de la Madrid were not undone, however, but were deepened to an extent that was considered impossible a few years back: NAFTA has been signed, all the big companies except for oil, electricity, and railroads have been privatized, and a radical deregulation program has been implemented, eliminating many monopolies and sources of corruption.

We can analyze the reversion of reform using a model similar to the one in section 2.3. Suppose that the autonomous regime prevails under the status quo (i.e., rent-seeking groups do not have access to fiscal revenue and $\tau = \underline{\tau}$), and consider the following two-stage game: In the first stage, after $p(0)$ and $p(1)$ are announced, and after $\tau(0)$, $g_a(0)$, and $g_b(0)$ are chosen, each group decides whether or not to incur a loss $q'\pi(T_{aut}(p_0)/2, z)$ at time 0, in order to become more powerful at time 1. In the second stage, $\tau(1)$, $g_a(1)$, and $g_b(1)$ are chosen. Again, there are three possible outcomes.

1. Only one group incurs the loss, and it becomes the leader. Thus the other group becomes the follower.
2. Both groups incur the loss, and both get common access to fiscal revenue.
3. Neither group incurs the loss, and the status quo prevails.

As in section 2.3, under the common access regime $g_i = \hat{T}(p)/2$, and under the leader-follower regime $g_f = 0$ and $g_l = \hat{T}(p)$. Therefore, the payoffs of the leader and the follower are

(12) $$L = [1 - q']\pi(T_{aut}(p_0)/2, z) + \delta\pi(\hat{T}(p_1), 0),$$

and

(13) $$F = \pi(T_{aut}(p_0), z).$$

Under the status quo, the autonomous regime prevails in both periods. Thus the payoff of each group is

(14) $$S = \pi(T_{aut}(p_0)/2, z) + \delta\pi(T_{aut}(p_1)/2, z).$$

Lastly, in the matching case the payoff of each group is

(15) $$M = [1 - q']\pi(T_{aut}(p_0)/2, z) + \delta\pi(\hat{T}(p_1)/2, z).$$

In terms of this model, a reform is not undone if the status quo is the only equilibrium outcome. Recall that this is the case if and only if the status quo is preferred to leading, and following is preferred to matching. Subtracting (14) from (12) and (13) from (15), $L - S$ and $M - F$ are increasing in $p(1)$ and decreasing in $p(0)$. Thus, at high levels of $p(1)$, the status quo ceases to be an equilibrium outcome. There is a shift to common access or to the leader-follower regime.

Let us now consider the policy implications of this model. Suppose that the costs of getting access to fiscal revenues (q') can be affected by the government. Since $L - S$ and $M - F$ are decreasing in q', it follows that, if during the period that the government enjoys autonomy it implements policies that lead q' to increase at a faster rate than potential fiscal revenue, then the likelihood of a reversion to the old system of privileges diminishes. On the contrary, if potential fiscal revenue were to grow faster than q', the likelihood of a failed reform would increase because of the heightened temptation of the groups to gain back their old privileges.

We might identify policies that alter q' as those that have to do with structural and judicial reform. For instance, signing a free trade agreement limits the possibility that groups will gain back import protection or production subsidies. Eliminating complicated regulations, introducing clear bankruptcy laws, and creating an independent judicial system will make the reestablishment of a patronage network much more expensive, since there will be no room for "interpretation of the law."

Increases in the parameter p can be identified with events that increase the ability of the government to obtain more fiscal revenue or that allow the government to borrow more. These events include an increase in foreign aid, discoveries of natural resources such as oil, and improvements in the terms of trade. These events might increase the cost a rent-seeking group is willing to pay in order to get access to this enlarged source of revenue.

For instance, if after a crisis foreign aid were granted, with no conditions of change in the regulatory framework or in the subsidization scheme, then the temptation of rent-seeking groups to gain back their old privileges would increase. Thus, foreign aid packages might have the unintended effect of preventing growth-enhancing structural change.

2.6 Conclusions

In Mexico, since the late sixties it became evident that the protectionist development strategy was not beneficial for the country anymore. However, trade liberalization did not take place until 1985, and the badly needed fiscal reform did not take place until 1989.

In this paper, I offer an explanation of why these reforms were delayed until an economic crisis took place and were not implemented during the 1970s, when the country could afford the costs associated with these reforms. My premise is that welfare-improving reforms for the country can be blocked by powerful interest groups that stand to lose from these reforms.

The interest groups that blocked the reforms during the seventies were the private import-competing elite and the parastatal elite. In the seventies, both groups were interested in keeping the status quo. Since fiscal resources were plentiful, both groups enjoyed high subsidies, which kept the profitability of their fixed assets at a high level. Under these circumstances, it was not profitable for either group to redirect its assets away from productive activities in order to reduce the power of the other group and to guarantee for itself a greater share of fiscal revenue. Hence the status quo prevailed.

The equilibrium between these two powerful groups broke down when the debt crisis erupted in 1982, since the government could no longer maintain high levels of subsidies. The struggle between interest groups took place in the spheres of private bank expropriation and trade liberalization. The short-run costs of trade liberalization were the adjustment costs implied by the efficiency effects of free trade. The private elite benefited because the power of the parastatal elite to expropriate and obtain studies was reduced. This mutual weakening gave temporary autonomy to the government to implement a fiscal reform.

Appendix A

Here I derive the fiscal revenue function (4). During each period, given the realization of $p(t)$ and the tax rate $\tau(t)$, the representative investor maximizes equation (2) by allocating her working capital so as to equalize after-tax rates of return:

$$(A1) \qquad p[1 - \tau]\alpha\hat{w}^{\alpha-1} = 1 + r.$$

In order to derive the fiscal revenue function, I further assume that the size of the investors' population is one. Thus, from (A1),

$$(A2)\, T(\tau, p) = p\tau\hat{w}(\tau, p)^\alpha = \frac{\tau}{[1 - \tau]^{\alpha/\alpha-1}}Ap^{\frac{1}{1-\alpha}}, \qquad A = \left[\frac{1 + r}{\alpha}\right]^{\frac{\alpha}{\alpha-1}} > 0,$$

where T is total fiscal revenue. Under the common access and the leader-follower regimes, the tax rate is set so as to maximize tax revenue. The first and second order conditions are

$$(A3) \qquad \frac{dT}{d\tau} = \left\{[1 - \tau]^{\alpha/(1-\alpha)} - \tau[1 - \tau]^{(2\alpha-1)/(1-\alpha)}\frac{\alpha}{\alpha - 1}\right\}Ap^{1/(1-\alpha)} = 0$$

and

(A4) $\quad \dfrac{d^2T(p,\ \tau)}{d\tau^2} = \dfrac{\alpha}{1-\alpha}[1 - \tau]^{(2\alpha-1)/(1-\alpha)}\left[\dfrac{2\alpha - 1}{1 - \alpha}\dfrac{\tau}{1 - \tau} - 2\right]Ap^{1/(1-\alpha)}$

$\qquad\qquad = -\dfrac{2\alpha A}{1 - \alpha}p^{\frac{1}{1-\alpha}}[1 - \tau]^{\frac{3\alpha-2}{1-\alpha}} < 0.$

Since the solution to (A3) is $\tau = 1 - \alpha$, and since $T(p,\ \tau)$ is concave in τ, the fiscal revenue function under the leader-follower and the common access regimes is obtained by substituting $\tau = 1 - \alpha$ in (A2).

(A5) $\qquad \hat{T}(p) = Bp^{1/(1-\alpha)}, \qquad B \equiv [1 - \alpha]\left[\alpha^2/(1 + r)\right]^{\alpha/(1-\alpha)} > 0$

Appendix B

Table 2.A1   **Mexican Fiscal Indicators (% of GDP)**

Year	Terms of Trade	Financial Balance	Primary Balance	Total Revenue	Total Expenditure	Parastatal Expenditure
1965	83.9	−0.8	0	16.8	17.5	9.3
1966	85.0	−1.1	−0.2	16.2	17.3	9.5
1967	83.9	−2.1	−0.8	16.5	18.6	9.1
1968	89.3	−1.9	−0.7	16.8	18.6	9.9
1969	88.0	−2.0	−0.7	17.2	19.1	10.1
1970	96.7	−3.4	−1.3	18.1	21.4	9.8
1971	100.0	−2.3	−0.4	17.6	19.6	10.5
1972	103.2	−4.5	−2.2	17.9	21.9	10.1
1973	114.8	−6.3	−3.5	19.3	24.7	11.9
1974	109.8	−6.7	−3.7	20.2	25.9	13.8
1975	97.5	−9.3	−6.0	22.2	30.6	17.0
1976	112.7	−9.1	−4.6	22.8	30.7	14.9
1977	112.0	−6.3	−2.2	23.6	28.7	14.6
1978	103.9	−6.2	−2.2	24.9	30.1	16
1979	113.1	−7.1	−2.7	25.6	31.3	16.5
1980	126.5	−7.5	−3.0	26.9	32.9	19.0
1981	123.3	−14.1	−8.0	26.7	39.2	22.0
1982	107.5	−16.9	−2.6	28.9	43.6	22.2
1983	98.2	−8.5	4.0	32.9	40.5	23.4
1984	96.3	−8.5	4.2	32.2	38.8	22.9
1985	91.1	−9.6	3.9	31.2	38.6	22.6
1986	65.6	−16.9	2.5	30.3	43.9	20.4
1987	72.5	−18.1	5.7	30.7	44.9	19.9
1988	65.5	−12.5	8.1	31.1	40.4	16.9
1989	68.9	−5.6	3.6	29.6	34.6	15.5
1990	74.3	−1.0	10.6	30.0	32.4	15.5
1991	61.8	−1.5	5.6	27.0	27.3	14.0
1992	—	—	—	26.1	24.2	13.2

Sources: Banco de México; Secretariat de Hacienda y Credito Publico.

References

Aizenman, J. 1992. Competitive Externalities and the Optimal Seignorage Segmentation. *Journal of Money Credit and Banking.*

Alesina, A., and A. Drazen. 1991. Why Are Stabilizations Delayed? *American Economic Review* 81 (5): 1170–88.

Aspe, P., and J. Beristain. 1984. Towards a First Estimation of the Evolution of Inequality in Mexico. In *The Political Economy of Income Distribution in Mexico,* ed. P. Aspe and P. Sigmund. New York: Holmes and Meier.

Bazdresch, C., and S. Levy. 1991. Populism and Economic Policy in Mexico, 1970–1982. In *The Macroeconomics of Populism in Latin America,* ed. R. Dornbusch and S. Edwards. Chicago: University of Chicago Press.

Cosio Villegas, D. 1972. *El Sistema Politico Mexicano.* Mexico City: Joaquin Mortiz.

Fernandez, R., and D. Rodrik. 1991. Resistance to Reform: Status Quo Bias in the Presence of Individual-Specific Uncertainty. *American Economic Review* 81 (5): 1146–55.

Maxfield, S., and R. Anzaldua Montoya, eds. 1987. *Government and Private Sector in Contemporary Mexico.* San Diego: University of California.

Ortiz Mena, A. 1970. El Desarrollo Estabilizador. *El Trimestre Economico* no. 146.

Skidmore, Thomas E., and Peter H. Smith. 1984. *Modern Latin America.* New York: Oxford University Press.

Tornell, A. 1992. The Rise and Decline of Economies with Endogenous Property Rights. NBER Working Paper no. 4354. Cambridge, MA: National Bureau of Economic Research.

Tornell, A., and A. Velasco. 1992. The Tragedy of the Commons and Economic Growth: Why Does Capital Flow from Poor to Rich Countries? *Journal of Political Economy* 100 (6): 1208–31.

Velasco, A. 1993. The State and Economic Policy: Chile 1952–1992. In *The Chilean Economy: Policy Lessons and Challenges,* ed. B. Bosworth, R. Dornbusch, and R. Labán. Washington, D.C.: Brookings Institution.

Comment   Kenneth A. Froot

Aaron Tornell has written a thought-provoking paper about the forces that opened the way for the Mexican liberalization of the 1980s. How were Presidents de la Madrid and Salinas able to overcome the political Achilles' heel of trade liberalizations—obtaining the backing of import-competing sectors—in their pursuit of openness? This is the question that Tornell asks. His approach is helpful in understanding how governments might gain consensus for programs that nevertheless impose substantial costs on powerful interest groups.

I want to make two points in this comment. First, I want to summarize what makes Tornell's model and argument work. Second, I want to identify and elaborate on another kind of explanation for how reforms can proceed and how a new consensus is achieved.

Kenneth A. Froot is professor of business administration at Harvard University's Graduate School of Business and a research associate of the National Bureau of Economic Research.

Tornell's model features two private sector (i.e., maximizing) groups that compete to receive government subsidies. Under the preliberalized regime, these groups cooperatively share a fixed pie of government subsidies. However, either group has the option of deviating from this cooperative arrangement. By doing so, the deviating group gains access to the entire (fixed) pie of government subsidies in the *future,* taking for itself the future subsidies of the other group. The cost of doing this is that the deviating group loses a fraction of its *current,* shared subsidies. This cost can be thought of as the adjustment cost imposed on an import-competing sector as the result of a liberalization program. So, if this group decides to support liberalization, it loses protection today, but gains sole access to large subsidies tomorrow. Provided that the net costs of the liberalization are temporary, the import-competing sector is willing to support it. Because the two groups play in a noncooperative game, this argument makes both groups more willing to support change over the preliberalized status quo.

This argument has two basic features. First, it looks at the liberalization process as redistributive, not expansionary, in the long run. Second, it has the government playing a relatively unimportant role in initiating the liberalization. Tornell has done this in order to emphasize the interplay between opposing rent-seeking groups. And I agree that this is an important effect that determines the strategic behavior of interest groups. Nevertheless, I wonder whether import-competing groups generally allow liberalizations to occur because they want to leapfrog over (or avoid being leapfrogged by) another subsidy-seeking group. That is, I wonder whether liberalizations actually evolve out of a strategic interaction between private interest groups with only a minimal role for government.

My own reaction is that, to understand the liberalization process, one must first say something about why import-competing sectors come to be subsidized in the first place. One explanation is that subsidies are created by governments that have output and employment objectives that are not fully consistent with economic efficiency. Looking around the world, one can find many apparent examples of such objectives—governments (including that of the United States) routinely protect sunset sectors (in the United States, steel and footwear) from international competition, bail out large failing companies (such as Chrysler), and even forestall the collapse of large industries (such as that of the S&Ls). Governments are frequently willing to spend substantial resources on these less-than-efficient objectives. Liberalization—especially in Latin American countries, and certainly in eastern Europe and the former Soviet republics—in my view follows when there is a consensus that these objectives are too costly to pursue. That is, trade liberalizations occur when the government can no longer afford protection. Note that consensus under this story can evolve because reform substantially increases efficiency over that of the highly distortionary, status quo policies.

Next comes the question of why import-competing sectors would ever go along. I think one answer is that, in these circumstances, the status quo cannot be maintained and is simply not an option at all. Such sectors do not view this as a choice between liberalization and the status quo, but between liberalization and something much worse, perhaps social unrest or political upheaval. And in many cases—think of the reforms in eastern Europe—such sectors really have little input into the reform decisions, which are broader in scope and much more far-reaching.

A second answer to why the import-competing sector would go along with liberalization involves growth. Preliberalized economies are often stagnating or contracting. The import-competing sector thus must choose between a protected, but shrinking, market versus a more open, but growing, market. It is not obvious that additional incentives are needed to get them to go along with liberalization measures.

Finally, recall that most liberalization programs include a healthy dose of exchange rate depreciation. Often trade protection has evolved partly in response to an overvalued currency. And liberalization is often a rationalization of the price structure in the economy, allowing relative prices to better reflect international standards. Because intermediate goods are often taxed, some import-competing sectors may actually be taxed rather than protected prior to liberalization.

In the end, both Tornell's story and the more standard one I suggest can rely on a crisis to motivate the policy switch. In Tornell's model, the crisis made both sectors more interested in pursuing government subsidies (such other revenues were harder to come by). In the standard story, the crisis comes when the government's antiefficiency goals are literally bankrupting the country, becoming too costly to finance in the domestic and international capital markets, and eroding the tax base through slow growth. As Tornell says, in the case of Mexico in the 1980s, there are surely elements of both.

II Political Economy of Reform

3   Macroeconomic Instability and Social Progress

Mauricio Cárdenas and Miguel Urrutia

3.1   Introduction

The organizers of this conference suggested that we explore the extent to which the adjustment of the last eight years in developing countries has resulted in increased poverty and inequality. Upon reflection we concluded that many of the costs of adjustment cannot be blamed on the adjustment process itself, but on the policies that made such adjustment inevitable. In other words, the social costs are more related to the size of the adjustment required by the misguided policies that lead to that adjustment.

The object of the paper is then to determine whether a certain set of long-term policies that have a built-in bias against large macroeconomic imbalances tend to be related to a better than average rate of progress of social indicators.

A recent paper by Stanley Fischer (1991) tested the relationship between macroeconomic policies and growth. His cross-section analysis and some case studies suggest that reasonable macroeconomic stability is probably necessary for sustained growth, but beyond that, the overall economic strategy pursued by the country—market and outward orientation, the size and role of government both in providing physical and social infrastructure especially for human capital and in limiting its role in other areas—is crucial.[1]

Mauricio Cárdenas is an associate of Fedesarrollo, Bogotá, Colombia. Miguel Urrutia is general manager, Banco de la República, Bogotá. Both authors also teach at Universidad de los Andes.

The authors would like to thank Felipe Barrera and Maria Teresa Ramirez for outstanding research assistance, as well as Alberto Carrasquilla and the participants of seminars at Fedesarrollo and the Inter-American Development Bank. The usual caveat applies.

1. Levine and Renelt (1992) provide a comprehensive review of the empirical cross-country growth literature. Using a variant of Leamer's (1983) extreme-bounds analysis, they find that most results from existing studies are not robust to the choice of variables in the regression. A strong relation between growth and investment, and between investment and trade openness, is one of the few results robust to small changes in the conditioning information set.

In this paper we explore the role of macroeconomic policy in social progress. Although one would expect that macroeconomic stability contributes to social progress through its effect on economic growth, some authors have postulated that stabilization generates social costs that overcompensate for the social benefits generated by economic growth. Therefore, we explore the relationship between macroeconomic stability and social progress, after controlling for the effects on economic growth.

The paper adopts two different approaches for testing the hypothesis. In the first part, cross-section analysis is used to see whether countries with less variance in some crucial macroeconomic variables have higher rates of growth in their human development index (independently from the effect of economic growth on this index). In the second part of the paper, the economic growth and social progress of four developing countries dependent on coffee exports are analyzed with a view to evaluating the social impact of institutional arrangements that attempt to diminish the fluctuations in various macroeconomic variables as changes in terms of trade occur. The hypothesis is that countries that avoid large swings in income, consumption, imports, and fiscal deficits may achieve greater social progress in the medium and long run.

The interesting question is not what are the costs of adjustment, but what are the costs of institutional arrangements that avoid having to carry out periodic large macroeconomic adjustments. If social indicators improve more in countries that minimize the variance of some strategic macroeconomic variables, then there would seem to be a good case for the argument that the costs of policies and institutions that facilitate macroeconomic stability are less than the benefits of such stability.

3.2   Social Progress in a Cross-Section of Countries

As mentioned in the introduction, this part of the paper explores the relationship between macroeconomic stability and social improvement in a large sample of countries. Our measure of social progress (i.e., the dependent variable) is the human development index (HDI), as calculated by the United Nations Development Programme (see UNDP 1991 for the exact methodology). The index aggregates a set of social indicators that measure life expectancy, educational achievement, and income. The index is comparable between countries and through time.

This comparability is achieved by measuring all of the country social indicators against the best and worst country indicators in the time period studied. The formula used to measure social progress between 1970 and 1985 is based on the construction of the following indices:

(1)
$$Z_{ijt} = \frac{(X_{ijt} - \min_{jt} X_{ijt})}{(\max_{jt} X_{ijt} - \min_{jt} X_{ijt})},$$

where i stands for the specific social indicator, j refers to a country, and t refers to a year. More precisely, X_1 is life expectancy, X_2 is adult literacy rates, and X_3

is the log of income per capita. The presumption is that the valuation of income diminishes as income rises above an international poverty line (i.e., diminishing utility of income). HDI_{jt} gives identical weights to each of the three indicators; that is,

$$(2) \qquad\qquad HDI_{jt} = \frac{1}{3}\sum_i Z_{ijt}.$$

In this paper social progress is measured by the percentage change in the HDI between 1970 and 1985. UNDP measures such progress for 110 developing countries.

3.2.1   Social Progress and Macroeconomic Performance: Preliminary Results

In the spirit of the new growth literature, we start by exploring the effects on social progress of differences in the average *levels* in inflation rates, fiscal deficits, government expenditures, and GDP growth rates, across countries. Also, we include the level of the HDI in 1970 (*HDI70*) as an additional determinant of social progress. The hypothesis in this case is that countries that were relatively worse off at the initial date have experienced faster social progress. This result would then mimic a recent empirical finding on growth dynamics, which indicates a force toward convergence in per capita income (after controlling for differences in other important determinants of growth rates).[2]

Gregory Ingram (1992) has shown that in fact there is better evidence for convergence of social indicators than of rates of growth. In the case of growth rates, high-income countries show some convergence, but developing countries show divergence of growth rates. On the other hand, there is a sharp convergence in life expectancy across countries, and that variable is one of the three components of our HDI. Ingram suggests that such convergence is due to the international transmission of techniques that reduce infant mortality at relatively low costs in terms of nontradable inputs. Such techniques include inoculation, oral rehydration therapy, and the provision of potable water and rudimentary waste-disposal facilities.

Furthermore, Ingram also finds convergence in primary school enrollment rates, another of the components of the social indicator used in the study.

In all cases cross-section data was used to test the statistical significance of the relationship of the independent variables with the HDI. The statistical relationships tested were of the type

$$(3) \qquad\qquad Y_{it} = \alpha + \beta x_{it} + \mu_{it},$$

where i denotes a country and t a time period; α is a constant; Y is the percentage change in the HDI between 1970 and 1985, x is a matrix of the independent variables used (explanatory variables), and μ is the error in the regression.

---

2. See, for example, Romer (1989); Barro (1991); Mankiw, Romer, and Weil (1992); Easterly, Kremer, Pritchett, and Summers (1992).

White tests were implemented to check for problems of heteroskedasticity (frequent in this type of estimations). The regressions reported have common variance of the residuals, which means there are no problems with hetero-skedasticity.

The empirical evidence confirms that in the case of the HDI there is a tendency toward convergence. In fact, a representative regression gave the following results:[3]

$$(4) \quad HDI = 66.0 - 0.88HDI70 - 0.02AVGINF + 0.58AVGG,$$
$$\quad\quad\quad (8.5)*** \quad (-7.5)*** \quad\quad (-1.1) \quad\quad (2.14)**$$

$R^2 = 0.57$; $n = 50$;   D.W. = 1.54; $F = 20.18***$; where one additional percentage point in the *HDI70* diminishes the rate of growth in the HDI by 0.88 percentage points. Average CPI inflation rate over the period 1970–85 (*AVGINF*) does not come out significant, but has the expected negative sign. Average government expenditures as percentage of GDP (*AVGG*) are positively correlated with the change in the HDI. This is interesting because it indicates that government expenditures help in promoting social progress. However, when those expenditures are financed through inflationary mechanisms, the effects may be undermined.

3.2.2   Macroeconomic Instability and Social Progress: The Evidence

This section of the paper tests the hypothesis that countries with greater *stability* in some crucial macroeconomics variables achieve greater social progress. The idea is that a country that develops institutional and political arrangements that allow it to avoid large swings in government expenditure or fiscal deficits may be able to achieve greater social progress (regardless of the *level* of those indicators). For example, the presumption is that large fluctuations in GNP also are harmful for social progress.

In relation to this last point, we try to see whether large terms of trade (TT)[4] shocks also hinder social progress, either directly or through the effect on GNP instability. The effect of instability of inflation rates on social progress was also tested.

Interestingly enough, when we include the measures of instability of some of the macroeconomic variables discussed above, it becomes possible to explain a relatively large proportion of the variations in the HDI. For instance, the following equation produced an R^2 of 0.84 with $N = 36$ (D.W. = 1.6; $F = 13.8***$):

$$HDI = \quad 74.1 - 0.99HDI70 + 3.15AVGGNP$$
$$\quad\quad (6.4)*** \quad (-8.59)*** \quad\quad (2.72)***$$

---

3. Throughout the paper asterisks denote significance at these levels: * = 10%, ** = 5%, and *** = 1%.

4. Measured as the ratio of the unit price of export to the unit price of imports.

(5) $+ 1.74DVGNP - 3.78DVFD + 1.66AVGFD + 1.14AVGG$
              $(0.84)\quad\quad (-1.77)^*\quad\quad (1.79)^*\quad\quad (2.4)^{**}$

              $- 0.77DVG - 4.25DVTT + 0.01DVINF$
              $(-0.44)\quad\quad (-1.24)\quad\quad\quad (0.97)$

where the prefixes *DV* and *AVG* denote the standard deviation and the average of that variable over the period 1970–85. *GNP* is the growth rate of output, and *FD* is the fiscal deficit as a percentage of GNP.

The results show, as expected, that high growth of GNP is positively related to improvements in the HDI, as well as to the level of public expenditure as a proportion of GNP. This latter result suggests that the HDI improves only with active involvement of the government in social expenditure, a circumstance that is accompanied by high government expenditure as a proportion of GNP.

Instability in the fiscal deficit deteriorates the HDI, as well as high average levels of fiscal deficit. (The fiscal deficit has a negative sign, so a positive relation between the average fiscal deficit and HDI improvement is to be expected.) The instability in government expenditures, terms of trade, and inflation variables have the right (negative) signs but are not statistically significant.

In equation (6) we use coefficients of variation, or the standard deviation divided by the average (*CV* is the prefix in this case), as a measure of instability, instead of deviations. This would be more appropriate in variables such as inflation, which may have very different levels across countries. Equation (6) is an alternative to equation (5) ($R^2 = 0.81; N = 36$).

$HDI =\quad 77.0 \quad- 1.0HDI70 + 3.26AVGGNP + 0.13\ CVGNP$
         $(6.78)^{***}\ (-8.52)^{***}\quad (2.82)^{***}\quad\quad\quad (1.00)$

(6)
              $- 0.3\ CVFD + 1.99AVGFD + 0.94AVGG - 5.1CVTT$
              $\quad (-0.65)\quad\quad (2.3)^{**}\quad\quad (2.96)^{***}\quad\quad (-1.18)$

              $- 1.31CVINF$
              $\quad (-0.28)$

The results are quite similar. Once again, in addition to average GDP growth, the average relative level of government expenditure is related positively to improvement in the HDI and average fiscal deficits are related negatively with improvements in the HDI. In both equations the initial level of the HDI affects HDI growth negatively and in a significant manner, confirming the tendency for convergence in our social indicator.

An interesting question is whether the relationship between the different variables and the HDI differs across continents. To see whether this is the case, we decided to test for regional differences in the effects of these variables. This involved using a set of regressors based on the interaction of *HDI70, CVFD, AVGFD,* and *CVINF* with the regional dummies for Africa (*DAF*), Latin America (*DAL*), and Asia (*DAS*). For example, the effect of the coefficient of variation of the fiscal deficit in Latin America is captured by the variable $CVFD*DAL = CVFDAL$. The regression gives an impressive R^2 of 0.71 with $N = 54$.

$$HDI = 74.4 - 0.93HDIAF_{70} - 0.38HDIAS_{70} - 0.73HDIAL_{70}$$
$$(9.4)*** \quad (-3.2)*** \quad (-1.31) \quad (-5.05)***$$

$$- 4.72CVFDAF - 0.08CVFDAS + 0.12CVFDAL$$
(7)
$$(-3.94)*** \quad (-0.04) \quad (0.22)$$

$$- 2.3AVGFDAF + 0.35AVGFDAS + 0.88AVGFDAL$$
$$(-2.25)** \quad (0.4) \quad (0.82)$$

$$- 18.7CVINFAF - 14.54CVINFAS - 4.44CVINFAL$$
$$(-.355)*** \quad (-0.81) \quad (-0.8)$$

By region it appears that the low initial social conditions in Africa and Latin America explain a good part of social improvement in those regions. In Africa variation in fiscal deficits are negatively related to social progress, and the levels of fiscal deficits (which have a negative sign) are related to lower improvements in social indicators.

Variations in inflation are also negatively related to changes in the HDI in Africa. It would therefore appear that in Africa macroeconomic instability is clearly related to lack of improvement in the HDI. Surprisingly, these relationships are not clear in the case of Latin America.

Since we were able to create a complete data base for eighteen Latin American countries, a separate set of regressions was run for the region. One specification that gave relatively good results was the following ($R^2 = 0.74$; $N = 18$):

$$HDI = 60.94 - 1.06HDI_{70} + 4.85AVGGNP + 0.1CVGNP$$
$$(4.8)*** \quad (-3.84)*** \quad (2.03)** \quad (0.93)$$

(8)
$$- 0.23CVFD + 0.36AVGFD + 0.96AVGG - 4.22CVINF$$
$$(-0.52) \quad (0.4) \quad (1.9)* \quad (-0.81)$$

$$- 3.5CVRER$$
$$(0.66).$$

The $HDI70$ variable confirms the convergence of social indicators, and the positive relationship between GNP growth and improvement in social indicators again suggests that high growth rates are a good way to improve social indicators. In Latin America the average level of government expenditures also explains social progress, suggesting that low fiscal burdens are not conducive to improvements in HDI. The signs on the macrovariables are the correct ones, but the coefficients are not significantly different from zero. In this equation we included the stability of the real exchange rate (RER) on the assumption that stable RERs minimize long-run macroeconomic imbalances. The positive sign suggests as much, but the t-statistic is quite low.

3.2.3   Cross-Section Results: Summary

The cross-country empirical analysis confirms that there is convergence in social indicators and that, in addition, high growth rates of GNP improve these indicators. However, there is some evidence suggesting that countries with high levels of government expenditure and low levels and variations in fiscal deficits tend to experience more rapid improvement in the HDI.

Fischer (1991) has given some evidence of the positive effect of macroeconomic orthodoxy on growth rates. Our analysis points toward the effects of macroeconomic orthodoxy on the improvement of social indicators, independent from the effect of macroeconomic policies on growth. This result is strong for Africa, and is less robust in the case of Latin America. However, there seems to be little evidence that low variations on GNP per capita growth are related to social improvement. We analyze this point in more detail in section 3.3.

Some comments should be made with respect to the HDI. The index, which covers a large sample of countries, is somewhat primitive. UNDP has tried to improve the indicator by adding an index of income distribution and indicators of gender discrimination or human freedom. The improved index, however, covers a much smaller sample of countries. Although it would be interesting to do the type of cross-section studies discussed here once an HDI with more components is available for a sufficiently large sample of countries, further work should be carried out in the development of an HDI that better reflects welfare.

In particular, life expectancy at birth is converging across countries, but the health conditions of a person sixty-five years old may be very different in countries with different levels of access to health services. In a developing country the older person may have deficient eyesight that could be corrected at low cost, or arthritic conditions that could be improved through medical treatment. Some index of health condition, even if subjective, should be used with the life expectancy index.

A social indicator should also include some index of housing quality. Such an indicator should also include an index of human freedom and violence, factors that clearly affect people's welfare. In summary, much work is still pending with respect to social indicators. The HDI was chosen for the analysis in this paper primarily because it was available for a large number of countries, but there is a clear awareness of its imperfections.

3.3   Business Cycles and Social Progress in a Group of Coffee-Producing Countries

An interesting feature of the analysis carried out in the first part of this paper is the lack of an empirical relation between the standard deviation in the rate of growth in GDP (arguably a proxy for the business cycle) and our measure of social progress. In this section we look in detail at this issue, refining the concept of business cycle and reducing the sample to four developing countries with remarkable similarities in their economic fluctuations. In particular we analyze the behavior of some leading social indicators and try to test whether macroeconomic stability (i.e., less variance in the cyclical component of GDP) is helpful in explaining differences in the rates at which income distribution, health, education, and demographic indicators improve over time.

The emphasis of this section is that the link between growth and improvement in social indicators is not a policy-free result. For example, in regard to the Kuznets curve, some countries (e.g., Indonesia) have been able to avoid the worsening in income distribution as growth takes off. If health and education are normal goods, then one would expect business and social cycles (as well as the trends in the corresponding indicators) to be correlated. Macroeconomic stability would then provide the appropriate environment for sustained social policies, a key condition for social progress.

The analysis focuses on the experiences of Colombia, Costa Rica, Côte d'Ivoire, and Kenya, four countries that are highly dependent on coffee for foreign exchange, fiscal revenue, and rural income. Consequently, temporary fluctuations in world coffee prices affect key macroeconomic variables (including the business cycle) in a similar way. In a typical pattern, high export prices result in above-trend levels of output, consumption, investment, and government expenditures. In addition, the income effect on imports, as well as changes in the RER, often cause countercyclical movements of the balance of trade (giving rise to a procyclical pattern in foreign lending).

Colombia provides, however, an exception to the rule. In fact, the historical evidence shows a countercyclical management of both the fiscal accounts and (public) external borrowing. In addition, private consumption in Colombia is substantially smoother than in the other three countries. Consequently, the amplitude of the business cycle in this country has been lower than in Costa Rica, Côte d'Ivoire, and Kenya. The frequency has been, however, remarkably similar in these otherwise structurally different countries (see table 3.1).[5] In sum, given the common external shock (which drives the frequency of the cycle), macroeconomic policies have had an effect in reducing (or augmenting) its impact (i.e., the amplitude of the cycle).

It is customary to think about macroeconomic stability as a desirable out-

---

5. In fact, as can be observed in table 3.1, the two Latin American countries are clearly more industrialized (and urbanized). Manufacturing sectors in Côte d'Ivoire and Kenya account for 10–13% of GDP, only half of the shares observed in Colombia and Costa Rica. The degree of openness is lower in Colombia, a relatively larger economy with trade coefficients that fluctuate around 13–15%. In contrast, imports and exports usually account for more than 30% of GDP in the other three countries. Colombia is, however, the country with the highest share of coffee in total exports. Inflation rates and money growth have traditionally been the highest in Colombia, with the exception of Costa Rica during the last decade. Per capita income is highest in Costa Rica, US$1,550 in 1987, followed by Colombia (US$1,230). The figure for Côte d'Ivoire (US$750) is high by sub-Saharan African standards, which on average correspond more closely to the level reported for Kenya (US$330).

Table 3.1   **Structural Characteristics (averages)**

	1950–59	1960–69	1970–79	1980–87
Colombia				
GDP composition (%)				
Agriculture	32.5	27.8	23.7	22.5
Manufacturing	18.4	20.9	22.7	21.4
Trade coefficients (% of GDP)				
Exports of goods and NFS	14.5	12.6	15.0	13.9
Imports of goods and NFS	13.5	13.5	14.0	13.7
Coffee exports/total exports of goods (%)	81.3	66.7	55.8	49.1
Inflation rate (%)	8.6	11.2	19.3	22.6
Growth in M1 (%)	14.9	17.7	14.3	25.2
Population (total, midyear, millions)	12.911	17.708	24.298	25.175
Costa Rica				
GDP composition (%)				
Agriculture	N.A.	24.6	21.4	20.5
Industry[a]	N.A.	17.9	25.2	27.8
Trade coefficients (% of GDP)				
Exports of goods and NFS	24.2	24.0	29.7	34.8
Imports of goods and NFS	26.1	29.4	37.9	37.2
Shares in total exports of goods (%)				
Coffee	43.6	43.0	29.5	27.7
Bananas	42.2	25.1	23.9	22.5
Inflation rate (%)	2.0	2.0	9.8	29.2
Growth in M1 (%)	8.2	7.6	21.0	29.8
Population (total, midyear, millions)	1.016	1.467	1.949	2.455
Côte d'Ivoire				
GDP composition (%)				
Agriculture	N.A.	36.6	31.0	27.6
Manufacturing	N.A.	10.2	7.5	10.8
Trade coefficients (% of GDP)				
Exports of goods and NFS	N.A.	33.0	38.4	38.7
Imports of goods and NFS	N.A.	28.1	35.7	36.7
Shares in total exports of goods (%)				
Coffee	54.3	38.7	28.9	18.6
Cocoa	25.6	19.6	19.0	28.5
Inflation rate (%)	N.A.	3.4	11.7	6.9
Growth in M1 (%)	N.A.	12.3	21.6	4.3
Population (total, midyear, millions)	2.957	3.881	6.626	9.61
Kenya				
GDP composition (%)				
Agriculture	N.A.	37.4	35.8	32.8
Manufacturing	N.A.	10.5	11.3	13.1
Trade coefficients (% of GDP)				
Exports of goods and NFS	N.A.	30.6	29.9	25.6
Imports of goods and NFS	N.A.	29.9	33.4	29.7
Shares in total exports of goods (%)				
Coffee	N.A.	17.6	23.4	26.2
Tea	N.A.	9.6	11.8	17.9

(continued)

Table 3.1   (continued)

	1950–59	1960–69	1970–79	1980–87
Inflation rate (%)	N.A.	1.8	6.0	11.2
Growth in M1 (%)	N.A.	N.A.	17.3	11.3
Population (total, midyear, millions)	6.913	9.392	13.218	19.349

Memo items (current US$)		1970	1980	1987
Colombia				
Current GNP per capita		340	1220	1230
External debt (outstanding at end of year, millions)				
Public/publicly guaranteed long-term		1297	4088	13828
Private nonguaranteed long-term		283	515	1524
Costa Rica				
Current GNP per capita		560	1950	1550
External debt (outstanding at end of year, millions)				
Public/publicly guaranteed long-term		134	1692	3629
Private nonguaranteed long-term		112	412	290
Côte d'Ivoire				
Current GNP per capita		270	1170	750
External debt (outstanding at end of year, millions)				
Public/publicly guaranteed long-term		255	4328	8449
Private nonguaranteed long-term		11	414	3264
Kenya				
Current GNP per capita		130	410	330
External debt (outstanding at end of year, millions)				
Public/publicly guaranteed long-term		319	2238	4482
Private nonguaranteed long-term		88	437	496

Sources: World Bank, World Tables (1976 and 1987); International Monetary Fund, International Financial Statistics; and World Bank, *World Development Report 1989.*
[a]Data on manufacturing sector is not available before 1970.

come, justified by the presumption that preferences are well behaved so that individual agents value less variability in their consumption profiles. Also, economic theory has suggested that less unstable (or risky) environments are more favorable to investment (hence, to growth). An alternative way of thinking about this issue, suggested in the introduction, establishes a connection between macroeconomic stability and social progress. Thinking along these lines, this section of the paper tries to answer three interesting questions. First, is it generally true that social progress is greater during periods of macroeconomic stability? Second, is there evidence suggesting that the growth rate in the trend component of some social indicators over the period 1960–89 is higher in the country with greatest macroeconomic stability (i.e., Colombia)? Third, is there a relationship between the "social" cycle (the cyclical component of those indicators) and the business cycle? In a corollary to this last point, do the "social" cycles in these countries seem to be correlated? Or in other words, do external shocks have an effect on social indicators?

Section 3.3.1 presents the main results of the GDP trend-cycle decomposition. Section 3.3.2 describes the sharp differences in the levels of the main social indicators across this group of countries. In fact, almost always Costa Rica ranks first, closely followed by Colombia, while the two African countries are substantially behind. A key distinction between their actual socioeconomic stance and its rate of improvement is established. The remainder of the paper tests the hypotheses outlined in the previous paragraph. Section 3.3.3 pools cross-section and time series data to see whether, across countries, periods of lower variance in the business cycle are matched with greater rates of growth in the social indicators. Section 3.3.4 looks at the time series evidence on the behavior of those indicators, country by country. This section discusses separately the main properties of the trend and cyclical components of some social indicators.

3.3.1   Business Cycle Fluctuations in Colombia, Costa Rica, Côte d'Ivoire, and Kenya

This section presents the main results of a standard Beveridge-Nelson GDP trend-cycle decomposition for the four coffee-producing countries under analysis. The exercise is somewhat limited by the availability of data, particularly for Kenya and Côte d'Ivoire, where the tests have to be carried out with a maximum of thirty observations (World Bank Data covers the period 1950, 1955, 1960–89). To have a uniform source and time period, the exercises were restricted in all cases to the period 1960–89.[6]

Interestingly, the tests fail to reject in all cases (with the exception of Côte d'Ivoire under some specifications) the presence of unit roots, indicating that a *difference-stationary* representation is preferred. Consequently, the model estimated for the log of GDP corresponded to

(9a) $$\Delta y_t = \mu + \sum_{i=1}^{k} \gamma_i \Delta y_{t-i} + \sum_{i=1}^{h} \Psi_i \varepsilon_{t-i} \varepsilon_t,$$

(9b) $$(1 - \gamma_1 L - \ldots - \gamma_k L^k) \Delta y_t = \mu + (1 + \Psi_1 L + \ldots + \Psi_h L^h) \varepsilon_t,$$

(9c) $$\Delta y_t = \frac{\mu}{1 - \gamma_1 L - \ldots - \gamma_k L^k} + \frac{1 + \Psi_1 L + \ldots + \Psi_h L^h}{1 - \gamma_1 L - \ldots - \gamma_k L^k} \varepsilon_t,$$

where k and h give the order of the autoregressive and moving-average polynomials, respectively. Sixteen ARIMA permutations were estimated, for values of k and h between zero and four, as well as the corresponding measures of persistence suggested in the literature (see Campbell and Perron 1991).

6. It is possible to reconstruct the Colombian national accounts since 1930 (see, e.g., Cuddington and Urzúa 1989). Bulmer-Thomas (1987) has calculated historical GDP data (1920–84) for Costa Rica (and four other Central American countries).

Table 3.2   **Trend-Cycle Decomposition: log(GDP)**

Country	Period	ARIMA	Measures of "Persistence"		Cyclical Component in % Deviation from Trend		
			Beveridge-Nelson	Cochrane	Standard Deviation	Min.	Max.
Difference-stationary models							
Colombia	1960–89	(0,1,1)	0.783	0.558	1.69	−1.88	2.97
Colombia	1960–89	(1,1,3)	0.183	0.016	4.71	−6.29	8.03
Costa Rica	1960–89	(0,1,1)	0.341	0.085	8.04	−12.86	13.33
Costa Rica	1960–89	(0,1,2)	0.514	0.189	6.63	−10.45	10.97
Côte d'Ivoire	1960–89	(0,1,1)	0.756	0.528	5.68	−10.33	7.87
Côte d'Ivoire	1960–89	(0,1,3)	0.447	0.176	10.38	−19.27	15.05
Kenya	1960–89	(2,1,0)	0.759	0.543	1.57	−3.18	5.11
Kenya	1960–89	(1,1,2)	0.537	0.225	3.21	−6.64	7.67
Trend stationary models							
Colombia	1960–89	(0,0,1)	0.000	0.000	4.73	−2.90	10.60
Costa Rica	1960–89	(0,0,1)	0.000	0.000	9.87	−9.96	20.36
Côte d'Ivoire	1960–89	(0,0,1)	0.000	0.000	15.22	−10.45	39.49
Kenya	1960–89	(0,0,1)	0.000	0.000	7.50	−11.76	14.12

Source: Data for the group of less-developed countries come from the World Bank National Accounts database.

Table 3.2 reports the results for those models able to produce white-noise residuals where the coefficients of persistence lay between zero and one.[7] Figure 3.1 depicts the corresponding trend-cycle GDP decomposition for a selected group of ARIMA models using the 1960–89 data. A cursory look at this figure suggests a remarkably similar pattern in the cyclical component. In addition, the evidence seems to suggest that business cycle fluctuations have been relatively less volatile in the case of Colombia (as indicated by the standard deviation of the cyclical component of GDP). However, the measures of persistence and, consequently, the variability of the business cycle seem to depend critically on the particular ARIMA specification, so that caution should be exercised in the interpretation of these results.

Table 3.3 shows the correlation coefficients between the business cycles of the countries in question. It is worth noticing the high correlation (above 87%) in the temporary component of GDP of Colombia, Costa Rica, and Côte d'Ivoire. In the case of Kenya these coefficients are somewhat lower (ranging between 67% and 74%).[8]

To support the hypothesis of a common external shock, table 3.4 displays the results of regressing the alternative measures of the business cycle on the cyclical component of real (world) coffee prices (contemporaneous and

7. More-than-permanent innovations were excluded on the grounds that innovations to coffee prices have zero persistence and, arguably, are the main force driving the business cycle.

8. Interestingly, the correlation coefficients between these cycles and those of their main trading partners (France, Germany, the United States, and the United Kingdom) are much lower (and even negative for some model specifications). See Cárdenas (1991) for more on this issue.

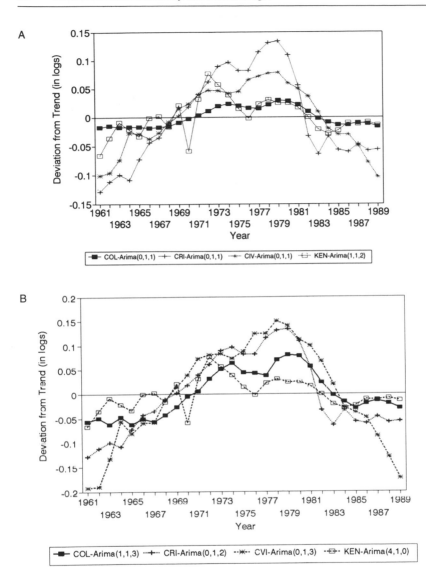

Fig. 3.1   Coffee producers: Cyclical component of GDP
Source: World Bank Andrex database.

lagged) and on the U.S. real Treasury bill rate. The set of explanatory variables also includes the cyclical movements in coffee production.[9] The evidence indicates that this set of right-hand-side variables has substantial explanatory

9. Arguably, variations in the size of the crop can induce business cycles either directly (coffee is an important component of GDP) or because coffee production is effectively the tax base for (coffee) taxation purposes.

Table 3.3   **Correlation Coefficients, GDP Cyclical Component, 1960–89**

		Colombia (0,1,1)	Colombia (1,1,3)	Costa Rica (0,1,1)	Costa Rica (0,1,2)	Côte d'Ivoire (0,1,1)	Côte d'Ivoire (0,1,3)	Kenya (2,1,0)	Kenya (1,1,2)
Colombia	(0,1,1)	1.000							
Colombia	(1,1,3)	0.984	1.000						
Costa Rica	(0,1,1)	0.907	0.905	1.000					
Costa Rica	(0,1,2)	0.906	0.900	0.999	1.000				
Côte d'Ivoire	(0,1,1)	0.869	0.847	0.897	0.896	1.000			
Côte d'Ivoire	(0,1,3)	0.876	0.865	0.904	0.902	0.996	1.000		
Kenya	(2,1,0)	0.106	0.126	0.276	0.281	0.216	0.218	1.000	
Kenya	(1,1,2)	0.672	0.671	0.736	0.740	0.661	0.665	0.755	1.000

Table 3.4   **Business Cycle and Coffee Prices, 1961–88 (t-statistic under the corresponding coefficient)**

Country	Constant	Cycle in Coffee Prices	Cycle in Coffee Production	U.S. Real Interest Rate[a]	R^2	F-Stat	Log-Likelihood
Colombia	0.0092	0.0163	0.0428	−0.0051	0.4292	5.7657	80.0058
	2.6409**	1.8110*	0.8906	−3.0700***			
Costa Rica	0.0380	0.0668	0.0177	−0.0205	0.6226	12.6466	49.2508
	3.7723**	2.4081**	0.5026	−4.8134***			
Côte d'Ivoire	0.0334	0.1189	0.0774	−0.0136	0.5140	8.4609	39.8671
	2.3471**	2.8688**	2.0047*	−2.4968**			
Kenya[b]	0.0110	0.0290	0.0187	−0.0046	0.6520	8.2429	73.7648
	2.4327**	1.9272*	1.2673	−2.4490**			

Sources: See text.

Notes: ARIMA models used in the derivation of the dependent variable (coefficients are similar for other specifications): Colombia (0,1,1); Costa Rica (0,1,2); Côte d'Ivoire (0,1,2); Kenya (1,1,2). Dependent variable: GDP cyclical component.

[a]Treasury bill rate deflated with the U.S. CPI.

[b]Two dummy variables (for 1970 and 1972) were used in the regressions for Kenya. The observed deviations from trend for those years are unusual (low and high, respectively), maybe due to measurement errors, or factors outside the scope of this project (e.g., the liquidation of commonly owned assets with Uganda and Tanzania, after the breakup of the economic integration in 1972). Explanatory variables in the case of Kenya have been lagged one year.

*Significance at 10%. **Significance at 5%. ***Significance at 1%.

power, accounting for more than 60% of the variance in the business cycle in Costa Rica and Kenya (51% in Côte d'Ivoire and 43% in Colombia).

In particular, coffee price shocks have a positive and significant impact on the business cycle, possibly with a one-year lag as in the case of Kenya. The size of the coefficient is smaller in Colombia (regardless of the model used in obtaining the cycle). In fact, other things constant, a 100% deviation from trend in coffee prices results in 1.6% deviation from trend in Colombia's GDP. The same shock would lead to a change in GDP (over trend) of 6.7% in Costa Rica, 11.9% in Côte d'Ivoire, and 2.9% in Kenya.

The coefficients on the cyclical component of coffee production[10] are positive (as expected) but low in statistical significance. In fact, only for Côte d'Ivoire can one reject the hypothesis of a nonzero coefficient with 90% confidence. This is interesting, for Côte d'Ivoire is the country where coffee taxation is the most pervasive (followed by Colombia, which also has the second largest coefficient on that variable).

Finally, the coefficients for the interest rate variable come out negative, as

10. Presence of a unit root in the production series was rejected only for Côte d'Ivoire. Consequently, cycles in coffee output were derived using a difference-stationary model (ARIMA [0,1,3]) for Colombia, Costa Rica, and Kenya. For Côte d'Ivoire a trend-stationary specification (ARMA [0,1]) was chosen.

expected, and significant. The size of the coefficient is larger for Costa Rica and Côte d'Ivoire, the two countries with the worst debt indicators in the group.

3.3.2   Social Indicators

In spite of the similarities in their business cycles, the group of four coffee producers show large disparities in the degree of development. In fact, most social indicators are quite different for the two African and the two Latin American countries, indicating the presence of other historical, political, and economic factors (ignored in this study) that play a decisive role in determining the scope of social progress.

To control for differences in methodology in the construction of the social variables, the same data source (the World Bank's Andrex database) is used in all cases (the original database covers 1950–89, but social variables are rarely available for the entire period).

This section describes the main facts regarding the level of those variables. The analysis is restricted to variables available for more than two years, so that a rough measure of the improvement throughout time is possible. Finally, the analysis is divided in four areas: income distribution, health, education, and demographic indicators.

Income Distribution

Figure 3.2 shows the pattern of income distribution at three points in time during the sample period. Figure 3.2A refers to an early period (1959–64), figure 3.2B to a midpoint (1969–73), and figure 3.2C to the latest available data (1986–88, except for Kenya where no information is available after 1976). By all standards, income distribution was more concentrated in Colombia during the early part of the period than in any other country under analysis. In fact, the share of the top quintile was 67.7%, while the poorest 20% (40%) of the population had only 2.1% (6.8%) of total income. Côte d'Ivoire lay at the other extreme with a relatively more egalitarian distribution of income (the share of the top quintile was approximately 50%, while the share of bottom quintile was 11.7%). Costa Rica was an intermediate case (no data is available for Kenya during this period).

The data for the midpoint (1969–73) show that, in spite of the reduction in the gap between Colombia and the other countries, the ranking in the distribution of income remained unchanged (from more to less egalitarian: Côte d'Ivoire, Kenya, Costa Rica, and Colombia). By the late 1980s this pattern had changed dramatically, to the point that the disparities among Colombia, Costa Rica, and Côte d'Ivoire (and 1976 Kenya) had disappeared. This process reflects a substantial improvement in the income distribution of Colombia and a worsening in the other countries throughout the period.[11]

---

11. See Londoño (1992) for a detailed analysis of the changes in income distribution in Colombia.

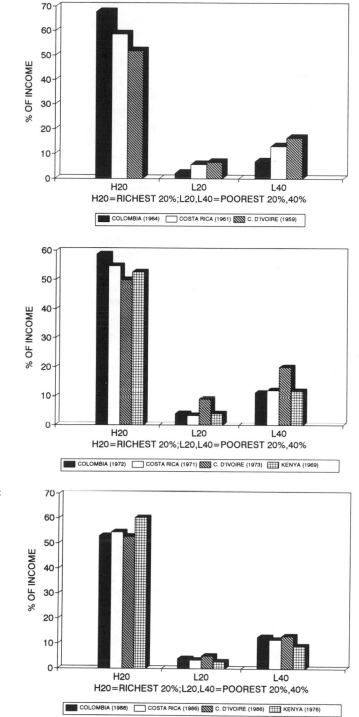

Fig. 3.2   Share of income: (A) early period; (B) middle period; (C) late period
Source: World Bank Andrex database.

Health

Figure 3.3 plots infant (age 0 to 1) mortality rates per thousand live births for the countries under analysis during 1951–89. The figure suggests that this indicator has been declining steadily in all cases, except for Colombia and Costa Rica during the 1980s. Costa Rica seems to have more instability in this indicator (perhaps due to better data), but ranks first, followed by Colombia, during the entire period. Infant mortality is much higher in Côte d'Ivoire and Kenya (100 and 80 deaths per thousand live births in 1989, respectively). The same pattern is observed for crude death rates per thousand people.

Life expectancy at birth (in years) shows an almost identical (but reciprocal) pattern. Life expectancy in 1989 ranged between seventy-five years (Costa Rica) and fifty-one years (Côte d'Ivoire). The rate of progress has been steady in all countries, and there is no tendency (in the sample period) toward convergence. Finally, data on the number of physicians per thousand people (figure 3.4) restates the fact that Costa Rica has much better health indicators. In this case progress in Colombia was very slow between 1960 and 1975 (although major improvements have taken place since 1975), while progress in health coverage (measured by the number of physicians) has been negligible in Côte d'Ivoire and Kenya.

Education

Data on education play a critical role in the analysis of this part of the paper for several reasons. First, the number of variables available provide a more comprehensive picture of the characteristics of social progress. Second, the number of observations per variables is much higher. And third, the data seem to be of better quality, evidencing fluctuations in the behavior of the indicators throughout time.[12]

Once again, educational levels reflect great disparities among the countries under analysis. For example, the number of teachers in primary education per thousand people aged 5–14 (figure 3.5A), arguably a proxy for the coverage and quality of education, shows interesting tendencies. In fact, one can observe some movement toward convergence in Costa Rica (which started at a much higher level than the others), Colombia, and Kenya. In this last country progress has been impressive (moving from four teachers in 1960 to over twelve in 1985). Costa Rica has fallen in absolute terms since the late 1970s, while Colombia stagnated after making strong improvements in the 1960–78 period. Côte d'Ivoire also improved until the early 1980s but then declined (in absolute terms). Its rate of progress has not been strong enough to overcome the low starting point.

Figure 3.5B shows the corresponding indicator for teachers in secondary education (divided by population aged 15–19). A cursory look at the plot sug-

---

12. Contrary to most of the health variables, which look like fitted values more than actual data.

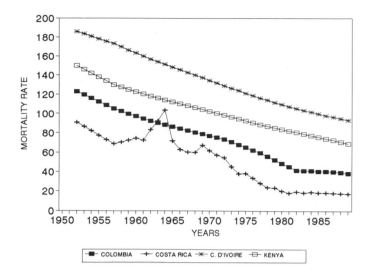

Fig. 3.3   Infant (0–1 year) mortality rate per thousand people
Source: World Bank Andrex database.

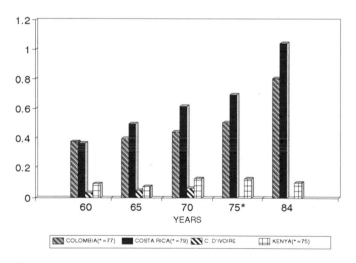

Fig. 3.4   Number of physicians per thousand people
Source: World Bank Andrex database.

gests that the two blocs (Africa and Latin America) are more dissimilar than
before. Progress has been steady in Colombia but in the other countries seems
more erratic.

   Figure 3.6 displays the gross enrollment rates in primary and secondary education. As opposed to the previous indicator, this variable isolates advances in
coverage of education (from those relating to the quality of education). In the

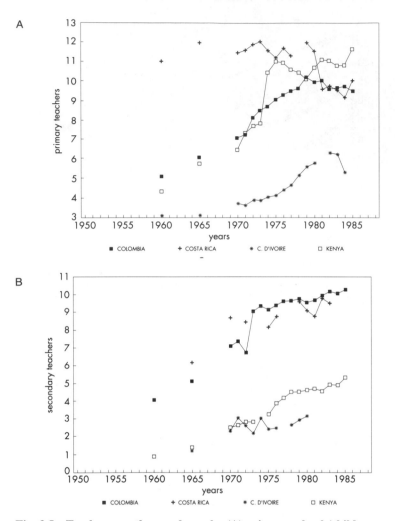

Fig. 3.5   Teachers per thousand people: (A) primary school (children aged (5–14); (B) secondary school (children aged 15–19)
Source: World Bank Andrex database.

case of primary education the ratio tends to stabilize (in the long run) around values of 100%, after periods of higher enrollment ratios (while older pupils become literate). This is why stability in Costa Rica is no sign of stagnation (the relevant variable in this case is secondary education enrollment rates). Improvement in the coverage of primary education has been impressive in Colombia and Kenya. However, in this last country the tendency was reversed in the late 1970s (and the ratio started to fall), while illiteracy rates were still higher than 50%. In this sense the continuity in the Colombian improvement (on this front) seems to be the exception rather than the rule. This is restated

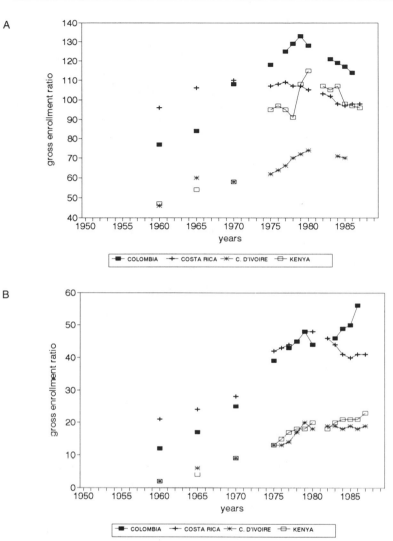

Fig. 3.6 Gross enrollment ratio: (A) primary school; (B) secondary school
Source: World Bank Andrex database.

when one looks at the gross enrollment ratios in secondary education (fig. 3.6B). In fact, Colombia now has the highest ratio, surpassing Costa Rica and evidencing a substantial improvement since 1960.

Demographic Indicators

It is well known that population variables involve complex determinants (such as the age structure of the population and women's labor force participation, not to mention cultural issues). Nonetheless, these variables can give an idea of how economic forces tend to affect family-size decisions and, in a narrow sense, reflect what we mean by "social" progress. Looking at two indicators, crude birth rates per thousand people and total fertility rates, we observe two interesting stylized facts. First, both rates were quite stable throughout the period 1951–89 in Côte d'Ivoire and Kenya (declining in this last country since 1982). Second, and in sharp contrast, the rates have decreased substantially in Colombia and Costa Rica throughout the period. The decline has been, however, steadier in the former than in the latter country. In fact, contrary to what happened at the beginning of the sample, crude birth rates are now lower in Colombia than in Costa Rica.

3.3.3   Macroeconomic Stability and Social Progress: Cross-Section Results

This section presents the results of testing the first hypothesis mentioned in the introduction (i.e., whether social progress is greater in periods of macroeconomic stability). The tests are carried out by pooling cross-section and time series data and estimating regressions of the form

$$(10) \qquad y_{it} = \alpha + \beta x_{it} + u_{it},$$

where y_{it} is the average annual change in the social indicator (e.g., share of income by the richest quintile) in country i during subperiod t (e.g., 1960–65), α is a constant, x_{it} is the standard deviation in the business cycle of country i during subperiod $t,$ and u_{it} is the error in the regression. Two alternative measures of the business cycle were used (corresponding to a difference-stationary [*std1*] and a trend-stationary [*std2*] decomposition).[13]

The dependent variables chosen can be classified in three groups: income distribution, health, and education. The change in the variable was defined in absolute terms in some cases (e.g., the income distribution indicators and some education variables) and in percentage terms in others (e.g., health indicators).[14] The main results are summarized below (all of them should be taken with care, as they are based on very few observations).

Income Distribution

Figure 3.7 plots the absolute changes in the share of income of the fifth quintile (*H20*), and the first and second quintiles (*L40*) against the standard deviation of the business cycle. It is apparent that the data point corresponding to Côte d'Ivoire during 1985–86 is highly implausible, as it reflects a substantial improvement in income distribution in a very short period of time (from one year to the next). This data point was ignored in the linear regressions

---

13. The exact models used were the following ARIMA $(p,1,q)$ processes: Colombia $(1,1,3)$, Costa Rica $(0,1,1)$, Côte d'Ivoire $(0,1,3)$, and Kenya $(1,1,2)$. As shown in table 3.2, these models correspond to those with greater variance. The trend-stationary decomposition corresponds to MA(1) models in all cases.

14. That is, y_{it} is alternatively $(z_{i,1965} - z_{i,1960})/5$ or $(z_{i,1965}/z_{i,1960} - 1)/5$, depending on the particular indicator z.

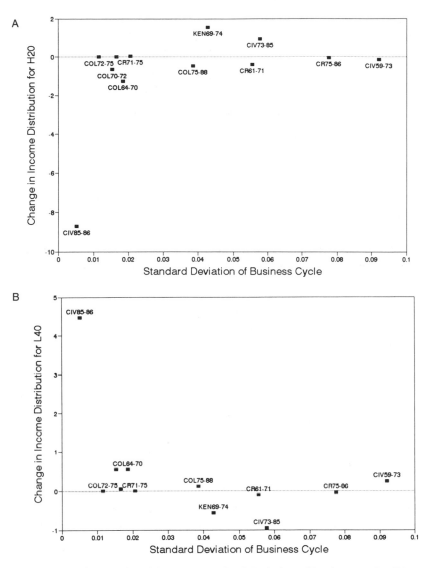

Fig. 3.7 **(A) Change in _H20_ versus standard deviation of business cycle; (B) change in _L40_ versus standard deviation of business cycle**
Source: World Bank Andrex database.

between the two variables, on the grounds that it is probably a measurement error (for our purposes it would have been better to leave that point in the sample, since we would have obtained a steeper slope).

The regressions came out with the right sign in all cases, implying that higher variance in the business cycle increases income concentration (the share of the richest quintile increases while that of the bottom 40% decreases). The results are relatively neutral to the specification of the business cycle (we report those obtained with a trend-stationary decomposition).

$$(11) \qquad\qquad H20_{it} = -0.4\text{E} - 02 + 0.108^* \, std2_{it};$$
$$(-0.67) \qquad\qquad (1.23)$$

$R^2 = 0.15$; D.W. $= 1.50$; Q (significance level) $= 0.81$; $N = 11$.

$$(12) \qquad\qquad L40_{it} = 0.13\text{E} - 01 - 0.28^* \, std2_{it};$$
$$(0.96) \qquad\qquad (-1.36)$$

$R^2 = 0.17$; D.W. $= 1.74$; Q (significance level) $= 0.80$; $N = 11$.

The coefficients on the business cycle are small and show relatively low statistical significance (ranging from 20% to 24%). Everything else constant, a 1 percentage point increase in the standard deviation of the business cycle raises the share of income of the top quintile by 0.001 percentage points (per year) and decreases the share of the bottom 40% by 0.003 percentage points.

Health

Contrary to the previous results, improvements in health do not seem to be dependent on the size of the business cycle. This is not surprising given Costa Rica's impressive record in health coverage (and its also impressive economic fluctuations). The estimated regressions use the percentage change in the number of physicians per thousand people (*Phy*) as the dependent variable. Surprisingly, when the standard deviations of the difference-stationary business cycles are used as regressors, the results show a positive (and significant) correlation between the two variables. That is,

$$(13) \qquad\qquad Phy_{it} = -0.2e - 02 + 1.45^* \, std1_{it},$$
$$(-0.11) \qquad\qquad (2.18)^{**}$$

$R^2 = 0.28$; D.W. $= 2.64$; Q (significance level) $= 0.99$; $N = 14$.

Interestingly, the variance in the business cycle explains 28% of the variance in health progress (as measured by the number of physicians relative to population).[15]

Education

The evidence on improvements in education is somewhat mixed, depending on the indicator chosen. For example, the absolute change in the illiteracy (*ILL*) ratios (illiterate population as percentage of the population older than fifteen) shows a negative correlation with the variance in the business cycle. That is, literacy rates rise with macroeconomic instability.

---

15. This result is even stronger when the absolute change (rather than the percentage change) in the health indicator is used.

(14) $ILL_{it} = -0.29 - 11.88* std2_{it}$,
                        (-0.86) $(-2.35)^{**}$

$R^2 = 0.38$; D.W. $= 1.00$; Q(significance level) $= 0.78$; $N = 11$.

The opposite is true for changes in enrollment rates in secondary education, where the number of observations is substantially larger than in the previous regressions. Two alternative measures of these enrollment ratios were used: (2) gross enrollment ratios (*GERS1*) as obtained directly from the database (which use as denominator the total population in the country-specific age bracket corresponding to that level of education); and (2) enrollment rates (*GERS2*) obtained dividing enrollment levels by the total population aged fifteen to nineteen (so that we control for country-specific variables). In both cases we used the absolute changes in the ratios as dependent variables. The results are summarized by the following two equations, which are robust to the specification of the business cycle (we report those obtained with a trend-stationary model).

(15) $GERS1_{it} = 1.43 - 13.81* std2_{it}$;
                        $(4.25)^{***}$ $(-1.97)^*$

$R^2 = 0.17$; D.W. $= 1.92$; Q (significance level) $= 0.95$; $N = 21$.

(16) $GERS2_{it} = 1.1 - 15.22* std2_{it}$;
                        $(4.05)^{***}$ $(-2.40)^{***}$

$R^2 = 0.23$; D.W. $= 1.74$; Q (significance level) $= 0.22$; $N = 21$.

These results indicate that the amplitude of the business cycle explains as much as 23% of the variance in enrollment ratios in secondary education. Other things constant, a 1% increase in the standard deviation of the cycle reduces enrollment ratios by 0.14–0.15 percentage point (per year).

Figure 3.8 plots the absolute change (per year in five-year intervals) in gross enrollment ratios in primary education for each country against the standard deviation in the business cycle for that country and subperiod. A cursory look suggests the lack of correlation between the two variables. As mentioned in the previous section, this could reflect that, for reasons different than the business cycle (i.e., changes in literacy ratios), gross enrollment ratios in primary education have been declining in Colombia and Costa Rica since the late 1970s. It is perhaps more puzzling to explain why the number of teachers (in primary and secondary education) relative to population have no apparent relation to the business cycle.

3.3.4   Macroeconomic Stability and Social Progress: Time Series Evidence

In this section we look at the time series evidence on the behavior of the same group of leading social indicators. The analysis starts with a deterministic trend-cycle decomposition of those variables available for a relatively long period of time (lack of data prevents use of unit root tests and difference-

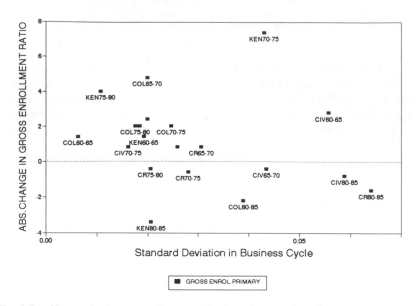

Fig. 3.8   Change in gross enrollment ratios in primary education versus standard deviation of business cycle
Source: World Bank Andrex database.

stationary models). Therefore, the decompositions were carried out using a standard trend-stationary specification. Table 3.5 presents the results of fitting linear trends to eleven social indicators.

Trend Components

The trend coefficients measure the average annual rate of change for a particular indicator, and the standard deviation of the residuals is a measure of the amplitude in the cyclical component of the same variable. It is interesting to observe that, for all the indicators related to secondary education, Colombia has the highest rate of improvement among the group of coffee-producing nations under analysis. The number of teachers in secondary education (per thousand people) increases at a rate of 0.26 per year, while the rates in Kenya, Costa Rica, and Côte d'Ivoire are 0.19, 0.15, and 0.09, respectively. Each year there are, on average, 8.5 additional pupils enrolled in secondary education (per one thousand people in the age group fifteen to nineteen) in Colombia (5.3 in Kenya, 4.4 in Costa Rica, and 2.1 in Côte d'Ivoire). The perhaps more accurately measured gross enrollment ratios in secondary education (as given by the World Bank) show an annual increase of 1.7 percentage points in Colombia (almost twice the figure for Costa Rica and Côte d'Ivoire).

The regressions for gross enrollment rates in primary education indicate that Kenya has the best record regarding improvements in basic education coverage (2.3 additional pupils per year per one hundred people of primary school age).

Table 3.5   **Deterministic Trend-Cycle Decomposition for Leading Social Indicators, 1950–89 (all variables in rates)**

	Trend	t-Stat	R^2	N	Standard Deviation of Residuals Levels	Standard Deviation of Residuals %
Teachers in primary education per 1000 people aged 5–14						
Colombia	0.203	9.812	0.857	18	0.568	7.67
Costa Rica	−0.090	−3.071	0.386	17	0.797	7.47
Côte d'Ivoire	0.149	8.212	0.828	16	0.454	8.23
Kenya	0.304	8.853	0.830	18	0.941	11.82
Teachers in secondary education per 1000 people aged 15–19						
Colombia	0.257	10.439	0.872	18	0.675	10.66
Costa Rica	0.150	4.630	0.728	10	0.569	7.50
Côte d'Ivoire	0.088	3.007	0.501	11	0.408	19.05
Kenya	0.189	21.474	0.968	17	0.241	13.12
Enrollment in primary education per 1000 people aged 5–14						
Colombia	2.604	3.182	0.403	17	18.058	6.75
Costa Rica	−1.734	−3.862	0.499	17	9.911	3.02
Côte d'Ivoire	4.450	11.371	0.896	17	8.638	4.31
Kenya	12.210	7.570	0.793	17	35.597	12.08
Enrollment in secondary education per 1000 people aged 15–19						
Colombia	8.527	8.430	0.826	17	22.325	12.38
Costa Rica	4.441	3.090	0.389	17	31.711	15.03
Côte d'Ivoire	2.123	13.044	0.966	8	2.772	13.32
Kenya	5.326	11.595	0.900	17	10.136	15.01
Gross enrollment ratio: primary						
Colombia	1.672	4.014	0.617	12	11.250	10.54
Costa Rica	−0.177	−1.066	0.080	15	4.829	4.71
Côte d'Ivoire	0.964	6.440	0.822	11	3.621	6.17
Kenya	2.300	5.914	0.729	15	11.316	14.00
Gross enrollment ratio: secondary						
Colombia	1.664	13.991	0.951	12	3.212	13.64
Costa Rica	0.850	4.536	0.632	14	5.449	15.26
Côte d'Ivoire	0.665	10.932	0.902	15	1.770	26.00
Kenya	0.803	18.097	0.962	15	1.292	24.04
Crude birth rate per 1000 people						
Colombia	−0.643	−32.834	0.968	38	1.324	3.77
Costa Rica	−0.591	−12.955	0.823	38	3.083	7.99
Côte d'Ivoire	−0.078	−20.107	0.918	38	0.263	0.51
Kenya	−0.091	−3.899	0.297	38	1.581	3.15

(continued)

Table 3.5   (continued)

	Trend	t-Stat	R^2	N	Standard Deviation of Residuals	
					Levels	%
Crude death rate per 1000 people						
Colombia	−0.276	−26.856	0.952	38	0.694	3.11
Costa Rica	−0.208	−20.594	0.922	38	0.684	8.92
Côte d'Ivoire	−0.397	−72.120	0.993	38	0.372	1.00
Kenya	−0.401	−189.780	0.999	38	0.143	3.57
Infant (0–1) mortality rate						
Colombia	−2.347	−52.921	0.987	38	2.998	6.18
Costa Rica	−2.259	−14.849	0.860	38	10.282	22.16
Côte d'Ivoire	−2.607	−76.455	0.994	38	2.305	0.71
Kenya	−2.064	−48.627	0.985	38	2.869	0.86
Total fertility rate						
Colombia	−0.127	−23.360	0.938	38	0.367	7.69
Costa Rica	−0.131	−21.505	0.928	38	0.413	7.38
Côte d'Ivoire	0.011	6.997	0.576	38	0.102	1.42
Kenya	−0.011	−2.304	0.129	38	0.327	4.34
Life expectancy at birth						
Colombia	0.502	30.696	0.961	40	1.194	2.59
Costa Rica	0.510	73.472	0.993	40	0.506	1.06
Côte d'Ivoire	0.462	54.466	0.987	40	0.620	1.50
Kenya	0.514	73.194	0.993	40	0.512	1.73

The figure for Colombia is 1.7 percentage points, and Côte d'Ivoire follows with 1 percentage point per year.

Colombia also shows the fastest decrease in crude birth rates per one thousand people (−0.64 per year). In regard to (crude) death rates the record is less impressive. In this case, Colombia ranks third after Kenya and Côte d'Ivoire. The improvements in infant mortality rates and in life expectancy are very similar across countries. On average, each year the number of babies that die per one thousand born falls by 2–2.6 in these countries. Also, each year babies can expect to live half a year more than those born the year before.

All in all, there seems to be a negative correlation between the trend coefficient in these variables and the standard deviation of the business cycle. Colombia, the country with more macroeconomic stability, fares relatively well in terms of long-term social progress, as measured by the trend component of those indicators.

Cyclical Components

The fluctuations in the social indicators around their long-run path (i.e., the residuals of the linear trend regressions) can be interpreted as an approximation to the concept of "social" cycle. Consequently, the standard deviation of those residuals (shown in the last two columns of table 3.5) measures the relative stability of each particular social indicator.

It is interesting to observe that when the regressions are estimated in logarithmic form (so that the standard deviation is expressed in percentage deviations from trend), Colombia's social indicators stand out as being relatively more stable. Frequently, it has the least variance (e.g., enrollment rates in secondary education), or is close to the minimum level (e.g., teachers in primary and secondary education). There are, however, some indicators that show a relatively high variance (e.g., fertility rates, life expectancy).

In addition, the evidence suggests that those indicators where fastest progress has been achieved are also the ones with more stability. In a way, there is some indication that social stability is associated with social progress (although we do not have enough information to provide a definite proof for this point).

Another remarkable fact about the "social" cycle is its high degree of correlation across countries. Table 3.6 shows the correlation matrices for the cyclical components of the leading social indicators. The correlations are usually high and positive, suggesting the presence of a common determinant. As in the case of business cycles, the correlations are particularly high between Colombia and Costa Rica. The pattern for Côte d'Ivoire and Kenya is more erratic, occasionally showing negative coefficients. On average, and for most indicators, there is evidence of strong comovements in these indicators.

One way of exploring for possible common determinants in the fluctuations of social indicators is by estimating regressions where the "social" cycle is the dependent variable and the business cycle and a constant are used as regressors. The presumption is that business cycles can explain social cycles. Since we saw that the frequency of the business cycles is led by external shocks, these regressions would suggest that those shocks also affect social indicators. In a way, stabilization policies would be justified not only on the grounds of (private) consumption smoothing, but also given the effect of the stability in social indicators on their long-run performance.

As shown in table 3.7 the evidence strongly supports this hypothesis. A large fraction of the variance in social cycles can be explained by business cycles. For example, in the case of secondary education enrollment rates, R^2 is higher than 0.48 in all cases (as high as 0.72 in Costa Rica). In general, the regressions for Colombia and Costa Rica are highly powerful in explaining the dependent variable: social and business cycles are very highly correlated in these two countries (for several indicators R is higher than 0.75).

The regressions are perhaps less robust for Côte d'Ivoire and Kenya, especially in regard to variables related to the number of teachers in primary and secondary education. The regressions that use gross enrollment ratios (primary and secondary) are, however, uniformly significant. In conclusion, fluctuations in world coffee prices do seem to have procyclical effects on enrollment ratios.

Table 3.6　　　　　　**Cyclical Component in:**

	Colombia	Costa Rica	Côte d'Ivoire	Kenya
Teachers in primary education per 1000 people aged 5–14				
Colombia	1.000			
Costa Rica	0.815	1.000		
Côte d'Ivoire	−0.165	−0.254	1.000	
Kenya	0.636	0.317	−0.258	1.000
Teachers in secondary education per 1000 people aged 15–19				
Colombia	1.000			
Costa Rica	0.094	1.000		
Côte d'Ivoire	−0.229	0.760	1.000	
Kenya	0.353	0.425	0.255	1.000
Enrollment in primary education per 1000 people aged 5–14				
Colombia	1.000			
Costa Rica	0.542	1.000		
Côte d'Ivoire	0.370	−0.276	1.000	
Kenya	0.344	−0.203	0.308	1.000
Enrollment in secondary education per 1000 people aged 15–19				
Colombia	1.000			
Costa Rica	0.932	1.000		
Côte d'Ivoire	−0.120	0.094	1.000	
Kenya	0.113	0.354	0.569	1.000
Gross enrollment ratio: primary				
Colombia	1.000			
Costa Rica	0.805	1.000		
Côte d'Ivoire	0.417	0.516	1.000	
Kenya	0.581	0.272	0.408	1.000
Gross enrollment ratio: secondary				
Colombia	1.000			
Costa Rica	0.665	1.000		
Côte d'Ivoire	0.393	0.759	1.000	
Kenya	0.394	0.755	0.566	1.000
Crude birth rate per 1000 people				
Colombia	1.000			
Costa Rica	0.579	1.000		
Côte d'Ivoire	0.269	0.513	1.000	
Kenya	−0.320	−0.367	0.216	1.000
Crude death rate per 1000 people				
Colombia	1.000			
Costa Rica	0.778	1.000		
Côte d'Ivoire	0.685	0.734	1.000	
Kenya	−0.335	−0.531	−0.303	1.000
Infant (0–1) mortality rate				
Colombia	1.000			
Costa Rica	0.138	1.000		
Côte d'Ivoire	0.479	−0.092	1.000	
Kenya	0.537	−0.242	0.737	1.000

Table 3.6   (continued)

	Colombia	Costa Rica	Côte d'Ivoire	Kenya
Total fertility rate				
Colombia	1.000			
Costa Rica	0.811	1.000		
Côte d'Ivoire	0.601	0.144	1.000	
Kenya	0.144	−0.227	0.806	1.000
Life expectancy at birth				
Colombia	1.000			
Costa Rica	0.669	1.000		
Côte d'Ivoire	−0.797	−0.174	1.000	
Kenya	0.866	0.468	−0.919	1.000

Note: Original variables in rates.

In addition, large fluctuations in social indicators do impose constraints on their long-term improvement.

3.4   Conclusions

This paper suggests that macroeconomic stability is a necessary (but not sufficient) condition to achieve social progress. As the recent literature on the political economy of stabilization has shown, the mechanisms for achieving stability have to do both with institutions and policies. In particular, institutions should give policymakers the incentives to stabilize the economy. Institutions, in this sense, are not neutral to the results. Different arrangements give rise to different macroeconomic outcomes. Institutions, therefore, can be ranked according to the policies and the performance of the main macroeconomic indicators.

Two important institutions in the developing world are tax systems and commodity stabilization boards. Commodity stabilization mechanisms have the purpose of taxing windfall gains when prices are high, and cushioning the income of commodity producers when prices decrease, by subsidizing local prices with the savings accumulated during the good times. In many countries the stabilization objectives of the marketing boards are soon abandoned, and such institutions become taxing mechanisms that distort farm prices and maintain expensive bureaucracies. But in some cases, the stabilization mechanism does work according to theory, and helps avoid large changes in the aggregate consumption of commodity producers. Commodity boards that reflect the preferences of coffee producers (as in Colombia) are more likely to perform well by stabilizing producers' incomes (and hence the economy). This is not true in places where the management of the board reflects the preferences of a highly impatient policymaker. In fact, in such cases it is likely that the board introduces more instability, by generating a highly procyclical pattern in government expenditures (as in Côte d'Ivoire).

Table 3.7   **Social Cycle versus Business Cycle, 1960–85 (all variables in rates)**

	Coefficient	t-Stat	R^2	N	Standard Deviation Residuals
Teachers in primary education per 1000 people aged 5–14					
Colombia	11.900	6.748	0.752	17	0.287
Costa Rica	7.323	3.962	0.529	16	0.500
Côte d'Ivoire	0.803	0.451	0.015	15	0.420
Kenya	7.914	1.197	0.087	17	0.926
Teachers in secondary eduction per 1000 people aged 15–19					
Colombia	9.922	3.004	0.376	17	0.538
Costa Rica	2.205	0.882	0.089	10	0.543
Côte d'Ivoire	0.891	0.438	0.021	11	0.404
Kenya	1.122	0.644	0.029	16	0.238
Enrollment in primary education per 1000 people aged 5–14					
Colombia	377.403	7.140	0.773	17	8.610
Costa Rica	61.650	1.993	0.209	17	8.813
Côte d'Ivoire	68.357	2.438	0.284	17	7.310
Kenya	148.096	0.589	0.023	17	35.192
Enrollment in secondary education per 1000 people aged 15–19					
Colombia	393.596	4.280	0.550	17	14.979
Costa Rica	371.415	6.571	0.742	17	16.103
Côte d'Ivoire	−6.197	−0.357	0.021	8	2.743
Kenya	58.303	0.823	0.043	17	9.915
Gross enrollment ratio: primary					
Colombia	197.440	5.822	0.790	11	5.226
Costa Rica	35.755	4.350	0.612	14	2.438
Côte d'Ivoire	7.446	0.541	0.035	10	3.479
Kenya	292.961	3.347	0.483	14	8.438
Gross enrollment ratio: secondary					
Colombia	48.006	3.198	0.532	11	2.313
Costa Rica	57.563	5.349	0.722	13	2.951
Côte d'Ivoire	14.095	3.302	0.476	14	1.312
Kenya	32.962	3.248	0.468	14	0.978
Teachers in primary education per 1000 people aged 5–14					
Colombia	10.812	7.940	0.798	18	0.256
Costa Rica	6.566	5.067	0.631	17	0.484
Côte d'Ivoire	−0.983	−1.139	0.085	16	0.434
Kenya	5.583	2.123	0.220	18	0.831
Teachers in secondary education per 1000 people aged 15–19					
Colombia	9.626	3.607	0.449	18	0.501
Costa Rica	1.914	0.948	0.101	10	0.540
Côte d'Ivoire	0.697	0.461	0.023	11	0.404
Kenya	0.793	1.030	0.066	17	0.233

Table 3.7   (continued)

	Coefficient	t-Stat	R^2	N	Standard Deviation Residuals
Enrollment in primary education per 1000 people aged 5–14					
Colombia	365.280	8.210	0.818	17	7.704
Costa Rica	46.910	1.949	0.202	17	8.853
Côte d'Ivoire	42.865	2.202	0.244	17	7.509
Kenya	154.599	1.466	0.125	17	33.293
Enrollment in secondary education per 1000 people aged 15–19					
Colombia	377.330	4.469	0.571	17	14.621
Costa Rica	278.272	5.839	0.694	17	17.527
Côte d'Ivoire	−5.674	−0.456	0.033	8	2.725
Kenya	39.959	1.314	0.103	17	9.599
Gross enrollment ratio: primary					
Colombia	192.390	9.095	0.892	12	3.695
Costa Rica	34.563	4.658	0.625	15	2.956
Côte d'Ivoire	8.367	1.271	0.152	11	3.334
Kenya	126.190	4.840	0.643	15	6.760
Gross enrollment ratio: secondary					
Colombia	39.555	2.934	0.463	12	2.355
Costa Rica	42.408	5.109	0.685	14	3.058
Côte d'Ivoire	7.195	2.917	0.396	15	1.376
Kenya	12.882	3.711	0.514	15	0.900

Some tax systems can also be more stabilizing than others. If the income tax is a large proportion of tax revenues, the system works as an automatic (income and consumption) stabilization device. On the other hand, a tax system very dependent on trade taxes may be destabilizing. Tax revenues decrease precisely when export prices decrease, generating a fiscal deficit at the same time as a trade deficit.

Institutional change is, however, a difficult task. In some countries it is particularly difficult to pass a tax reform or to devalue the currency. There may be very strong pressure groups that oppose devaluations, such as the army or an urban middle class, and no institutional mechanisms for treating devaluation decisions in such a way that these groups have no veto power. In other countries, tax reforms are very difficult to implement. For example, in Venezuela, a value-added tax has been discussed and proposed for many years, but it has never been passed by Congress. In other countries the congress has an interest in certain social expenditure programs for electoral reasons, and tax reforms are possible.

In addition, government (social) expenditures are important for promoting social progress and human development. The conclusion that we obtain from our analysis is that macroeconomic stability has to be matched with sustained programs on the part of the state. However, the effects of public expenditures that are not properly financed and rely heavily on the inflation tax are completely undermined. Moreover, the paper provides a strong argument for diminishing fiscal deficits.

Political structure may determine the level and degree of fluctuation of fiscal deficits, variables that we have shown affect social progress. Countries that have difficulty adjusting tax systems may thus have to live with discontinuity in crucial social programs, and this affects their social welfare indicators.

The difficulty in solving budget deficits may also create an inflation bias, insofar as the government tries to use the inflation tax instead of adjusting other taxes. This inflation bias would also appear to affect negatively the indicators of social progress.

Policies also play a role. As has been mentioned, a bias toward stability would recommend to policymakers exchange rate and commercial policies that favor export diversification. Such policies would tend to diminish the variations in tax revenues, balance-of-payments disequilibria, income, and consumption that large changes in terms of trade generate. Clearly policies that attempt to maintain fairly constant RERs also generate stability in the balance of payments and tax revenues from trade taxes. Policies with a strong ideological bias against large fiscal deficits (but not necessarily expenditures) and inflation probably also favor social progress, if we accept some of the empirical relations found in this paper. This does not mean, however, that fiscal balance should always be pursued. As the Colombian experience illustrates, a countercyclical fiscal policy is the key to macroeconomic (business cycle) stability. What it means is that budget surpluses and deficits should not be too large and cancel out intertemporally (over relatively short periods of time).

Many of these stabilizing institutions and policies have costs. This would certainly be the case of marketing boards, or a political bias toward increases in tax burdens, which would be the corollary of political arrangements that facilitate revenue-enhancing tax reforms. The question is whether the social benefits generated by stabilizing institutions and policies are greater than the costs. The empirical evidence here suggests that the benefits of fiscal stability may be worth the costs. The case studies of the coffee producers indicate the mechanisms that compensate terms of trade shocks may also have social benefits.

Appendix
Data Sources

GNP per Capita. International Monetary Fund, *International Financial Statistics Yearbook 1990* (data 1970–85).

Real GDP per Capita Adjusted for Changes in the Terms of Trade. Taken from Robert Summers and Alan Heston, A New Set of International Comparisons of Real Product and Price Levels: Estimates for 130 Countries, 1950–1985, *Review of Income and Wealth* 34 (March 1988): 1–25.

Fiscal Deficit. International Monetary Fund, *International Financial Statistics Yearbook 1990* (data 1970–85).

Inflation. International Monetary Fund, *International Financial Statistics Yearbook 1990* (data 1970–85).

Terms of Trade. For Latin America: Comision Economica para America Latina, *Statistical Yearbook for Latin America and the Caribbean 1991* (data 1975–85). For the others: International Monetary Fund, *International Financial Statistics Yearbook 1990* (data 1973–85).

Real Exchange Rate. For Latin America: BID Progreso Económico y Social de América Latina, Informe 1991 (data 1975–85). For other countries: International Monetary Fund, *International Financial Statistics Yearbook 1990* (data 1973–85).

Current Account. International Monetary Fund, *International Financial Statistics Yearbook 1990* (data 1973–85).

References

Barro, Robert. 1991. Economic Growth in a Cross Section of Countries. *Quarterly Journal of Economics* 106 (May): 407–43.

Bulmer–Thomas, Victor. 1987. The Political Economy of Central America since 1920. Cambridge: Cambridge University Press.

Campbell, John Y., and P. Perron. 1991. Pitfalls and Opportunities: What Macroeconomists Should Know about Unit Roots. In S. Fischer, ed., *NBER Macroeconomics Annual.* Cambridge: MIT Press.

Cárdenas, Mauricio. 1991. Coffee Exports, Endogenous State Policies, and the Business Cycle. Ph.D. diss., University of California, Berkeley.

Cuddington, John, and Carlos Urzúa. 1989. Trends and Cycles in Colombia's GDP and Fiscal Deficit. *Journal of Development Economics* 30:325–43.

Easterly, W., M. Kremer, L. Pritchett, and L. Summers. 1992. Good Policy or Good Luck? Country Growth Performance and Temporary Shocks. Washington, DC: World Bank, March. Mimeo.

Fischer, Stanley. 1991. Growth, Macroeconomics, and Development. In Stanley Fischer, ed., *NBER Macroeconomics Annual.* Cambridge: MIT Press.

Ingram, Gregory. 1992. Social Indicators and Productivity Convergence in Developing Countries. World Bank Policy Research Working Papers, WPS 894. Washington, DC: World Bank.

Leamer, Edward. 1983. Let's Take the Con out of Econometrics. *American Economic Review* 73 (March): 31–43.

Levine, Ross, and David Renelt. 1992. A Sensitivity Analysis of Cross-Country Growth Regressions. *American Economic Review* 82 (4): 942–63.

Londoño, Juan Luis. 1992. Human Capital, Income Inequality, and the Development Process. *Quarterly Journal of Economics* forthcoming.

Mankiw, N. Gregory, David Romer, and David Weil. 1992. A Contribution to the Empirics of Economic Growth. *Quarterly Journal of Economics* 107 (May).

Romer, Paul. 1989. What Determines the Rate of Growth of Technological Change? Policy, Planning and Research Working Paper no. 279. Washington, DC: World Bank.

United Nations Development Programme. 1991. *Human Development Report.* Oxford: Oxford University Press.

4 Continuity, Change, and the Political Economy of Transition in Chile

Raúl Labán and Felipe Larraín

4.1 Introduction

Since the mid-1970s, the Chilean economy has suffered a profound transformation. From very high levels of protection and pervasive state intervention, it has been transformed into an economy integrated to world markets, where the engine of economic growth is the private sector. The process, however, has not been smooth on the economic front. Two major depressions—in 1975 and 1982–83—tested Chile's resolve in continuing free-market reforms, but the process endured. Political transition from authoritarian rule to democracy was also an important test for the economic model. To some, the opposition's victory in the presidential elections of December 1989 posed grave threats to the economy. These fears proved to be wrong, and in the early 1990s Chile's economic model has been deepened and legitimized in democracy.

This paper analyzes the economic policies pursued by the government of President Patricio Aylwin, which took office in March 1990, and discusses the issue of continuity and change in the policy regime. In an attempt to look forward, it also touches on the main challenges currently facing the Chilean economy. Despite major progress, a significant fraction of the Chilean population still lives below the poverty line. Consolidating a strong and stable path of economic growth is an essential component in the defeat of poverty and underdevelopment. Persistent economic growth on the order of 7% per year is attainable for Chile, but this requires a higher investment and saving effort.

Raúl Labán is macroeconomic advisor at the Ministry of Finance in Chile. Felipe Larraín is professor of economics at the Universidad Católica de Chile.

The authors would like to thank Stanley Fischer, Ricardo Lago, and conference participants for helpful comments, and Marcelo Tokman for efficient research assistance.

4.2   The Legacy of the Military Regime, 1973–90

In this section, we briefly review the main economic developments and reforms implemented during the military regime (1973–90) and describe the economic conditions under which Chile returned to democracy after sixteen years of authoritarian rule.

4.2.1   Economic Policy in the Authoritarian Era[1]

The Dramatic Changes of the 1970s: The Chilean Transition to Markets

From the outset of the military regime in late 1973, the Chilean economy began the transition to markets by implementing a number of major economic and institutional reforms aimed at attaining three different objectives: stabilization, privatization, and liberalization. The first two objectives were to be achieved immediately, while liberalization was supposed to be more gradual.

Stabilization amounted initially to the elimination of the imbalances in the goods markets, induced by an excess of government intervention during the previous administration, and in the public sector. By the end of 1974 and during 1975, the efforts concentrated mainly on correcting the balance-of-payments deficit provoked by the collapse in the world price of copper (Chile's main export) and the tripling of oil prices. Finally, it addressed the control of inflation. The stabilization attempt ended by fixing the nominal exchange rate in 1979, which was supposed to play the role of a nominal anchor for the economy. Inflation, however, did not converge to international levels due to widespread indexation in labor and financial markets and to an aggregate spending that was expanding faster than output. This caused an important decline in the real exchange rate and thus in the competitiveness of the tradable sector.

A first round of privatization (1974–78) was centered on the divestiture of most of the real assets that had been transferred to the state during the Unidad Popular administration (1970–73). By 1980, the public sector remained in control of only forty-three firms (including one commercial bank), compared to the more than five hundred firms under state control during President Allende's administration. Privatization was part of a comprehensive attempts to restructure the public sector.

Liberalization involved many reforms aimed at increasing the role of market forces in the economy. The starting point was the freeing of most controlled prices in late 1973, followed by a sweeping deregulation of the domestic financial market and the beginning of extensive trade liberalization. This trend was extended to international financial transactions by the end of the decade and especially during the early 1980s.

---

1. This section draws on Larraín (1991a, 1991b). For a detailed analysis of economic developments during this period, see also Edwards and Cox-Edwards (1987) and Meller (1990).

In 1979, a major labor reform established collective bargaining at the firm level, relaxed the prohibition on dismissals, and restricted strikes. These reforms to labor legislation reduced the negotiating power of workers vis-à-vis employers (in comparison to the pre-1973 legislation) and were strongly opposed by labor organizations.

By the beginning of the 1980s, Chile had undergone a deep process of economic restructuring. This embodied a dramatic change in the relative roles of the private and public sectors, and increased the role played by markets in the allocation of productive resources. At that time, Chile had market-determined domestic interest rates and prices (with the exception of public wages and the exchange rate), a unified exchange rate system, a uniform 10% import tariff as the only trade barrier (except for automobiles), and a relatively liberalized capital market.

Economic performance experienced wide fluctuations in the period 1974–81. A very large contraction took place during 1974–75, with GDP declining by about 13% and unemployment surging to 16.4% of the labor force in 1975. This was attributable not only to the terms of trade loss resulting from the rise of oil prices and the fall of copper prices, but also to a sharp decline in domestic demand as a consequence of restrictive fiscal and monetary policies, and exchange rate devaluation, which sharply reduced real wages—by 15.6% during 1974–75 (see table 4.1).

It is difficult to identify how much of the reduction in real wages and the employment losses was due to the economic reforms implemented at that time and how much was due to other shocks. But privatization of state enterprises with overemployment and trade liberalization may be expected to induce, at least in the short run, a decline in living standards and an increase in unemployment.

In 1976–77, the economy recovered from the 1975 depression and then experienced four years of growth at an average rate of 7.5%. The recovery gave way to a boom in 1980–81, spurred by a major shift in expectations, from a realistic assessment of Chile's prospects to an illusion of sustained, high growth. Unemployment, however, remained very high during the complete period.

The opening of the capital account and the abundance of foreign credit in the late seventies and early eighties provided the financing necessary for an unsustainable expansion in private expenditures at the time of the boom. By late 1981, Chile had accumulated a stock of foreign debt approaching US$16 billion. The economy was particularly vulnerable to an increase in interest rates, since almost 60% of the debt was contracted at variable rates, mostly tied to the London interbank offered rate, which in 1981 shot up to 16.5% at the same time that terms of trade declined by 6%. But the worst would come in the following year.

Table 4.1   Selected Macroeconomic Indicators in Chile, 1970–92

Years	GDP Growth[a] (%)	Inflation[b] (%)	Unemployment[c] (%)	Real Wages[d] (%)
1970–73[e]	1.1	218.1	4.4	−8.5
1974–79[e]	2.7	145.2	16.6	6.3
1974–89[e]	3.1	57.3	17.3	3.0
1980–89[e]	3.3	20.5	17.7	1.1
1985–89[e]	6.2	19.8	13.0	1.1
1990–92[e]	5.9	19.6	5.8	3.7
1974	1.0	369.2	9.2	−13.3
1975	−12.9	343.3	16.4	−2.7
1976	3.5	197.9	19.9	10.8
1977	9.9	84.2	18.6	21.5
1978	8.2	37.2	17.9	14.3
1979	8.3	38.9	17.7	10.9
1980	7.8	31.2	15.7	8.7
1981	5.5	9.5	15.6	8.9
1982	−14.1	20.7	26.4	−0.2
1983	−0.7	23.1	30.4	−10.6
1984	6.3	23.0	24.4	0.1
1985	2.4	26.4	21.4	−4.3
1986	5.7	17.4	16.0	2.1
1987	5.7	21.5	12.2	−0.2
1988	7.4	12.7	9.0	6.5
1989	10.0	21.4	6.3	1.9
1990	2.1	27.3	6.0	1.8
1991	6.0	18.7	6.5	4.9
1992[f]	9.7	12.7	4.9	4.5

[a]Central Bank of Chile. Monthly and quarterly reports.

[b]December to December, 1970–78: Cortázar and Marshall (CIEPLAN: Corporacion de Investiga-ciones Economicas para Latinoamerica 1979–92: Central Bank of Chile.

[c]1970–79: ODEPLAN (National Planning Office); 1980–92: Instituto Nacional de Estadisticas (INE). Includes emergency unemployment programs (PEM and POJH).

[d]1970–73: industrial sector; 1974–92: aggregate index; Instituto Nacional de Estadisticas (INE).

[e]Average annual rates.

[f]Preliminary estimates.

Crisis, Adjustment, Recovery, and Growth (1982–89)

In 1982–83, Chile experienced its worst economic crisis since the 1930s, with real output collapsing by 15%. This major depression was partly a result of several external shocks: the drying up of voluntary external financing, the deterioration of 23% in the terms of trade since 1980, and the major increase in foreign interest rates. But the impact of external developments was exacerbated by several domestic policy mishandlings: the fixed exchange rate policy coupled with mandatory indexation of wages at 100% of past inflation; the sweeping opening of the capital account at the time of the boom; the radical liberalization of domestic financial markets without the provision of proper regulations and controls; and the belief in the "automatic adjustment" mechanism, by which policymakers expected the market to produce a quick adjustment to the new recessionary conditions without interference by the authorities.

The government initially responded to the 1982 external payments crisis with a contractionary adjustment policy during 1982–83, aimed at closing the income-expenditure gap. Output dropped during both years, the unemployment rate reached over 30% of the labor force in 1983, and real wages declined by almost 11% during this period. In addition, the exchange rate policy was erratic, as shown by the implementation of five different exchange rate regimes after the abandonment of the fixed exchange rate policy in June 1982. The external disequilibrium was reduced in 1983, but the economy continued to be depressed. This is not surprising, since most of the adjustment to Chile's external crisis occurred initially through import reduction induced by an aggregate expenditure contraction, while substitution effects in demand and exports showed little response. In 1983, imports were less than 50% of their 1981 level.

In order to prevent the high costs that the adjustment program was inducing, the government pursued an expansionary policy during most of 1984, which helped to achieve a recovery in output but proved to be unsustainable. The current account deficit almost doubled, surpassing US$2 billion—10.7% of GDP. In September of that year, the exchange rate was devalued and tariffs were raised, in order to induce a switch in expenditure toward domestic goods.

At the beginning of 1985, a new macroeconomic policy was implemented. Its aim was to promote a recovery of output and employment through the export-oriented structural adjustment of the economy. Policy actions centered on three fronts: the promotion of noncopper exports, the enhancement of domestic saving and investment, and the strengthening of the corporate and financial sectors.

The heavy burden of a foreign debt in excess of GDP required a vigorous effort to promote exports. At the same time, the need to diversify exports beyond copper had been recognized, and a process of export diversification had been under way since the midseventies. To strengthen this effort, the authorities relied on several policies: a series of devaluations restored first the loss in international competitiveness suffered during the fixed exchange rate period (1979–82), and were followed by the stabilization of the real exchange rate at a competitive level; import tariffs were reduced from 35% to 15% in three steps; and various fiscal and administrative measures were effected, including a 10% import duties rebate on minor exports and an acceleration of existing tax refunds for exporters. While these measures were primarily oriented toward exports, they also provided an incentive for efficient import substitution stemming from the high level of the real exchange rate.

During 1985–89 the volume of exports of goods and services expanded at an average annual rate of 10.5%, and Chile became one of the countries with

Table 4.2   Evolution of Imports, Exports, and the Real Exchange Rate, 1980–92

Year	Import Volume[a]		Export Volume[a]		Real Exchange Rate[b] (1980=100)
	% of Real GDP	Annual Rate of Change	% of Real GDP	Annual Rate of Change	
1980	30.3		23.6		100.0
1981	33.1	15.7	20.3	−9.0	87.0
1982	24.7	−35.3	24.6	4.7	97.0
1983	20.9	−17.9	25.3	0.1	116.4
1984	22.3	13.2	24.4	2.3	121.7
1985	19.6	−10.3	26.9	12.3	149.5
1986	20.9	14.1	27.5	9.7	164.5
1987	23.1	17.0	28.3	8.8	171.5
1988	24.1	12.1	27.9	6.1	182.9
1989	27.4	25.3	29.4	15.7	178.6
1990	27.0	0.6	31.0	7.6	185.4
1991	27.7	8.5	33.0	12.9	175.0
1992[c]	30.7	21.6	34.0	13.1	161.1

[a]Import and exports of goods and services in 1977 pesos, National Accounts, Central Bank of Chile.
[b]Effective real exchange rate, Central Bank of Chile.
[c]Preliminary projections.

higher outward orientation, as exports of goods and services accounted in 1989 for 29.4% of GDP, compared to 23.6% in 1980 (see table 4.2 and figure 4.1).

National saving reached a remarkable low of 1.6% of GDP in 1982. As foreign saving became severely limited, it was imperative to improve the domestic effort in order to finance higher levels of investment. At a broad level, the restoration of macroeconomic stability was essential to increase saving. But specific policies were also pursued. The tax reform of December 1984 promoted corporate saving through a radical reduction in the tax rate affecting retained earnings. Attempting to encourage household saving, the reform also allowed a reduction from the tax base of 20% of certain qualified investments.

Public revenues were hurt by the depressed economic activity, the social security reform of mid-1981 (which required increased public contributions to the state social security system), the 1984 tax reform (which significantly reduced direct taxation), and the reduction of 20% of import tariffs.

In view of weakened public finances, the government implemented a series of measures to improve its financial position. Wage adjustments in the public sector were set systematically below inflation, and social security disbursements ceased to be adjusted automatically to lagged inflation. Several other categories of current and capital expenditures were also curtailed.

During 1982–83, nonfinancial corporations had become very weak—some outright insolvent—as a consequence of extremely high real interest rates, the effects of currency devaluation on dollar-denominated debt, and the economic depression. These factors, coupled with faulty banking practices in a permissive regulatory environment, set the stage for a major crisis in the financial sector, requiring regulators to assume control of several troubled financial institutions, including the two largest private commercial banks.

In the short run, the government reacted to the crisis with a substantial aid package for banks and local debtors. This package included a preferential exchange rate for dollar debts, at times 40% below the official rate; credit lines at below-market rates for the financial sector; and the Central Bank's purchase of bad loans from the banking system with a repurchase agreement, which also involved a subsidy. The various programs were phased out by the end of 1986, but their cost was substantial for the public sector. The total value of subsidies for financial rehabilitation was estimated at approximately US$6 billion, or about 35% of 1986 GDP. In an attempt to avoid the mistakes of the earlier financial liberalization, bank regulation was strengthened, and the regulatory powers of the Superintendency of Banks and Financial Institutions were enhanced. By mid-1985, the authorities started a major recapitalization program for private banks.

During the second half of the 1980s, a second round of privatization was carried out. A total of forty-six firms—a number of financial institutions that were intervened in by the government to keep them from bankruptcy after the economic and financial crisis—were sold to the private sector for slightly over US$3 billion. This process was relatively rapid, given the large number of firms and the volume of the assets sold.

Macroeconomic performance significantly improved after 1984. In 1985, the economy started a sustained recovery, accompanied by a steady improve-

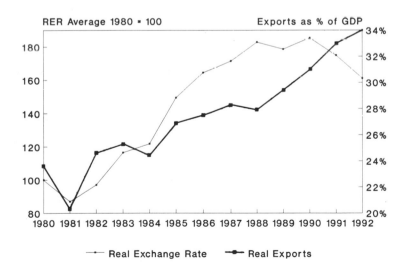

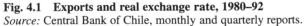

Fig. 4.1   Exports and real exchange rate, 1980–92
Source: Central Bank of Chile, monthly and quarterly reports.

ment in the external accounts. These results came from a combination of internal and external factors. Internally, the structural adjustment program was accompanied by macroeconomic stability, which enabled response to the new policies. The fiscal deficit declined from 4.3% of GDP in 1984 to about balance in 1989. On the external front, the decline of world interest rates during a good part of the program and the improvement of the terms of trade in 1986–89 certainly helped the current account and economic growth.

The structural adjustment program was quite successful in the promotion of noncopper exports and the efficient substitution of imports. The combination of a competitive real exchange rate, low and flat tariffs, and specific fiscal incentives produced a strong response from nontraditional exports. At the same time, the generalized economic recovery strengthened substantially both the financial and nonfinancial sectors.

4.2.2 Income Distribution, Poverty, and the Military Regime's Economic Policy

The record in terms of income distribution during the authoritarian period points toward a deterioration, both during the restructuring process of the 1970s and through most of the structural adjustment process of the 1980s. This is not surprising, given the two sharp depressions that Chile experienced in this period and the painful adjustments that followed. In each case, real wages declined significantly and unemployment increased to unprecedented levels. Additionally, some of the economic measures adopted during these periods had a regressive bias.

It has been shown that the income of the poor is very accurately explained by the unemployment rate and the wage index. On the whole, wages in Chile declined more than per capita output, and unemployment was quite high on average.[2] It is likely, then, that income distribution worsened.

Several measures confirm this trend in income distribution. The Gini coefficient increased from around 0.50 in 1970 to more than 0.54 during 1982–84. The share in national income of the highest quintile increased steadily from 55.8% in 1970 to 59.5% in 1982–84, while the income share of the poorest two quintiles declined from 11.5% in 1970 to 10% in 1982–84. The worst point of income distribution happened, then, at the height of the depression (see table 4.3).[3] In 1989, however, the share of the bottom 40% had climbed back to 12.6%, while the top 20% had retained its 59.5% share; this suggests a recovery of income distribution in the second half of the 1980s.

A number of social expenditure items were severely affected by the adjustment to the economic and financial crisis, especially in the first half of the

---

2. The average rate of unemployment increased from 6.5% in the 1960s to 17.3% during 1974–89.

3. For a more detailed discussion on the distributive impact of the adjustment program carried out in the 1980s in the Chilean economy, see Larraín (1991b) and Meller (1991).

Table 4.3   **Income Distribution in Chile: Selected Years, 1970–92**

Years	Gini Coefficient of Family Income[a]	Share of Income[a]			Real Wage Index[b] (1970=100)	Unemployment Rate[c] (%)
		Lowest 40%	Middle 40%	Highest 20%		
1970	0.500	11.5	32.7	55.8	100.0	5.7
1979–81	0.523	11.1	31.3	57.6	93.8	16.5
1982–84[d]	0.543	10.0	30.5	59.5	94.7	27.4
1989		12.6	27.9	59.5	97.6	6.3
1990		13.3	28.7	58.0	99.4	6.0
1991		14.7	30.6	54.7	104.3	6.5
1992[e]					109.0	4.9

Source: INE: Instituto Nacional de Estadisticas. Monthly report.

[a]Meller (1991).

[b]Central Bank of Chile. Monthly report.

[c]Cortázar and Marshall (1980).

[d]The share of income of different groups corresponds to 1982–83.

[e]Preliminary projections.

1980s. Thus, the per capita health, housing, and education budgets declined by more than 20% during the adjustment to the crisis of the 1980s.

The economic crisis and the policies directed to close the income-expenditure gap pushed the unemployment rate to over 30%—including emergency employment programs (PEM [*programa de empleo mínimo*, minimum employment program] and POJH [*programa de ocupación para obreros jefes de hogar,* employment program for heads of family])—in 1983, with unemployment remaining over 24% for almost four years (1982–85); real wages declined by 20% for at least five years, and minimum real wages dropped 40% during 1981–85.

Revenues of the public health system were also hurt with the privatization of middle- and high-income health care. When the option to switch to the private health institutions was given, 8% of the affiliates did so and carried with them 40% of the revenues of the public entity. While the reform certainly increased the quality of service for those who switched, the lower income groups suffered significantly from the decline in resources of the state system.

The military regime implemented several correct principles in the social sectors, such as targeting to the lower income groups, and decentralization and competition in the provision of social services. These principles found concrete application in successful programs such as free distribution of milk and attention to pregnant women, which influenced the sharp reduction in the country's infant mortality rate.[4] Nonetheless, this effort was not sufficient. A high

---

4. For a thorough—and favorable—analysis of social policies during the military government, see Castañeda (1990).

proportion of Chileans—estimated at around 45% by Torche (1987)—were living below the poverty level in the mid-1980s. Although poverty in Chile is not a new problem, this high proportion was, to a significant extent, the result of the 1982–83 depression and the adjustment pattern that followed. The economic recovery and the resumption of growth in 1986–88 improved this situation, but it takes decades of economic expansion to break the circle of poverty.

4.2.3   The Legacy of the Military Regime

It is widely recognized that the first democratically elected government after sixteen years of military rule in Chile inherited, in general terms, a very successful economy. This stands as a major contrast to other experiences of transition in the region.

At the end of the military government, the Chilean economy had been successful in completing its stabilization and structural adjustment. The country was a leader in the implementation of a number of economic reforms—trade and social security reforms and privatization, among others. The last half decade of the military regime was also the subperiod with better economic performance. During 1985–89, real GDP expanded at an average rate of 6.2%, inflation averaged 19.8%, the volume of exports expanded at an average annual rate of 10.5%, and the government was able to achieve a fiscal surplus of over 1% of GDP in 1989.

Nevertheless, as we just discussed, this success was not painless. The structural adjustment process carried out during this period resulted in significant costs. Available information is robust in pointing out a deterioration of income distribution during this period and the fact that the transition to democracy was initiated in the context of a high share of the population living in poverty.

By the end of the military regime, poverty had also become a very significant concern in public opinion. According to a September 1988 poll conducted by a prestigious private academic institution (Centro de Estudios Públicos, CEP), poverty and low income levels were the principal reasons behind the vote for the "no" option in the plebiscite of October 1988, which cleared the way for competitive presidential and congressional elections held in December 1989.

4.3   Economic Policies of the Aylwin Administration

The government of President Aylwin, a center-left coalition known as Concertación, was elected with an absolute majority in December 1989 and went into office in March 1990. The new administration started from a strong position on the economic front and maintained the economic model inherited from the previous regime. This produced a climate of stability in economic policy and institutions, necessary for strong private investment and sustained growth.

The democratic legitimization of the free-market economic model adopted by the previous regime was crucial. To attain this goal the government had to gain, in a short period of time, support for policy continuity from organized labor and from those that were hit worst during the prolonged adjustment process of the 1980s. Among the latter were those earning the minimum wage, which was, at the beginning of 1990, 35% lower than its real value for 1980; those receiving family allowances (which had not been adjusted since 1985), whose purchasing power in 1990 was a third of that in 1980; the average worker, whose real wage in 1989 was 1.6% lower than its average real wage in 1980–81; those receiving public sector pensions, which declined 10% in real terms from 1985 to early 1990; recipients of the subsidy for extremely poor families, which declined 50% in real terms between 1981 and 1989; and beneficiaries of social spending, which went down 20% in per capita terms since 1985. Clearly, the adjustment of the economy from the deep depression of 1982–83 had not been painless, but the economy was at the beginning of 1990 in a solid position to improve the situation of people.

The Aylwin administration was able to create a climate of consensus in the conduct of economic policy, which was central to shape the reforms that were implemented and to design the development strategy that was to be followed during this period. This strategy was built on four widely accepted principles. First, the market was to play the leading role in the allocation of resources and in the distribution of goods and services. Second, the maintenance of macroeconomic stability (building on fiscal austerity and monetary discipline) was crucial to ensure sustainable growth. Third, there was a commitment to increase social spending in health, housing, pensions, and education. Lastly, it was recognized that external markets provide the best opportunities for small economies, and thus the government must try to maintain a competitive real exchange rate and make efforts to increase the integration of the Chilean economy to the international markets in goods, services, and capital.

4.3.1   Macroeconomic Stability and the Management of Economic Policy

Managing Social Demands under Macroeconomic Equilibrium

The new democratic government faced several potential pressures from different groups of the population. An attempt to give in to all demands would have only produced short-term benefits at the cost of sacrificing macroeconomic stability and future growth. One need only witness the problems of Argentina, Brazil, and Peru in reconciling the different claims that arose with the restoration of democracy.

There was a wide agreement in the government and the opposition that the only way to allow a larger fraction of the population to benefit permanently from modernization, and to defeat poverty, was through sustained growth. But waiting for growth alone to eliminate poverty takes too long to be a viable solution ethically and politically. And growth does not necessarily come with improved income distribution in its earlier stages. If a large fraction of the population waits for years for the benefits of modernization, this process may be politically unsustainable in democracy. If perceived in this way by investors, such a postponement will ultimately limit, despite attractive fundamentals, the supply response to investment incentives until at least some of the uncertainty about the sustainability of pro-investment policies is resolved.[5]

Given the irreversible nature of productive real investment, stability and credibility in economic institutions and a solid basis of support for policy continuity may be more important to stimulate private investment than tax incentives and "high" ex ante rates of return. Put in other words, if there is a high degree of uncertainty in the economic-political environment, tax breaks and ex ante rates of return will have to be very attractive in order to have an important impact on the accumulation of physical capital (Dornbusch 1990; Pindyck 1991). Thus, an important cost associated with political and economic instability is its depressive impact on productive investment, and thus on economic growth.

The new administration avoided the conflict between macroeconomic stability and increased resources devoted to the lower-income groups in two ways: (1) changing the composition of government spending, whereas the share of social spending in the government budget during 1990–91 was 3.4 percentage points higher than in 1988–89;[6] and (2) implementing a tax reform that would contribute additional resources for social spending, as analyzed in section 4.3.2.

In addition, the government sent to Congress a labor reform in 1990, partly intended to balance negotiating power between employees and employers, and raised the minimum wage, the family allowance, and the subsidy for low-income families during 1990–92. These adjustments were set in national agreements among the government, the major representatives of organized labor (Central Unitaria de Trabajadores, CUT), and of entrepreneurs (Confederación de la Producción y el Comercio, CPC), which allowed for a 21.9% rise in the real minimum wage between March 1990 and March 1992.[7] In April 1991, the government, CPC, and CUT agreed that, after this first stage of recovery, further real increases in the minimum wage should be related to gains in labor productivity, and that future expected inflation (as opposed to past inflation) should be used as the criterion for nominal adjustments.

Although the minimum wage has a coverage of only 12% of the labor force and there are no mandatory wage changes, its adjustment serves as a "signal" of inflationary expectations for the rest of the economy. Thus, the use of future expected inflation to set the minimum wage, which was in fact the criterion used in the 1992 negotiations, is an important contribution to breaking index-

5. "Pessimistic" expectations may be self-fulfilling. The wait-and-see strategy deprives the economy of much needed investment, thus retarding growth and eroding the political support for policy continuity. Ultimately, this may bring about the reversal of pro-investment policies initially feared (Labán and Wolf 1993).

6. Some significant inflexibilities were built into the budget, such as the impossibility—by law—of reducing defense spending in real terms.

7. The minimum wage was in March 1992, however, still 12% below its average real value for 1980–81.

ation to past inflation (widely used in labor and financial contracts) and therefore inflationary inertia. The negotiations of public and minimum wages for 1993 were also based on expected inflation.

There was some room for wage improvement at the beginning of the democratic government, but it was necessary to be cautious in this area. Several important reasons suggested restraint from wage increases beyond productivity improvements. First, even though unemployment was significantly reduced during 1988–89, the economy hit productive capacity constraints; thus, to sustain low levels of unemployment, the required increase in investment put a strict limit on real wage adjustments beyond productivity improvements. Second, real wages recovered significantly in 1988 and 1989, increasing by an accumulated 8.5% over this two-year period. This was a clear indication of a tightening labor market, which through its own workings would further increase wages as long as the economic expansion continued. Third, there were doubts about the impact that the labor and tax reforms would have on the private sector and thus on the capacity of the economy to create enough productive employments. Some economists predicted that the combined effect of the rigidities that the labor reform would introduce, and the reduction of incentives to invest for firms that the tax reform would imply, would reduce the capacity of the economy to create productive employments and thus would result in a higher "equilibrium" level of unemployment.

The experience of other countries in Latin America helped Chile in this respect. Aggressive wage adjustments have proved short-lived and have quickly resulted in sharp wage contractions, as figure 4.2 shows for Argentina, Brazil, and Peru in the 1980s. In the first two cases, the rise lasted for just one year and then gave way to an enormous contraction that soon left workers with lower real wages than before the start of the expansion. In Peru, wages increased for two years and then suffered a major setback that left them substantially below their initial level in 1985. Thus it is in the collective interest of workers to avoid this pattern.[8]

During the first three years of President Aylwin's administration, average wages and the minimum wage are expected to grow approximately by 12% and 28% in real terms, respectively.[9] At the end of 1992, the unemployment rate is projected to be around 4.5%, almost 2 percentage points below that attained in 1989. At the same time, fiscal social spending rose an accumulated

8. Dornbusch (1989b) has argued that an artificial rise in real wages makes labor gain at the expense of capital. This has a negative impact on capital formation and may even induce capital flight. Thus the initial increase in real wages is partially dampened by a decline in the capital stock, so that the level of real wages that can be sustained in equilibrium may be lower than when this process started. For an analysis of the populist cycle, see Dornbusch and Edwards (1991) and Sachs (1990).

9. This rise in the average real wage is explained mainly by three elements: the increase in labor demand due to the expansion in economic activity, the decline in inflation, and the increase in real minimum wages.

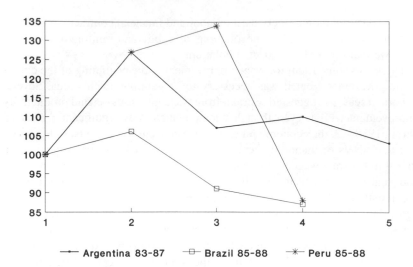

—•— Argentina 83-87   —▫— Brazil 85-88   —*— Peru 85-88

Fig. 4.2   Real wage index (year 1 = 100)
Source: Larrain 1991a.

20.5% real during 1990–91,[10] and it is expected to increase even further during the period 1992–93. Per capita fiscal social spending in the 1993 budget law is 40% higher in real terms than that stipulated in the 1990 budget law inherited from the military government. As agreed with CUT and CPC, the government has also implemented other measures directed to raise the income of poor families, such as increase in family allowances, subsidy to low-income families, payment of the 10.6% adjustment in the minimum pension that was not fulfilled in 1985, and wage rises to public sector teachers and health workers.

Higher wages and lower unemployment are bound to improve income distribution. Preliminary information suggests that income distribution improved during the first two and a half years of the Aylwin government. Estimates show that the income share of the richest 20% declined from 59.5% at the end of 1989 to 54.7% in 1991, which is the lowest level since 1970, while the lowest 40% of the population increased its share to 14.7%, the highest since 1970; the middle 40% of the families increased their share by 2.7 percentage points with respect to 1989. Nevertheless, there is still much to be done in Chile to improve income distribution and to reduce the still high share of the population living under the poverty line.

Cooperation with the government from organized labor, entrepreneurial associations, and the main opposition party (Renovación Nacional[11]) has been

10. This increase of public social spending can be decomposed into a 35.7% increase in health, 54.5% rise in housing, 8.2% increase in education, 21.6% rise in pensions, and 17.3% increase in other social items.
11. Renovación Nacional backed both the tax reform and the labor reform, as discussed below.

crucial in the preservation of macroeconomic stability and in the implementation of a social plan directed to integrate lower-income groups in a permanent way in the development process during the Aylwin administration.

Conducting Monetary Policy under High Capital Mobility

The new authorities thought that Chile could not sustain the high rates of GDP expansion it had experienced in 1988 (7.4%) and especially in 1989 (10%). They also considered the cumulative rates of expansion of private money (85%) and of domestic expenditure (23%) during 1988–89 to be unsustainable. This rapid expansion of aggregate demand had induced an increase in imports of 35% in value terms during 1989. In their view, the country was running the serious risk of an inflationary outburst.[12] The annualized rate of inflation reached 30% in the last quarter of 1989, and showed an upward trend. Nonetheless, the monthly indicator of economic activity (IMACEC)—a widely watched index in the country—showed that the economy was decelerating since the last quarter of 1989 (see table 4.4 and figure 4.3).

In early 1990, the Central Bank engineered a sharp monetary contraction aimed at reducing aggregate expenditure, and thus to moderate the rise of imports and to control inflation. Ex ante real interest rates on ten-year Central Bank bonds were raised from less than 7% in the last quarter of 1989 to 9.7% at the beginning of 1990. At the same time, the monetary authorities announced that the adjustment would be transitory, which indicated the prospect of substantial capital gains once interest rates declined to normal levels. Enthusiasm to acquire Central Bank bonds was immense, and the stock of Central Bank debt increased by 80% between December 1989 and December 1990. Attracted by high interest rates on long-term Central Bank bonds—which were offered through an open window—many funds invested on shorter-term instruments were shifted to longer term instruments, and annual short-term real rates surged, from 6% at the beginning of 1989 to 13.3% in March 1990, their highest level since 1981.

The adjustment was vastly complicated by international capital mobility.[13] Spreads between local interest rates and international rates increased so sharply that short-term speculative capital flew massively to Chile. As a result, during the first half of 1990 the nominal exchange rate went from the upper limit of its 10% fluctuation band to the bottom of the band and remained there for the rest of the year. Moreover, the monetary authority had to purchase dollars in order to defend the floor of the band. As a result of this intervention in the foreign exchange market, the Central Bank ended up accumulating US$2.4 billion in reserves during 1990. To control the consequent rise in the monetary base, the bank sterilized the effects of foreign exchange operations by selling

12. According to estimates by Marfán (1992), any excess productive capacity generated during the prolonged adjustment process of the 1980s had been exhausted by 1989.
13. On capital mobility in Chile, see Labán and Larraín (1993).

Table 4.4 Macroeconomic Quarterly Data for Chile, 1989–92 (%)

Quarter	GDP Growth[a]	Inflation[a]	Unemployment[b]	Real Wages[a]
1989				
I	9.8	13.3	6.2	4.1
II	12.2	20.8	7.0	0.9
III	10.3	21.7	6.4	−0.4
IV	7.6	30.5	5.3	3.1
1990				
I	5.5	22.9	5.3	1.5
II	0.8	24.3	6.5	1.7
III	0.2	40.1	6.6	−0.7
IV	2.1	22.9	5.7	5.0
1991				
I	2.4	7.1	6.2	7.2
II	5.6	27.7	6.8	4.1
III	6.2	18.8	7.5	6.6
IV	9.9	22.1	5.3	2.6
1992				
I	8.9	4.8	5.0	3.2
II	8.2	13.0	4.9	5.8
III	13.8	21.3	5.3	4.4
IV[c]	8.1	12.5	4.4	3.9

Source: Central Bank of Chile.
[a]Average twelve-month rate of growth.
[b]Quarterly average.
[c]Preliminary projections.

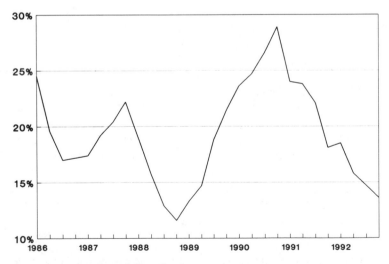

Fig. 4.3 Quarterly inflation, 1986–92
Source: Central Bank of Chile, monthly and quarterly reports.

more of its own bonds, preventing in this way a faster decline in interest rates. As a consequence, its balance sheet deteriorated: foreign exchange earned international interest rates, while Central Bank bonds paid a much higher peso rate.

The adjustment was costly in terms of output—GDP growth in 1990 was only 2.1%—but it served the monetary authority as a genuine proof that it was willing to pay a cost to fight what was regarded as an overheated economy, and thus to preserve macroeconomic equilibrium. Its contractionary effects, however, were milder on other variables and were soon reversed. The unemployment rate went from an average 6.2% during 1990–91 to an expected 4.8% by the end of 1992; real wages increased an accumulated 6.8% during 1990–91, and are expected to increase by 4.5% in 1992. An important increase in social spending and other government programs directed to lower-income groups also helped to mitigate the costs of the adjustment.

Fiscal Policy

Fiscal policy during the current government has been highly responsible, especially if compared to other transitions to democracy in the region. The government has spent no more than its income, generating a surplus in the consolidated nonfinancial public sector. Real government spending, however, increased at rates higher than GDP growth in 1991 (13.5%), while in 1992 it is expected to increase at a rate similar to GDP. Although the budgets approved by Congress have contemplated more moderate expansions, higher-than-projected revenues have enabled the government to spend more than budgeted without going into deficit.

Fiscal revenue has increased significantly during 1990–92, due to the tax reform of 1990, a strong expansion of economic activity and imports, a relatively high price of copper, and a reduction in tax evasion. In addition to low international interest rates, this has allowed the government to increase its social spending while generating enough saving to finance its investment and have a surplus in each of these three years. For 1990–91, the nonfinancial public sector attained an average surplus of 1.5% of GDP—3.1% of GDP if we add the copper stabilization fund. Expectations for 1992 are that the nonfinancial public sector will show a surplus of more than 2% of GDP. At the same time, comparing the expected execution for 1992 and the budget law for 1990, social spending and central government investment will increase by 30% and 53% in real terms, respectively.[14]

At the same time, the increase in social spending has been accompanied by a higher saving effort by the government. Nonfinancial public sector saving, which was on average 4.5% of GDP in the 1980s, rose from 5.0% of GDP in 1990 to 5.9% in 1991; in the first semester of 1992 it showed an increase in

---

14. The 1993 budget law (currently in congressional discussion) stipulates a real increase of almost 18% in government investment and of 7.6% in social spending.

real terms with respect to the same semester of 1991. Private saving has also increased, reaching 12.8% of GDP on average in 1990–91, which is almost double the average for the 1980s—6.9% (see table 4.5).

Nevertheless, the public sector's contribution to national saving has been partially dampened by an operational deficit at the Central Bank, which was 3.9% of GDP on average during 1983–89. Originally, this resulted from the government's intervention to avoid massive bankruptcies during the crisis of the early 1980s. After declining year by year since 1986, this quasi-fiscal deficit reached 2.1% of GDP in 1990, as the Central Bank suffered important operational losses to defend its nominal exchange rate policy and prevent a faster appreciation of the real exchange rate. This quasi-fiscal deficit declined to 1.3% of GDP during 1991 and is expected to decline even further in 1992 (see table 4.5).

The current government has contributed to this reduction in the quasi-fiscal deficit. Since 1990, the Aylwin administration has made extraordinary prepayments of more than US$600 million to the Central Bank, and the 1993 budget stipulates a prepayment of US$135 million. This has allowed the government to increase the consolidated public sector surplus in a politically viable way (increasing expenditure through prepayments), because, given the social needs of the population, it is politically costly for the government to show a high nonfinancial public sector surplus.

The strength of Chile's public finances is in sharp contrast to the situation of other economies, both in the developed and developing world. Countries with different degrees of development and diverse economic policies, and with governments of different political orientation, are fighting to reduce public deficits. In many cases, they have to reduce significantly social spending and public investment, placing a high welfare cost on those with lower income and negatively affecting long-term growth prospects. Estimates for the principal

Table 4.5   **Saving and Investment in the Chilean Economy, 1980–92 (% of nominal GDP)**

Year	Investment	Saving				
		Foreign	Domestic	NFPS[a]	Central Bank	Private
1980–89[b]	16.9	7.0	9.9	5.3	−2.4	7.0
1990–91[b]	19.5	1.3	18.2	7.1	−1.7	12.8
1990	20.2	2.8	17.4	7.5	−2.1	12.0
1991	18.8	−0.2	19.0	6.6	−1.3	13.6
1992[c]	21.0	3.5	18.5			

Source: Central Bank of Chile, Ministry of Finance.

[a]NFPS=nonfinancial public sector (includes Banco del Estado, the only commercial bank owned by the Chilean government).

[b]Average.

[c]Preliminary projections.

industrialized countries (OECD 1992) indicate that they will have fiscal deficits averaging 3% of GDP in 1992, with the exception only of Japan, which has a surplus.[15] Developing countries (including eastern Europe and the ex–Soviet Union), on the other hand, are expected to attain an average deficit of more than 4% of GDP (International Monetary Fund 1992). This same pattern is observed across geographic locations in developing countries; in 1992, fiscal deficits, as a share of GDP, are expected to be 3.7% in Africa, 2.1% in Asia, 6.7% in Europe, 6.4% in the Middle East, and 1% in Latin America.

Macroeconomic Performance

Higher interest rates had significant real effects in the economy. GDP growth decelerated from 10% in 1989 to a mere 2.1% in 1990. Paradoxically, inflation increased to 27.3% in 1990. This was greatly influenced by the effects of the Gulf War, which were quickly passed through to consumers. After high inflation rates in September and October (between 3% and 5% per month), inflation slowed down in the last two months of 1990, and declined to 18.7% in 1991. It is expected to decline to about 13% during 1992 (see table 4.1). Official projections point to a further decline in 1993 (around 11%), but this looks quite hard to achieve.

The rate of fixed capital formation declined from 19.5% of GDP in 1990 to 18.2% in 1991, and then rebounded to around 20% in 1992.[16] The drop of investment in 1991 was quite moderate; in our view, it responded mostly to the monetary contraction of 1990, while the tax and labor reforms—implemented also in 1990—had little to do with it. The unemployment rate, after having dropped consistently in the second half of the 1980s from its heights of almost 30% in 1982, reached an average of 6.2% during 1990–91, and it will be below 5% by the end of 1992. At the same time, real wages have increased by an accumulated 6.8% during 1990–91, and they are expected to rise by about 4% during 1992 (see table 4.1).

During 1990–92, domestic saving will attain an average of 18.6% of GDP, the highest in the last three decades. Although a stronger saving effort is still needed, this helps to set the basis for sustainable long-term growth. In this period, domestic saving will finance—on average—more than 90% of domestic investment, compared to only 41.4% in the 1980s. This will help to reduce the vulnerability of the Chilean economy to external shocks, which traditionally have accounted for a large fraction of the fluctuation that has characterized the country's growth process.

The external accounts have been very strong too. During 1990–91, the balance of payments showed a surplus, expected to be repeated in 1992 and in

15. Without considering the significant surplus in the social security system, however, Japan's general government is also expected to have a deficit of around 3% of GDP in 1992.

16. The rate of capital formation in 1990 was the highest since 1981, when it also reached 19.5% of GDP.

1993. The 1990 surplus was explained mainly by a large capital account surplus due to both an important inflow of medium- and long-term capital in the form of credits and direct foreign investment,[17] and an inflow of short-term speculative capital attracted by an interest rate differential that more than compensated for devaluation expectations and any other source of risk. During 1991, Chile experienced a small current account surplus—0.2% of GDP—the first since 1976. This was explained by a large trade surplus of around US$1.5 billion (an increase of almost 20% with respect to 1990), despite a reduction in tariffs from 15% to 11% in June 1991 and a decline of almost 9% in the real exchange rate. Exports have continued to grow fast, accumulating an increase of 10.5% during 1990–91; noncopper exports rose by 19.7% over the same period. In real terms, exports of goods and services accumulated an increase of 21.6% during 1990–91, increasing the outward orientation of the Chilean economy. In 1991, exports accounted for 33% of GDP, compared to 23.6% and 29.4% in 1980 and 1989, respectively. Foreign exchange reserves stood at US$9 billion at the end of 1992, equivalent to over one-quarter of GDP, or almost twelve months of imports.[18]

4.3.2   The Tax Reform Package of 1990

The program of the Concertación government contemplated a tax reform that could increase available resources for social programs in education, health, housing, and nutrition. The government understood that running a fiscal deficit to finance these programs would endanger the much-prized macroeconomic stability. This could result in increased inflation that disproportionately hurts those with lower income, who receive an important part of their income in nominal terms and have far less access to inflation-proof assets. Higher inflation could also threaten national saving and investment and, in this way, the prospects for future growth and social welfare.

A large majority of the country shared the objective of helping the less well-off. A minority, however, considered that increasing taxes was not the appropriate way to attain this goal. An agreement between the government and the main opposition party, Renovación Nacional (RN), enabled the legislative approval of the tax reform law.

The tax package included, among other measures, a change in *corporate taxation,* whose tax base went from only distributed earnings to total earnings, as was the case until 1988. Its rate was increased from 10% to 15% for the period 1991–93. This increase in corporate taxation was explicitly said to be transitory in the tax reform project sent to Congress by the executive, as a result of a previous negotiation with RN.

---

17. Direct foreign investment amounted to US$1.1 billion in 1990, a 26% increase with respect to 1989 and a record high for the country. On average, direct foreign investment was in the order of 1.6% of GDP in the 1980s, compared with about 4.5% in 1990–91.

18. On the basis of projected 1992 imports.

Personal income taxes[19] were raised by narrowing the income tax brackets but without touching tax rates—the highest marginal rate continues to be 50%—and the *value-added tax* (VAT) was increased from 16% to 18% (VAT had been 20% during most of the military regime and was reduced to 16% only in 1988). Both of these tax increases were permanent in the government project; as a result of the negotiation in Congress, however, they were raised transitorily until 1994.

Additionally, the corporate tax base for "large" agricultural, transportation, and mining companies was changed from presumed income to effective income, leaving the option to chose among both tax bases for small companies in these activities.

It is estimated that the tax reform package raised fiscal revenue by some US$800 million annually, or almost 2.7% of 1991 GDP, and the government was committed to spend all these extra resources in social programs.

Critics argued that the tax reform would reduce investment, but evidence in this respect does not support their claim. A drop in investment from 20.2% of GDP in 1990 to 18.8% in 1991 can be mostly attributed to a lagged response to the contractionary monetary policy of 1990. As mentioned, investment is expected to reach a record level of over 21% of GDP in 1992.

In other countries, the corporate tax rate fluctuates between 20% and 50% and cannot be used as a credit against personal income taxes, as it is the case in Chile. Additionally, the majority of these countries do not offer preferential treatment for retained earnings. In some cases, such as Germany and Japan, the situation is just the opposite: retained earnings are taxed at a higher rate than distributed earnings, as a way to favor the intermediation of resources through capital markets.

Small and medium-sized companies, however, may have been hurt by the increased cost of using retained earnings to finance investment brought by the tax reform, because of their restricted access to financial markets. To offset part of this effect, the reform allowed firms to discount up to 2% of the value of *new* productive investment from their corporate tax base, as a way to stimulate investment independently of its financing. Its low rate (2%) and a maximum deduction of about US$16,000 of 1990, however, made the effect of this incentive quite marginal.

There are also good arguments for a positive effect of the tax reform on investment. First of all, the increase was quite moderate and still leaves Chile as one of the countries with the lowest rate of corporate taxation. Second, the government made a commitment not to pursue further tax increases during its tenure after this reform was approved. Third, increased spending in health, education, and nutrition is also a form of investment, as it will likely mean improved human capital over the medium to long term. And last, an increase

19. The so-called *global complementario* tax, whose base adds up personal income from all sources.

in social spending, if used efficiently, would allow a larger proportion of Chileans to feel the benefits of the economic model, thereby increasing the popular support for policy continuity, which is expected to have a positive impact on private investment.

Other critics argued that an increase in the VAT would raise inflation and thus would have a regressive social impact. The reform, however, did not have an important negative effect on inflation. It is true that the VAT has a proportionately greater effect on lower-income families who consume a higher share of their income, but to evaluate the impact of a higher VAT on the poor, one needs to take into account also the share of higher spending—which this tax increase allowed—transferred to these families.

More than a year before the programmed reduction of the different tax rates increased in 1990, an important debate arose between the government and the opposition concerning the convenience of maintaining the current tax rates. The government is in favor of maintaining the tax reform, arguing that it is not possible to sustain the pattern of public spending already committed (a large part of which is permanent) and at the same time reduce the tax rates in 1994 without generating a fiscal deficit. The opposition is in favor of reducing the tax rates, on the grounds that the expansion in economic activity over the last couple of years allows for a reduction in tax rates while maintaining the social spending effort and without generating a significant fiscal deficit.

4.3.3   Reforms to Labor Legislation

By the end of 1990, a broad agreement had been reached about the need to introduce changes in labor legislation. The government had two major goals with this reform. On the one hand, it aimed to balance negotiating power between employers and employees, which the authorities considered to be biased in favor of employers. On the other hand, the government wanted to legitimize the labor legislation.

As mentioned earlier, the labor reform implemented in 1979 was largely opposed by workers. Their main criticisms were that it (1) repressed labor unions,[20] (2) restricted collective bargaining, (3) biased the relative bargaining power against workers,[21] and (4) allowed for arbitrary dismissal—workers could be dismissed without expression of cause and without appeal—and for a low severance payment.

The reform that was finally approved by Congress represented an intermediate position between the old law and the original project of the executive, as the

20. During the 1980s, the unionization rate in Chile was only 11%, compared to 18% during 1965–70 and 29% during 1971–73. This rate is much higher in developed countries. In Denmark and Sweden, for example, this rate is around 85–89%; in Belgium, 70–7 9%; in the United Kingdom, 40–49%; in Germany, Italy, and Canada, 30–39%; in Japan, 20–29%; in the United States, France and Spain, 15–19% (Ramos and Bravo 1992).

21. This law established that strikes should have a maximum duration of sixty days. If the strike was not over after sixty days, the contracts of striking workers were automatically terminated, losing them not only their jobs but also their severance payments.

government had to negotiate it with the main opposition party. This negotiation helped to moderate the reform.

The labor reform eliminated the right of employers to fire workers with no expression of cause, but allowed a general cause of "needs of the company." Severance payments remained at one month of salary per year of work in the company, but the maximum was increased from five to eleven months[22] (there was no maximum in the original reform project) and workers could appeal in court. In case firing was declared unjustified by the courts, the severance payment had to be raised by 20%. Additionally, severance payments in case of firing from the seventh year on can now be substituted (by agreement of the parts) for an all-event payment; that is, severance can be paid if the worker is fired or if he or she quits.

The other reforms to the labor law applied to collective bargaining and unionization. Groups of nonunionized workers were allowed to participate in collective bargaining, and negotiations started to be allowed at the industry level only by common agreement between employers and employees. Before the reform, negotiations were allowed only at the firm level. The reform also eliminated the prohibition to form union associations, extended the objectives of union organizations, gave more protection to labor unions, and increased the financing of union activities. On the other hand, the new legislation eliminated the maximum of sixty days for strikes, leaving them without limit.

Critics said that the labor reform would increase strike activity, push up real wages beyond productivity, and maybe raise unemployment.[23] The evidence, however, points the other way. Days lost to strikes have declined since the reform, and the unemployment rate declined to around 4.5% by the end of 1992, the lowest in more than two decades. Also, initial real wage adjustments in collective bargaining processes have been moderate and declined from around 4% in 1990 to an average of 2.5% for the period January 1991 to September 1992 (see table 4.6).

4.3.4   Trade Policy and Integration to the World Economy[24]

Since the mid-1970s, Chile has pursued a strategy of global trade liberalization, aiming to integrate the country into the world economy without making any distinctions among countries or regions. This strategy has been immensely successful. Chile's trade has been greatly diversified, both in terms of the composition of exports and in terms of trading partners. Asia, Latin America, and North America now account each for about 20% of Chile's exports, and Europe for 30%. Copper, which accounted for almost 80% of Chile's exports in the

22. The idea was to give dismissed workers enough income to subsist during the average unemployment period (8 months); this is important because Chile lacks an unemployment insurance program.

23. José Piñera, for example, minister of labor during the military regime, stated that the labor reform meant "putting a loaded gun in the hand of unions."

24. For further details on this topic, see Larraín and Assael (1992).

Table 4.6   Initial Real Wage Adjustments Agreed to in Collective
                   Bargaining (%)

Period	Labor Unions	Groups	Total
1990			
January–March	6.1	4.9	6.0
April–June	3.7	3.7	3.7
July–September	4.6	2.1	4.1
October–December	3.5	2.9	3.4
1991			
January–March	3.2	2.5	3.1
April–June	3.0	4.7	3.5
July–September	1.4	0.8	1.3
October–December	1.6	0.8	1.5
1992			
January–March	2.9	1.7	2.7
April–June	2.0	2.9	2.1
July–September	2.6	3.4	2.7

Source: Annual Report to Congress delivered by the President of the Central Bank of Chile.

early 1970s, is now down to less than 40% of total exports in spite of increased production from new private mines. Overall, exports have increased dramatically. From about 15% of GDP in 1965, exports are now over 35% of GDP, a ratio similar to that of South Korea. Chile is today the most open economy of Latin America. And the export sector has become the main engine of economic growth in the country.

In spite of this success, the country is now pursuing free trade agreements (FTAs) with several countries of the continent. An FTA has already been signed with Mexico, which establishes a gradual decline in bilateral tariffs to 0% in 1996, and an elimination of all nontariff barriers. Soon Chile is likely to sign similar agreements with Colombia and Venezuela, and it is second to Mexico in progress toward an FTA with the United States.

Chile has not abandoned the goal of global trade integration. In fact, the country's flat import tariff was unilaterally cut from 15% to 11% in June 1991; furthermore, there are no nontariff barriers. But the trade strategy has shifted emphasis toward bilateral agreements, provided that they do not result in increased barriers with the outside world.[25]

There are several reasons for the emphasis on FTAs. First, it responds to a worldwide phenomenon, the prospect of large trading blocks in Europe (and maybe in Asia), and to the U.S. Initiative for the Americans. Although it might not be optimal for a country like Chile to sign FTAs if other countries were not

25. This is one complicated aspect of MERCOSUR, which is a customs union (not an FTA) and has not yet agreed on its common external tariff.

following this strategy, it may be optimal to do so if the world is moving toward the formation of FTAs (Krugman 1991). Second, although global free trade is recognized as the first best, there is growing frustration with slow progress in the General Agreement on Tariffs and Trade (GATT) multilateral negotiations. Third, if a country intends to liberalize trade anyway, bilateral agreements are a way to obtain something in return, especially when starting from low tariff levels and no nontariff barriers. Nonetheless, FTAs must be understood as a complement, not a substitute, of trade integration with the world economy.

To deepen its integration in the world economy, Chile needs to gain increased market access, especially in developed countries. FTAs may cooperate in this task. The net welfare implications of bilateralism are ambiguous, and mainly depend on the characteristics of the integration partners and on the international context in which the FTA is carried out. The different costs and benefits of this type of strategy should be taken into account when choosing trading partners. A recent empirical evaluation of an FTA with the United States (Coeymans and Larraín 1992) shows important gains to Chile of such an agreement, especially on the investment front.

Chile is currently evaluating an important number of FTAs (with the United States, Venezuela, Costa Rica, Colombia, Uruguay, Ecuador, and Argentina, among others), but the country lacks a well-specified trade strategy vis-à-vis FTAs. This leads to excessive arbitrariness in the evaluation of such agreements and to increased uncertainty on the relative profitability of different productive activities, which could have a negative impact on investment and growth.

4.4   Investment, Saving, and the Needs for Sustained Growth

One of the central challenges for Chile is to consolidate a stable path of strong economic growth. A low and highly volatile growth rate has characterized the Chilean economy for many decades. The average growth rate was 4.9% in the 1960s, 2.5% in the 1970s, and 3.6% during the 1980s. And the country has suffered two major recessions (1975 and 1982–83) with output contractions of up to 15%. A major improvement has occurred since the mid-1980s, when the average expansion rate reached a record of 6% for the period 1985–92, the highest in the Latin American region over the same period.

Sustained growth is the only way to defeat poverty permanently. It is also the way to avoid destabilizing social conflict. Strong distributive pressures in a stagnant society are bound to prove explosive. Thus, redistributive policies can succeed beyond the short run only in a growing economy. Lower-income groups have suffered the most with the instability that has characterized Chile's growth process over the last two decades. The challenge then is to attain higher rates of economic growth and to reduce its volatility, which, to a large extent, has been associated with external shocks.

4.4.1   The Role of Investment and Saving

The Necessary Investment Effort

Higher economic growth over the medium term requires increased rates of accumulation of productive factors—both physical and human—and improved efficiency. This is not necessarily true in the short run, however. The country can rely on available unutilized capacity to expand production even with relatively low levels of investment, as happened in the second half of the 1980s. But this has a limit. When the utilization rate approaches capacity, strong economic expansions get translated into an acceleration of inflation (e.g., 1981 and 1989) unless accompanied by a stronger investment effort. And when the external constraint is the dominant restriction, an effort to grow faster in the short run leads to a balance-of-payments crisis (e.g., 1971).

Investment has recovered strongly since the mid-1980s (in 1983 it was barely enough to cover depreciation), and by 1992 it is expected to be around 21% of GDP, with capital formation projected at about 20% of GDP. It is clear to most analysts, however, that capacity utilization has reached its upper limits.[26] Moreover, Chile cannot expect to obtain the efficiency gains of structural transformation or the benefits of stabilization, because structural adjustment has been completed and the economy is already stable. The labor market is now quite tight, and unemployment declined to about 4.5% by the end of 1992, the lowest in two decades. Thus, investment has become a major constraint on growth.

If Chile wants to increase its output at a rate of 6% to 7% per year, it will be necessary to increase capital formation at between 24% and 25% of GDP, assuming that this is done very efficiently. A brief examination of various countries that experienced high growth in the 1970s and 1980s shows that their investment efforts are substantially higher than Chile's. To achieve average annual growth rates of almost 7% to 9% over the last two decades, Korea, Malaysia, Singapore, and Thailand had rates of capital formation between 25% and 40% of GDP.

Some people argue that the Chilean economy is so efficient that it can grow at 7% consistently with the current levels of investment. This is, on our view, overly optimistic. Average ICORs (incremental capital output ratios) in those four Asian countries have been between 2 in Thailand and 3.2 in Singapore. In the past, however, the efficiency of investment in Chile has been lower than this, and only in the last few years has efficiency improved markedly. Chile's average ICOR during 1985–91 was 2.4.[27] Using this, and a depreciation of between 7% and 8% of GDP, the country's fixed investment rate would need to be between 24% and 25% of GDP to grow at 6% to 7% per year. If Chile's

26. See, for example, Marfán (1992).
27. This period is favorable to use to calculate the ICOR, as it includes the recovery from a major recession.

investment efficiency reaches Korea's (ICOR = 2.1), fixed investment should be between 22.4% and 23.4% of GDP to attain the same goal.

Thus, the extra investment effort needed in Chile to grow at 6% to 7% annually on a consistent basis is around 4 points of GDP. In 1992, however, the economy grew at over 9% with fixed investment of almost 20% of GDP. The discussion above indicates that this performance cannot be sustained. This is the view of the authorities, too. The Central Bank's annual report to the Senate and the minister of finance states that, "in spite of a dynamic investment during 1992, it is not considered feasible for Chile to sustain growth rates of over 6% per year."[28] According to Marfán (1992), the national saving and investment observed in the last couple of years will allow for a sustainable annual expansion of productive capacity on the order of 5.5%.

To some people, aggregate numbers look a bit intangible, and it is perhaps useful to mention two areas where anybody living in Chile could feel a deficit of investment. One of them is productive infrastructure. The fiscal budget for 1992 stipulated a real increase of 18.9% for public investment in infrastructure, and the budgetary law for 1993, just sent to Congress, includes a similar increase in this area. The accumulated (stock) deficit in infrastructure, however, due to low levels of investment in the last decade, and the necessary (flow) effort required to sustain high rates of growth, makes the current effort of the government in this area insufficient. The government has opened the possibility for the private sector to invest in major infrastructure projects, and the reforms to capital markets (discussed below) will help this initiative, but private participation in this area is likely to be marginal.[29] Another area where a deficit of investment is clearly visible is the protection of the environment.

Without adequate incentives, the private sector would tend to underinvest in these two areas, and thus requires constant assistance from the government (direct investment and/or subsidies). At present, Chile does not have the right mechanisms to induce the private sector toward the level of investment that is socially optimum in these areas. It is necessary to design schemes that would promote private infrastructure investment, and that would induce the private sector to internalize the social costs (benefits) associated with the destruction (protection) of the environment.[30]

The increased overall investment effort is sizable and cannot be accomplished in one year. For more than a decade, the main obstacle to increased investment and economic growth in Chile was the foreign constraint. Today this is no longer the bottleneck to economic development, and the prospects

28. Banco Central de Chile, "Evolución de la Economiá en 1992 y Perspectivas para 1993," annual report to Congress delivered by the President, September 1992.

29. The magnitudes involved are huge, and the law restricts private investments to new projects where an alternative exists for the users.

30. The new concessions law allows the private sector to build and operate public works. Since its approval in mid-1992, however, there has not yet been one project in operation through this law. The first one—a major tunnel—is expected to be approved this December.

for sustained growth now rest on the country's capacity to increase productive investment. Nevertheless, the experience of Chile and other countries of the region in the early 1980s suggests that a massive and short-lived inflow of foreign capital induces strong real appreciations of the local currency and a deterioration of the trade balance. Given the need to preserve export dynamism and thus to maintain a competitive real exchange rate, foreign saving must be used prudently. Thus, the bulk of the required increase in saving will have to come from domestic savings.

National Saving and Foreign Saving

At present, Chile can finance sustainably a current account deficit of 3% to 4% of GDP, as an upper limit. This is consistent with expected medium- and long-term capital inflows, and with the experience of successful Asian economies following an outward-oriented economic strategy.[31] An attempt to go beyond this level, although possible to finance in the short term, would probably be unsustainable. On the one hand, it is unlikely that foreigners would be willing to finance such a current account gap over the medium to long term. On the other hand, it may threaten the expansion of the export sector, the engine of economic growth, because it would likely require an appreciation of the real exchange rate at a rate higher than what can be offset by productivity gains. If this happens, a negative impact on aggregate investment is almost certain, given the larger opportunities offered by world markets relative to domestic markets.

National saving has been chronically low in Chile, even more so than investment. This is the case whether one compares Chile with industrialized economies or with other middle-income countries. During the 1970s, and especially in the early 1980s, saving was clearly insufficient to finance domestic investment. The gap was translated into significant current account deficits, reaching a record of 14% of GDP in 1981. The recovery of saving from the lows of the 1982 depression has been impressive, and by 1991 gross national saving reached 19% of GDP. Yet in that year foreign saving was negative (there was a current account surplus). For 1992, gross national saving is expected to reach around 19.5%. If Chile is able to attract and digest foreign saving of about 3% of GDP, the extra national saving effort would be around 2.5 points of GDP. This would finance inventory accumulation assumed at 1% of GDP per year, and fixed investment of 24% of GDP that would allow the country to grow consistently at a rate of 6% to 7% per year.

Increased national saving has been the result of higher public and private saving. The nonfinancial public sector saving rate attained an average of 7.1% of GDP during 1990–91 compared to 5.3% in the 1980s. On the other hand, the private saving rate reached 12.8% during 1990–91, which almost doubles

31. Larraín and Vergara (1993) study the cases of Korea, Malaysia, and Thailand, where average current account deficits for the last two decades have been between 2% and 4% of GDP.

that for the 1980s (7.0%). At the same time the government has contributed to reduce the quasi-fiscal deficit of the Central Bank, as mentioned earlier, which is an important source of national dissaving.

It would be desirable to achieve a significant increase in public saving to support the national saving effort. But one could not count on it, given the significant pressures to expand social spending, and the commitments that the government has already made in this area. Thus, it is likely that the bulk of the extra saving effort would have to fall on the private sector.

Reforms to Domestic Capital Markets

A higher contribution of private saving to finance investment can be accomplished both by stimulating the private saving effort and by more efficient channeling of private saving to investment. Two of the major sources of domestic saving in Chile are pension funds and life insurance companies. As of March 1992, these institutional investors had accumulated resources of US$15 billion, about 45% of GDP, which are expected to grow to 100% of GDP by the end of the decade. To attain adequate profitability and low risk, a further diversification of their portfolio—now constrained by strict rules—is needed. This requires a larger number of eligible financial instruments (creating new ones and increasing eligibility among those available), which would also increase the availability of medium-term domestic financing for investment projects. This goal has been partially accomplished by allowing pension funds to invest in new projects, which was previously banned. Three months after having developed such a mechanism, some important mining and infrastructure projects that used to be financed with external borrowing are completing the necessary studies that will allow them to place US$200 million in bonds among local institutional investors.

On the other hand, the government will soon send to Congress a project aimed at the modernization and deepening of the Chilean financial system. Its goals are to diversify the investment portfolio of institutional investors, to improve the regulation of pension funds, to strengthen the autoregulation mechanisms in the capital market, and to develop new financial instruments to channel private saving to investment projects. It contemplates the creation of bonds and funds for project financing, mortgage-backed bonds for the financing of housing, and the development of other types of securitization.

Labor Markets, Export Incentives, and Other Constraints to Growth

The tightening of the labor market—especially of skilled labor—suggests that, in contrast to what has been traditionally the case in Chile, labor may become a binding constraint to economic growth, maybe even more restrictive than domestic and foreign saving.

Additionally, given the central role of exports in Chile's development strategy and the difficulties experienced over the last two years in maintaining the real exchange rate, further gains of international competitiveness in the export sector and efficient import substitution industries will have to come from increased productivity. At present, a major objective is to improve the technological content and increase the value added of Chile's export supply. A highly trained labor force will be essential for this.

Chile's educational system, however, does not appear suited to accomplish this goal. At present, it is not preparing the kind of workers the economy is demanding, which may help to explain why the youth unemployment rate is almost twice the average rate. Thus, a reform to the educational system, and more and better training programs to improve labor productivity, should be given more attention in the near future.[32]

4.4.2 Vulnerability of the Growth Rate to External Shocks

To attain sustainable growth, the Chilean economy would also need to reduce its vulnerability to external shocks in commodity and financial markets. Since the mid-1980s, progress has stepped up in this respect.

The traditional transmission mechanism of external shocks is a drop in the trade of goods (or, equivalently, in the terms of trade) and a surge in the service of external debt. Since 1985, Chile has reduced the absolute level and relative burden of the external debt. More recently, public foreign debt has declined quite rapidly, generating space for external borrowing by the private sector while continuing the reduction in the debt burden. In 1992, the external debt to GDP ratio will be around 46%, which is the lowest in the last ten years.[33] At the same time, foreign direct investment has grown substantially in recent years, reaching an average of nearly 4% of GDP in the 1990s. Precise measures of the stock of domestic capital in the hands of foreigners are unavailable, but the large capital gains in the stock market and the reinvestment of profits suggest that it has increased significantly. Although it is difficult to estimate total net Chilean liabilities with the rest of the world, their proportion of debt to equity has declined. And foreign investment appears to have better properties than foreign credits during the cycle (Larraín and Velasco 1990).

Nowadays, the contribution of foreign saving to financing Chilean investment is much smaller than in the past. While in the 1980s this source of saving accounted on average for over 40% of total investment, it accounted for only 1.3% of total saving in 1990–92.

Chile's vulnerability to external shocks has been further reduced by the significant increase in export diversification, both in terms of goods and in the destination markets. Noncopper shipments represented 37% and 54% of total exports in the 1970s and 1980s, respectively; they account today for 62% of exports. The geographic diversification of exports has also increased; trade with Asia, for example, has surged to 20% of total trade. Higher availability of

---

32. Increased labor productivity can also be attained by labor reallocation from less to more dynamic sectors.
33. This coefficient was 81% on average during the 1980s.

foreign reserves in the Central Bank also helps to cushion against external shocks. While these reserves allowed the financing of seven months of imports—on average—during the 1980s, in 1992 they represented a whole year of imports, or a quarter of GDP.

The lower vulnerability of the Chilean economy is evident from its vigorous behavior of the last two years, in an international context characterized by low growth and slow expansion of trade. While in the 1990–91 world trade expanded at an average rate of only 3.1%, Chile's total trade increased by 7.5%. And world income will have grown at an average rate of 1.2% in 1990–92, compared to 5.6% in Chile.

Chile has also increased its degree of integration to international financial markets, which also helps to reduce the vulnerability of the economy to external shocks. On the one hand, the international diversification of Chilean assets—for example, the investment abroad of pension funds allowed in 1991—should contribute to reduce the variability of returns, and thus the volatility of national income. At the same time, external borrowing allows smoothing the impact of transitory external shocks, distributing its impact over time and thus allowing for a more stable consumption path.

A tighter integration with world capital markets allows for a more efficient allocation of capital and for risk diversification, but it imposes new challenges for a small economy like Chile. Higher international capital mobility puts strict limits on short-term stabilization policy if the country wants to avoid large fluctuations in the real exchange rate.

How effective monetary and fiscal policy are in this context depends importantly on the prevailing exchange rate arrangement. The fact that fiscal policy is—at least in the short term—less flexible than monetary policy favors a flexible exchange rate. But the central role played by the export sector in Chile's development strategy and the fact that short-term excess exchange rate volatility can have permanent effects on the pattern of trade (Krugman 1987) and investment (Pindyck, 1991) favor the protection of tradables from short-term variability. Chile now follows a target zone system with amplitude of ±10%. To protect against real appreciation, the center of the exchange rate's fluctuation band is adjusted by the difference of domestic inflation and an estimate of external inflation. This arrangement results in partial effectiveness of both monetary and fiscal policy.

Chile, like several other Latin American economies, has experienced lately difficulties in managing domestic stabilization policy in a context of large capital mobility and extremely low international interest rates—inconsistent with internal equilibrium (Calvo et al. 1992). This has resulted in increased investment spending, deterioration of the trade balance, appreciation of the local currency and the stock market, accumulation of external reserves in order to prevent further currency appreciation, and a need for sterilization to avoid the inflationary impact of massive purchases of foreign reserves by the Central Bank. The last two policies have led to important losses at the Central Bank and the requirement of maintaining high real interest rates, which attract more capital.

In the last year the government has carried out a number of measures directed to increase the degree of autonomy in domestic economic policy. First, it has increased the width of the exchange rate band from ±5% to ±10%, thus buying more independence for monetary policy. Second, it has moved to peg the exchange rate to a basket of currencies that includes the U.S. dollar, the yen and the deutsche mark, rather than only to the U.S. dollar; this makes the relevant international mix of economic policy a combination of fiscal and monetary policy in Germany, the United States, and Japan, which results in a higher average international interest rate than the U.S. policy mix alone. Third, it has adopted taxes and reserve requirements to foreign credits, increasing the "relevant" international interest rate and thus allowing Chile to keep a domestic interest rate consistent with internal equilibrium.

4.5   Conclusions: Continuity, Change, and Future Challenges for the Chilean Economy

Chile's economic performance in democracy during the 1990s has been outstanding. The economy is in its ninth uninterrupted year of growth, unemployment is below 5% (the lowest in more than two decades), inflation has declined to less than 13%, and the external position of the country is extremely solid. These achievements have occurred during a transition from military rule to democracy, in an international environment of very low growth and depressed international trade.

Many reasons account for this success. The strong initial position of the economy at the end of the 1980s, with macroeconomic stability and a completed structural transformation, was no doubt a crucial asset. Another major factor is a broad political consensus on economic matters. Of course, good initial conditions and broad consensus are necessary but not sufficient conditions. Highly responsible and well-oriented conduct by the economic authorities also deserves much credit.

In the end, we found more continuity than change in the economic policies applied during the current regime. This is not meant as a criticism. The sensible thing was to preserve most of the economic policies of the previous regime, while significantly improving the social effort, thus legitimizing the free-market economic model. Therefore, we regard the tax and labor reforms as important, positive, and moderate policy changes.

Despite a very healthy economic outlook, however, there are still substantial challenges ahead for the country. The first one is the consolidation of a strong and stable economic growth path. Second is the elimination of poverty, a condition that still affects some 40% of the Chilean population. Succeeding in this goal will take time even with the best policies. But it clearly requires the preservation of strong economic growth, since eliminating poverty will be impossible in a stagnant or slowly growing economy. Reducing inflation to single-digit rates has also become a widely shared objective, and it is a feasible option within the next two years. A more ambitious goal of achieving world inflation rates looks feasible only in the medium term.

To maintain high rates of growth it is necessary to increase Chile's investment effort. Capital formation has been growing strongly since the mid-1980s, and in 1992 it is expected to reach around 20% of GDP. This is healthy, but still insufficient to maintain rates of output growth of 6% to 7% per year on a consistent basis. Higher investment can count on foreign saving, but this source faces limits. In 1992, Chile will run a current account deficit of about 1.5% of GDP, which will likely double in 1993. Foreign saving of up to 3% to 4% of GDP per year is sustainable in an economy such as Chile. Thus, higher investment would require more domestic saving. The country's national saving rate in 1991 was 19% of GDP, and in 1992 will likely rise a bit. It is necessary to increase it between 2 and 3 points to support investment rates of around 25% of GDP.

A new challenge for Chile is the preservation of the environment. The worst environmental problem is air pollution in Santiago, which has so far been approached with half measures like a circulation restriction for 20% of all vehicles during weekdays. (Since September 1992, however, new cars imported or sold in Chile must have a catalytic converter.) Industries in certain areas also have maximum emission standards for toxic wastes. A comprehensive solution to the problem of air pollution, however, is estimated to cost over half a billion dollars and so far has not been tried. The preservation of species has been approached with special laws that regulate fishing and the exploitation of forests and native woods. For the first time, comprehensive environmental legislation is about to be approved by Congress.

Another challenge for the country is deepening its integration into the world economy in trade of goods, services, and capital. To this end, the country unilaterally reduced import tariffs from 15% to 11% in 1991, and is studying a number of FTAs that may help Chile gain access to some important markets. Bilateral deals, however, should be viewed as a complement to global liberalization, as the ultimate goal is to integrate Chile with the world as a whole.

References

Calvo, G., L. Leiderman, and C. Reinhart. 1992. Capital Inflows and Real Exchange Rate Appreciation in Latin America: the Role of External Factors. *IMF Working Paper.*

Castañeda, T. 1990. *Para Combatir la Pobreza: Política Social y Descentralización en Chile durante los 80.* Santiago: Centro de Estudios Públicos.

Coeymans, J. E., and F. Larraín. 1992. Impacto de un Acuerdo de Libre Comercio entre Estados Unidos y Chile: Un Enfoque de Equilibrio General. Universidad Católica de Chile, September. Mimeo.

Cortázar, R., and J. Marshall. 1980. Indice de Precios al Consumidor en Chile: 1970–78. *Colección Estudios CIEPLAN.* November.

Dornbusch, R. 1990. The New Classical Macroeconomics and Stabilization Policy. *American Economic Review* 80:143–47.

———. 1989. Real Exchange Rates and Macroeconomics: A Selective Survey. *Scandinavian Journal of Economics* 2:401–32.

Dornbusch, R., and S. Edwards. 1991. *The Macroeconomics of Populism in Latin America.* Chicago: University of Chicago Press.

Edwards, S., and A. Cox-Edwards. 1987. *Monetarism and Liberalization: The Chilean Experiment.* Cambridge, MA: Ballinger.

Krugman, P. 1987. The Narrow Moving Band, the Dutch Disease, and the Competitive Consequences of Mrs. Thatcher. *Journal of Development Economics* 27 (October): 41–55.

Krugman, P. 1991. Is Bilateralism Bad? In E. Helpman and A. Razin, eds., *International Trade and Trade Policy,* Cambridge: MIT Press.

Labán, R., and F. Larraín. 1993. The Chilean Experience with Capital Mobility. In B. Bosworth, R. Dornbusch, and R. Labán, eds., *The Chilean Economy: Policy Lessons and Challenges.* Washington, DC: The Brookings Institution.

Labán, R., and H. C. Wolf. 1993. Large-Scale Privatization in Transition Economies. *American Economic Review* 83:1199–1210.

Larraín, F. 1991a. The Economic Challenges of Democratic Development. In P. Drake and I. Jaksic, eds., *The Struggle for Democracy in Chile, 1982–1990.* Lincoln: University of Nebraska Press.

———. 1991b. Public Sector Behavior in Highly Indebted Country: The Contrasting Chilean Experience. In F. Larraín and M. Selowsky, eds., *The Public Sector and the Latin American Crisis.* San Francisco: ICS Press.

Larraín, F., and P. Assael. 1992. Integración Comercial Selectiva: El Caso de Chile. *Estudios Públicos* (46). Santiago: Centro de Estudios Públicos.

Larraín, F., and A. Velasco. 1990. Can Swaps Solve the Debt Crisis? Lessons from the Chilean Experience. Princeton Studies in International Finance no. 69. December. Princeton, NJ: Princeton University Press.

Larraín, F., and R. Vergara. 1993. Investment and Macroeconomic Adjustment: The Case of East Asia. In L. Servén and A. Solimano, *Striving for Growth After Adjustment: The Role of Capital Formation.* Washington, DC: World Bank.

Marfán, M. 1992. Reestimación del PGB Potencial en Chile: Implicancias para el Crecimiento. CIEPLAN: Corporacion de Investigaciones Economicas para Latinoamerica. Mimeo.

Meller, P. 1990. The Chilean Case. In J. Williamson, ed., *Latin American Adjustment: How Much Has Happened?* Washington, DC: Institute for International Economics.

———. 1991. Adjustment and Social Costs in Chile during the 1980s. *World Development* 19 (11): 1545–61.

Pindyck, R. 1991. Irreversibility, Uncertainty, and Investment. *Journal of Economic Literature* 29 (no. 3): 1110–48.

Ramos, J., and D. Bravo. 1992. Análisis de las Reformas Laborales. ECLAC: Economic Commission for Latin America and the Caribbean. Mimeo.

Sachs, J. 1990. Social Conflict and Populist Policies in Latin America. In R. Brunetta and C. Dell'Aringa, eds., *Labour Relations and Economic Performance.* London: Macmillan.

Torche, A. 1987. Distribuir el Ingreso para Satisfacer las Necesidades Básicas. In F. Larraín, ed., *Desarrollo Económico en Democracia.* Santiago, Chile: Ediciones Universidad Católica.

III   Country Experiences

5   Inflation and Unemployment as Determinants of Inequality in Brazil: The 1980s

Eliana Cardoso, Ricardo Paes de Barros, and Andre Urani

5.1   Introduction

Inequality in Brazil has shown extreme oscillations in short periods of time. The benefits from growth in the 1960s went disproportionately to the rich, and the costs of the 1980s stagnation fell disproportionately on the poor. The income of the richest 10% of the active population divided by the income of the poorest 10% of the population increased from a factor of 22 in 1960, to 40 in 1970, 41 in 1980, and 80 in 1989. It declined in 1991.[1]

This paper studies the oscillations of income distribution in Brazil during the 1980s. Using monthly data for the six largest metropolitan areas, it claims that inequality responded to megainflation and the sharp oscillations in employment. As opposed to what happened in the 1960s, education cannot explain the change in inequality in the 1980s.

Economists agree that behind the vast inequality of income distribution in Brazil lies an extremely unequal education distribution. Barros et al. (1992)

Eliana Cardoso is the William Clayton Professor of Economics at the Fletcher School of Law and Diplomacy at Tufts University and a research associate of the National Bureau of Economic Research. Ricardo Paes de Barros is assistant professor of economics at Yale University and a research associate of the Instituto de Pesquisa Economica Aplicada in Rio de Janeiro. Andre Urani is adjunct professor of economics at the Universidade Federal do Rio de Janeiro and a research associate of the Instituto de Pesquisa Economica Aplicada in Rio de Janeiro.

The authors thank Renata Patricia Jeronimo, Danielle Carusi Machado, and Carlos Henrique Leite Corseuil for excellent research assistance.

1. These numbers are calculated from the annual household surveys called Pesquisa Nacional de Domicilios and do not cover the same universe as the monthly employment surveys called Pesquisa Mensal de Emprego (PMEs), which are used in this paper. The PMEs show that the income of the richest 10% of the active population in the metropolitan areas divided by the income of the poorest 10% of the population, after peaking in mid-1990, was declining during 1991. It averaged a factor of 72 during the last quarter of 1991.

show that, if all wage differentials by education level were eliminated, the inequality in labor income in Brazil would be reduced by almost 50%.[2]

But even if we believe that education plays a major role in explaining inequality, we do not want to attribute the big deterioration of distribution that occurred from 1987 to 1989 to changes in the distribution of education. The poor do not lose their skills so fast, nor do the rich acquire in such a short period of time the education that transforms them into productivity prodigies. On the other hand, recessions and megainflations do play a role in explaining exacerbated income inequality.

Over the past decade, inequality in Brazil has shown only a minor change in trend but extreme short-run variations (fig. 5.1). The contribution of this paper is to decompose inequality into two components: inequality within and between groups with the same number of years of schooling. Our objective is to identify macroeconomics as an important explanation for the short-run variations. Specifically, we offer two conclusions: inflation promotes increased inequality and unemployment increases inequality.

These conclusions do not surprise, but they have not been formally documented before nor has their extreme effect, as shown in figure 5.1, been noted. Needless to say, on the evidence shown here, anyone concerned with inequality would focus on macroeconomic stability as a central policy for increased equality.

A recession worsens income distribution because of its effect on employment. In a recession, unskilled workers are the first to lose their jobs, as firms hoard the trained labor force. In the recovery, unskilled workers get back their jobs, and inequality diminishes. One must also take into account the fact that a recession has lasting effects on income distribution. During the recession the middle-class groups sell their assets to smooth consumption, assets that they might not be able to earn back during a recovery.

Figure 5.2 shows the recession of 1983–84 and the decline in real income during 1989–91. Add to the recession all the failed stabilization programs and observe that the poor have little room to cope with the radical policy moves that produce sectoral dislocation of resources and employment.

Figure 5.3 shows inflation during the 1980s. Inflation can increase inequality in three ways. First, if high wages benefit from more perfect indexation, inequality increases. The empirical evidence shows that perfect indexation does not exist and that all labor groups suffer real losses during episodes of high inflation. This paper also shows that in Brazil the group with five to eight years of education lost more than other groups in the 1980s.

Second, the inflation tax reduces disposable income. Although the inflation tax does not affect those individuals below the poverty line due to their negligible average cash holdings, it may wipe out the savings of the middle class

2. See Paes de Barros and Reis (1989); Sedlacek and Paes de Barros (1989); Lauro Ramos (1991).

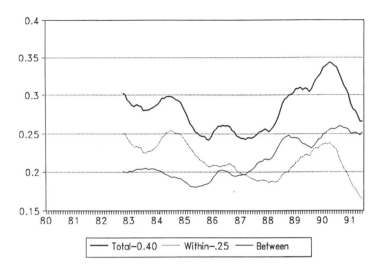
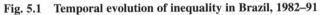

Fig. 5.1   Temporal evolution of inequality in Brazil, 1982–91
Note: Twelve-month moving averages for six metropolitan areas of the Theil indices
for total, within, and between educational groups inequality.

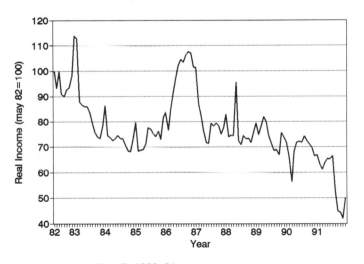
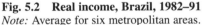

Fig. 5.2   Real income, Brazil, 1982–91
Note: Average for six metropolitan areas.

and increase the number of poor. In this sense it increases poverty and widens
inequality of income (see Cardoso 1992).

Third, inflation will redistribute assets in favor of the group better able to
play the financial markets. Inflation is difficult to predict, and nominal interest
rates may fail to reflect changing inflation rates. As a result there will be trans-

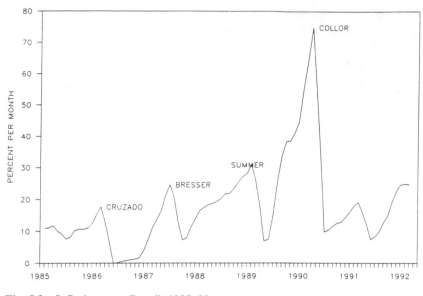

Fig. 5.3   Inflation rate, Brazil, 1985–92
Note: Three-month moving average; percentage per month.

fers of wealth between creditors and debtors. This will be true of all debtors and creditors linked by indebtedness in the form of bonds, mortgages, and sales contracts, and will also be reflected in the stock market. When inflation reaches 1,000%, big gains and losses can be made overnight. The middle-income groups will certainly lose compared to the groups who have better information, access to expensive technical advice, and flexibility.

The costs of inflation for wage earners also include oscillations in their real income. For individuals who are liquidity constrained, the significant oscillation in their real wages means that they cannot smooth consumption or that their real disposable income will be eroded if they try to carry cash from one month to the next.

This paper explores the impact of unemployment and inflation on Brazilian inequality in the 1980s. The data we use is from Pesquisa Mensal de Emprego (PME), a monthly employment survey conducted by the Instituto Brasileiro de Geografia e Estatistica.[3] These surveys do not cover money holdings and capital gains. Our measures of inequality capture only inequality in labor earnings, and thus the impact of inflation that we can estimate derives from imperfect indexation. Further information is needed to identify the impact on inequality from the inflation tax and the redistribution of assets.

The paper is organized as follows. Section 5.2 sets the background with a

---

3. The universe of analysis and the data are described in the appendix.

summary of what is known about income distribution in Brazil. It also describes the inequality measures used in the paper. Section 5.3 contains the empirical evidence, which is based on monthly survey data for the six largest metropolitan areas of Brazil between 1982 and 1991. The empirical analysis considers the relationship between inequality in labor income and three variables: the inflation rate, the unemployment rate, and the income differentials by educational level. The methodology and the evidence are summarized in section 5.4, which gives our conclusions.

5.2 Brazilian Income Distribution

5.2.1 Background

In no country has the academic debate on growth versus equality been sharper than in Brazil. In the 1970s the core of the discussion was whether the poor benefited from growth during the 1965–74 "miracle" and whether they might have done better under different policies.[4] Today the discussion must evaluate the costs of bad macroeconomics in the 1980s.

The complexity of statistical problems surrounding income distribution data in Brazil is serious enough to provoke skepticism. However, a few stylized facts are widely accepted.

Unequal income distribution. Brazil (with a Gini coefficient equal to 0.6 in 1990) has one of the most unequal income distributions in the world. Social indicators look worse than in any other country with the same income per capita. Table 5.1 compares economic and social indicators in Brazil with those of Latin American countries with a population of more than 10 million people. Brazil does poorly. Although in 1990 it had the highest dollar income per capita in the region, infant mortality was three times that of Chile, the illiteracy ratio was four times that of Argentina, and Brazilians could expect to live four years less than Mexicans.[5]

Regional inequality. National averages of economic and social indicators hide extreme disparities. Regional inequality is severe.[6] For instance, the interstate range of income in Brazil is seven to one.[7] Table 5.2 shows the range of economic and social indicators for the poorest and richest regions and states. Cavalcanti de Albuquerque (1991) compares the index of human development for

---

4. See for instance Camargo and Giambiagi (1991); Fields (1977); Fishlow (1980); Morley (1982); Pfeffermann and Webb (1979); Taylor et al. (1980).
5. For measures of poverty see Hoffmann (1989) and Ravallion and Datt (1991).
6. See for instance Vinod (1987); Maddison and associates (1989).
7. Interstate disparity is two to one in the United States, where Mississippi's per capita income was half that of Connecticut's in 1991 (U.S. Department of Commerce, *Survey of Current Business,* vol. 72 [4] [April 1992] table A).

Table 5.1   Economic and Social Indicators in Latin American Countries with More than 10 Million People

Country	Population (millions) (1990)	GDP per Head ($) (1990)	Gini (index) (1989)	Population Growth (%)[a]	Life Expectancy (years) (1990)	Adult Illiteracy Rate (%)[b]	Mean Years in School[c]	Infant Mortality Rate[d]
Brazil	150.4	2,680	0.625	2.2	66	19	3.9	60
Mexico	86.2	2,490		2.0	70	13	4.7	40
Argentina	32.3	2,370	0.461	1.3	71	5	8.7	31
Colombia	32.3	1,260	0.515	2.0	69	13	5.7	39
Peru	21.7	1,160		2.3	63	15	6.4	82
Venezuela	19.7	2,560	0.498	2.7	70	12	6.3	35
Chile	13.2	1,940		1.7	72	7	7.5	20
Ecuador	10.3	980		2.4	66			

Sources: World Bank (1992); Fiszbein and Psacharopoulos (1992); Barros et al. (1992).
[a]Percentage per year between 1980 and 1989.
[b]Percentage of the total population that is fifteen years old or older.
[c]For individuals twenty-five years old or older.
[d]For one thousand live births.

Table 5.2   Economic and Social Indicators in Brazil: Poorest and Richest Regions and States, 1988

	GDP per Head ($ of 1988)	Life Expectancy (years)	Literacy Ratio (%)
Poorest states			
Piauí	594	62.6	55.9
Paraíba	718	51.9	63.1
Richest states			
São Paulo	3,503	67.0	90.5
Distrito Federal	4,215	68.9	89.5
Poorest region: Northeast	1,005	58.8	63.5
Richest region: Southeast	2,989	67.1	88.2
Brazil	2,241	64.9	81.1

Source: Cavalcanti de Albuquerque (1991).

Brazilian states with indices of other nations. Rio Grande do Sul is as advanced as Portugal, South Korea, or Argentina, while Paraíba performs as badly as Kenya and worse than Bolivia.

Destitution remains predominantly a rural phenòmenon even if the gap between the urban and the rural living standards has declined in the last twenty years (table 5.3). In 1988 rural income was still 60% of urban income.

Inequality has roots in history. In the colonial economy, rents from abundant natural resources were monopolized by the state and by large landlords from

Table 5.3   Indices of Urban-Rural Disparity, Brazil, 1970–88

	Income Index (urban income = 100)			Human Development Index[a] (urban index = 100)		
	Rural Northeast	Rural South	Rural Brazil	Rural Northeast	Rural South	Rural Brazil
1970	30	53	37	39	71	52
1980	47	70	53	55	83	64
1988	52	78	60	64	84	69

Source: Cavalcanti de Albuquerque (1991).

Portugal. The labor force was slaves. After the abolition of slavery, there was no land reform. Official policy kept labor cheap and uneducated.

Poorly managed social programs. Brazil spends as much as Korea on social programs, but it spends poorly. The Brazilian share of social service expenditure by government in GDP is as high as or even higher than that of other middle-income developing countries, but Brazilian social welfare indicators are strikingly low.

The reasons for such an unsatisfactory social performance are twofold: public resources are poorly managed and are not efficiently targeted. The poorest 19% of the population (with less than one-quarter of a minimum wage per household member) receives 6% of social benefits. An estimated 78% of all spending on health is devoted to high-cost curative hospital services and only 22% to basic preventive health care, such as immunization programs, malaria control, and maternal and child health. In education, the government supports free tuition in universities although the cost of educating each university student is eighteen times higher than government expenditure per student at the primary and secondary level combined.[8]

Increasing inequality. From 1960 to 1975 the degree of inequality increased continuously. While Fishlow (1972) emphasized the role of government policy in squeezing real wages, Langoni (1973) stressed nonpolicy forces inherent in a situation of fast growth with a shortage of educated labor. Despite the political debate that surrounded the two studies, there is no necessary conflict between the two views. The gap between rich and poor increased not only as a result of the increase of the real wage of skilled labor but also because the real wage of unskilled labor fell, in part as a result of the rise in inflation before 1964 and from the mid-1960s recession, which validated the incomes policy of imperfect indexation. Along with this explanation, education plays a central

8. The World Bank (1988) and Barros et al. (1992) offer analyses and critiques of social spending in Brazil.

role in explaining the worsening in the distribution of income in Brazil between 1960 and 1975.

The education system has a double relationship with the degree of inequality in income. Since the level of education is so low, educational expansion tends to increase the inequality in education and consequently the inequality in income. This is the composition or Kuznets effect. On the other hand, education expansion was considered to be too slow in comparison to the rate of economic growth and technological change. As a consequence, a relative shortage of educated and skilled workers led to a widening of the wage differential between workers with different years of schooling.

Barros et al. (1992) shows that two-thirds of the increase in inequality between 1960 and 1970 can be attributed to education. But the same paper also shows that education has a minor role in explaining what happened in the late 1970s and in the first half of the 1980s. In this paper we will show that unemployment and inflation generated the extreme oscillations in inequality observed in the 1980s.

5.2.2   Measuring Inequality

Changes in income inequality are usually described by changes in a scalar measure of inequality such as the Gini or the Theil index. A scalar measure completely ranks a set of income distributions in terms of increasing inequality, but alternative scalar measures do not necessarily rank a set of distributions in the same way. We lessen this problem by using six different measures.

The Lorenz curve, $L(p)$, shows the share of the total income that is appropriated by the poorest $p\%$ of the population and is defined as

$$(1) \qquad L(p) \equiv (1/\mu) \int_0^p F'(t) \, dt$$

for $0 \leq p \leq 1$. F is the cumulative distribution of the random variable Z, which represents labor earnings, and μ is the mean of Z. Figure 5.4 illustrates the behavior of the Lorenz curves. The continuous line represents income distribution in the early 1980s. In 1990 the Lorenz curve shifts out as inequality increases, and in 1991 it shifts in as inequality decreases.

Based on the Lorenz curve, we can estimate a second measure of inequality: the relation between the income share of the richest 10% of the population and the income share of the poorest 40%. We call this measure the spread, S.

$$(2) \qquad S \equiv [1 - L(0.9)]/L(0.4)$$

We also use the Gini coefficient as a measure of inequality. The Gini coefficient is defined as

$$(3) \qquad G \equiv \int_0^1 (1 - 2L(p)) \, dp.$$

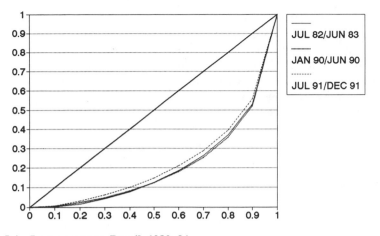

Fig. 5.4   Lorenz curves, Brazil, 1980–91

The next inequality measure is the Theil index, T, defined as

(4) $$T \equiv E[(Z/\mu) \ln(Z/\mu)],$$

where E is the expectation operator, and Z has already been defined as a random variable representing labor earnings.[9]

Inspection of monthly estimates for the spread, the Gini coefficient, and the Theil index, from January 1980 to December 1991, indicates the presence of outliers. We consider as outliers any estimate that diverges from the mean by more than two standard deviations. Since outliers can strongly influence our empirical analysis, we discarded them. The identification of outliers was done for each metropolitan area separately. Having identified an outlier, all inequality measures for that point in time and metropolitan area were discarded.

Next we decompose inequality.[10] The objective of the decomposition is to isolate the contribution of changes associated with education from all other sources of change in inequality. We divide the population in each metropolitan region into five subgroups. In each of these subgroups, all workers have the same level of education according to the number of completed years of schooling: less than one, one to four (elementary school), five to eight, nine to eleven, and twelve or more years. Based on this division we compute a measure of the average income inequality within groups, I, defined as

(5) $$I \equiv \sum_{i=1}^{5} \alpha_i \, TW_i,$$

9. Monthly estimates for the spread, the Gini coefficient, and the Theil index for the six largest metropolitan areas of Brazil are available upon request.

10. The variables used in the decomposition analysis spread over the period May 1982 and December 1991, because the surveys do not cover information on the level of education of workers before May 1982.

where TW_i is the inequality within subgroup i as measured by the Theil index; $\{\alpha_i\}$ is a system of weights, $\alpha_i \geq 0$ and $\Sigma\alpha_i = 1$.

The measure of inequality within groups, I, can change either because the inequality within groups, $\{TW_i\}$ has changed or because the weights, $\{\alpha_i\}$, have changed. Because we do not want our measure I to be affected by changes in the distribution of the population by educational level, we define the weight of each subgroup i as the average of the 1980–91 shares in total population in each metropolitan area. Therefore, the weights are constant, and only variations in $\{TW_i\}$ can affect the measure of inequality within groups, I.

The measure of the inequality between groups, B, is defined as

(6) $B \equiv T - I.$

Figure 5.5 shows the twelve-month moving average of the Gini coefficient for the largest metropolitan areas between January 1980 and December 1991. The degree of inequality is smallest in São Paulo, followed by Rio de Janeiro. The extent of inequality is very similar in Belo Horizonte, Salvador, and Recife.

Despite some regional nuances in the temporal pattern of inequality, all regions followed the same broad pattern summarized in table 5.4. During the first half of the 1980s, the degree of inequality oscillates around a high level. After 1984, inequality first goes down with a trough around mid-1987. It reaches a peak around mid-1990 (with the Gini coefficient exceeding 0.62 in Belo Horizonte, Recife, Rio de Janeiro, and Salvador). After that it declines: at the end of 1991 the degree of inequality was smaller than the minimal level

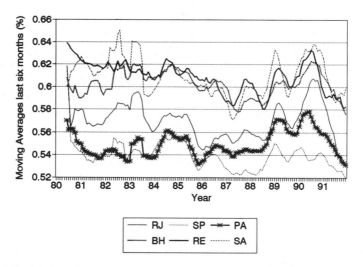

Fig. 5.5   Gini coefficients, Brazilian metropolitan areas, 1980–91
Notes: Twelve-month moving averages. RJ = Rio de Janeiro; SP = São Paulo; PA = Porto Alegre; BH = Belo Horizonte; RE = Recife; SA = Salvador.

Table 5.4   **Inequality Indices: Twelve-Month Average for Six Metropolitan Areas, 1981–91**

	Theil	Gini
1981	0.68	0.58
1982	0.73	0.59
1983	0.69	0.58
1984	0.69	0.59
1985	0.64	0.58
1986	0.65	0.57
1987	0.63	0.57
1988	0.67	0.57
1989	0.69	0.58
1990	0.73	0.60
1991	0.65	0.56

reached during the 1980s (the average for the six metropolitan areas was 0.56 in 1991).

The temporal pattern for the other inequality indicators (the Theil index and the spread) follow a very similar pattern. The appendix table 5A.1 shows the high degree of correlation between the different inequality indicators for each metropolitan region.

5.3   The Empirical Evidence

5.3.1   Sources of Inequality

We believe that education has an important role in determining inequality but that it cannot explain the cyclical pattern followed by inequality in the 1980s. To determine whether education contributed to the cyclical pattern of the degree of income inequality in the 1980s, we compare the temporal evolution of the Theil index, T, with the temporal evolution for the average inequality within groups, I. By construction, I is not affected by changes either in the educational composition of the labor force or in the wage differentials by education level. Hence, if I and T follow the same pattern, we can say that the events affecting the evolution of the inequality in the 1980s are unrelated to changes associated with education.

We begin by investigating the temporal evolution of the average inequality within groups, I, and the inequality between groups, B. We can do this only after March 1982, when questions on education were introduced in the PME questionnaire. Both I and B behave similarly across regions, and we can thus concentrate our discussion on the average across regions.[11]

---

11. Monthly estimates of the two components of the Theil measure for each of the six metropolitan areas are available upon request.

Figure 5.1 shows the temporal evolution of the average across metropolitan areas of the Theil index, T, of the index of inequality within groups, I, and of the index of inequality between groups, B. Both the Theil index and the index for inequality within groups display the same cyclical pattern. In addition, the index for inequality within groups shows a decreasing trend. On the other hand, the index of inequality between groups, B, displays almost no cyclical pattern and a clear increasing trend.

In summary, the temporal pattern of the overall inequality can be decomposed into three components: (1) a complete cycle from mid-1984 to the end of 1991 that is perfectly matched by the temporal evolution of the inequality within group; (2) a decreasing trend in inequality caused by a decline in the Theil within groups; and (3) an upward trend in inequality caused by an increase in the inequality between groups. As a result, from mid-1982 to the end of 1991, the overall inequality went through a complete cycle with a slightly decreasing trend.

A consequence of the opposite trends in inequality within groups and inequality between groups is an increase in the power of explanation of education to account for the level of inequality at a point in time. We can measure the "explanatory power of education" by the ratio between the indices of inequality between and within groups, B/I. This ratio increases over the period. Therefore, over the 1980s, even though education does not explain the variations in inequality during the period, the static relationship between education and the level of the overall inequality in 1991 is even stronger than in 1982.

We also use an alternative procedure to investigate the relative contribution of education to the cyclical fluctuations in inequality. We first identify four periods, which are characterized by relatively big or small inequality: July 1982 to June 1983 (big); July 1986 to June 1987 (small); January 1990 to June 1990 (big); July 1991 to December 1991 (small). Then we decompose the change in overall inequality between each of these periods in two components: a change in inequality within groups and a change in inequality between groups. Table 5.5 shows that the decline in inequality between 1982–83 and 1986–87 is almost entirely explained by a decline in inequality within groups. The increase in inequality between 1986–87 and 1990 is explained by an increase in inequality in both indices of inequality. Finally, the decline in inequality between 1990 and 1991 is fully explained by the variation in inequality within groups.

Estimates by metropolitan area (in the appendix tables) corroborate that for

Table 5.5   Decomposing the Variation in Inequality (average of all metropolitan areas)

From	To	ΔT	$\Delta I/\Delta T$	$\Delta B/\Delta T$
July 82–June 83	July 86–June 87	−0.053	0.94	0.06
July 86–June 87	Jan. 90–June 90	0.102	0.50	0.50
Jan. 90–June 90	July 91–Dec. 91	−0.095	1.02	−0.02

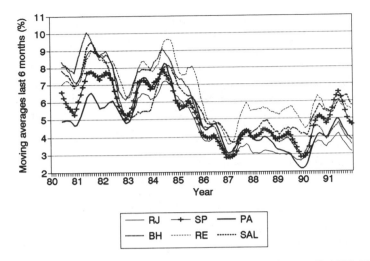

Fig. 5.6   Unemployment rate in largest metropolitan areas, Brazil, 1980–91
Notes: Twelve-month moving averages. For definitions of abbreviations, see note to
fig. 5.5.

all areas the within component contributes more than the index for inequality
between groups to the decline in inequality from 1982–83 to 1986–87 and
from 1990 to 1991. The results are mixed for the period in which inequality
increases. In Belo Horizonte and Recife the between component accounts for
the major part of the increase in inequality; in Salvador both components account equally for the change in inequality; in Rio de Janeiro the within component accounts for the major part of the change in the overall level of inequality.

Having argued that the cyclical pattern followed by the level of the income
inequality in Brazil is unrelated to changes associated with education, we turn
to the analysis of unemployment and inflation.

5.3.2   Unemployment and Inflation as Determinants of Inequality

We first describe the evolution of inflation and unemployment in the 1980s.

The inflation rates calculated from regional price indices are practically the
same in all metropolitan areas. Between 1981 to mid-1983, the inflation rate
was relatively stable at approximately 6% per month (fig. 5.3). From mid-1983
to the beginning of 1986, inflation doubled, it disappeared in March 1986 with
the Cruzado Plan and returned at full speed in 1987, when it accelerated fast,
reaching 40% per month in 1989. Inflation declined in 1990 to 15% per month.

The evolution of the unemployment rate between 1980 and 1991 by metropolitan area is shown in figure 5.6.[12] Recife has the highest unemployment
rates and Rio de Janeiro the lowest. In all metropolitan areas the unemploy-

---

12. An individual is defined as unemployed if he or she is ten or more years old and was not
employed at the time of the interview but was actively looking for a job in the week prior to
the interview.

ment rates declined over the period. The decline was larger in Belo Horizonte and smaller in São Paulo. Overall the oscillation of unemployment during the period follows a similar pattern in all metropolitan areas.

From 1980 to 1985 the unemployment rate went through two small cycles. It peaked at approximately 9% in the third quarter of 1981, declined to 6% in the third quarter of 1982, and increased to almost 8% in mid-1984. From mid-1984 to the end of 1986, there was a sharp decline in unemployment to less than 4%. Finally, from 1987 to 1991, the unemployment rate showed a slight increasing trend.

The short-run fluctuations in unemployment in the first half of the 1980s and the sharp decline from 1985 to 1987 quite closely match variations in inequality. Hence, variations in the unemployment rate are promising explanations for the variations in inequality that occur before 1988. After 1988 the unemployment rate became stable, but the degree of inequality reveals sharp fluctuations. On the other hand, the inflation rate was stable in the first half of the 1980s, but fluctuated sharply in the second half of the 1980s and beginning of the 1990s, matching the fluctuations in the level of inequality. Over the period 1980 to 1991, the combined behavior of unemployment and inflation can explain the oscillations of the degree of inequality.[13]

We now look at the results of the regression analysis. We have run two sets of regressions. In the first set we look at unemployment and inflation as determinants of inequality. In the second set we look at impact of unemployment and inflation on the real income of each educational group.

In the first set, in each regression, our dependent variable is one of our inequality indices. We ran each regression separately for each metropolitan area and inequality index. In each regression we used the raw monthly estimates for the inequality index. In the second set, in each regression, our dependent variable is the logarithm of the real income of one of the six educational groups. Again, we ran each regression separately for each metropolitan area. The independent variables are the level of the unemployment rate and the level of the inflation rate. We used the raw estimate of the unemployment rate. For the rate of inflation we used the average inflation of the previous year.[14]

Table 5.6 presents the coefficient of determination, R^2, of the eighteen re-

13. The period of fast increase in inflation (January 1987 to March 1990) coincides with the period of sharp increase in the inequality between educational groups (there is a strong correlation between the inequality between groups and the rate of inflation). One could argue that high rates of inflation increase the differentials in average wages between educational groups because the more educated groups are able to protect themselves better through more complete indexation. This conclusion is not warranted, because the decline in inflation in 1990 does not reduce inequality between groups. It does, however, reduce inequality within groups.

14. Our search indicates that results are not sensitive to the use of raw monthly unemployment rates or of three-month, six-month, or twelve-month moving averages. On the other hand, results did improve when we used the previous year's average inflation rate instead of the current inflation rate.

Table 5.6   **Coefficient of Determination, R^2: Regressions of Inequality on Unemployment and Inflation**

	Dependent Variable			
Metropolitan Area	Gini	Spread	Theil	N
Porto Alegre	0.35	0.33	0.16	131
São Paulo	0.11	0.15	0.06	129
Rio de Janeiro	0.33	0.32	0.32	126
Belo Horizonte	0.34	0.37	0.32	126
Salvador	0.30	0.24	0.37	117
Recife	0.37	0.60	0.28	127

Note: Metropolitan areas are ordered from south to north.

gressions where the independent variable is a measure of inequality. The coefficient of determination of the regressions of real income is in table 5.7.

Table 5.6 shows that, except for São Paulo, variations in unemployment and inflation can explain approximately one-third of all variation in the level of inequality. This is an impressive result, given that our dependent variable is the raw monthly estimates of inequality, which include quite erratic variations, and we have not used any dummies to capture changes in government wage policies.

Table 5.8 shows the estimated coefficient on unemployment in the regressions of inequality. All coefficients are positive, and almost all of them have t-statistics above 2. Therefore they corroborate the hypothesis that inequality increases with unemployment.

The regressions of real income of each educational group show that unemployment affects all groups negatively (table 5.9). Unemployment reduces the real income of the group with less than one year of education more strongly than the income of other groups in São Paulo, Rio de Janeiro, Belo Horizonte, and Salvador. Unemployment does not affect the real income of the group with more than twelve years of education in Rio de Janeiro and Belo Horizonte.[15]

Table 5.10 shows the estimated coefficients on inflation and their t-statistics of the regressions of inequality. Except for inequality within groups in São Paulo and Recife (where the t-statistics are small), all other coefficients are positive and have large t-statistics. They corroborate the hypothesis that inflation has an adverse effect on distribution.

These results are supported by regressions for the real income by education

15. Katz and Ravenga (1989) argue that the education-related wage differential is less likely to grow in very tight labor markets; that is, unemployment increases inequality between educational groups. Our evidence does not support this hypothesis. Unemployment does increase inequality within groups but does not affect inequality between groups. The coefficient on unemployment of regressions of inequality between groups actually has a negative coefficient (but t-statistics are small). See appendix table 5A.3.

Table 5.7   **Coefficient of Determination, R^2: Regressions of Real Incomes on Unemployment and Inflation (N in each regression $= 116$)**

Metropolitan Area	Years of Education				
	Less than 1	1 to 4	5 to 8	9 to 11	12 or More
Porto Alegre	0.22	0.31	0.37	0.19	0.23
São Paulo	0.25	0.30	0.26	0.25	0.20
Rio de Janeiro	0.26	0.14	0.33	0.20	0.07
Belo Horizonte	0.31	0.35	0.36	0.27	0.13
Salvador	0.35	0.44	0.44	0.39	0.27
Recife	0.07	0.34	0.33	0.31	0.13

Notes: The dependent variable is the logarithm of the real income of the group with the given years of education. Metropolitan areas are ordered from south to north.

Table 5.8   **Coefficient on Unemployment in Regressions of Inequality**

Metropolitan Area	Dependent Variable		
	Gini	Spread	Theil
Porto Alegre	0.13	6.11	0.28
	(2.0)	(3.2)	(1.2)
São Paulo	0.23	7.86	0.39
	(3.8)	(4.8)	(2.3)
Rio de Janeiro	0.48	16.70	1.28
	(6.8)	(7.2)	(6.2)
Belo Horizonte	0.41	22.31	0.87
	(7.1)	(8.4)	(4.8)
Salvador	0.50	27.52	1.46
	(4.6)	(5.4)	(4.4)
Recife	0.63	52.33	1.59
	(8.4)	(12.9)	(6.3)

Notes: Metropolitan areas are ordered from south to north. The numbers in parentheses are *t*-statistics.

differentials in table 5.11. These regressions show that inflation adversely affects the real income of all educational groups, but it particularly affects the real income of the group in the middle (five to eight years of education, column 3).

Regressions of relative earnings, not reported in this paper, show that unemployment reduces earnings of the two groups that have less than five years of schooling relative to earnings of any of the three groups with more than five years of schooling. They also show that inflation reduces earnings of the group with five to eight years of schooling relative to any of the other groups. Moreover, although inflation reduces real earnings of the group that has more than twelve years of schooling, it increases earnings of this group relative to all other groups. This supports the view that the better-educated groups are able to obtain more perfect indexation than other groups.

5.4   Conclusions

Using monthly data for the six largest metropolitan areas of Brazil, this paper shows that education cannot explain the evolution of inequality in the 1980s, which increased with unemployment and inflation. Despite regional features in the temporal pattern of inequality, inequality in all regions remained

Table 5.9   **Coefficient on Unemployment in Regressions of Real Incomes**

Metropolitan Area	Less than 1	1 to 4	5 to 8	9 to 11	12 or More
Porto Alegre	−2.24	−1.11	−0.56	−5.80	−1.54
	(−1.6)	(−1.0)	(−0.5)	(−4.5)	(−1.5)
São Paulo	−3.87	−3.46	−2.58	−2.75	−3.28
	(−3.3)	(−3.4)	(−2.3)	(−2.5)	(−3.2)
Rio de Janeiro	−2.29	−0.66	1.63	1.22	0.82
	(−2.3)	(−0.5)	(1.3)	(0.9)	(0.6)
Belo Horizonte	−4.11	−2.95	2.04	−0.21	−0.86
	(−4.8)	(−3.6)	(1.8)	(−0.2)	(−1.0)
Salvador	−3.74	−4.12	−1.88	−1.96	−4.50
	(−2.1)	(−2.3)	(−1.0)	(−1.0)	(−2.9)
Recife	−2.25	−5.21	−1.70	−1.23	−2.62
	(−1.6)	(−2.7)	(1.3)	(−1.0)	(−2.9)

Notes: The dependent variable is the logarithm of the real income of the group with the given years of education. Metropolitan areas are ordered from south to north. The numbers in parentheses are *t*-statistics.

Table 5.10   **Coefficient on Inflation in Regressions of Inequality**

	Dependent Variable		
Metropolitan Area	Gini	Spread	Theil
Porto Alegre	0.10	2.79	0.20
	(8.0)	(7.8)	(4.8)
São Paulo	0.02	0.41	0.07
	(1.8)	(1.3)	(2.3)
Rio de Janeiro	0.13	3.62	0.39
	(6.9)	(6.0)	(7.1)
Belo Horizonte	0.08	2.85	0.31
	(6.4)	(4.6)	(7.4)
Salvador	0.11	3.40	0.41
	(6.3)	(4.1)	(7.7)
Recife	0.06	0.10	0.23
	(4.1)	(0.1)	(4.9)

Notes: Metropolitan areas are ordered from south to north. The numbers in parentheses are *t*-statistics.

Table 5.11   Coefficient on Inflation in Regressions of Real Incomes

Metropolitan Area	Years of Education				
	Less than 1	1 to 4	5 to 8	9 to 11	12 or More
Porto Alegre	−1.33	−1.34	−1.52	−0.97	−1.04
	(−5.5)	(−6.8)	(−7.6)	(−4.2)	(−5.6)
São Paulo	−1.11	−1.14	−1.16	−1.09	−0.83
	(−5.7)	(−6.7)	(−6.3)	(−6.0)	(−4.9)
Rio de Janeiro	−0.99	−0.81	−1.23	−0.92	−0.50
	(−6.2)	(−4.1)	(−6.1)	(−4.2)	(−2.8)
Belo Horizonte	−1.16	−1.31	−1.48	−1.09	−0.69
	(−6.6)	(−7.7)	(−6.4)	(−6.0)	(−4.1)
Salvador	−1.78	−2.16	−2.50	−2.14	−1.23
	(−7.1)	(−9.4)	(−9.5)	(−8.4)	(−6.2)
Recife	−0.68	−1.56	−1.65	−1.47	−0.84
	(−2.7)	(−7.5)	(−7.5)	(−7.0)	(−3.9)

Notes: The dependent variable is the logarithm of the real income of the group with the given years of education. Metropolitan areas are ordered from south to north. The numbers in parentheses are t-statistics.

relatively high and stable over the first half of the 1980s and moved cyclically thereafter. Inequality reached a bottom in the middle of 1987, peaked in the middle of 1990, and declined in 1991.

We divide the population into five groups. The active labor force in each group has the same level of education. We measure the inequality within and between groups, and we decompose the temporal pattern of inequality in the 1980s into three components: a complete cycle from the middle of 1984 to the end of 1991, which is perfectly matched by the evolution of the within group component of the inequality; a decreasing trend in inequality within groups; and an upward trend in inequality between groups.

Having shown that the cyclical pattern followed by the level of the income inequality is unrelated to changes associated with education, we argue that the opposite trends of the two components of inequality increase the power of differentials in education to explain the level of inequality in 1991 relative to 1982. (The ratio between the index of inequality between groups divided by the index of inequality within groups rises over the period.)

Moreover, we show that variations in unemployment and inflation can explain approximately one-third of all variation in the level of inequality in all metropolitan areas, except São Paulo. Furthermore, inflation reduces the real incomes of all educational groups but affects more strongly the group in the middle (with five to eight years of education).

Our results support the hypotheses that unemployment increases inequality and that inflation widens inequality by pushing the middle-income groups into poverty.

Appendix
Data Sources and Description

Here we describe the data and the universe we used.

Information on the consumer price index in each metropolitan area was obtained from the Instituto Brasileiro de Geografia e Estatistica (IBGE, the Brazilian census bureau). The consumer price indices for São Paulo, Rio de Janeiro, and Belo Horizonte are also published in Fundação Getulio Vargas, *Conjuntura Economica,* Rio de Janeiro, various issues.

Information on labor income, the unemployment rate, and the income differentials by educational level was obtained from the Pesquisa Mensal de Emprego (PME), a monthly employment survey conducted by the Instituto Brasileiro de Geografia e Estatistica. The survey exists since 1980 for the six largest Brazilian metropolitan areas. Ordered from south to north they are Porto Alegre, São Paulo, Rio de Janeiro, Belo Horizonte, Salvador, and Recife. In 1982, the PME was evaluated and revised, leading to several improvements, in particular the inclusion of questions on the education level of workers.

Each month, approximately 10,000 workers, ten or more years old, are interviewed in each metropolitan area. The PME asks each sampled individual nineteen questions about his or her individual characteristics and the nature of his or her position in the labor market. For each individual in the sample we use the information on whether the individual was employed or not at the time of the interview. For those who were employed we also use the information on the labor income actually received in the previous month in his or her primary occupation, and his or her education level. For those who were not employed we use the information on whether or not they were actively looking for a job during the week prior to the interview.

The analysis is conducted separately for each metropolitan area. For each month between January 1980 and December 1991 and each metropolitan area, we compute the unemployment rate and different measures of income inequality. The universe of analysis is the employed population ten or more years old, and the concept of earnings is labor earnings actually received in the previous month in the primary occupation.

Table 5A.1   Correlation between Inequality Indices

Metropolitan Area	Theil-Gini	Gini-Spread	Theil-Spread
Porto Alegre	0.84	0.97	0.76
São Paulo	0.77	0.98	0.68
Rio de Janeiro	0.90	0.98	0.84
Belo Horizonte	0.85	0.95	0.73
Salvador	0.92	0.94	0.83
Recife	0.91	0.84	0.65

Note: Metropolitan areas are ordered from south to north.

Table 5A.2   **Decomposing the Variation in Inequality**

	From	To	ΔT	$\Delta I/\Delta T$	$\Delta B/\Delta T$
São Paulo	July 82–June 83	July 86–June 87	−0.017	0.62	0.38
	July 86–June 87	Jan. 90–June 90	0.007	−1.46	2.46
	Jan. 90–June 90	July 91–Dec. 91	−0.028	0.95	0.05
Rio de Janeiro	July 82–June 83	July 86–June 87	−0.091	0.93	0.07
	July 86–June 87	Jan. 90–June 90	0.129	0.96	0.04
	Jan. 90–June 90	July 91–Dec. 91	−0.172	1.03	0.10
Belo Horizonte	July 82–June 83	July 86–June 87	−0.041	0.74	0.26
	July 86–June 87	Jan. 90–June 90	0.085	0.19	0.81
	Jan. 90–June 90	July 91–Dec. 91	−0.113	0.82	0.18
Salvador	July 82–June 83	July 86–June 87	−0.042	1.16	−0.16
	July 86–June 87	Jan. 90–June 90	0.164	0.54	0.46
	Jan. 90–June 90	July 91–Dec. 91	−0.063	2.01	−1.01
Recife	July 82–June 83	July 86–June 87	−0.077	1.03	−0.03
	July 86–June 87	Jan. 90–June 90	0.123	0.28	0.72
	Jan. 90–June 90	July 91–Dec. 91	−0.097	0.62	0.38

Table 5A.3   **Regressions of Inequality within and between Groups**

			Inequality within Groups			Inequality between Groups		
Metropolitan Area	N	R^2	Coefficient on Unemployment	Coefficient on Inflation	R^2	Coefficient on Unemployment	Coefficient on Inflation
Porto Alegre	115	0.08	0.67	0.04	0.36	−0.44	0.17
			(3.0)	(0.9)		(−2.7)	(5.6)
São Paulo	113	0.08	0.43	−0.03	0.20	−0.01	0.10
			(2.6)	(1.0)		(−0.1)	(5.1)
Rio de Janeiro	110	0.28	1.69	0.21	0.27	−0.06	0.18
			(6.3)	(4.3)		(−0.3)	(5.4)
Belo Horizonte	113	0.18	1.18	0.07	0.38	−0.05	0.23
			(5.0)	(1.5)		(−0.3)	(7.4)
Salvador	110	0.13	1.35	0.12	0.31	−0.11	0.30
			(3.6)	(2.3)		(−0.4)	(6.8)
Recife	112	0.27	1.60	−0.04	0.34	−0.08	0.28
			(5.9)	(−0.8)		(−0.4)	(7.2)

Note: The numbers in parentheses are t-statistics.

References

Barros, Ricardo, et al. 1992. Welfare, Inequality, Poverty, and Social Conditions in Brazil in the Last Three Decades. Paper presented at the Brookings Institution Conference, July 15–17, 1992, Washington, DC.

Camargo, José, and Fabio Giambiagi, eds. 1991. *Distribuição de Renda no Brasil.* Rio de Janeiro: Paz e Terra.

Cardoso, Eliana. 1992. Poverty and Inflation. NBER Working Paper. Cambridge, MA: National Bureau of Economic Research.

Cavalcanti de Albuquerque, Roberto. 1991. A Situação Social: O Que Diz o Passado e o Que Promete o Futuro. In Instituto de Pesquisa Economica Aplicada, *Perspectivas da Economia Brasileira, 1992.* Brasilia: Instituto de Pesquisa Economica.

Fields, Gary. 1977. Who Benefits from Economic Development? *American Economic Review* 67.

Fishlow, Albert. 1972. Brazilian Size Distribution of Income. *American Economic Review* 62.

———. 1980. Who Benefits from Economic Development? Comment. *American Economic Review* 70.

Fiszbein, Ariel, and George Psacharopoulos. 1992. Income Inequality Trends in Latin America in the Eighties. Paper presented at the Brookings Institution Conference, July 15–17, 1992, Washington, DC.

Hoffmann, Helga. 1989. Poverty and Prosperity in Brazil. In Edmar Bacha and Herbert Klein, eds., *Social Change in Brazil, 1945–1985.* Albuquerque: University of New Mexico Press.

Katz, Lawrence, and Ana Ravenga. 1989. Changes in the Structure of Wages: The United States versus Japan. *Journal of the Japanese and International Economics* 3 (December): 522–53.

Langoni, Carlos. 1973. *Distribuição de Renda e Desenvolvimento Economico do Brasil.* Rio de Janeiro: Editora Expressão e Cultura.

Maddison, Angus, and associates. 1989. The Political Economy of Poverty, Equity, and Growth in Brazil and Mexico. World Bank, Washington, DC, final draft, July. Mimeo.

Morley, Samuel. 1982. *Labor Markets and Inequitable Growth.* Cambridge: Cambridge University Press.

Paes de Barros, Ricardo, and Jose G. A. dos Reis. 1989. Educação e Desigualdade de Salarios. In *Perspectivas da Economia Brasileira, 1989.* Rio de Janeiro: Instituto de Pesquisa Economica e Social and Instituto de Pesquisa Economica Aplicada.

Pfeffermann, Guy Pierre, and Richard Webb. 1979. The Distribution of Income in Brazil. World Bank Staff Working Paper no. 356. September.

Ramos, Lauro. 1991. Educação, Desigualdade de Renda e Ciclo Economico no Brasil. *Pesquisa e Planejamento Economico* 21 (3): 423–48.

Ravallion, Martin, and Gaurav Datt. 1991. *Growth and Redistribution Components of Changes in Poverty Measures.* LSMS Working Paper no. 83. Washington, DC: World Bank.

Sedlacek, Guilherme Luis, and Ricardo Paes de Barros, eds. 1989. *Mercado de Trabalho e Distribuição de Renda: Uma Coletanea.* Serie Monografica. Rio de Janeior: Instituto de Pesquisa Economica Aplicada.

Taylor, Lance, et al. 1980. *Models of Growth and Distribution in Brazil.* New York: Oxford University Press.

Vinod, Thomas. 1987. Differences in Income and Poverty within Brazil. *World Development* 15 (2): 263–73.

World Bank. 1988. *Brazil: Public Spending on Social Programs: Issues and Options.* Report 7086-BR.

———. 1992. *World Development Report 1992.* Oxford: Oxford University Press.

Comment   Rubens Ricupero

In the early 1970s, Nixon put in a nutshell the conventional wisdom of the time when he said that, "as Brazil goes, so goes Latin America." The so-called Brazilian economic miracle led observers—with a few worthy exceptions, such as Professor Albert Fishlow—to overlook the increasing inequality, the absence of democracy, and the violation of human rights.

Twenty years later, another cliché stubbornly clings to descriptions of the current Brazilian situation. Once again, economic performance is given pre-eminence, but the new, reverse cliché risks glossing over other relevant aspects of our reality.

The purpose of this seminar is precisely to probe clichés and stereotypes in an attempt to grasp—to the extent possible—the diversity and contradictoriness of Brazil's overall situation today.

This is perhaps too ambitious a goal for only one day of discussions, but we can at least broach the subject by pointing out a few issues worthy of consideration.

First, there is a risk of excessive absorption in the short term. Among the ten largest economies in the world, Brazil's was the one that grew the most in the 117-year period between 1870 and 1987. The 1986 and 1987 Interamerican Development Bank and ECLAC reports still stressed that it was Brazil's growth during that period that kept the Latin American average growth from being negative. Those who still remember how quick was the transition from Europessimism to Europhoria or that only twenty-four months separate the 1989 annus mirabilis from the 1992 annus horribilis should resist the temptation of drawing too definitive conclusions about the present.

Second, it should be recalled that although we share Latin America's circumstances—an inescapable frame of reference—some peculiar features of the Brazilian situation make it impossible to fit it into a continental typology.

In my view, three of these features stand out as differentiating elements between the Brazilian situation and that of the rest of Latin America, namely, the centrality of the political and institutional crisis, the significance of regional problems, and the implications of size.

Other Latin American countries may experience dramatic conflicts, guerrillas, and coups and attempted coups, as we recently saw in Venezuela and Peru. But none of them is seriously considering the adoption of parliamentarism, as Brazil is getting ready to do in six months' time. None has undertaken such an extensive and ambitious process of overhauling its constitution as Brazil. Argentina did not change its 1853 constitution after the military regime, while Chile opted for approving a constitutional amendment before transition—in

Rubens Ricupero is the minister of finance of Brazil. He was the coordinator of the Contact Group on Finances at the United Nations Conference on Environment and Development (Rio de Janeiro, 1992) and chaired the GATT Contracting Parties (Geneva, 1990–91).

both instances the extent and the destabilizing effects of the changes were kept within strict boundaries.

Pronounced regional contrasts and tensions and, more important, the degree of power and autonomy enjoyed by some states and municipalities are other characteristics setting Brazil apart from the prevailing Latin American pattern. Only recently did the Colombian and Venezuelan governments relinquish the practice of appointing provincial governors and accepted that they should be chosen through direct elections. In other countries, federalism is of a mild, loose variety as compared to Brazil's. One of the military regime's mentors used to say that Brazilian history could be defined as the alternation between centralization and decentralization or, in his characteristic prose, by systole and diastole. This issue has now reached a critical point, for it not only fuels the increasingly hot debate on popular representation in the Chamber of Deputies but also raises one of the most delicate issues concerning fiscal and economic adjustment, owing to the resistance to any change in the incentive system and in the current tax revenue sharing system.

In essence, this is one of the manifestations of another of Brazil's distinguishing features: the gigantic size of a territory physically difficult to control and to exploit and a population equivalent to that of Russia, a great part of which concentrated in megalopolises whose administration constitutes a greater challenge than governing any of several smaller nations on the continent. Problems pertaining to territory and population combine to put Brazil more appropriately in the same category as Russia, China, and India than in one class with Argentina, Chile, and Venezuela. This inevitably affects the prospects for foreign policy and of integration with the world economy.

Such a rich and dynamic picture as that presented by Brazil today necessarily allows different but also seemingly contradictory readings. For example, many see the impeachment procedure under way against President Collor as just one more manifestation of the failure of a fragmented political system incapable of producing consensus and acceptable standards of administrative ethics; others, however, commend the lack of violence, the military's exemplary conduct, and the sanctioning of the removal of an incumbent president on grounds of corruption as evidence of the renewed vigor and effectiveness of democratic institutions and the civilian society.

As a further illustration of this diversity of possible interpretations, consider first an article by Jorge Castañeda in *El País* (September 24, 1992), suggestively entitled "El ejemplo brasileño" (*The Brazilian example*). The article starts with the prevailing negative approach: "From this perspective, the misappropriation of public funds . . . would represent but a further trauma, in contrast to the current success achieved by Mexico, Chile and Argentina. Differently from these fortunate nations, Brazilians would have been humiliated by the unexpected fall of a frivolous president, caused by the proverbial failure of a paralyzed political system—the whole made worse by the abandonment of the attempt to carry out the ultimate economic reform." But, after outlining the widespread corruption problem on the Latin American continent and pointing out the failure in combating it, the author chooses another interpretation, stating that "Brazil's serious crisis can also be viewed differently as a real watershed in Latin American politics, as the first time in history when corruption . . . is finally going to be punished instead of rewarded. It can also be taken as a herald of future developments, to the extent that the Brazilian scandal sets a precedent and an example to be followed." Castañeda goes on to say that "never before had the very institutions that raised someone to power turned against him and finally removed him from the Presidential Office." And he concludes that "Fernando Collor's likely impeachment is by no means a symptom of weakness in Brazilian politics, nor is it a result of the so often commented paralysis of the political system. On the contrary, it is evidence of the strength and viability of both Brazilian politics and the Brazilian political system as well as the logical outcome of underlying, contradictory, often decisive political trends." One of these trends is the "process of democratization of Brazilian politics in the past decade. The sturdiness of civilian society—the strength of the church and the political parties, of the press and the unions, of women and students, of environmentalists and the Congress—has made Brazil a singular case in Latin America."

An example of that same reading is another article in *El País* (September 1, 1992), written by Alain Touraine and entitled "La crisis brasileña" (*The Brazilian crisis*); the author states that "this painful crisis deepens the misery felt by many, but Brazil's outlook remains very positive. Brazil was not an underdeveloped country making progress, but a poor developed country, as it already possessed all the elements of a modern society: investment capability, entrepreneurship, technical capacity, social negotiation forces, and a very rich intellectual and cultural environment. Brazil was the last country on the continent to complete the liberal revolution but it will be the first to rebuild itself and to forge ahead within the framework of a modern economy, owing above all to the soundness of its social agents," the latter of which, according to Touraine, find a parallel only in Chile.

What is under discussion is not the Brazilian reality. There is no denying that failures in recent years owe a great deal to the fragmentation of the political system and to insufficient political craftsmanship. This recognition, however, does not advance much further our understanding of why this is occurring now instead of at other moments of our past.

The articles quoted might offer a clue to a possible explanation. After the military regime came to an end, it could be said that Brazil not only began a transition to a civilian form of government, or a change from a semiautarkic to a more open and market-oriented economy. Far beyond that, a process of profound social change was taking place, subjecting the political system to unprecedented pressures and disturbances. Such a process of social democratization boosts the number of players, exacerbates class and regional conflicts, and intensifies the awareness of disparities, thereby making consensus more difficult to achieve.

The scale of this process of change should not be underestimated. A country that started the nineteenth century with a population consisting of 1.3 million free whites and 3.9 million blacks, mostly slaves, and entered the twentieth century with a life expectancy of slightly over thirty years, Brazil now offers a scene in which a blue-collar worker and a black woman from the *favelas* had a real change of being elected president of the Republic and mayor of Rio de Janeiro, respectively. One might ask, in which countries in Latin America or in the Western world would such situations be a realistic possibility?

This kind of process does not occur in an orderly, Cartesian, rational manner—as the legend "Order and Progress" on our flag portends; rather, its course is often destabilizing and unpredictable. Some academic analysts might prefer a strictly controlled process conducted by a small promodernization elite in the Atatürk model or, to take up a new fashionable term, a sequencing after the Asian model, in which economic modernization precedes political participation. Whatever the merit of these approaches, this kind of debate is irrelevant in Brazil's case, as history has clearly chosen to embark on a complex course, in which political and social democratization coincides with the economic stabilization and modernization effort.

Among the successful development models cited for comparison purposes, some countries have achieved economic adjustment under an authoritarian regime and have maintained it under a democratic form of government but have yet been unable to settle the inherited social debt. Others, which are carrying out an exemplary modernization task from a technocratic point of view, enjoy a high degree of social control and are not overly disturbed by the unions and the press, nor by a vigorous, autonomous legislature or judiciary. In others, economic indices are encouraging, but popular dissatisfaction with poor wealth distribution, the persistence of corruption, and the weakness of the judiciary system or the press raise doubts and fuel uncertainty about the results.

To prove that far-reaching political and social democratization based on sound institutions is capable of engendering the consensus needed to effect and maintain economic adjustment and ensure the proper distribution of its benefits is a challenge that has never been fully met—not in Brazil, in Latin America, or anywhere else in the developing world.

6   Israel's Stabilization: Some Important Policy Lessons

Gil Bufman and Leonardo Leiderman

6.1 Introduction

The Israeli stabilization program is considered a success: it resulted in a
sharp and rapid reduction in the rate of inflation from over 400% per year in
the mid-1980s to less than 20% per year thereafter. While the benefits from
this heterodox program on the inflation front were visible from the beginning,
some of the costs associated with stabilization appeared with a considerable
lag. After a pronounced consumption boom and an economic activity boom at
the start of the program, a recession emerged in early 1988, and no major
transition from stabilization to growth was observed. Clearly, some of these
developments could be explained by changing conditions that were not necessarily associated with the stabilization program per se. In order to determine
which elements of the program could be applied to other countries, it is important to evaluate whether there could have been ways to improve the benefits
and/or reduce the costs of the program.

Two important lessons from stabilization in Israel are quite uncontroversial.[1]
First, an important role in the design and success of the heterodox program
was played by a set of social-political agreements (a sort of social pact) that
were reached at that time. This took the form of a national-unity coalition that
was built by the main political parties, and broad agreements among representatives of labor, government, and industry, setting patterns for prices, wages,

Gil Bufman is a senior economist at the Bank of Israel's monetary department. Leonardo Leiderman is professor of economics at Tel Aviv University and a research fellow of the Center for
Economic Policy Research.

The views expressed in the paper are solely the responsibility of the authors.

1. Earlier work evaluating the Israeli stabilization program includes Bruno (1986); Bruno and
Piterman (1988); Bruno and Meridor (1991); Helpman and Leiderman (1988); Kiguel and Liviatan
(1989); Leiderman and Liviatan (1990); and Leiderman (1993).

and the exchange rate. Second, the stabilization effort was supported by external aid in the first two years of the program. Without this aid, more stringent (and probably less feasible) fiscal adjustments would have been required to achieve the same degree of disinflation that was observed ex post. Similarly, foreign aid provided support to the exchange rate targets that were chosen and helped avoid any balance-of-payments crises.

With the benefit of hindsight, this paper draws some lessons from two key aspects of Israel's disinflation; the transition (or lack thereof) from stabilization to growth, and exchange rate policy. Accumulated experience indicates that both these issues can play a key role in the success of a disinflation program. That is, major political and economic difficulties were encountered by stabilizations that were associated with a slowdown in economic activity and did not eventually produce a transition to growth. Similarly, there are several well-known episodes in which an exchange rate–based stabilization failed because of speculative attacks on foreign currencies—attacks that emerged in the face of lack of compatibility between exchange rate policy and the underlying fiscal and monetary fundamentals.

This paper is organized as follows. Section 6.2 provides an updated set of empirical regularities associated with the stabilization plan of 1985. Section 6.3 discusses issues related to the transition from stabilization to growth. Various aspects of exchange rate policy are discussed in section 6.4. Section 6.5 provides our main conclusions.

6.2 Results from Stabilization

In this section, we discuss the main empirical regularities after the 1985 stabilization program in Israel. We focus on periods immediately before and after stabilization; for the latter we consider 1986–88. Clearly, care is suggested in interpreting the evidence, as not all facts were associated with inflation stabilization per se, and other things were not equal. The main regularities are discussed here.

Rapid disinflation. A marked reduction in inflation was already observed in the first few months following the implementation of the program in mid-1985. From annual rates of inflation in the triple-digit range, the program quickly succeeded in bringing inflation down to about 16–20% per year in the period from 1986 to 1991. Only in 1992 were there strong forces to bring annual inflation to the single-digit range; see figure 6.1. Various price increase indicators are shown in table 6.1.

Real exchange rate appreciation. While the nominal exchange rate of the new Israeli shekel (NIS) was held fixed for long periods, domestic prices rose at a higher rate than foreign prices, resulting in a real exchange rate appreciation (table 6.1). The real exchange rate of the NIS against the U.S. dollar appreciated at the considerable rates of 16% in 1986, 7% in 1987, and 11% in 1988.

Table 6.1   **The Exchange Rate and Relative Prices (rates of change)**

	Nominal Exchange Rate (avg./avg.) (%)			Real Exchange Rate (avg./avg.) (%)			Terms of Trade (exports) (%)
	Currency Basket[a]	Dollar	Nondollar Basket	Currency Basket[b]	Dollar[c]	Nondollar Basket[c]	
1980	103.6	101.5	106.2	−2.6	−2.4	−7.8	—
1981	105.7	122.9	84.9	−0.4	8.1	−14.4	—
1982	103.0	112.4	89.5	−5.6	−2.9	−12.9	—
1983	124.4	131.7	112.4	−7.9	−5.4	−13.3	1.0
1984	399.7	421.4	361.3	4.0	7.1	−4.4	−1.7
1985	305.5	302.1	312.3	10.6	10.6	9.1	1.1
1986	37.2	26.2	58.8	−8.2	−15.5	9.7	4.1
1987	14.4	7.2	25.5	−2.1	−7.1	5.8	−3.1
1988	2.4	0.3	5.2	−9.0	−11.4	−9.9	5.2
1989	16.1	19.9	11.4	0.9	3.7	−8.1	−0.6
1990	10.9	5.3	18.6	1.0	−2.6	5.5	1.1

	Prices (%)				Price of Exports vs. Domestic Uses (%)	Services Price Index Compared to Wholesale Price Index
	CPI (Dec./Dec.)	Wholesale (Dec./Dec.)	Tradable[d] (avg./ avg.)	Nontradable		
1980	132.9	138.1	—	—	—	—
1981	101.5	130.5	—	—	−2.7	—
1982	131.5	136.9	117.2	121.8	−5.0	—
1983	190.7	199.7	238.5	149.8	−3.0	100.0
1984	444.9	446.9	389.9	386.2	0.8	88.1
1985	185.2	152.8	285.0	246.3	1.5	95.5
1986	19.7	14.3	40.7	54.5	−11.6	119.3
1987	16.1	20.7	17.5	28.3	−4.3	135.0
1988	16.4	15.7	11.5	22.6	−3.3	141.1
1989	20.7	19.3	17.5	22.5	0.6	143.2
1990	17.6	12.6	—	—	−2.7	151.9

Sources: Bank of Israel Annual Report; Statistical Abstract of Israel.

[a]The five-currency basket was established in August 1986. For the period prior to August 1986 the basket exchange rate is computed using the weights of the currency basket.

[b]Using the effective rate in export.

[c]Using the official rate.

[d]Based on CPI prices (Ben-Basat 1992).

When expressed against a basket of foreign currencies, the real exchange rate appreciated at about 8% in 1986, 2% in 1987, and 9% in 1988. In August 1986, a trade-weighted currency basket was officially adopted for fixing the exchange rate, instead of the U.S. dollar. The composition of one currency basket unit is 0.6 U.S. dollar, 0.4177 deutsche mark, 0.067 pound, 0.3394 French franc, and 7.7 yen. The effective weights of the various currencies in the currency basket vary according to the cross-currency rates. Accordingly,

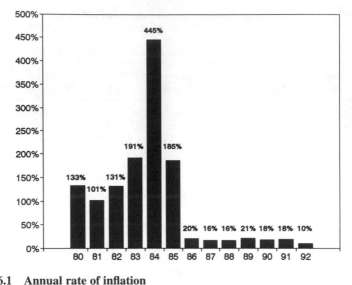

Fig. 6.1   Annual rate of inflation
Source: Statistical Abstract of Israel; Central Bureau of Statistics.

the composition of the currency basket has been 55–60% of the U.S. dollar, 35–40% of European currencies, and about 5% of Japanese yen. Consequently, the real exchange rate against nondollar components of the basket depreciated at 10% in 1986 and 6% in 1987, and it appreciated at 10% in 1988.[2] The considerable real exchange rate appreciation that followed the program is evident in various measures of relative prices. Specifically, the cumulative increase in the relative price of nontraded to traded goods over 1986–88 was 32%; the relative price of exports against domestic uses decreased over that period by 20%; and the relative price of services to manufacturing goods rose by 48%. Notice that, at the same time, no major shifts were observed in Israel's terms of trade.

Fiscal adjustment. Three main features highlight the major fiscal adjustment after the program. First, there was a major fall in the domestic government budget deficit, from 16% of GDP in 1984 to 1.3% of GDP in 1986–88; see table 6.2. This reflects an increase of about 8% of GDP in domestic revenues from 1984 to 1986–87, and a reduction of about 7% of GDP in domestic gov-

2. In comparison, the real exchange rate of the NIS vis-à-vis the U.S. dollar evolved quite differently, as it appreciated 16% in 1986, 7% in 1987, and 11% in 1988. This marked difference in real exchange rate development may have contributed to changes in the geographic composition Israel's trade. More specifically, during 1986–88 the share of exports to European destinations as percentage of total exports of Israeli goods increased from 36% to 38%, while the share of exports to the United States decreased from 33% to 31%. Exports to Asia rose from 10% to 16%, and exports to all other destinations, which are conducted mainly in U.S. dollars, declined from 21% to 16%.

ernment expenditures. As far as the latter is concerned, the main items of government expenditures that were reduced (as percentage of GDP) after the program were grants and subsidies (including credit subsidies and subsidies for production of basic goods and utilities), and domestic defense expenditures. These trends show up in government's total budget deficit, which also includes foreign revenues and expenditures. In this context, an important role was played by the special foreign aid received from the United States, amounting to $1.5 billion in 1985 and 1986. Second, the stronger fiscal stance was reflected in a reversal in the time path of domestic and foreign public debt ratios, from increasing trends before 1985 to marked reductions after 1985; see figure 6.2. Specifically, domestic public sector debt decreased from 112% in 1985 to 90% of GDP in 1989, and foreign public sector debt fell from 53% in 1985 to 24% in 1989; see table 6.2. Third, seigniorage played no major role in inflation or disinflation: it remained relatively stable at about 2–3% of GDP before and after stabilization. Put differently, changing trends in the behavior of inflation were more closely associated with fluctuations in public debt ratios than with government seigniorage.

Consumption boom. Prior to the stabilization program (i.e., between 1980 and 1984), total private consumption grew at an average annual rate of about 5% and consumption of durables (which were on average 13% of total consumption) grew at about 8% per year; see table 6.3. The consumption boom began at the first quarter after the program (i.e., the last quarter of 1985), when total private consumption increased by 13% in comparison to the previous quarter. This was led by a sharp increase in consumption of durable goods, which registered a *36% increase* in comparison to the previous quarter. The year of 1986 is the most salient example of the consumption boom phenomenon. In that

Table 6.2   **Public Expenditure, Revenue, and Deficit (% of GDP)**

			Deficit(−)/Surplus(+)			Public Sector Debt (net)		
	Expenditure	Revenue	Total	Domestic	Foreign	Domestic[a]	Foreign	Seigniorage
1983	66.0	61.4	−4.6	−7.0	2.4	112.9	38.6	3.1
1984	72.0	60.2	−11.9	−16.0	4.2	106.9	48.7	3.0
1985	69.8	71.5	1.7	−6.3	8.0	111.8	52.9	3.1
1986	64.3	67.6	3.3	−1.2	4.5	110.6	40.3	2.6
1987	61.1	61.1	0.0	−1.2	1.3	100.5	31.2	2.3
1988	58.0	57.6	−0.3	−1.4	1.1	88.9	25.5	−1.4
1989	57.4	53.4	−4.0	−6.0	2.0	89.8	23.6	0.7
1990	57.0	54.3	−2.7	−5.5	2.8	88.9	20.1	0.5

Source: Bank of Israel Annual Report.
[a]Excluding government liabilities to the public associated with the 1983 bank share arrangement.

Fig. 6.2   Public sector domestic net debt and inflation

Source: *Statistical Abstract of Israel;* Central Bureau of Statistics; *Bank of Israel Annual Report*
Note: The domestic debt shown here includes government liabilities to the public that are associated with the 1983 bank share arrangement. This definition differs slightly from that shown in table 6.2.

year, private consumption rose by 15% (i.e., over 13% per capita), and consumption of durables *increased by 50%*. These figures clearly imply that the consumption boom applied to *both* durable and nondurable goods. Most of the increase in durable goods consumption was translated into an increase in imports of consumer goods; however, notice that imports of nondurable consumption goods also increased, outpacing nondurable domestic consumption. The consumption boom continued, though somewhat moderated, in 1987. Total consumption rose by 9% in that year, and consumption of durables grew at 13%. The boom lasted for about two and a half years and came to a half after the first quarter of 1988. In 1989, total private consumption remained unchanged from the level of the previous year, while consumption of durable goods declined by 13%.

Completing a cycle: Postboom recession. To a large extent, these developments in private consumption spending were reflected in fluctuations in economic activity. In the two years after the program, that is 1986–87, the rate of growth of GDP was 5% per year, which is double the rate of growth that prevailed for 1984; see table 6.4. This boom in economic activity was not spread evenly across various sectors in the economy. That is, while there was a strong growth performance in the nontradables sector, whose output grew at 7.5% per year in 1986–87 compared to less than 2% per year in 1981–85, rates of growth for

Table 6.3   **Private Consumption (rates of change, real terms)**

	Population Growth (%)	Consumption (%)			Imports of Consumption Goods (%)			Durable Consumption Growth beyond Total Consumption Growth (%)
		Total	Nondurables	Durable Goods	Total	Nondurables	Durable Goods	
1981	2.4	13.0	9.4	43.6	—	—	—	13.5
1982	1.8	8.0	7.2	13.3	9.1	11.5	6.1	14.2
1983	2.0	8.7	6.7	20.9	8.5	−5.9	24.2	15.7
1984	1.2	−7.0	−2.4	−31.8	−18.8	−13.3	−27.5	11.5
1985	2.0	0.7	0.8	−0.0	−4.6	1.4	−12.9	11.5
1986	1.8	14.8	10.3	49.7	39.3	31.6	52.5	14.9
1987	1.6	9.0	8.5	13.2	13.5	11.7	16.0	11.7
1988	1.7	4.3	4.1	5.8	12.7	10.0	15.5	11.9
1989	1.7	0.0	1.7	−12.8	−8.4	2.3	−19.7	10.4
1990	3.1	5.3	4.0	17.1	12.6	2.1	27.1	11.5

	Consumption Prices[a]			
	Total (%)	Nondurables (%)	Durable Goods (%)	Relative Price Index: Durables/Nondurables
1981	118.3	121.1	100.6	100.0
1982	118.5	120.7	105.4	93.1
1983	144.0	145.6	135.7	89.4
1984	391.8	388.9	414.4	94.0
1985	295.9	301.8	250.2	81.9
1986	46.0	46.5	42.9	79.9
1987	19.9	20.2	17.6	78.2
1988	16.3	17.0	11.0	74.2
1989	20.8	22.0	10.5	67.2
1990	15.9	16.8	8.7	62.5

Sources: Bank of Israel Annual Report; Statistical Abstract of Israel.

[a]Based on national account consumption prices, annual averages.

the tradables sector remained unchanged at about 4.5% per year.[3] Along similar lines, the rate of growth of output in manufacturing rose modestly from 4–5% per year from the period before to after the program, yet the rate of growth of output in the services and commerce sector almost doubled, from 4% to 7% per year, from 1981–85 to 1986–87. *These trends were reversed in 1988–89.* On average, GDP growth slowed down to about 2% per year in that period, and there was a *decline* in output of the traded goods sector of about 1% per year, led by a decline in industrial sector's production of about 2.4%

3. The tradable sector includes manufacturing, agriculture, sea and air transportation, and tourism.

Table 6.4   Economic Growth (rates of change, real terms, %)

	Population Growth	Gross Product Growth				Total Factor Productivity	
	Population Growth	Total Domestic	Business Sector	Industrial Sector	Services & Commerce	Business Sector	Industrial Sector
1981	2.4	4.5	6.0	3.5	8.4	1.5	—
1982	1.8	1.1	−0.1	−2.2	2.6	1.6	—
1983	2.0	2.8	3.4	3.4	4.1	1.5	—
1984	1.2	2.5	2.9	7.3	0.9	−2.3	—
1985	2.0	4.0	6.0	7.2	7.6	1.0	1.6
1986	1.8	3.8	6.3	7.1	9.4	1.4	2.2
1987	1.6	6.2	8.6	7.0	8.8	3.7	3.3
1988	1.7	2.6	2.4	−0.8	5.8	−0.6	−1.0
1989	1.7	1.7	2.1	−2.0	3.8	0.0	−2.4
1990	3.1	5.4	6.8	5.9	4.3	4.3	4.3

Sources: Bank of Israel Annual Report; Statistical Abstract of Israel.

per year. The slowdown was also present in the nontraded sector, whose output's growth was reduced yet remained positive at 3.4% per year. Interestingly, the program was followed initially by a rise in both total factor productivity and labor productivity relative to their levels prior to stabilization. Productivity further increased in 1990, along with a process of restructuring and rationalization of operations in business and activity.

Rise in wages beyond productivity. Coupled with wage controls, the devaluation and rises in controlled prices at the start of the program were associated with a decrease in the real wage in 1985 of 9% over all sectors; see table 6.5. However, the relaxation of controls and the heating up of the economy in 1986–87 were accompanied by marked real wage increases of 8% per year, which clearly *outpaced* increases in labor productivity (by about 6 percentage points per year). The program did not result in a noticeable change in the economy's rate of unemployment. Only after four years into the program did the rate of unemployment markedly rise, to 9.6% in 1990. Increased employment was associated, to a large extent, to a cumulative decline of about 5% in industrial sector employment during the recession years of 1988–89, and with an increase in the participation rate in the labor force.

Monetary expansion. Disinflation in Israel was followed by substantial expansion of monetary aggregates, both in nominal and real terms. This is particularly the case of M1 and M2 growth in 1986–87. Broader aggregates, such as M3 and M4, showed much more moderate increases. To a large extent, these movements reflect a shift in the financial portfolio of the private sector, away from indexed bonds and foreign exchange assets to nonindexed short-term do-

Table 6.5   **Labor and Wages (rates of change, real terms, %)**

	Real Wage per Employee Post[a]			Employment			Output per Labor Hour		
	All Sectors	Business Sector	Industrial Sector	All Sectors	Business Sector	Industrial Sector	Business Sector	Industrial Sector	Unemp. Rate
1980	−3.1	−0.5	0.1	1.1	1.7	−1.0	3.9	0.3	4.8
1981	11.6	12.4	10.4	2.0	2.6	2.5	2.3	5.0	5.1
1982	−1.5	−0.3	3.5	1.4	1.5	1.2	0.3	−0.8	5.0
1983	6.2	4.7	5.2	3.2	4.3	2.2	1.4	2.3	4.5
1984	−0.4	−1.2	1.9	1.5	1.8	0.3	−1.6	2.7	5.9
1985	−9.0	−6.5	−7.4	0.7	1.9	−0.2	2.1	3.2	6.7
1986	7.8	9.1	7.0	1.4	1.7	4.2	1.5	1.6	7.1
1987	7.9	8.0	7.1	2.6	3.9	1.9	3.1	4.9	6.1
1988	6.0	4.7	3.7	3.5	3.2	−2.1	2.2	1.5	6.4
1989	−1.3	−1.7	0.9	0.5	−0.0	−2.5	0.5	4.4	8.9
1990	−1.0	−1.6	0.0	2.1	2.1	2.8	3.9	7.4	9.6

Sources: Bank of Israel Annual Report; Statistical Abstract of Israel.
[a]Excluding labor from territories.

Table 6.6   **Monetary Aggregates (nominal terms)**

	Inflation (avg./avg.) (%)	Asset Growth (%)				Velocity (Y/M)				Total Credit Growth (%)
		$M1$	$M2$	$M3$	$M4$	$M1$	$M2$	$M3$	$M4$	
1981	116.8	93.2	117.4	120.7	117.3	26.8	18.1	5.4	3.3	58.8
1982	120.3	100.4	140.7	133.7	130.1	30.2	16.9	5.2	3.3	148.3
1983	145.7	113.5	165.4	171.4	147 6	36.5	16.5	5.0	3.4	136.1
1984	373.8	225.0	315.0	435.2	372.4	55.6	19.7	4.6	3.6	366.2
1985	304.6	351.6	553.2	309.7	301.2	45.8	11.2	4.2	3.3	317.5
1986	48.1	169.4	128.5	44.3	56.1	26.6	7.7	4.5	3.3	64.1
1987	19.9	60.2	71.6	37.1	38.0	21.1	5.7	4.2	3.1	39.4
1988	16.3	31.9	25.9	19.3	17.5	19.7	5.5	4.3	3.2	22.7
1989	20.2	27.8	20.3	20.7	24.8	18.8	5.6	4.4	3.2	41.4
1990	17.2	28.3	25.1	23.1	24.5	18.1	5.6	4.4	3.1	23.8

Sources: Bank of Israel Annual Report; Statistical Abstract of Israel.

mestic currency assets, most of which are included in M2 (see table 6.6, in particular the drop in velocities of M1 and M2). This picture of monetary expansion held despite the initial attempt to use a restrictive credit policy as a key ingredient of monetary policy under disinflation—an attempt that was not effective enough over time. In fact, real credit to the public showed marked increases from mid-1986 onward. While monetary expansion was accompanied by a sharp reduction in nominal interest rates, ex post real interest rates remained extremely high (i.e., at about 35% for debitory rates) during 1986–87

Table 6.7   Interest Rates: Short-Term Credit

	1983	1984	1985	1986	1987	1988	1989
Nominal interest rates							
Total credit	205.5	576.8	234.5	31.9	39.0	33.2	33.4
Directed[a]	176.2	567.0	188.9	11.9	16.2	13.1	34.1
Nondirected	214.8	582.8	260.5	40.6	46.5	38.4	32.8
Debitory rate	181.6	771.0	443.7	61.5	61.9	46.2	34.3
Real interest rates							
(ex post)							
Total credit	5.1	24.2	17.3	10.2	19.7	14.4	10.5
Directed	−5.0	22.4	1.3	−6.5	0.1	−2.8	11.1
Nondirected	8.3	25.3	26.4	17.5	26.2	18.9	10.0
Debitory rate	−3.1	59.8	90.6	34.9	39.4	25.6	11.3
Average interest rate,							
real terms (ex post)[b]							
Business sector	7.9	32.6	17.5	6.9	16.2	11.6	—
Industrial sector	4.7	33.8	11.7	1.4	10.1	6.3	11.1
Share of directed credit							
in short-term credit usage							
Business sector	41.6	43.3	43.9	39.1	34.1	28.7	—
Industrial sector	75.0	76.8	76.1	66.4	59.3	54.1	50.1
Total short-term credit							
per output							
Whole economy	24.8	22.6	25.6	26.6	31.5	35.0	39.3
Industrial sector	30.8	28.3	28.1	27.6	30.1	34.3	36.7

Sources: Bank of Israel Annual Report; Statistical Abstract of Israel; Ben-Rawe (1989); Bruno and Meridor (1991).

[a]Directed credit is credit allocated by the government. The interest rate of this credit is typically below the market (i.e., nondirected) rate. Total credit is the sum of short-term directed and nondirected credit.

[b]Weighted average based on the actual composition of credit usage according to directed/nondirected credit and credit in domestic/foreign currency.

(table 6.7). Starting in 1988, there was a gradual process of reduction in ex post real interest rates, which still remained relatively high. In any case, it should be stressed that ex ante real interest rates may well have behaved quite differently from ex post rates precisely at times of change in policies.[4]

Reduction in investment and improvement of the current account. In the two years following the implementation of the stabilization program, the current account registered an average annual surplus in the order of 5% of GDP. This surplus contrasts the current account deficit in the order of 6% of total national that existed in 1981–84. Not surprisingly, this surplus was partly associated

4. Interest rate trends over this period also reflected the impact of various monetary and capital market reforms.

with the marked increase in foreign aid. On average, a current account surplus of 1.5% of GDP prevailed during 1988–89, mainly due to a decrease in the import surplus, which partially offset the decrease in unilateral transfers to Israel; see table 6.8.

Alternatively, we can examine current account developments in terms of fluctuations in gross national saving and investment. Following this approach, the current account surplus of 1986–87 was a result of a decline in investment and unchanged savings (as a percentage of total national income). Following the implementation of the stabilization program there was a marked decline in investment from over 20% of GDP during 1981–84 to 18% in 1986–87; this was due mainly to a decline in investment in residential construction. Gross national savings varied slightly around 18% of GDP during 1981–84, increased somewhat to about 20% in 1986–87, and returned to about 18% in 1988–89. Although total national savings did not change much, there were marked changes in the composition of savings, as the public sector shifted from being a negative-saving sector prior to the stabilization program to a positive-saving sector in the first two years after the program. As the saving ratio of the public sector increased, there was a decrease in the saving ratio of the private sector. Put differently, the private consumption boom of 1986–87 resulted in a saving ratio deduction from 27% to about 16% of GDP. These offsetting trends in components of national saving, much as in a Ricardian equivalence framework, are depicted in figure 6.3.

In our view, a unified overall theoretical explanation of the foregoing empirical regularities is still missing. While the observed inflation/unemployment developments do not conform with traditional, money-based disinflations, they can be partly explained by invoking models of exchange rate–based disinflation. Other developments can be explained by lack of full credibility of policymakers. Models such as Fischer's (1986) and Calvo's and Végh's (1991) predict that an immediate drop in inflation and a real exchange rate appreciation follow an exchange rate–based stabilization program. By pointing out the lack of credibility, Calvo and Végh (1991) are able to account for a consumption boom in the aftermath of disinflation. However, their explanation is not complete, in that it does not seem to fully account for the rise in real interest rates[5] after the program. Another somewhat puzzling feature of the data is that both inflation and disinflation were not tightly linked to fluctuations in seigniorage. This feature provides some scope for models based on economic agents' expectations of future monetary and fiscal adjustments in response to observed underlying trends in public debt. In this context, there is a remarkable comovement between public debt ratios and the behavior of the rate of inflation, much in the spirit of Sargent and Wallace (1981).

---

5. Notice that money-based stabilization models are capable of explaining increases in the real interest rate but at the same time cannot explain a consumption boom, as in exchange rate–based models.

Table 6.8   **External Balance**

	Billions of Dollars, Deficit(−)/Surplus(+)[a]					% of GDP				
	Trade Balance	Import Surplus	Unilateral Transfers (net)	Current Account	Foreign Debt (net)	Trade Balance	Import Surplus	Unilateral Transfers (net)	Current Account	Foreign Debt (net)
1981	−2.46	−4.06	3.10	−0.96	12.59	−10.6	−17.5	13.4	−4.1	54.4
1982	−2.92	−4.36	2.46	−1.90	15.24	−11.9	−17.7	10.0	−7.7	62.0
1983	−3.49	−4.65	2.71	−1.94	17.54	−12.7	−17.0	9.9	−7.1	64.0
1984	−2.45	−4.56	3.28	−1.28	18.69	−9.4	−17.5	12.6	−4.9	71.8
1985	−1.94	−3.88	5.00	1.12	18.42	−8.0	−16.1	20.7	4.6	76.5
1986	−2.35	−3.73	5.38	1.65	18.21	−7.9	−12.5	18.0	5.5	61.1
1987	−3.25	−5.63	4.77	−0.86	18.21	−9.2	−15.9	13.5	−2.4	51.4
1988	−2.84	−5.17	4.51	−0.66	18.52	−6.5	−11.9	10.4	−1.5	42.7
1989	−2.36	−3.77	4.86	1.10	16.24	−5.3	−8.5	11.0	2.5	36.6
1990	−3.53	−5.09	5.79	0.70	15.56	−6.8	−9.8	11.1	1.4	29.9

Sources: Bank of Israel Annual Report; Statistical Abstract of Israel.

[a]Current prices.

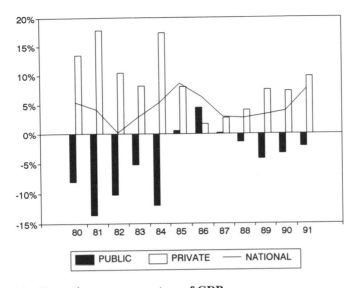

Fig. 6.3 Net savings as a percentage of GDP
Source: Statistical Abstract of Israel; Central Bureau of Statistics.

6.3 Transition (or Lack Thereof) from Stabilization to Growth

Disinflation in Israel was not accompanied by a fast transition to sustained growth. In fact, the growth performance of the economy deteriorated considerably after the late 1970s. In the decades of the 1950s and 1960s, real GDP grew annually at an average rate of about 10%, and total factor productivity grew at about 4.55 per year. In the late 1970s, GDP growth became 3% per year, and total factor productivity grew by less than 1% per year. While the consumption boom at the initial stages of the 1985 stabilization program contributed to maintain and even accelerate the level of economic activity, the latter was not sustained. In fact, a recession developed in 1988–89, and the growth rate became less than 2% per year. Underlying these developments were decreases in the rates of growth of public and private sector investments, which made the transition to growth more difficult. In this section, we examine the links between private and public investment and growth, as well as the relation between exports and growth.

Figure 6.4 provides evidence on various indicators of investment and growth. The period after the stabilization program was characterized by relatively low ratios of public and private sector investment to GDP. These ratios were low both by Israeli historical standards and by international comparisons. While total investment reached about 27% of GDP in the 1970s, it declined to a level of 17% of GDP between 1985 and 1990. The deterioration in the pattern of investment is reflected in a marked decrease in the capital/output ratio, depicted in figure 6.4. In particular, *notice the marked decrease in the capital/*

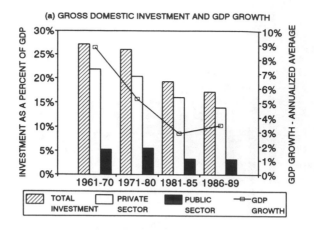

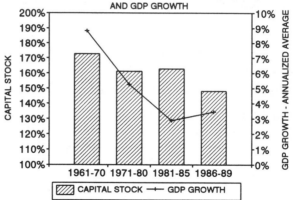

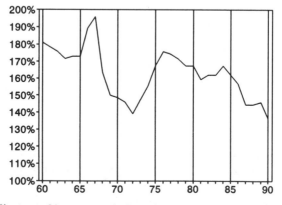

Fig. 6.4 Indicators of investment in Israel
Source: Statistical Abstract of Israel; Central Bureau of Statistics; *Bank of Israel Annual Report.*

output ratio after 1985. As far as international comparisons are concerned, investment as a percentage of GDP was about 21% in industrialized countries, and it was 22% in the rapidly growing East Asian developing countries (see figure 6.5).

The finding that there is an empirical relation between economic growth and the share of investment in GDP has been documented in numerous studies of various countries; hence, is is not unique to Israel. For example, in a cross-section regression including 101 countries over the period 1960–89, Levine and Renelt (1990) confirmed the robustness of earlier findings that the coefficient on the ratio of investment to GDP has significant explanatory power for the rate of growth of real per capita income. Similar results were reported by Fischer (1991), based on a pooling of cross section and time series for the period 1972–85. This relation is also clear from figures 9 and 10 in Dornbusch (1991), which plot the investment/GDP ratio against GDP growth for thirty-three developing countries for the periods 1965–73 and 1974–84. Perhaps Chile is the best-known example of a close relation between strong economic growth in recent years and a marked increasing trend of the investment share in GDP; see figure 6.6. The relation is also characteristic of comparisons involving industrialized countries. To take two extremes, over the period 1963–90 Japan's GDP grew at a rate of 6% per year, and the investment/GDP ratio was equal to 0.22. Over the same time period, the United Kingdom's GDP growth rate was 1% per year, and the share of investment in GDP was about 0.125 (see Auerbach 1992).[6] The notion that, other things equal, an increase in the share of investment in GDP will be associated with an increase in the rate of growth of output is familiar from standard growth accounting. The latter implies that an $x\%$ increase in the investment ratio increases output growth by that $x\%$ times the product of the output/capital ratio and capital's share in production. Yet growing evidence indicates that the observed effects of increases in the investment/GDP ratio on growth are much larger than what is implied by such arithmetics of growth (see, e.g., Auerbach 1992 and De Long and Summers 1991). Put differently, it can be argued that capital accumulation has not only direct effects on growth but also, and not less important, indirect effects in the form of increased inducements for innovation and for the adoption of new technologies that lead to an increase in total factor productivity. Some of these indirect effects may well take the form of "spillovers," social returns to investment that are not fully captured by individual investors, as emphasized in the recent endogenous growth literature; see Helpman (1992).

Work by De Long and Summers (1991) has emphasized that investments in machinery and equipment are one category of investment that is characterized by these spillover effects. Based on the cross-sectional distribution of growth rates across economies in the post–World War II period, the authors find evidence in support of the hypothesis that investments in machinery and equip-

---

6. Obviously, these findings must be interpreted with care because other things may not be equal.

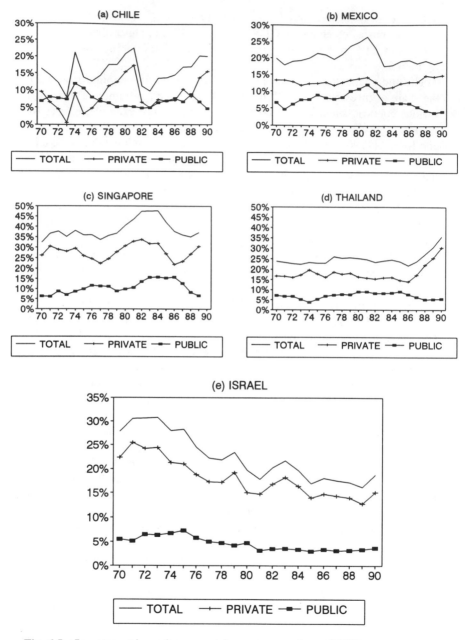

Fig. 6.5   Investment in various countries as a percentage of GDP
Source: International Financial Statistics, International Monetary Fund.

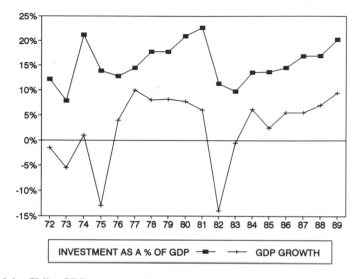

Fig. 6.6   Chile: GDP growth and investment as a percentage of GDP
Source: International Financial Statistics, International Monetary Fund.

ment are a strategic factor in growth, and do carry substantial benefits. Figure 6.7 illustrates these relations based on time series for Israel (using three-year moving averages). It is seen that the marked decrease in the rate of growth of total factor productivity observed after 1987 was preceded by a marked decrease in net growth of machinery and equipment, and that other periods have a close link between these variables.

Public sector investments, in particular in infrastructures, are another important category of total investment, one that has been associated with public good–type spillovers. As shown in table 6.9 and figure 6.8, there has been a clear trend of decrease in the ratio of investment in infrastructure to GDP in Israel, which was equal in the 1980s to only 50% its level in the 1960s. Although some increase in the ratio was registered after the 1985 program, the level is much lower than what is given by the historical standards.[7] Investments in infrastructures picked up only recently, in response to the wave of migration from the former Soviet Union. The role of public sector capital for growth has been assessed for Israel using time series and a production function–growth accounting framework, in which the rate of growth of output is related to the rates of growth of private and public capital and employment, by Hercowitz, Leiderman, and Siddi (1992), who find evidence in support of constant returns to scale on the private sector inputs and a coefficient of 0.4, which is statisti-

7. Similarly, a temporary increase (of 13.5%) in overall gross investment in fixed assets is also noted in 1987. This increase is mainly compensatory after three years of decline in investment, which cumulatively amounted to an 18% decline. The 1987 increase merely restored the real level of gross investment in fixed assets to the 1982–83 average.

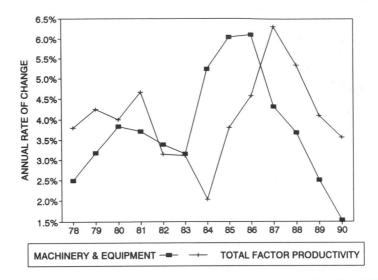

Fig. 6.7 Israel: net growth of machinery and equipment stock and total factor productivity change
Source: Bank of Israel Annual Report.
Note: Three-year moving averages used.

Table 6.9   **Investment in Infrastructure as a Percentage of Israel's GDP (five-year averages)**

1965–70	4.3
1970–75	3.9
1975–80	3.3
1980–85	2.8
1985–90	2.6

cally significant, on public sector capital.[8] Similar results were obtained by Bregman and Marom (1992), based on a pooling of time series and cross section for Israel. These results are quite similar to those obtained by Aschauer (1989) for the United States. While these findings are certainly controversial, because of their strength and the simplicity of the methodology used they all point to a relation that is less controversial in both theory and casual evidence.

Does the recovery of growth after stabilization necessarily require real exchange rate depreciation and export-led growth? The independent role of exports as percentage of GDP in the process of growth is less clear and more controversial, in theory and facts, than that of the investment share discussed above. Figure 6.9 provides evidence for three countries: Chile, Mexico, and

8. The authors used annual data for these variables from 1960 to 1988.

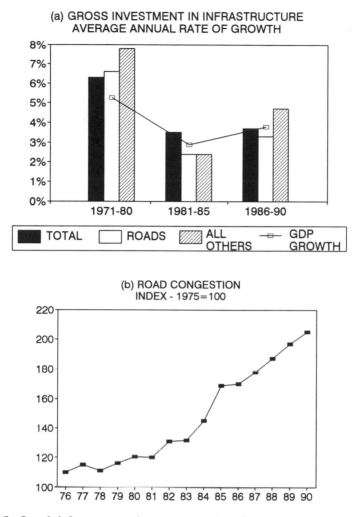

Fig. 6.8   Israel: infrastructure, investment, and strain
Source: Bank of Israel Annual Report (1990).

Israel. Chile represents an example of export-led growth. Between 1981 and 1986, the authorities succeeded in producing a real devaluation of nearly 40%. At the same time, there was a boom in exports. Similar evidence about the relation between GDP growth, investment growth, and the export/GDP ratio holds for Mexico, yet after considering different subperiods. At variance with Chile, however, there was a real exchange rate appreciation throughout.

What are the lessons for stabilization policy? We have documented the fact that, as far as investment and growth are concerned, *the initial conditions of the 1985 program were not strong.* This was especially the case for the stock

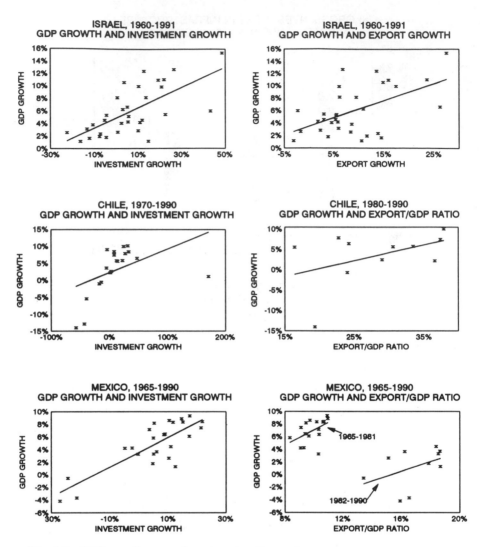

Fig. 6.9   GDP growth versus investment and exports
Source: International Financial Statistics, International Monetary Fund.

of public sector capital, including infrastructures. Moreover, after the program (and until the beginning of the immigration from the former Soviet Union) there was no marked renewal of investment and growth. Although some of these developments were due to factors not necessarily related to the stabilization program,[9] the program embodied no specific direct policy measures aimed

9. These factors include (1) the uprising in the administered territories, which had adverse effects on tourism, increased absenteeism of labor supply from the territories, created a decline in

at reversing this state of affairs. The policy was one of "stabilize inflation first, and deal with growth later." It was also argued at the time that the reduction in inflation per se would lead to a reallocation of resources, away from the financial sector and back into the real sector, that would increase measured output and productivity. Perhaps the main lesson here is that, already at the stage of disinflation, it is important to undertake policies that would facilitate a rapid transition to growth, for example, increasing public investment in infrastructure. This would be especially important in countries such as Israel, where the initial conditions are not extremely conducive to investment and growth, and in countries in which investors face a relatively large option value of waiting (see Dornbusch 1991). The recovery of investment takes time, especially at times of transition in economic policies. There are fiscal and industrial policies that can speed up the transition from stabilization to growth. However, the real dilemma for policy is to find the resources that would enable adopting these measures without jeopardizing a key ingredient of stabilization: a reduction in government spending and in the budget deficit. Perhaps the resolution of this dilemma is in the role of international institutions in providing support in the form of long-term loans, heavily conditioned on implementation of new policies, aimed at enhancing the transition from stabilization to growth (see Dornbusch 1991).

6.4 Evolution of Exchange Rate Policy

We begin this section by discussing the various stages of exchange rate policy in Israel after stabilization. Then we shift to a discussion of Israel's exchange rate band, a regime that was adopted in January 1989. Last, we provide new evidence on the relation between real exchange appreciation, world demand, and the performance of exports.

6.4.1 Exchange Rate–Based Stabilization

As indicated, the nominal exchange rate was used as a key anchor for disinflation in Israel. There were three main stages in the evolution of exchange rate policy after 1985. First, a fixed exchange rate of 1.5 NIS per U.S. dollar was adopted at the start of the program after an initial devaluation of 19.1%. The authorities themselves made no commitment to keep the exchange rate irrevocably fixed. In fact, announcements were made that the exchange rate would be adjusted if there were wage increases or other pressures, on prices, beyond the original targets.

Still as part of the original fixed exchange rate policy, there was a technical

---

demand for Israeli output by the territories, and produced greater uncertainty and increased domestic defense expenditure; (2) the cancellation of the Lavi aircraft project; and (3) severe financial distress in several major segments of the manufacturing sector (Koor, the kibbutzim). Factors 2 and 3 are not unrelated to the stabilization program per se.

change in August 1986, when it was decided to peg the domestic currency's exchange rate to a basket of foreign currencies (instead of to the U.S. dollar). The change was clearly motivated by the sharp fluctuations in international exchange rates at that time (i.e., the U.S. dollar was depreciating in world currency markets) and by the fact that, in addition to the United States, European countries are important trading partners of Israel.

Throughout the second half of 1985 and during 1986 domestic prices rose at a higher rate than foreign prices, resulting in a gradual loss of competitiveness of domestic products. In January 1987, there was a 10% devaluation of the domestic currency against the basket. Domestic prices continued to rise at a higher rate than foreign prices in 1988, at which time devaluation expectations built up considerably. Figure 6.10 shows the increasing trend in foreign currency purchases by the private sector associated with this buildup of expectations. In late December 1988 and early 1989, another devaluation was effected, this time as part of a shift to the second stage of exchange rate policy: the unilateral adoption of an exchange rate band.

Israel's exchange rate band from 1989 to 1991 was characterized by a preannounced fixed nominal reference (or central parity) exchange rate and a specific band width; see Helpman and Leiderman (1992) and Helpman, Leiderman, and Bufman (1994) for further analysis and details. Initially the width of the band was set at ±3% around the reference rate. The width was expanded to ±5% in 1990. Various parameters and characteristics of the exchange rate band are shown in table 6.10. The adoption of an exchange rate band was viewed as a useful way to allow for short-run flexibility of the nominal exchange rate without necessarily abandoning the role of the exchange rate as a

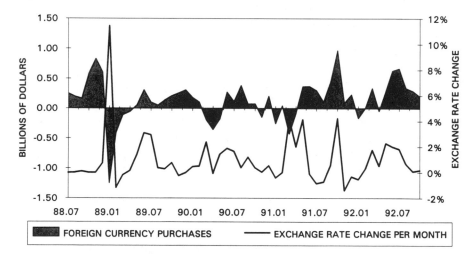

Fig. 6.10   Sales of foreign currency to the Israeli public
Source: Bank of Israel, Research Department database.

Table 6.10   **Israel's Exchange Rate Band: Band Characteristics, Exchange Rate, Interest Rates, Prices, and Foreign Currency Reserves**

	Band 1	Band 2	Band 3	Band 4	Band 5	Band 6 Crawling Band
	1989.01–89.06	1989.07–90.02	1990.03–90.08	1990.09–91.02	1991.03–91.11	1991.12–92.10
Band characteristics and the exchange rate (using daily data)						
Midband rate (NIS/basket)	1.95	2.07	2.19	2.41	2.55	—
Band width +/−(%)	3	3	5	5	5	5
Crawl of midband rate, annualized (%)	—	—	—	—	—	9
Average exchange rate	1.92	2.07	2.20	2.29	2.52	2.69
Average deviation of exchange rate from midband (%)	−1.51	−0.05	0.29	−4.88	−1.06	−1.45
Standard deviation from midband (%)	1.06	0.69	2.29	0.32	2.31	1.71
Interest rates (using weekly data, % per month)						
Average domestic interest rate (monetary auction rate)	1.07	1.12	1.15	1.09	1.19	0.91
Standard deviation of domestic interest rate	0.18	0.22	0.09	0.08	0.29	0.09
Average foreign interest rate (LIBID)[a]	0.71	0.71	0.71	0.69	0.58	0.50
Average interest differential (Israel-foreign)	0.36	0.40	0.43	0.40	0.61	0.41
Annualized average interest differential	4.42	4.95	5.31	4.85	7.61	5.06
Standard deviation of interest rate differential	0.20	0.21	0.09	0.07	0.30	0.08

(continued)

Table 6.10 (continued)

	Band 1	Band 2	Band 3	Band 4	Band 5	Band 6 Crawling Band
	1989.01–89.06	1989.07–90.02	1990.03–90.08	1990.09–91.02	1991.03–91.11	1991.12–92.10
Inflation (using monthly data, % per month)						
Average domestic inflation rate (CPI)	1.11	1.01	1.34	0.88	1.47	0.66
Average foreign inflation rate (CPI)[a]	0.44	0.30	0.35	0.25	0.27	0.25
Average inflation differential (Israel-foreign)	0.67	0.71	0.98	0.63	1.19	0.41
Annualized average inflation differential	8.38	8.83	12.47	7.85	15.28	5.07
Standard deviation of inflation differential	0.07	0.15	0.04	0.02	0.12	0.28
Foreign currency reserves (nongold) (using monthly data, in millions of dollars per month)						
Average change in reserves	203	0	–28	238	–32	–96
Standard deviation of change in reserves	525	212	258	363	500	398

Sources: Bank of Israel; Central Bureau of Statistics, Israel.

[a]Weighted average, using Israel's currency basket weights. LIBID = London interbank interest on deposits.

key nominal anchor—a role that was now attributed to the preannounced central parity rate.

Figure 6.11 depicts the behavior of the nominal exchange rate of the NIS against the basket of foreign currencies under the band. It is evident that during the first months after the adoption of the band the exchange rate was positioned in the lower half of the band. This may have well been the result of market forces, but there is evidence that official intervention, aimed at avoiding inflationary pressures of currency depreciation, played a role in ensuring such an outcome. As domestic prices continued to increase at a higher rate than foreign prices, there were several realignments (i.e., upward adjustments, or devaluations, in the central parity rate) of the band with the objective of avoiding a deterioration in the less international competitiveness of exports. In fact, *there were five such realignments in less than two years!* (see table 6.10 and figure 6.11). Although these periodic adjustments of the central parity rate contributed to avoiding real exchange rate appreciation and were not accompanied by a rise in inflation, during the 1989–91 period, there was substantial uncertainty about the timing and size of these exchange rate adjustments. Increased uncertainty, lack of full credibility, and a buildup of expectations toward a realignment were associated with increases in the domestic-foreign interest rate differential, which then decreased after realignments. Figure 6.12 illustrates the important degree of interest rate volatility that was associated with this period. The increased speculative purchases of foreign currencies and increased domestic interest rates that were observed in Israel in anticipation of devaluations

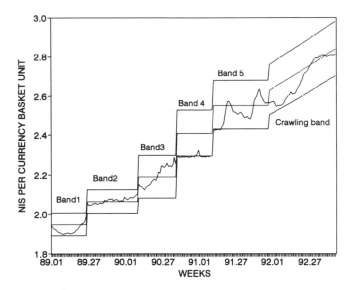

Fig. 6.11   Israel's exchange rate band
Source: Bank of Israel, Research Department database.

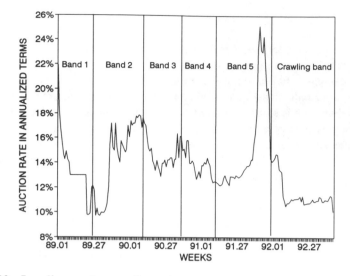

Fig. 6.12   Israel's monetary auction rate
Source: Bank of Israel, Monetary Department database.

are quite similar to those observed before realignments in Europe under the European monetary system (EMS); see Helpman and Leiderman (1992) for a comparison.[10]

The frequent realignments and speculative attacks, coupled with the increased volatility in interest rates that they induced, motivated a shift toward a third, and so far last, stage in exchange rate policy, the shift to a crawling band effected in December 1991. The adoption of a crawling central parity rate was seen as a more credible commitment than the earlier regime, and this rate was still assigned the role of a key nominal anchor. After making a 3% upward adjustment in the central parity rate, the authorities announced that the latter would not be fixed at a nominal value; instead, it would crawl daily at a preannounced rate of 9% per year.[11] It was hoped that such an annual nominal depreciation of 12% would be more than enough to prevent deterioration in the competitiveness of exports associated with a positive differential between domestic and foreign inflation. The crawling band is shown in figure 6.11. The main motivation for this regime was to reduce as much as possible the uncertainty about the size and timing of realignments of the central parity rate, and

10. See Pessach and Razin (1990) for an earlier empirical application of target zone models to Israel.

11. This crawling band differs from the one adopted in Chile in one important aspect: while Israel's band features a preannounced crawling path for the nominal central parity exchange rate, Chile's central parity rate is set within the year to accommodate differences between domestic and foreign inflation. Thus, Chile's system is more accommodative, and therefore could have a weaker stabilizing impact on inflation expectations, than Israel's. For a more detailed comparison of performance under these two systems, see Helpman and Leiderman (1992).

consequently to attempt to reduce the extent of domestic interest rate volatility. Indeed, the level and volatility of domestic interest rates were considerably reduced since the adoption of this new system (see fig. 6.12).

The experience accumulated thus far illustrates the costs and benefits of exchange rate–based stabilization. Fixing the exchange rate at the outset of the 1985 stabilization program played a key role in quick disinflation and served as a visible anchor to the nominal system and to inflation expectations. However, as long as domestic inflation does not reach world inflation levels, pressures arise for exchange rate adjustments in order to attenuate the degree of real exchange rate appreciation.[12] These adjustments, that is devaluations, give rise to serious policy dilemmas because of concerns with their possible destabilizing impact on inflation expectations and on increased interest rate volatility. While the shift to an exchange rate band allowed more day-to-day flexibility in exchange rate determination, it did not remove from the system the uncertainty about future realignments and therefore was also accompanied by substantial interest rate volatility. If credible, a crawling band system, such as the one adopted in December 1991, has the potential of reducing this interest rate volatility while at the same time avoiding a deterioration in the competitiveness of exports. Overall, with the benefit of hindsight, we conclude that the adoption of a fixed exchange rate at the beginning of the stabilization program played a major role in its success. However, we believe that beginning with 1988 there was room for a more flexible exchange rate policy, such as the adoption of a crawling exchange rate band, designed to prevent real appreciation and some of the increased unemployment.

6.4.2 Devaluation Expectations and the Exchange Rate Band

We argued that the observed level and volatility of domestic interest rates during the period 1989–91 can be related to expectations of realignments, or more broadly a lack of credibility of the existing exchange rate band. Under an exchange rate band, the domestic-foreign interest rate differential set at a point in time may reflect both expectations of exchange rate depreciation within the existing band, and expected realignments of the central parity rate (or devaluations). While expected depreciations within the band need not be equal to zero even under full band credibility, it is clear that nonzero expected devaluations do represent lack of full credibility. This section provides a quantitative assessment of these expectations, using a methodology similar to Svensson (1991).

At each point in time, the log of the spot exchange rate (s_t) can be expressed

---

12. In this context, Dornbusch has argued that "[t]he key issue then is to select the initial level of the exchange rate so that even with moderate inflation for a few months, the real exchange rate is not overvalued from the start. Moreover, very soon, exchange rate policy should shift from a fixed rate to a crawling peg to offset inflation differentials and maintain competitiveness. . . . But if the decision is postponed too long, the real exchange rate becomes starkly overvalued, and the program ultimately fails" (1991, 27).

as the sum of two components: the log of central parity (c_t) and percentage deviation from such central rate (x_t).[13] That is,

(1)
$$s_t \equiv x_t + c_t.$$

Accordingly, the percentage depreciation in the exchange rate from t to $t + 1$ can be expressed as the sum of exchange rate depreciation within the band and of the rate of realignment (defined as the percentage change in the central parity rate):

(2)
$$\Delta s_{t+1} \equiv \Delta x_{t+1} + \Delta c_{t+1}.$$

Taking expectations of both sides of equation (2) conditional on time t information yields an expression for expected exchange rate depreciation:

(3)
$$E_t \Delta s_{t+1} \equiv E_t \Delta x_{t+1} + E_t \Delta c_{t+1}.$$

That is, the expected total rate of depreciation equals the expected rate of depreciation within the band (i.e., $E_t \Delta x_{t+1}$) plus the expected rate of realignment (i.e., $E_t \Delta c_{t+1}$).

In order to make this equation operational, additional assumptions are required since all three variables are unobservable. Assuming that uncovered interest parity holds, the left-hand side of the above equation is equal to the domestic-foreign interest rate differential. While this assumption makes total expected depreciation observable, further assumptions are needed to decompose this depreciation into its two components. To do so, we assume that expectations of exchange rate depreciation within the band are approximated by a linear equation of the form

(4)
$$x_{t+1} - x_t = \sum_{j=1}^{n} [\beta_{0j} d_j] + \beta_1 x_t + \varepsilon_{t+1},$$

where d_j is a dummy for regime j (each period between realignments) and the $n + 1$ parameters to be estimated are β_{0j} for $j = 1$ to n and β_1. Assuming that the error term in this equation is orthogonal to the explanatory variables, these parameters can be estimated by least squares. Alternatively, the expected future exchange rate within the band may be estimated, as in equation (5). Clearly, the estimation of equation (5) is equivalent to the estimation of equation (4).

(5)
$$x_{t+1} = \sum_{j=1}^{n} [\gamma_{0j} d_j] + \gamma_1 x_t + \eta_{t+1}$$

The coefficients and error terms of (4) and (5) are related by $\gamma_{0j} = \beta_{0j}$, $\gamma_1 = \beta_1 + 1$, and $\eta_{t+1} = \varepsilon_{t+1}$.

To summarize, using the interest differential for $E_t \Delta s_{t+1}$ and the fitted values from equation (4) or (5), we are able to construct a series for expected devalua-

---

13. We obviously assume that the log of one plus the percentage deviation of the exchange rate from the central parity is well approximated by such percentage deviation itself.

tion, which is equal to expected total exchange rate depreciation minus expected depreciation within the band (conditional on no realignment).

This procedure was implemented on weekly time series for Israel for the period of January 1989 through July 1992. The interest rate differential, $\delta_t = i_t - i_t^*$ is defined as the difference between the weekly Israeli monetary auction rate and a weighted basket (using the currency basket weights) of foreign treasury bill rates. The exchange rate used is Israel's currency basket. The number of band regimes is $n = 6$, where band number 6 is the crawling band regime that was described earlier. In all cases, we excluded from the sample all weeks in which a devaluation occurred. The estimation results using equation (5) are shown in table 6.11.

In addition, we considered expanding equation (5) to include a lag of the depreciation within the band, x_{t-1}, and nonlinear elements as explanatory variables. The modified equation is

$$(6) \qquad x_{t+1} = \sum_{j=1}^{n} \gamma_{0j} d_j + \gamma_1 x_t + \gamma_2 x_t^2 + \gamma_3 x_t^3 + \gamma_4 x_{t-1} + \eta_{t+1},$$

and the estimation results are shown in table 6.12.

Figure 6.13 describes the outcomes of these calculations. Despite the use of weekly data, the estimated version of equation (6) fits quite well the actual behavior of exchange rate depreciation within the band. The estimated expected rate of devaluation exhibits the following patterns. During the first band, there was a gradual decrease in devaluation expectations, which was reversed a few weeks before the end of the band, resulting in a buildup of expectations and increase in the domestic-foreign interest rate differential.

The second band exhibits positive expected devaluation throughout its existence, with a gradual upward trend until the next realignment. The third band shows an initial decrease in expected devaluation, followed by a sharp increase

Table 6.11   **Estimation Results of Equation (5)**

	Parameter Estimate	Standard Error
γ_{01}	−0.0016	0.0017
γ_{02}	0.0001	0.0011
γ_{03}	−0.0004	0.0031
γ_{04}	−0.0064	0.0031
γ_{05}	−0.0010	0.0017
γ_{06}	−0.0022	0.0017
γ_1	0.8700	0.0613
R^2	0.87	
D.W.	1.191	
N	180	
σ	0.0236	

Table 6.12   **Estimation Results of Equation (6)**

	Parameter Estimate	Standard Error
γ_{01}	0.0006	0.0008
γ_{02}	0.0002	0.0023
γ_{03}	0.0039	0.0006
γ_{04}	−0.0036	0.0008
γ_{05}	0.0006	0.0023
γ_{06}	0.0009	0.0006
γ_1	1.4374	0.2264
γ_2	−8.4456	3.0722
γ_3	−174.84	58.905
γ_4	−0.5003	0.2542
R^2	0.89	
D.W.	1.628	
N	180	
σ	0.0236	

in these expectations, also reflected in the interest differential. The shift to the fifth band was apparently unexpected. However, the shift to the sixth band was preceded by a speculative run on foreign currencies and by sharply increased expectations of devaluation. In this episode, these expectations were met with massive central bank intervention in the foreign exchange market, intervention that succeeded in bringing expected devaluation down subsequently. Thus, there was an important surprise element in the shift to a crawling band. During the first eight months of the new regime, no expectations of major devaluations arose.

To test for the joint credibility of the various bands, we estimated the following equation for expected devaluation:

$$(7) \qquad \Delta \hat{c}_{t+1} = \alpha + \beta(\bar{e}_t - e_t).$$

Under the null hypotheses that the bands were credible, intercept = slope = 0, and the residuals ought to be white. Notice that we used the position of the exchange rate within the band as the main explanatory variable, as it appeared from figure 6.11 that there is a link between this variable and expectations of devaluation.[14] The estimation results of equation (7) are shown in table 6.13.

___

14. For a model that has such an implication, see Cukierman, Kiguel, and Leiderman (1992). We have conducted similar tests using monthly Israeli data and have found the qualitative results to be similar to those shown here. In addition, we have examined whether macroeconomic variables (such as the money supply, industrial production, the real exchange rate, and foreign reserves) can explain the expected rates of devaluation. We do so by adding macroeconomic variables to the right-hand side of equation (7) as explanatory variables. We find the main results are unchanged: the value of the parameter β is unchanged, the constant remains significantly higher than zero, and there is evidence of serially correlated errors. For a comparison of these results

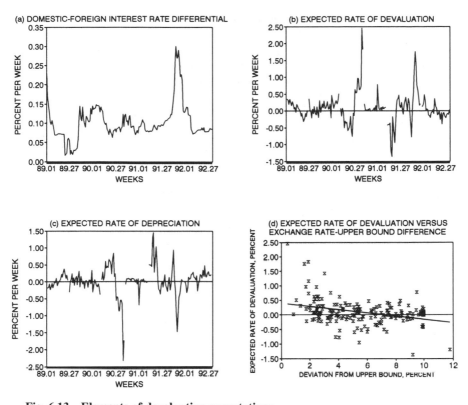

Fig. 6.13   Elements of devaluation expectations

Source: For *a,* Bank of Israel, Research Department database.

Note: Weekly data, January 1989 through July 1992. Breaks in data indicate a devaluation.

The results indicate an important degree of lack of credibility of exchange rate bands.[15] Lack of credibility shows in that the intercept and slope coefficients are significantly different from zero, and the residuals are serially correlated. The sample mean for expected devaluation throughout the total sample period and each of the various bands is shown in table 6.14. Figure 6.14 presents the expected rate of devaluation with 95%-significance confidence intervals for zero devaluation expectations within each band.

We conclude that, although the adoption of exchange rate bands in 1989 was an important step in making exchange rate policy more flexible, the fixity of the central parity rate in each band was not considered credible by market participants. This was reflected in the behavior of expected devaluation and in

---

with results of other countries with unilateral bands (such as Finland, Norway, Sweden, and Chile), see Bufman, Kiguel, and Leiderman (1992).

15. This confirms the conclusions of Helpman and Leiderman (1992) using less formal methods.

Table 6.13   **Estimation Results of Equation (7)**

	Parameter Estimate	Standard Error
α	0.0041	0.0001
β	−0.0554	0.0140
R^2		0.12
D.W.		0.558
N		180
σ		0.0044

Table 6.14   **Mean of Expected Rate of Devaluation (% per week)**

Period	Mean	t-Statistic of Mean
Total period	0.08	2.568
Band 1	0.06	1.511
Band 2	0.11	3.657
Band 3	0.19	1.266
Band 4	0.09	2.925
Band 5	0.07	0.716
Crawling band regime	−0.01	−0.401

interest rate volatility. These considerations certainly played an important role in the transition toward a band regime with a crawling central parity rate, like the one adopted in December 1991.

6.4.3   Real Exchange Rate Appreciation and Exports

As shown in section 6.2, inflation stabilization was accompanied by substantial appreciation of the real exchange rate and by a shift of resources toward the nontraded sector. Thus, it was argued that these developments discouraged production and entry of firms into the exports sector, which shared a sizable burden in exchange rate–based stabilization. While these arguments have their merits, it is difficult to determine how much of observed real exchange rate appreciation was due to the nominal exchange rate policy per se and how much was due to fundamentals. In any case, the purpose of this section is to take a new look at the relation between real exchange rate appreciation and exports, controlling for other factors that may affect exports as well.

Specifically, we estimate here a reduced-form equation for the rate of growth of exports of industrial goods as a function of the rates of growth of the real exchange rate, world imports, the real wage per labor hour in industry, and the real ex post interest rate in industry. We used quarterly data expressed as annual rates of growth (except for the interest rate). We focused on industrial exports excluding diamonds, and examined their statistical relation to fluctuations in the real interest rate, the real cost of labor, real effective exchange rate, and an external impulse (world imports). The real interest rate applied here is a

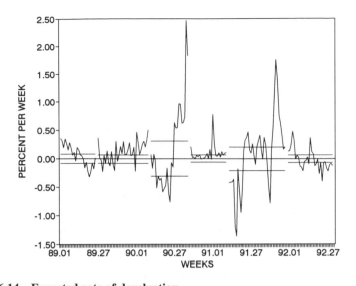

Fig. 6.14   Expected rate of devaluation

Note: Horizontal lines mark 95%-significance confidence intervals of zero devaluation expectations. Breaks in data indicate a devaluation.

weighted average of the following four rates (using the relevant weights for industry in each period): credit in NIS allocated by the government (i.e., directed credit), directed credit in foreign currency, credit obtained in the free market (i.e., nondirected credit) in NIS, and nondirected credit in foreign currency. Ex post real interest rates were obtained by subtracting the rate of change in the wholesale price of industrial outputs (WPI) from these calculated effective nominal interest rates. The cost of labor in the industrial sector was measured by the cost of labor per work hour in industry. This measure includes wages, salaries, and other labor expenses in industry. The real effective exchange rate is used as an indicator of the relative prices of industry in Israel vis-à-vis those of Israel's main trade partners and as a partial measure of profitability in the industrial sector. The real exchange rate was computed by deflating the exchange rate of the NIS against the currency basket by the WPI in Israel and the countries represented in the currency basket. The foreign WPI is a weighted average of the WPIs in the United States, France, Germany, the United Kingdom, and Japan. In order to get the real effective exchange rate relevant to the industrial sector, export subsidies were taken into account. The ratio of subsidies to industrial exports compared to the value of industrial goods exported was computed and applied to the real exchange rate.

In order to focus on real fluctuations, the dollar value of the industrial exports (excluding diamonds) was deflated using the correspondence export price index as shown in Israel's trade statistics. The export function that was estimated is:

$$(8) \quad DEXPORT_t = \beta_o + \beta_1 DWORLD_t + \beta_2 DRER_{t-1} + \beta_3 DWAGE_t + \beta_4 DINT_t,$$

where $DEXPORT_t$ = [(industrial exports)$_t$]/[(industrial exports)$_{t-4}$] − 1; $DWORLD_t$ = [(world imports)$_t$]/[(world imports)$_{t-4}$] − 1; $DRER_{t-1}$ = [(real exchange rate)$_t$]/[(real exchange rate)$_{t-4}$] − 1; $DWAGE_t$ = [(labor costs per hour in industry)$_t$]/[(labor costs per hour in industry)$_{t-4}$−1; and $DINT_t$ = [(real interest rate (industry))$_t$] − [(real interest rate (industry))$_{t-4}$] − 1. All variables are expressed in real terms. Equation (8) was estimated using quarterly data from first quarter 1979 to fourth quarter 1990.

In order to insure the heteroskedasticity and autocorrelation consistency of the covariance matrix during the estimation of equation (8), we used Parzen's lag window approach (this technique and similar ones such as Newey and West [1987] are discussed in Andrews [1991]). The interpretation of the coefficients is as follows: β_1 is the reduced-form elasticity of export growth with respect to world import, β_2 is the elasticity with respect to the real exchange rate, β_3 is the elasticity with respect to wages in industry, and β_4 is the reduced-form elasticity with respect to the real interest rate in industry. Notice that the real exchange rate was entered with a lag. The use of four differences is motivated by the notion that the impact of world demand or real exchange rate on exports is effected with lags, and by the attempt to remove seasonality from our calculations. The results are shown in table 6.15.

Our results indicate that the rate of growth of world imports has a significant positive coefficient, as does the rate of change of the real exchange rate. The elasticity of exports with respect to world demand is estimated at 1.861, and its 95%-confidence interval is (0.629, 3.093). The estimated elasticity for the real exchange rate is 0.857 and its confidence interval is (0.216, 1.499). These elasticities fall in the range of previous export function estimates for Israel. The coefficients on the remaining variables (i.e., real wage and real interest rate) are not precisely estimated.

Table 6.15	Estimation Results of Israeli Export Equation (8) (industrial exports, excluding diamonds)	
	Parameter Estimate	Standard Error
β_0	−0.0232	0.0532
β_1	1.8610	0.6164
β_2	0.8575	0.3206
β_3	0.0607	0.2925
β_4	−0.0345	0.1651
R^2	0.77	
N	43	
σ	0.1507	

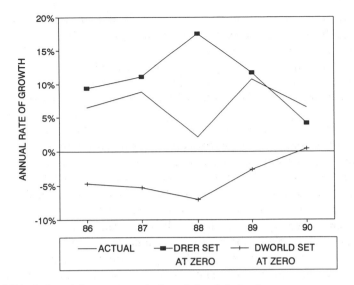

Fig. 6.15   Industrial exports: actual and simulated values

Note: The simulated values are based on the estimation results of equation (8) while alternately holding the real exchange rate and world imports at their values at the start of the stabilization program. Quarterly simulated values are accrued to create the annual projections shown.

To assess the relative importance of world demand and real exchange rate in the performance of exports over the sample period, we used the coefficients of equation (8) to simulate the behavior of the rate of growth of exports under various scenarios. The simulation is given in figure 6.15, which includes three elements: (1) the actual rate of growth of exports expressed in annual terms; (2) the predicted rate of growth of exports under the restriction that the real exchange rate is fixed at its value at the start of the program—which isolates the impact of world demand on Israeli exports over the sample; and (3) the predicted rate of growth of exports under the assumption that there is no change in the level of world demand—thus capturing the separate effect of real exchange rate fluctuations. Due to the existence of a regression residual, the simulated paths do not exactly sum up to the actual path. From the figure, two types of patterns are evident. First, from 1986 to 1987 and from 1989 to 1990, the rate of growth of exports moved in the same direction as that of world demand. In the former period, exports expanded (along with expansion of world demand), and in the latter period, the rate of growth of exports decreased along with world recession. Second, from 1987 to 1989, the rate of growth of exports moved in the same direction as the real exchange rate. That is, it decreased along with a more pronounced real exchange rate appreciation.

Although the estimated relations allow for one-year lags, it is well to examine whether longer lags and more complicated dynamics show up in the data as well. To deal with this issue, we estimated bivariate vector autoregressions

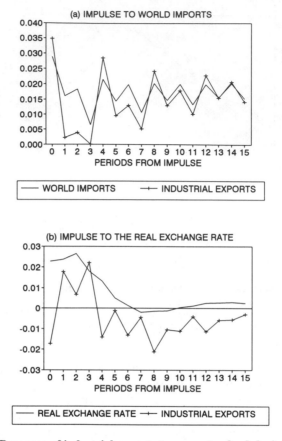

Fig. 6.16   Response of industrial exports to a one-standard-deviation shock of (a) world imports and (b) the real exchange rate

Notes: The vector autoregressive system estimated is a bivariate log-log system with four lags:

$$\ln(EXP_t) = \text{const} + \sum_{i=1}^{4} \{[\beta_i \ln(EXP_{t-i})] + [\gamma_i \ln(x_{t-i})]\}.$$

In panel *a*, *x* is world imports, and in panel *b*, *x* is the real exchange rate. The system was estimated using quarterly data of the Israeli economy from first quarter 1979 to first quarter 1990.

for the rate of growth of exports and the rates of growth of world demand and the real exchange rate using four lags for each variable. Figures 6.16 and 6.17 depict the dynamic effects of real exchange rate and world demand shocks on exports, in the form of impulse response functions. The evidence indicates that the most important effects operate with a one-period lag, and that indeed real exchange rate depreciation and increased world demand are associated with higher rate of growth of exports.

Overall, the foregoing findings indicate that the behavior of exports after the

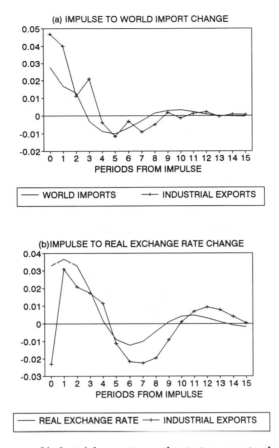

Fig. 6.17   Response of industrial export *growth* rate to a one-standard-deviation shock of (a) the rate of world import growth and (b) the rate of real exchange rate change

Notes: The vector autoregressive system estimated is a bivariate system with four lags, applied to annual rates of growth:

$$\left(\frac{EXP_t}{EXP_{t-4}} - 1\right) = \text{const} + \sum_{i=1}^{4} \left\{ \beta_i \left(\frac{EXP_{t-i}}{EXP_{t-4-i}} - 1\right) + \gamma_i \left(\frac{x_{t-i}}{x_{t-4-i}} - 1\right) \right\}.$$

In panel *a, x* is world imports, and in panel *b, x* is the real exchange rate. The system was estimated using quarterly data of the Israel economy from first quarter 1979 to first quarter 1990.

1985 stabilization program cannot be attributed solely to fluctuations in the real exchange rate; changes in world demand played an important role as well. However, the partial impact of the real exchange rate on exports was negtive for most of the sample period, thus capturing the effect of the marked real appreciation observed during the sample period. Whether such real appreciation was avoidable, and whether it was the result of nominal exchange rate policy per se or of underlying fundamentals, are important issues whose resolution must await further research.

6.5 Conclusions

In assessing the main lessons from Israel's disinflation, and the applicability of similar stabilization programs to other economies, this paper draws two main conclusions. First, in countries where the initial conditions in terms of investment and growth are not strong, the adoption of policy measures aimed at increasing the stock of public sector capital, especially infrastructures, right at the time of stabilization may well contribute to acceleration of transition from stabilization to growth. In this context, Israel's program embodied no specific direct policy measures aimed at reversing this state of affairs, and we argued that this may have played an important role in the lack of fast transition to growth after disinflation.

Second, any exchange rate–based stabilization faces the issue of how and when to relax exchange rate targets and to adapt them to changing economic conditions without losing their value as key nominal anchors. We found that Israel's adoption of an exchange rate band in 1989 was an important step in making exchange rate policy more flexible. Yet as domestic inflation continued to exceed foreign inflation, the fixity of the central parity rate in each band was not considered credible by market participants. Under these circumstances, it may be most appropriate to shift to a band regime with a preannounced crawling central parity rate, like the one adopted in December 1991.

References

Andrews, Donald W. K. 1991. Heteroskedasticity and Autocorrelation Consistent Covariance Matrix Estimation. *Econometrica* 59:817–58.

Aschauer, David A. 1989. Is Public Expenditure Productive? *Journal of Monetary Economics* 23:177–200.

Auerbach, Alan J. 1992. Investment Policies to Promote Growth. Presented at the conference, "Policies for Long-Run Economic Growth," Federal Reserve Bank of Kansas City, Jackson Hole, August.

Ben-Basat, Idit. 1992. Price Indexes of Traded on Non-traded Goods (in Hebrew). *Bank of Israel Survey* 66:19–34.

Ben-Rawe, Yoram. 1989. The Burden of Short-Term Bank Credit Interest on the Economy's Branches (in Hebrew). Research Department Discussion Paper no. 89.07. Bank of Israel.

Bregman, Arie, and Arie Marom. 1992. Growth Factors in Israel's Business Sector, 1958–1988 (in Hebrew). Bank of Israel. Manuscript.

Bruno, Michael. 1986. The Israeli Economy, the End of a Lost Decade? Hebrew University of Jerusalem. Mimeo.

Bruno, Michael, and Leora (Rubin) Meridor. 1991. The Costly Transition from Stabilization to Sustainable Growth: Israel's Case. In *Lessons of Economic Stabilization and Its Aftermath,* ed. Michael Bruno, Stanley Fischer, Elhanan Helpman, Nissan Liviatan, and Leora (Rubin) Meridor. Cambridge: MIT Press.

Bruno, Michael, and Sylvia Piterman. 1988. Israel's Stabilization: A Two-Year Review. In *Inflation Stabilization: The Experience of Israel, Argentina, Brazil, Bolivia, and Mexico,* ed. Michael Bruno, Guido Di Tella, Rudiger Dornbusch, and Stanley Fischer. Cambridge: MIT Press.

Bufman, Gil, Miguel A. Kiguel, and Leonardo Leiderman. 1992. Devaluation Expectations and Mean Reversion under Unilateral Exchange Rate Bands: Some Evidence. Working paper, Tel Aviv University.

Calvo, Guillermo A., and Carlos A. Végh. 1991. Exchange-Rate-Based Stabilization under Imperfect Credibility. IMF Working Paper 91/77.

Cukierman, Alex, Miguel A. Kiguel, and Leonardo Leiderman. 1992. The Choice of Exchange Rate Bands: Credibility versus Flexibility. Working paper, Tel Aviv University.

De Long, J. Bradford, and Lawrence H. Summers. 1991. Equipment Investment and Economic Growth. *Quarterly Journal of Economics* 106:445–502.

Dornbusch, Rudiger. 1991. Policies to Move from Stabilization to Growth. In *World Bank Economic Review: Proceedings of the World Bank Annual Conference on Development Economics 1990.* Washington, DC: World Bank.

Fischer, Stanley. 1986. Exchange Rate versus Monetary Targets in Disinflation. In S. Fischer, *Indexing, Inflation, and Economic Policy.* Cambridge: MIT Press.

———. 1991. Growth, Macroeconomics, and Development. Working paper, MIT, February.

Helpman, Elhanan. 1992. Endogenous Macroeconomic Growth Theory. *European Economic Review* 36 (2–3): 237–67.

Helpman, Elhanan, and Leonardo Leiderman. 1988. Stabilization in High Inflation Countries: Analytical Foundations and Recent Experience. *Carnegie-Rochester Series on Public Policy* 28:9–84.

———. 1992. *Israel's Exchange Rate Band.* Tel Aviv: Israeli International Institute.

Helpman, Elhanan, Leonardo Leiderman, and Gil Bufman. 1994. A New Breed of Exchange Rate Bands: Chile, Israel, and Mexico. *Economic Policy* 19 (October).

Hercowitz, Zvi, Leonardo Leiderman, and Ilan Siddi. 1992. Notes on Public Investment and Growth: Evidence for Israel. Unpublished notes, Tel Aviv University.

Kiguel, Miguel A., and Nissan Liviatan. 1989. The Old and the New in Heterodox Stabilization Programs: Lessons from the 1960s and the 1980s. Working paper 323, Policy Planning and Research Department, World Bank.

Leiderman, Leonardo. 1993. *Inflation and Disinflation: The Israeli Experiment.* Chicago: University of Chicago Press.

Leiderman, Leonardo, and Nissan Liviatan. 1990. Comparing Macroeconomic Performance in Israel. Working paper, World Bank.

Levine, Ross, and David Renelt. 1990. A Sensitivity Analysis of Cross-Country Growth Regressions. World Bank. Manuscript.

Newey, W. K., and K. D. West. 1987. A Simple Positive Semi-definite, heteroskedasticity and Autocorrelation Consistent Covariance Matrix. *Econometrica* 55:703–8.

Pessach, Shula, and Assaf Razin. 1990. Targeting the Exchange Rate: An Empirical Investigation. IMF Working Paper 90/61.

Sargent, Thomas J., and Neil Wallace. 1981. Some Unpleasant Monetarist Arithmetic. *Federal Reserve Bank of Minneapolis Quarterly Review* 5:1–17.

Svensson, Lars E. O. 1991. Assessing Target Zone Credibility: Mean Reversion and Devaluation Expectations in the EMS. Seminar paper no. 493, Institute for International Economic Studies, Stockholm University.

Comment on Chapters 5 and 6   José De Gregorio

The two papers presented in this session are very interesting and cover a wide range of issues. In my discussion I want to focus on three issues raised by the authors: the relationship between inflation and income distribution, the evolution of consumption after the Israeli stabilization, and exchange rate management.

Inflation and Income Distribution

The paper by Cardoso, Paes de Barros, and Urani (CPU henceforth) presents time series evidence on the role of macroeconomic conditions on income distribution in Brazil. After a detailed review of the evidence for the six largest metropolitan areas of Brazil, they conclude that inflation and unemployment have had a negative impact on income distribution. In addition, they argue that, although an unequal education distribution may be an important cause for inequality, it is not important in explaining the evolution of inequality during the 1980s.

The data used by CPU correspond to the distribution of labor earnings; hence, the authors conclude that the data capture only the effects of inflation on income distribution stemming from imperfect wage indexation. That is, wages of high-income people appear to be more protected from inflation (through indexation) than those of the poor.

Given that indexation and other forms of protection of labor earnings from inflation usually appear in countries that have experienced at least two-digit inflation, one may wonder whether CPU's finding applies to other countries.[1]

To examine this issue, I present some empirical evidence on the relationship between income distribution and inflation in a cross section of countries. The sample consists of forty-six countries, where data on income distribution are available for the 1960s and 1980s.

The first specification reported below has as dependent variable an index of inequality (*INEQ80*). This index is constructed as the ratio between the share of income earned by the richest 20% of the population and the share of income earned by the poorest 20% of the population. The year for each data point is different, but the data are centered on 1980. The secondary school enrollment ratio in 1960 (*SEC60*) was used to capture the effects of the distribution of education. Although this index does not compare enrollment ratios at different education levels, it is a good proxy for education distribution because it represents an intermediate stage in the educational process. Inflation is another explanatory variable and is measured as the logarithm of the average inflation

José De Gregorio is an economist in the research department of the International Monetary Fund.

The author is very grateful to Brooks Dana Calvo for research assistance and to Roberto Perotti for providing data.

1. Blejer and Guerrero (1990) find similar results for the Philippines.

rate from 1960 to 1985 (*LINF*). Finally, dummy variables for Latin America and Africa (*LAMER* and *AFRICA*) were included to control for cultural, institutional, and other factors that were excluded in the regressions and that could account for the fact that income distribution in these regions is worse than in the rest of the world. This regression can be interpreted as the effect that education, inflation, and continental characteristics have on the long-run level of equality. The result for the sample of forty-six countries is (t-statistics in parentheses).[2]

(1)   INEQ80 = 9.966 + 0.123 LINF − 6.535 SEC60
            (3.32)   (0.12)   (−1.70)
            + 10.73 AFRICA, + 10.66 LAMER,
                (3.71)   (5.21)

$R^2 = 0.61$, $N = 46$. The result for the sample excluding Latin American countries is

(2)   INEQ80 = 10.30 − 0.108 LINF − 6.133 SEC60
            (4.73)   (−0.14)   (−2.78)
            +10.84 AFRICA,
                (6.71)

$R^2 = 0.74$, $N = 36$.

The overall fit of the regressions is good. They explain over 60% of the variability of income distribution across countries. Three main conclusions emerge from these results. First, education distribution, measured by *SEC60*, is an important determinant of income distribution in the long run. Second, after controlling for education, the level of inequality in Latin America and Africa is greater than in the rest of the countries of the sample. Third, inflation performance has no effect on the level of inequality.[3]

The finding that inflation is not important to whether a certain country has relatively better or worse income distribution does not necessarily imply that inflation has no effects on inequality. In fact, what CPU's results suggest is that the improvement or deterioration of income distribution depends on the rate of inflation. That is, *changes in income distribution are correlated with inflation.* The following two regressions look at this correlation by regressing the change in inequality between 1980 and 1960 ($\Delta INEQ = INEQ80/INEQ60$) on the logarithm of the rate of inflation, the change is secondary school enrollment

2. The data sources are as follow: *INEQ80*, Larraín and Vergara (1992): *INEQ60* (same variable as *INEQ80* but centered on 1960), Alesina and Perotti (1992); *LINF*, International Financial Statistics (to eliminate outliers in inflation, which distort the average rate of inflation for the whole period 1960–85, the observations for Argentina and Bolivia in 1985 and Chile in 1974 were eliminated); *SEC60* and *SEC85;* Barro and Wolf (1989).

3. The results are robust to the use of secondary school enrollment ratio in 1970 and inflation between 1970 and 1985. In addition, when Gini coefficients were used as proxies for inequality, the significance of *SEC60* increased, and inflation remained not significantly different from zero.

ratios during a similar period ($\Delta SEC = SEC85/SEC60$), and the continental dummies, for the full sample and the sample that excludes Latin American countries:[4]

(3) ΔINEQ = 0.573 + 0.186 LINF − 0.041 ΔSEC
                  (2.02)   (1.60)   (−0.71)
            + 1.692 AFRICA + 0.499 LAMER,
                  (2.40)   (2.17)

$R^2 = 0.42, N = 40$; and

(4) ΔINEQ = −0.094 + 0.489 LINF − 0.028 ΔSEC
                  (−0.27)   (3.19)   (−0.53)
            + 1.589 AFRICA,
                  (2.50)

$R^2 = 0.42, N = 31$.

The results show that inflation leads to increased inequality and that changes in education do not explain the changes in inequality. The result excluding Latin America is even stronger,[5] suggesting that this correlation is not caused by the presence of high-inflation countries. Thus, the evidence reported here suggests that the negative effects of inflation on the change in income distribution is not particular to Brazil or high-inflation countries. However, this evidence should be considered preliminary for at least two reasons. Since data on income distribution have serious problems that make comparisons difficult across countries and over time, this evidence, although suggestive, has to be considered preliminary. More work will have to be done to establish the robustness of the results presented above.

Stabilization and Consumption Boom

Bufman's and Leiderman's paper provides a nice description of the stabilization program in Israel, and draws some important policy lessons. One interesting fact that they report is the existence of a consumption boom at the onset of the program and a posterior recession. This evolution of consumption is not particular to Israel, and as reported by Kiguel and Liviatan (1992) is a common phenomenon in some other episodes, in particular in exchange rate–based stabilizations. Moreover, the consumption boom appears to be followed almost inevitably by a recession. This consumption cycle, however, is not observed in money-based stabilizations. The hypothesis that has received most attention is so-called temporariness. This hypothesis, advanced by Calvo (1986), suggests that the lack of credibility on the sustainability of the low inflation rate will,

4. Another rationale for using the change of inequality rather than the level as dependent variable is that inequality indices are not comparable across countries, since they come from different sources and are constructed using different methodologies.

5. In regression (3), *LINF* is only significant at 12%. The results were the same when the change in the Gini coefficients were used instead of the ratio between the extreme quintiles. However, in that case, *LINF* was significant at 5% and 10% in all of those regressions.

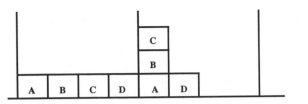

Fig. 6C.1 Consumption of durables

through intertemporal substitution, lead individuals to anticipate consumption. The mechanism is the temporary reduction of the effective price of consumption goods (through a decline in the nominal interest rate). Bufman and Leiderman find this explanation unsatisfactory because it requires a decline in the real interest rate, which was not the case in Israel. Furthermore, one can argue that in the case of Israel there were no expectations that the plan would be unsuccessful (Bruno, 1993). Indeed, the expectations that Israel's stabilization would fail would have turned out to be wrong, since the reduction of inflation has lasted for more than seven years.

I want to present another explanation for the consumption cycle associated with exchange rate–based stabilizations. It is based on the observation that most of the rise in consumption occurs in the category of durables (Dornbusch 1986; Drazen 1990).[6]

An important characteristic of durable goods is that they are indivisible and, therefore, bought infrequently. In addition, the purchase of durable goods involves transaction costs. Now, consider an economy consisting of four consumers (fig. 6C.1), each of them buying a unit of durable goods every four periods, but at different times. Thus, discrete purchases at the individual level appear as smooth behavior of consumption of durables at the aggregate level.

Now assume that an exchange rate–based stabilization is implemented. Contrary to money-based stabilizations, exchange rate–based stabilizations generally induce positive wealth effects, at least in the short run. This wealth effect may be caused by several mechanisms, for example, the expectation of higher income as the result of the return to stability; the relaxation of liquidity constraints as a consequence of the increase in real wages, disposable income, and the supply of banks' credit; and the reduction of interest payments stemming from the reduction of the nominal interest rate. The wealth effect will cause an expansion of both durable and nondurable consumption goods, but what drives the consumption cycle (a boom followed by a recession) is the change in the timing of consumption of durables. In contrast, in money-based stabilizations, the slow adjustment of prices and the consequent contraction of real balances leads to an immediate reduction of output.

---

6. This explanation is developed formally in De Gregorio, Guidotti, and Végh (1992), from which the following discussion is based. That paper also presents additional evidence on the consumption cycle in exchange rate–based stabilizations.

Individuals' reaction to a wealth shock will be to anticipate the purchase of the next durable good, and to buy a more expensive one. For simplicity, consider the case illustrated in figure 6C.1, where individuals A, B, and C decide to buy a new durable at the onset of the stabilization, while D will wait for one period, since she bought a new durable good just before the stabilization. The behavior of the economy will be quite different after the stabilization. There will be a consumption boom followed by a recession. This explanation appears to be consistent with the evolution of consumption of durables in Israel as well as in other stabilization programs.[7]

Understanding the evolution of consumption is important not only at the theoretical level, but also in terms of policy implications. If the consumption cycle were the result of lack of credibility, the slowdown of consumption would be an indication that, at least from the public's point of view, the program is close to the end. In contrast, if the consumption cycle were the result of a dynamic in consumption of durables as described above, the consumption slowdown would not imply that the stabilization is at risk.

Using the Exchange Rate to Stop Inflation

Perhaps the most important lesson we learned from the stabilization in Israel is the need for flexibility in the exchange rate policy. Although the exchange rate was chosen as the nominal anchor, the authorities kept the option of adjusting the exchange rate whenever necessary. This is an important element, since a real appreciation is an inevitable consequence of exchange rate–based stabilizations. By not basing the success of the stabilization on having an irrevocable fixed exchange rate, the Israeli authorities were able to adjust the nominal exchange rate to protect competitiveness and to defend the program against the main threat to an exchange–based stabilization: the unsustainability of the current account.

It seems there is broad agreement that the first stage in a stabilization should reduce the rate of inflation from three digits to, say, 20%. Attempts to achieve one-digit inflation in a short period of time may be unsustainable in the medium term. Once a moderate rate of inflation has been achieved, on a permanent basis, the focus should be on the recovery of competitiveness, and then the more ambitious objective of bringing inflation down to one digit should be pursued. The adoption of an exchange rate band with the central parity following a crawling peg is a good solution during moderate inflation.

Although I agree that it is better to have crawling rather than jumping central parity (such as the case of Israel during the period 1989–91), the evidence provided by Bufman and Leiderman to support this conclusion is not convincing. The main piece of evidence presented in the paper is the estimation of devaluation expectations in the period of fixed central parities. They argue that

---

7. Allowing for idiosyncratic shocks, the economy will converge to a steady state where the consumption cycle vanishes (see Caballero and Engel 1992).

the central parities were not credible and that lack of credibility resulted in increased interest rate volatility.

The problem with Bufman's and Leiderman's interpretation is that the authorities did not announce that the central parity would remain unchanged; hence, there is no issue of credibility involved (in contrast, for example, with the functioning of the European Monetary System). They estimate expectations of realignment, but not credibility of a certain policy. Moreover, it could be argued that the public quite accurately predicted the realignments because it knew the implicit policy followed by the authorities. In this case, however, the conclusion that the operation of the band introduced excessive (in the sense of undesirable) volatility is not warranted.

Finally, another puzzling result of the estimations is that during some weeks there were *expectations of revaluation* of the central parity (most notably right after the fourth realignment!), which seems to be inconsistent with the perception that the real exchange rate was appreciating from some equilibrium level. Perhaps analyzing more carefully some of the assumptions used to derive the estimated regression, such as the assumption of uncovered interest parity, or the approximation used to estimate expectations, may help better understanding of the operation of exchange rate bands.

References

Alesina, Alberto, and Roberto Perotti. 1992. The Political Economy of Growth: A Critical Survey of the Recent Literature. Columbia University and Harvard University, August. Mimeo.

Barro, Robert J., and Holger Wolf. 1989. Data Appendix for Economic Growth in a Cross Section of Countries. Harvard University. Mimeo.

Blejer, Mario I., and Isabel Guerrero. 1990. The Impact of Macroeconomic Policies on Income Distribution: An Empirical Study of the Philippines. *Review of Economics and Statistics* 72:414–23.

Bruno, Michael. 1993. *Crisis, Stabilization, and Economic Reform: Therapy by Consensus.* Oxford: Oxford University Press.

Caballero, Ricardo J., and Eduardo M. R. A. Engel. 1992. Dynamic (S, s) Economies. *Econometrica* 59:1659–86.

Calvo, Guillermo A. 1986. Temporary Stabilization: Predetermined Exchange Rate. *Journal of Political Economy* 94:1319–29.

De Gregorio, José, Pablo E. Guidotti, and Carlos A. Végh. 1992. Inflation Stabilization and the Consumption of Durables. International Monetary Fund, December. Mimeo.

Dornbusch, Rudiger. 1986. External Debt, Budget Deficits, and Disequilibrium Exchange Rates. In *International Debt and the Developing Countries,* eds. G. Smith, and J. Cuddington. Washington, DC: World Bank.

Drazen, Allan. 1990. Can Exchange Rate Freezes Induce Business Cycles? Maryland University. Mimeo.

Kiguel, Miguel A., and Nissan Liviatan. 1992. The Business Cycle Associated with Exchange Rate-Based Stabilizations. *World Bank Economic Review* 6:279–305.

Larraín, Felipe, and Rodrigo Vergara. 1992. Distribución del Ingreso, Inversión, y Crecimiento. *Cuadernos de Economía,* (87): 207–28.

7   Progress Report on Argentina

Rudiger Dornbusch

7.1 Introduction

Argentina, it used to be said, has problems: the money is outside and the unions are inside; the unions are British and the taxpayers Italian. Half a year ago one might have believed that all this was changing. The money had been coming back at a rapid pace, the unions had moved off the stage, and the tax system was showing a rapid improvement in yield. On courageous reform, Argentina was moving far ahead of Italy. Unfortunately, today Argentina is once again under the shadow of financial instability, though decidedly not on the ropes. Acute overvaluation, melting of confidence, questions about the sustainability of reforms are all back. Today the questions are how much of the recent progress can be carried forward and how best to defuse the currency crisis.

The economic reforms are less than two years old, started in April 1991 in the aftermath of the most recent hyperinflation. From hyperinflation, the rate of price increase has been brought down to a modest 15–20% per year. Pervasive reform in the economy, ranging from deregulation and privatization to trade opening, has raised productivity and helped reduce budget deficits. A radical and broad-based attack on poor fiscal performance is gradually showing results in increased tax collection and containment of spending. All of that is only a beginning, and the effort will have to continue for years. For a moment the payoff was phenomenal: growth returned at an astounding pace and with it confidence that Argentina can make it. The return of confidence is the most gratifying reward: Argentines have traditionally been highly contemptuous of their country's economy and cynical beyond belief. Today they keep their heads high even though they once again are worrying about their currency.

Rudiger Dornbusch is the Ford International Professor of Economics at the Massachusetts Institute of Technology and a research associate of the National Bureau of Economic Research.

Argentina has not yet escaped from its most traditional problem, already described a century ago in 1899 in the *Banker's Magazine* (quoted by Cardoso 1987): "They are always in trouble about their currency. Either it is too good for home use, or as frequently happens, it is too bad for foreign exchange. Generally, they have too much of it, but their own idea is that they never have enough. . . . The Argentineans alter their currency almost as frequently as they change presidents. . . . No people in the world take a keener interest in currency experiments than the Argentineans."

Only a year ago, there was the prospect that a century of instability would be put behind and a golden age would open up for Argentina.[1] Not implausible, but it will take persistent, hard work, and at this time the prospects are unclear.

7.2   Looking Back

At the beginning of the century, Argentina was among the most prosperous countries in the world. It is not true that Argentina had an income level *equal* to that of the United States or the leading country, Britain—in fact, as table 7.1 shows, Argentine per capita income was more nearly half the U.S. level. Argentina is often compared to Australia—both are resource rich and were among the ten most prosperous regions at the beginning of the century. Again, Australia already had almost twice the level of per capita income that Argentina showed. Interestingly, Italy closely matched Argentina at the outset of the century and in 1950.

Even so, Argentina was one of the very rich countries in the world and deserved a weekly report in the *Economist*. The country had made it when the invention of the Libby process made it possible to conserve meat and thus bring Argentine beef to the world market. The end of the past century, including the move to the gold standard in the 1890s which stabilized the currency, marked the dramatic ascent of Argentina to world-class performance.

What did Argentina look like then? Here is a contemporary description by Hyndman in 1892.

> Buenos Aires surpassed every other city in its luxury, extravagance, and wholesale squandering of wealth. There was literally no limit to the excesses of the wealthier classes. While money, luxuries, and material poured in on the one hand, crowds of immiserization from Italy and other countries flocked in to perpetuate the prosperity of the new Eldorado of the South. Railways, docks, tramways, waterworks, gas-works, public building, mansions, all were being carried on at once in hot haste. (89)

Over the past eighty years much if not most of that status has been lost. Argentine per capita growth has been dismal, lower even than that of Britain.

---

1. Cavallo (1984) enunciated a new growth paradigm for Argentina already in the 1980s.

Table 7.1   Per Capita GDP (U.S. 1913 = 100)

	1913	1950	1987	Growth, 1900–87
Argentina	47	62	88	1.1
Brazil	14	28	91	2.4
Australia	90	116	253	1.4
United Kingdom	81	106	243	1.4
United States	100	178	359	1.8
Italy	47	62	239	2.2
Japan	21	30	259	3.1

Source: Maddison (1982).

What went wrong in this century? First, in the interwar period, the Depression hit Argentina extra hard. Having built a fortune on a very open economy oriented toward exports of agricultural commodities—wheat and beef—protection in industrial countries and the collapse of world trade and of prices had a devastating impact. Even so, the country maintained its international credit by steadfast adherence to debt service and internationalism.

Protection of manufacturing and the building up of a sheltered industrial sector was the common response of Latin America to the 1930s crisis in world trade. The strategy worked at the outset to create employment and dampen the Depression. Moreover, World War II filled the coffers with reserves and allowed the strategy to be carried forward for a while. But Peron was too much—a nationalist-populist policy of protection, regulation, and macroeconomic instability increasingly brought down growth and prosperity and ultimately destroyed macroeconomic stability. Inflation became endemic, deficits became structural, and the country fell into cycles of populism and stabilization.

The 1960s were the last cycle of expansion, and since then there has been only bad news: dictatorships and a "dirty war" on domestic dissent and guerrillas, a mad war on Britain over the Malvinas, massive capital flight, and a few hyperinflations. Raped over and over again, Argentina ultimately fell into full and complete disillusionment. By 1991 the economy was almost completely dollarized, and a massive part of wealth had moved abroad.

In the 1980s the debt crisis was particularly severe. Having financed massive capital flight in 1978–82 by borrowing abroad, the country had no way of facing the large debt service burdens that emerged with the end of voluntary lending, world recession, and record high dollar interest rates in the early 1980s.

Net investment has been negative for almost a decade, and real income has been falling (see fig. 7.1). A once great country had been run down to the point where millions of people in Buenos Aires were fed at soup kitchens. Real GDP per capita was back to the level of the early 1960s.

Table 7.2   **Long-Term Performance (%)**

	1960–80	1980–90
Growth per capita	1.8	−2.3
Investment/GNP	22.0	13.6
Inflation	71.7	440.0

Table 7.3   **Current Indicators**

	1989	1990	1991	1992[a]
Inflation	5,386	800	56	15
Public debt[b]	79,377	74,832	75,048	
External	50,532	48,300	49,007	
Trade balance[b]	5,376	8,189	4,406	−1,000
Budget[b]	−1,883	−333	−1,107	
Revenue	7,073	10,345	15,334	
Expenditure	8,956	10,679	16,441	
Real wage[c]	68	66	73	76
Real exchange rate[d]	170	122	75	65
Industrial production[e]	90	86	96	120

[a]April 1992.
[b]Million US$.
[c]1986 = 100.
[d]1976 = 100.
[e]1988 = 100.

7.3   The Menem-Cavallo Miracle[2]

In March 1991, following yet another burst of extreme inflation (see fig. 7.2), the country moved to a radical stabilization. The program was centered on the "convertibility plan." Under this plan the government guaranteed the convertibility of pesos at a fixed exchange rate into U.S. dollars *and* undertook not to print any money except in the course of buying dollars in the foreign exchange market. Since foreign exchange reserves in the central bank exceeded the dollar value of the domestic money supply, the program was "credible" provided the government stuck to the constitutional commitment not to print money to finance the budget.

So far, for more than a year, the promises have been kept. The currency has become strong in the sense that there has been a major rebuilding of monetary assets in the form of peso currency holdings and bank deposits. Moreover, the government has initiated sweeping economic reforms.

Privatization is proceeding at breakneck speed. Without much regard for

2. See de Pablo (1992); Cline (1992); table 7.3 in this chapter.

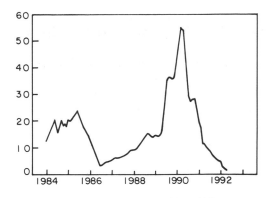

Fig. 7.1   Argentine per capita GDP (index 1980 = 100)

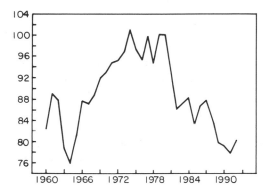

Fig. 7.2   Twelve-month inflation rate (percentage per month)

getting "good" or "fair" prices, the government is selling enterprises from oil to steel, from airlines to military production facilities (see Petrecolla, Porto, and Gerchunoff 1992). The key recognition is that the public sector enterprises make up much of the deficit; the sooner they pass out of public hands, the sooner there is a chance to balance the budget.

Deregulation is pervasive. A while back, restrictions on economic activity abounded. Hours for shops, licensing, permits, prohibitions wherever one looked. In one sweeping piece of legislation the government cleaned out an entire range of impediments to productivity.

Trade liberalization has been pushed aggressively and is seen as a key building block in more rational and productive use of the national resources. Access to cheaper and better intermediate goods has started lowering production costs and raising international competitiveness. More broadly, in manufacturing, international competition that comes with trade opening has started to exert price discipline.

Beyond unilateral trade liberalization, the ongoing effort to construct a MERCOSUR free trade area complements the trade strategy.[3]

Fiscal reform is equally ambitious, although progress is inevitably only gradual. The enforcement of tax laws has been stepped up dramatically, taxation has been simplified, and the tax yield is up. Between 1989 and 1991 the real (in U.S. dollars) revenue from taxation doubled!

Institutional reform is being implemented in the social security system, with a major impact on the budget, national saving, and the labor market.

Inflation has been brought down dramatically and possibly on a lasting basis.

Discarding entirely a leftish, nationalist perspective, the country has been thrown open to *foreign investment* in the asset markets and in the area of direct investment.

The country has *normalized relations* with the rest of the world. Politically, an understanding has been reached with Britain. In the Gulf War, Argentina was among the first to commit troops. In the economic area a quiet and responsible Brady debt relief plan secured access to International Monetary Fund (IMF) and World Bank funding.

Most important, *democracy* is firmly established, and the possibility of putsches or other adventures is just not part of the scene.

All of this is splendid. If kept up and pushed further, year after year, the reform program cannot fail to give Argentina the same stability that Chile or Mexico have secured from a decade of adjustment. For the time being, the willingness to do more is strong, and the program and the government command wide support.

The external environment has been immensely favorable in supporting the reforms with capital inflows and hence support for what otherwise might have been a fledging currency. The external support derived in part from the decline in alternative yields in developed economies.[4] But in large measure, restored access to the world capital market derived from the receptivenss of the world capital market to "reform economies"—Chile and Mexico had paved the way. There is certainly something to the view that either a developing country gets too much capital from abroad or too little, but rarely the middle ground. Taussig (1928, 130) long ago remarked on this fact: "The loans from creditor countries . . . begin with a modest amount, then increase and proceed crescendo. They are likely to be made in exceptionally large amounts toward the culminating stage of a period of activity and speculative upswing, and during that stage become larger from month to month so long as the upswing continues. With the advent of crisis, they are at once drawn down sharply, even cease entirely."

---

3. The recent imposition of import duties, prompted by Brazil's "excess competitiveness," clearly represents a setback in progress toward regional liberalization.

4. On this argument see Calvo, Leiderman, and Reinhardt (1992). Hanson (1992) reviews the problems of a capital account opening.

Of course, there are areas of vulnerability. The picture would not be complete without talking of three acute problems.

Fiscal correction notwithstanding, the budget continues to be in deficit. Over time there will be further improvement, but for now the deficit is lowered by privatization income, which will not be permanent. The financing by external credit helps financial stability, but ultimately is not sustainable. Hence, a first clear message: far more must be done with the budget to secure a very comfortable position of equilibrium without extraordinary revenues or special financing. That point is widely understood and may happen.

Competitiveness is a serious issue. Over the past year, on a fixed exchange rate but with inflation of 20%, competitiveness has been eroded. Wholesale prices in dollars are very high relative to levels of the mid-1980s. Some real appreciation is warranted by the fact that Argentina is now a stabilizing or even almost stable country, but too much real appreciation threatens stability because it suggests that the convertibility plan might fail.

External debt remains an issue. The public debt amounts to $61 billion, including a sizable portion of arrears. The financing of debt service either requires foreign private capital flows or else a large trade surplus. Both are in question. The resource transfer problem therefore remains acute.[5]

All is well while growth proceeds at a fast pace. But does Argentina's political and economic miracle have the stamina to go through a few hard years? A look at the reforms will give a better basis to judge that question.

7.4   Fiscal Reform

Correcting the budget deficit is a critical step in establishing financial stability. Any deficit financed by money creation is bound to be inflationary. The fact that the economy is substantially demonetized translates even quite small deficits into extremely large inflation rates (see Rodriquez 1992).

Only a few years ago, Argentines would have thought that paying taxes was a serious mistake. There were no sanctions; the government was in disgrace. The public did not get "their money's worth." Public finance is on the way to major improvement. Efficiency in government is derived by layoffs, privatization, and accountability. The budget is being nudged toward balance. Macroeconomic performance as a result is better and certainly more stable, and the chances for growth are enhanced.

Part of the fiscal improvement can be attributed to privatization. In 1990–92 the government derived $4 billion in cash revenue and achieved debt reduction by conversion in the amount of $7,343 (Salomon Brothers 1992). Of course, the benefit of privatization is not measured exclusively by these numbers. There is typically an accompanying deficit reduction because the public sector is a major source of deficits. Moreover, privatization brings a chance of invest-

5. See United Nations, *CEPAL* (1992) on the historical pattern of these transfers.

Table 7.4   **Public Finance**

	1985	1986	1987	1988	1989	1990	1991[a]	1992[b]
Overall balance	−7.9	−4.1	−6.5	−7.0	−21.8	−3.3	−1.8	−0.4
Tax revenue	18.6	18.5	17.8	16.8	16.3	16.6	19.1	20.9
Nonfinancial Public Sector								
Primary balance	0.7	1.8	−0.9	−1.0	−0.4	2.2	2.4	2.2
Interest	5.9	4.3	4.7	5.4	15.6	4.5	3.7	2.2
Central Bank quasi-Fiscal								
Deficit	−2.8	−1.6	−0.9	−0.7	−5.9	−1.0	−0.6	
Central government								
Revenues	11.3	11.8	10.9	9.2	9.8	9.6	14.2	
Primary balance	3.2	3.2	2.2	0.8	1.5	2.6	3.7	

[a]Preliminary.
[b]International Monetary Fund program.

ment by a party that faces less financial constraint than the government. This ought to translate into a reduction of bottlenecks, improved technology, and ultimately a better supply response.

Beyond privatization, reform of the social security system is a key priority of reform. The number of recipients exceeds the number of sixty-year-olds; the ratio of recipients to the supporting labor force is extravagant. Reforms are now passing the Congress and are likely to improve both the budget and the real income of qualified recipients. In the process Argentina will move to a more realistic retirement age—sixty-five years, instead of the present sixty.

Another critical area of fiscal reform involves revenue sharing and sharing of spending responsibilities between the federal and provincial governments. The early attempt at fiscal federalism invariably involves a major transfer of revenues of the provinces without an equivalent transfer of burdens. In the correction phase now under way the center recovers revenues and increasingly shifts responsibilities to the provinces.

7.5   Trade Opening

In the 1930s Argentina became a highly protected economy. An extreme example of the impact of such protection is that the Ford Falcon, produced with 1960s U.S. secondhand machinery, kept being produced in Argentina right up to 1990. But that is not the only example. Throughout manufacturing costs were high, quality was poor, models were obsolete, and all this was maintained by a tight regime of protection. Tariffs and quotas were the rule. And when, as often happened, the exchange rate was overvalued, the impact on imports was not extreme because protection was so fierce.

Over the past two decades, but notably in the last few years, Argentina has moved sharply in the direction of trade liberalization. Quotas have been largely

Table 7.5   **Average Tariff Rates (%)**

	1976	1980	1989	1991
	55.9	27.8	23.8	9.4

Source: GATT (1992).

Table 7.6   **Protective Duties by Category**

	Mean	Standard Deviation	Minimum	Maximum
Total	12.2	7.3	5	35
Raw materials	6.5	3.1	5	22
Semimanufactures	10.3	5.8	5	22
Finished goods	14.1	7.7	5	35

Source: GATT (1992).

Table 7.7   **Effective Tariff Rate, 1991**

	Tariff Only	Tariff & Tariff-Type Measures
Mean	12.4	28.2
Standard deviation	4.1	8.1
Minimum	−1.7	0
Maximum	32.3	52.0

Source: GATT (1992).

Table 7.8   **Balance of Payments**

	1988	1989	1990	1991	1992[a]
Trade balance	3,813	5,379	8,274	3,879	−402
Exports	9,135	9,579	12,353	11,972	7,518
Imports	5,322	4,200	4,079	8,093	8,275
Current account	−1,572	−1,305	1,903	−2,500	

Source: Banco Central Republica Argentina; International Monetary Fund: International Financial Statistics.

[a]January to July, *not* annualized.

eliminated, and tariff rates have come down both in level and, perhaps even more important, in their dispersion.

Trade opening, the boom of 1991–92, and the overvaluation (discussed below) combined to worsen sharply the external balance. Argentina had a tradition of trade surpluses. In the past thirty years, with the exception of 1975, there was never a deficit. This time the deficit will be large—$1 billion or more. Moreover, the shift in the trade balance is nothing short of huge. Awareness of this growing trade problem and the accompanying question of how this might be financed if foreign capital inflows taper off is the basis for the confidence crisis that is now emerging.

It might be thought that the trade deficit is benign in that it reflects a high component of capital goods imports—a reflection of modernization and no risk since ultimately the expanded capacity pays its own dividends. In fact, however, capital goods imports doubled since 1989. But consumer goods increased more than fourfold and intermediates also doubled. It is clear that protection held back imports and that now the liberalization, the boom, and the exchange rate all combine to yield a 1979-Chile-style blowup of the external balance.

7.6 Overvaluation

A simple model helps formulate the problem of currency appreciation.[6] Let P, W, and E be the log level of prices, wages, and the exchange rate. Lowercase letters stand for their rates of change with π, the rate of inflation. The unemployment rate (or the GDP gap) is represented by y.

(1) $$\pi = (1 - \alpha)(w - \pi) + \alpha(e - \pi)$$

(2) $$w = \pi - \sigma y$$

(3) $$y = \theta(i^* + e + \Delta - \pi) - \lambda(E - P) + f$$

(4) $$CA = \mu(E - P) + v(i^* + \Delta + e - \pi) + \rho f$$

i^* and i are foreign and home interest rates and Δ denotes the political risk premium. Fiscal restraint is denoted by f, and the current account surplus is denoted by CA.

Equation (1) represents a standard accelerationist pricing equation: inflation has inertia.[7] Deceleration is possible only if wage inflation or the rate currency depreciation can be brought down below the prevailing rate of inflation. Equation (2) describes wage inflation. The rate of increase of wages, because of explicit or implicit indexation, is equal to the rate of inflation but with an adjustment for cyclical conditions. In the third equation the unemployment rate is determined by real interest rates and by the level of competitiveness.

Figure 7.3 shows the phase diagram of this model, using equation (3) and the combination of (1) and (2):

(5) $$\pi = \gamma(e - \pi) + (1 - \alpha)\lambda(E - P) - (1 - \alpha)\theta(i^* + \Delta);$$
$$\gamma = [\alpha - (1 - \alpha)\theta].$$

---

6. See also Dornbusch (1979); Rodriguez (1982); Dornbusch and de Pablo (1990); Edwards (1989).

7. On the disinflation problem see Calvo (1983); Chadha, Masson, and Meredith (1992); Dornbusch and Fischer (1992); Edwards and Montiel (1989); Végh (1992).

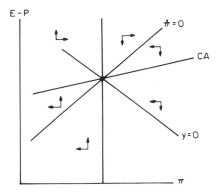

Fig. 7.3   Phase diagram of the currency model

The diagram is drawn for a given rate of depreciation e_0, and it is assumed that the term γ is positive.

Consider now a program of disinflation. Starting in a steady state at point A, the government reduces the rate of depreciation to zero and sustains the now fixed exchange rate. The new long-run equilibrium is at point B, where inflation has come down to zero.

The immediate impact of the rate fixing is to cut nominal interest rates and hence the real interest rate so that demand increases (see fig. 7.4). Higher demand and the elimination next lead to real appreciation. The instant rise in the level of demand, output, and employment gradually wears off. Ultimately the loss in competitiveness returns the economy to normal levels of output and then creates a recession. The economy will return to full equilibrium, with reduced inflation, only after deflation has restored the initial level of competitiveness. Protracted unemployment is the rule. Moreover, in the early phases of the adjustment program, the current account turns toward deficit.

The model is oversimplified in a number of respects. First, there are no large movements in the adjustment of demand and the current account to changes in the real exchange rate. In addition, the adjustment to real exchange rate changes assumes an immediate dominance of substitution effects, contrary to the Diaz-Alejandro hypothesis. Second, the monetary mechanism operates entirely through interest rates, and there is no special role for credit or confidence. Third, wealth effects and asset process play no role. But even though these aspects of the adjustment process are absent, the highly stylized model captures the patterns of the adjustment process. It highlights in particular that, on the way to full disinflation, high unemployment and large deficits constitute major confidence blocks to the continuation of the program. And if confidence does break down, so does the financing of external imbalances. Interest rates will soar, output will fall faster, and ultimately the program will be abandoned.

Argentina today is in a situation of currency overvaluation. Table 7.9 shows the extreme increase of the Argentine CPI measured in U.S. dollars. The ques-

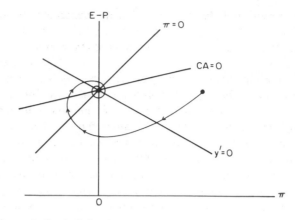

Fig. 7.4   The impact of rate fixing

Table 7.9   **Argentina: Relative Prices and Real Wages (1986 = 100)**

	Goods	Services[a]	Real Wage[b]
1987	96.2	119.7	91.7
1988	99.7	103.1	90.9
1989	107.5	91.9	82.9
1990	94.9	129.7	78.7
1991	85.0	158.8	74.7
1992[c]	81.0	173.8	75.4

Source: Banco Central Republica Argentina.
[a]Private.
[b]Manufacturing.
[c]July.

tion is whether high *domestic* prices will now start affecting wages and from there the competitiveness of the international sector.

Interestingly, the strong inflation impetus is entirely concentrated in the service sector (see fig. 7.5). The boom of 1991–92—28.9% growth in industrial production between midyear 1990 and 1992—in an economy that had not invested in capacity for many years must be the chief reason. What remains puzzling, however, is the combination of (measured) declining real wages with an expanding economy. The ability to repatriate assets from abroad is an essential ingredient in sustaining that process.

But the idea that competitiveness has not suffered because inflation has occurred predominantly in services is not right. Measures of the effective real exchange rate have been prepared by the Banco Central Republica Argentina (BCRA) and are shown in table 7.10. These data show a drastic loss in competitiveness over the past few years. Moreover, detailed data reveal that there are no significant differences across sectors. Thus it is no surprise that the trade balance should have shifted so massively toward deficit.

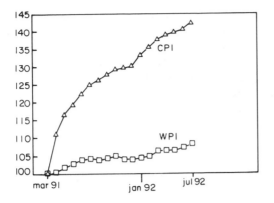

Fig. 7.5   Argentine CPI and WPI

Table 7.10   **Real Effective Exchange Rates (1986 = 100, trade weighted)**

	Imports	Exports
1987	101.6	108.2
1988	101.4	104.9
1989	120.5	118.9
1990	74.8	85.3
1991	52.1	65.0
1992[a]	54.6	58.9

Source: Banco Central Republica Argentina.
[a]September.

What next? If high consumer prices make their way into wages and costs, the overvaluation is bound to spread to a sharp loss of competitiveness, a trade crisis, and a currency crisis. The beginning of that process is already visible. If so, another payments problem and with it expectations of devaluation and instability will emerge. For the time being, reflow of Argentine money and investment in Argentina's assets by the rest of the world easily finance the trade deficit. But, of course, hot money can also go the other way.

There are five ways of coping with the process under way. The first is to just let it run its course. Hang on to the convertibility law both in respect to the level of the peso and the money supply rule and fully play the gold standard. If a loss in confidence occurs, this will mean capital flight, a tightening of credit, and a recession—the rules of the game.

Second, the government could hasten a recession by a sharp tightening of fiscal policy. That would crush demand and hence service sector inflation. This strategy has the advantage of keeping interest rates low, thus avoiding a new wave of balance sheet problems. Under both these options the government would follow an uncharted, unprecedented path of maintaining the integrity of exchange rate commitments. That would be new in a country where most years, around December, confidence in the currency vanishes, and the lack of confidence soon becomes self-fulfilling.

A third possibility is to abrogate the convertibility law (how can this be done expeditiously?), devalue, and declare that this is the very last time. Nobody would be fooled, and the loss of confidence not only in the exchange rate but in the entire promise of reform and modernization might be vehement and destructive.

A fourth possibility is to depart marginally from the convertibility law in that one maintains the monetary rule but moves to a crawling peg without initial devaluation. This strategy would do little to reduce the initial overvaluation, and there would also be no mechanism to stabilize inflation. If money is endogenous and the exchange rate is indexed to inflation, with a minimal lag, the rate of increase of inflation might be sluggish, but inflation itself could reach any level in time.

Of these four options, following the rules, reinforced by a sharp fiscal tightening, is the strategy most likely to avoid destabilizing inflation. In another country one would add an appeal for a social pact. In Argentina that might be asking for the impossible. The basic fact is that the popularity of the Menem-Cavallo strategy derived from the image and the supergrowth. The bad news is that the country now will go into far more disappointing performance as it gradually builds up stability, institutions, and supply capacity just as Chile and Mexico have done.

Another devaluation would break the confidence that has been built and risk an outbreak of another inflation wave. A sharp tightening of the budget and a slowdown of the premature boom in demand will maintain confidence and result in better performance in the long run.

A fifth and final option goes even further than mere adherence to the convertibility law. In this option the government elimintates *all* domestic money and proceeds to complete dollarization. The proposal does nothing to solve the problem of an accumulated lack of competitiveness, but it works forcefully on the credibility front.[8] The usual arguments about the loss of seigniorgage apply only in a mitigated fashion, since the country is de facto dollarized. The only issue is whether to proceed from 95% to 100% dollarization.

7.7 Concluding Remarks

Today Argentina needs to save and invest, not to spend and spend. Politically that message is unpopular. But Argentina is like Germany or Austria in 1920 or in 1947—destroyed economically and in need of reconstruction; saving and productivity growth are essential, running down assets to finance a consumption boom is dead wrong.

---

8. See Dornbusch, Sturzenegger, and Wolf (1990) for such a proposal.

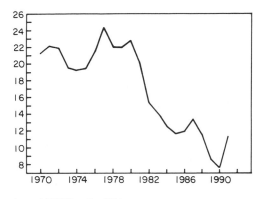

Fig. 7.6   Investment/GDP ratio (%)

Argentines have become far too optimistic in regard to the ease of modernizing and recovering their lost position. The benchmark is not to return to 1980
but rather to put the country in place to compete with Asia. For over a decade
investment performance has been minimal (see fig. 7.6). In an economy where
net investment has been negative, real wages cannot plausibly be the same as
they were ten years ago. If Argentina succeeds, and it may well because the
disillusionment accompanying the last inflation was extreme, it will take a
decade or more to stabilize and put in place a firm basis for sustained growth.
Chile, which has made the turn to sustained high growth, took fifteen years to
get there. Mexico, which has not made it yet, has been at work for nearly a
decade. Argentina is just starting, and already impatience is shining through.
One hundred years ago, Argentina was stabilized and set off into a period of
striking growth. The agenda today is the same, but the task is harder because
agricultural endowments count for less and in industry Italian talent and flair
just are no longer enough.

Argentina now has come around to the view that inflation is deadly and that
an inefficient state represents a weight that will ultimately crush prosperity. On
the inflation front the country is wrestling with adjustments and mechanisms
to put in place lasting stability. On the modernization front the country is grap-
pling with cleaning out the state and establishing efficient arrangements between the federal government and the provinces. Argentina clearly has come
around to the view that technocrats do better than populists. It has at the helm
an immensely competent, pragmatic technocrat. Continuity and perseverance
can put the country back in the race. As these efforts bear fruit, the need will
emerge to open a discussion on a new role of the state in areas such as education and social welfare, which is now all but dismissed.

References

Calvo, G. 1983. Staggered Contracts and Exchange Rate Policy. In J. Frenkel, ed., *Exchange Rates and International Macroeconomics*. Chicago: University of Chicago Press.

Calvo, G., L. Leiderman, and C. Reinhart. 1992. Capital Inflows and Real Exchange Rate Application in Latin America: The Role of External Factors. International Monetary Fund. Mimeo.

Cardoso, E. 1987. Latin America's Debt: Which Way Now? *Challenge* 30 (2): 11–17.

Cavallo, D. 1984. *Volver a Crescer.* Buenos Aires: Sudamericana.

Chadha, B., P. Masson, and G. Meredith. 1992. Models of Inflation and the Costs of Disinflation. *International Monetary Fund Staff Papers* (June).

Cline, W. 1992. *Argentina: Socioeconomic Report.* Interamerican Development Bank. Manuscript.

de Pablo, J. C. 1992. Menem y la Transformación Económica Argentina. Buenos Aires. Mimeo.

Dornbusch, R. 1979. *Open Economy Macroeconomics.* New York: Basic Books.

Dornbusch, R., and J. C. de Pablo. 1990. Debt and Macroeconomic Instability in Argentina. In J. Sachs, ed., *Developing Country Debt and Economic Performance.* Chicago: University of Chicago Press.

Dornbusch, R., and S. Fischer. 1993. Moderate Inflation. *World Bank Review* 7: 1–44.

Dornbusch, R., F. Sturzenegger, and H. Wolf. 1990. Extreme Inflation: Dynamics and Stabilization. *Brookings Papers on Economic Activity* (2): 1–84.

Edwards, S. 1989. *Real Exchange Rates, Devaluation, and Adjustment.* Cambridge: MIT Press.

Edwards, S., and P. Montiel. 1989. Devaluation Crises and the Macroeconomic Consequences of Postponed Adjustment in Developing Countries. *IMF Staff Papers* (December).

GATT. 1992. *Trade Policy Review: Argentina.* 2 vols. Geneva: GATT.

Hanson, J. 1992. Opening the Capital Account. Working paper WPS 901. World Bank.

Hyndman, H. 1892. *Commercial Crises of the 19th Century.* Reprinted. New York: Augustus Kelley, 1967.

Maddison, Angus. 1982. Phases of Capitalist Development. New York: Oxford University Press.

Petrecolla, A., A. Porto, and P. Gerchunoff. 1992. Privatization in Argentina. Buenos Aires, Instituto Torcuato di Tella. Mimeo.

Rodriguez, C. 1982. The Argentine Stabilization Plan of December 20th. *World Development* (9): 21–42.

———. 1992. The Macroeconomic Effects of Public Sector Deficits: Argentina. Mimeo no. 76. CEMA, Buenos Aires.

Salomon Brothers. 1992. Argentina's Economy: In Transition to Growth and Stability. New York. Newsletter.

Taussig, F. 1928. *International Trade.* New York: Macmillan.

United Nations. Comision Economica para America Latina. 1992. *Postwar Transfers of Resources Abroad by Latin America.* Santiago: CEPAL.

Végh, C. 1992. Stopping High Inflation. *IMF Staff Papers* 39 (September): 626–95.

8   Bolivia: From Stabilization to What?

Federico A. Sturzenegger

8.1   Introduction

Bolivia is a landlocked and sparsely populated nation of South America. With an area the size of the United Kingdom, Germany, and France combined, Bolivia had by 1989 a population of only 7 million. The country is divided into three clearly differentiated geographical areas. The western portion of the country is a flat plateau at 12,600 feet above sea level. This area is mineral-rich and historically has been the political and economic center of the country. Known as the *altiplano,* this region includes the departments of La Paz, Oruro, and Potosí. East of the altiplano lies the *valles* (valleys), an intermediate region between the high Andean ridge and the *precordillera.* At 8,500 feet above sea level the area is rich in agricultural products and comprises the departments of Cochabamba, Chuquisaca, and Tarija. This region also contains the famed region of the Chaparé, one of the best in the world for the production of coca leaf. As a consequence this region has recently been a strong receptor of population, particularly from the altiplano (see Pereira, Montano, and Calle 1991). Finally, east of the valles lies the extensive (and mainly still unexploited) area of the lowlands, or *llanos.* With a thriving economic center at Santa Cruz, this area has increasingly become a major economic and political center for the country. The extensive department of Santa Cruz, together with the northern, selvatic, cattle-growing regions of El Beni and Pando, conform this region.

Table 8.1 shows Bolivia's interregional disparities and underscores two im-

Federico A. Sturzenegger is assistant professor of economics at the University of California, Los Angeles, and a faculty research fellow of the National Bureau of Economic Research.

The author thanks Geoffrey Carliner, José De Gregorio, Sebastian Edwards, Rafael Garcia Mora, Ricardo Goody, Al Harberger, Juan Antonio Morales, Juan Carlos Requena, Ken Sokoloff, Jacques Trigo, and John Williamson for useful suggestions and conversations. He thanks Martin Kaufman for excellent research assistance.

Table 8.1   Bolivia's Regional Disparities

Region	GNP (% of total)	GNP/L (US $)	Urban GNP (US $)
La Paz	26.0	545	896
Santa Cruz	24.9	872	1036
Cochabamba	17.8	767	1332
Potosí	7.0	366	972
Chuquisaca	7.0	603	1714
Oruro	5.9	685	1119
Tarija	5.9	937	1549
El Beni	4.6	752	529
Pando	0.9	839	3748

Source: Ministerio de Planeamiento y Coordinación (1989).

portant characteristics of the Bolivian economy. First, Bolivia remains a very poor country. With a per capita income of US$630 in 1990, it ranked lowest among all South American economies. Second, Bolivia presents striking income disparities across regions. Notice from table 8.1 that the intraregional disparity in income is substantially lower than the interregional differences. While these disparities have found response in labor migration, the economy remains to some extent segmented along the lines of its geographical division. This of course is fundamental in evaluating the ability of the economy to adjust to shocks.

Bolivia has been, and to a great extent still is, a mining country. Development of mining products is among the main reasons both Incas and Spaniards were interested in the region. An analysis of productivity and growth potential can by no means be separated from the mining issue. Mining has historically been the main source of foreign exchange and savings for the country, a point first emphasized by Eder (1968). Not surprisingly, the recent collapse in Bolivia's mineral markets has had a major impact on Bolivia's economy.

Bolivia also brings to mind political instability, with twenty-one presidents since 1952. Between 1979 and 1982, nine presidents held office, a mere 4-month average tenure! Even the period between 1960 and 1980, which is considered a period of relative political tranquility, experienced eight coups and thirteen presidents. In section 8.2 I will show that the econometric link between political instability and growth is weak. Still I argue that this will not be enough to disregard the role of political instability as detriment to growth.

More recently, Bolivia has become an important coca-producing country with a large sector of the economy completely separate from that of the formal (and legal) economy. Samuel Doria Medina (1986) estimates for 1985 that the informal GNP was actually larger than that of the formal sector. He estimates an informal GNP of US$3,147 million, while that of the formal sector was

$3,055 million.[1] He also finds that the total and relative importance of coca production was growing very significantly until the end of the study in 1985. While in 1980 the value added associated with the production of cocaine was $353 million, by 1985 this figure had reached US$2 billion. Considering that the price of cocaine has fallen by half during the same period, it is clear that there has been a strong shift in factors of production (land, capital, and labor) toward this sector during the last decade. If the informal sector of the economy remains rather constant, at least for some computations, one could presume that use of the formal sector data should not strongly bias the results. Unfortunately, this presumption is not necessarily true. An increase in the inflation rate, for example, is a major incentive to avoid the formal sector, usually characterized by longer contracting periods and payment intervals. Below I try to adjust for this component where I think that misleading results would otherwise obtain. Unfortunately, lack of reliable data requires making heroic assumptions.

In summary, any analysis of Bolivia's growth performance has to cope with these issues: the role of mining, the low level of income, the role of political instability, and coca production and the informal sector. I study, first, the growth experience since the early 1950s. I try to uncover the driving forces of growth in Bolivia and then, from understanding such forces, to derive implications for future policy action.

Bolivia is a country of paradoxes. These go beyond geographical contrasts to the reign of politics, its interplay with macroeconomics and growth. After the Chaco war of the 1930s, the country entered an economic slide that triggered in the early 1950s a revolutionary movement with a socialist orientation, led by the Movimiento Nacional Revolucionario (MNR) and headed by the *caudillos* Victor Paz Estenssoro and Hernán Siles Zuazo. The revolution came to power with a clear socialist platform, implemented an agricultural reform, and nationalized mining production. Victor Paz Estenssoro was appointed president and immediately embarked on an expansionist spending program. Only a few years later the country was in a situation of increasing inflation and general economic disorder.[2] Hernán Siles Zuazo, sworn in as president in 1956, in order to cope with inflation implemented a very strict fiscal austerity and rationalization program, which with external supervision quickly put inflation under control. These reforms were the prelude to a long period of stability and high growth, which lasted until the early 1980s.

The late 1970s and early 1980s saw the collapse of a boom in mineral prices, which had allowed Bolivia to increase its standard of living significantly. The fall in the international price of tin was closely followed by the onset of the

---

1. The Doria Medina estimate is considered to be, at best, an upper bound for the amount of coca production. I discuss this issue in detail below.
2. See Eder (1968) for an incisive account of both the economic reality and policy making in Bolivia during this period.

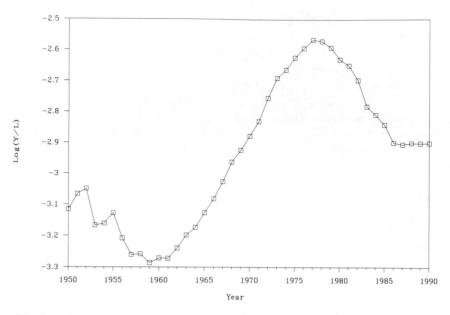

Fig. 8.1   Output per capita
Source: Data from Juan Antonio Morales, based on information provided by Banco
Central de Bolivia and Instituto Nacional de Estadísticas.

international debt crisis. With increased impoverishment of the economy, the
political struggle and the redistributive conflict intensified so that the military
delegated power to a democratically elected government. The new democratic
regime, headed once again by Hernán Siles Zuazo, was responsible for dealing
with the strong adjustment that international markets were imposing on the
Bolivian economy. Unfortunately, in spite of six stabilization attempts during
his presidency (see Morales 1988), the underlying causes of Bolivian inflation
were not tackled. This eventually resulted in the most traumatic experience
of Bolivian modern history, as the economy hit hyperinflation by mid-1985.
Hyperinflation created the consensus for a broad reform program that, in
a reversal of roles from the 1950s, was this time put forward by Victor Paz
Estenssoro.[3] The set of policies implemented and known as "new economic
policy" (NEP) are well known (see Morales 1991; Morales and Sachs 1989)
to have quickly brought inflation and fiscal accounts under control.

Figures 8.1 and 8.2 show (in log scale) output per capita for Bolivia from
1950 to 1990. Figure 8.1 contains official data only. Figure 8.2 has been adjusted to include the product of Bolivia's cocaine sector. The size of Bolivia's
cocaine sector has been estimated for the period 1980–85 (Doria Medina

3. To understand why hyperinflation induces the political consensus for reform, see Labán and
Sturzenegger (1992a, 1992b).

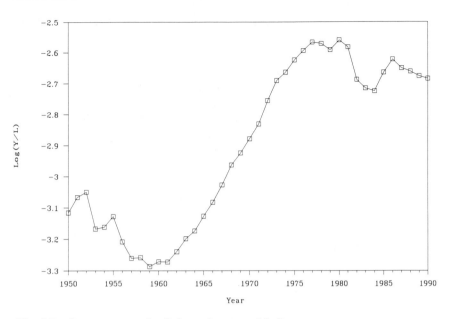

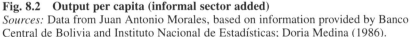

Fig. 8.2   Output per capita (informal sector added)
Sources: Data from Juan Antonio Morales, based on information provided by Banco
Central de Bolivia and Instituto Nacional de Estadísticas; Doria Medina (1986).

1986). We have assumed that this product was zero prior to 1980 and constant
at the 1985 level for years after 1985. Regarding this last assumption, work by
Gutierrez and Pando (1989) suggests that the production of coca leaf has remained constant or has slightly declined. Godoy and De Franco (1990) suggest
values for 1985 production similar to those of Doria Medina. Serious discrep-
ancies arise in evaluating the value of this production. Doria Medina uses the
price of cocaine hydrochlorate, though data from the National Narcotics Intelligence Consumer Committee (NNICC 1989) suggest that only 15% of coca
paste is transformed into cocaine hydrochlorate in Bolivia itself (most of this
process takes place in Colombia). Godoy and De Franco use instead the price
of coca paste and obtain estimates roughly one-third of the Doria Medina estimates for 1987–89. I have used the Doria Medina numbers because they constitute a clear upper bound to the estimate range.

   Both figures 8.1 and 8.2 show that the 1950s are characterized by a fall in
real income induced by the social and political convulsion that characterized
the Bolivian economy during this period. Civil war in 1952 brought the MNR
to power. Both 1955 and 1956 were years of extreme inflation, the rest of the
decade being dominated by a strict austerity program. The country then experienced steady growth from the early 1960s to the early 1980s. Growth halted
in the 1980s as prices of tin collapsed, the debt crisis started, and inflation
picked up. The stabilization attempt of 1985 was considered a major step to-

ward recovering growth. As shown by the two graphs, this hope has not been validated by the facts; this paper examines why.

In section 8.2 I review the main factors contributing to Bolivia's economic growth. In section 8.3 I take the main elements identified in the empirical analysis and develop a model that I hope provides a unifying framework for the discussion of terms of trade, real exchange rates, optimal taxation, and coca production and its relation to growth. In section 8.4 I discuss the theoretical and empirical relation between inflation and growth. In section 8.5 I discuss the relation between structural reform and poststabilization productivity. After computing productivity for specific industrial sectors for the poststabilization period, I conclude that improvement in productivity has been sluggish. In section 8.6 I discuss other possible explanations for Bolivia's recent poor growth performance, a puzzling result given that it constitutes a "model" case of fiscal austerity and market liberalization. Section 8.7 contains some policy conclusions that can be derived from the paper.

8.2 Sources of Growth

In this section I identify the main sources for Bolivia's growth performance by looking at the evolution of productivity. In order to study the performance of productivity I compute the total factor productivity (TFP) for Bolivia for the period 1950–90. While data are available for measures of the capital stock (see Huarachi 1988) and for population,[4] information on factor shares in unavailable. I perform the computation by estimating the shares as in Griliches and Ringstad (1971).[5] I assume that there exists a production function with constant elasticity of substitution and possible nonconstant returns to scale; that is,

(1)
$$Y = B[\delta K^{-\rho} + (1 - \delta)L^{-\rho}]^{\frac{\mu}{\rho}},$$

where B is an aggregate productivity parameter, K is capital stock, L is employment, μ represents the elasticity of scale, and $\sigma = 1/(1 + \rho)$ is the elasticity of substitution. In order to estimate this production function, Griliches and Ringstad suggest taking a second-order Taylor expansion around $\rho = 0$ for a log version of equation (1). This gives the equation

(2)
$$\ln(Y/L) \cong a_0 + a_1 \ln L + a_2 \ln(K/L) + a_3 \ln(K/L)^2.$$

From (2) we can obtain estimates for the elasticity of output with respect to both factors, labor and capital. a_1 is a measure of increasing returns to scale. Estimates of (2) turned out to be very unstable for the sample periods considered. For the sample 1950–87, equation (2) gives the following result for the official data:

---

4. Population data are available for the whole sample. The labor force was computed from estimates obtained from census data, interpolating for the intermediate years.

5. The particular formalization used here allows for nonconstant returns to scale as discussed in Dollar (1988) and Wang (1990).

$$(3) \quad \ln(Y/L) \cong - \underset{(0.14)}{5.06} + \underset{(0.16)}{0.49 \ln L} + \underset{(7.33)}{3.43 \ln(K/L)} + \underset{(1.70)}{0.57 \ln(K/L)^2},$$

where standard errors are shown in parentheses. As can be readily observed from the standard errors, the coefficients on ln (K/L) are very imprecisely estimated.

For the data including the informal section I use only the Cobb-Douglas specification ($a_3 = 0$). Estimation gives

$$(4) \quad \ln(Y/L) \cong - \underset{(0.11)}{9.84} + \underset{(0.10)}{0.65 \ln L} + \underset{(0.17)}{1.02 \ln(K/L)}.$$

Notice that the estimates in (4) are favorable to "endogenous growth" theories, indicating the presence of increasing returns to scale and an almost constant capital-output ratio.[6] From (3) and (4) we can compute the elasticities with respect to capital and labor as $\varepsilon_K = a_2 + 2a_3 \ln(K/L)$ and $\varepsilon_L = (a_1 + 1 - a_2) - 2a_3 \ln(K/L)$. And from these we can compute the factor shares as

$$(5) \qquad\qquad \alpha = \frac{\varepsilon_K}{\varepsilon_K + \varepsilon_L},$$

and

$$(6) \qquad\qquad \beta = 1 - \alpha.$$

An estimate of TFP is then obtained from[7]

$$(7) \qquad\qquad TFP = \frac{Y}{K^\alpha L^\beta}.$$

These estimates for the elasticities (α and β) and TFP (TFP_2 corresponds to the data that include the informal sector) are presented in the last four columns of Table 8.2. The table also shows data for the capital/labor ratio ($\ln(K/L)$), employment ($\ln(L)$), output per capita ($\ln(Y/L)$, official data), and the growth rates of output per capita (both for the official data [γ_1] and with the informal sector [γ_2]). TFP estimates are plotted in figures 8.3 and 8.4. The estimates obtained assign a share to capital of between 55 and 80% for the official data case, and of 62% for the data including the informal sector.[8]

Figures 8.3 and 8.4 indicate a very clear pattern, with an upward swing in productivity that culminates in the early 1980s. Since then the two graphs disagree, as one omits the effect of the informal economy. The official figures suggest a drastic collapse in the productivity of the Bolivian economy, down by 35% since 1979. Figure 8.4 suggests, on the contrary, a stagnant profile for productivity, though with an important fall during the first half of the 1980s.

6. See, among others, Romer (1986); Rebelo (1991); Lucas (1988); Jones and Manuelli (1990). For a comprehensive survey see Sala-i-Martin (1990a, 1990b).

7. Use of the Cobb-Douglas specification is appropriate as long as we could not reject the hypothesis that $a_3 = 0$.

8. Certainly my measure of TFP may have several biases. Most important, human capital has been patently excluded from the estimation and therefore is subsumed in the residual term.

Table 8.2   **Total Factor Productivity and Sources of Growth**

Year	Ln(K/L)	Ln(L)	Ln(Y/L)	γ_1	γ_2	α	β	TFP	TFP$_2$
1950	−2.15	13.80	−3.12			0.66	0.34	0.18	0.17
1951	−2.15	13.81	−3.07	.05	.05	0.66	0.34	0.19	0.18
1952	−2.15	13.83	−3.05	.02	.02	0.66	0.34	0.19	0.18
1953	−2.17	13.85	−3.17	−.12	−.12	0.64	0.36	0.17	0.16
1954	−2.19	13.86	−3.16	.01	.01	0.63	0.37	0.17	0.16
1955	−2.18	13.88	−3.13	.03	.03	0.63	0.37	0.17	0.17
1956	−2.18	13.90	−3.21	−.08	−.08	0.63	0.37	0.16	0.16
1957	−2.19	13.92	−3.26	−.05	−.05	0.63	0.37	0.15	0.15
1958	−2.21	13.94	−3.26	.00	.00	0.61	0.39	0.15	0.15
1959	−2.24	13.96	−3.29	−.03	−.03	0.59	0.41	0.14	0.15
1960	−2.26	13.99	−3.27	.02	.02	0.57	0.43	0.14	0.15
1961	−2.29	14.01	−3.27	−.00	−.00	0.55	0.45	0.13	0.16
1962	−2.30	14.03	−3.24	.03	.03	0.54	0.46	0.14	0.16
1963	−2.30	14.05	−3.20	.04	.04	0.54	0.46	0.14	0.17
1964	−2.31	14.08	−3.17	.02	.02	0.54	0.46	0.14	0.17
1965	−2.31	14.10	−3.13	.05	.05	0.54	0.46	0.15	0.18
1966	−2.35	14.12	−3.08	.04	.04	0.50	0.50	0.15	0.20
1967	−2.34	14.13	−3.03	.06	.06	0.51	0.49	0.16	0.21
1968	−2.30	14.13	−2.96	.06	.06	0.54	0.46	0.18	0.21
1969	−2.28	14.14	−2.92	.04	.04	0.55	0.45	0.19	0.22
1970	−2.26	14.15	−2.88	.05	.05	0.57	0.43	0.20	0.23
1971	−2.22	14.15	−2.83	.05	.05	0.60	0.40	0.22	0.23
1972	−2.18	14.16	−2.75	.08	.08	0.64	0.36	0.25	0.24
1973	−2.15	14.16	−2.69	.06	.06	0.66	0.34	0.28	0.26
1974	−2.10	14.18	−2.66	.03	.03	0.69	0.31	0.30	0.26
1975	−2.07	14.20	−2.62	.04	.04	0.72	0.28	0.32	0.26
1976	−2.04	14.23	−2.59	.03	.03	0.74	0.26	0.34	0.26
1977	−2.00	14.25	−2.57	.03	.03	0.77	0.23	0.36	0.26
1978	−1.95	14.27	−2.57	−.00	−.00	0.81	0.19	0.37	0.26
1979	−1.92	14.30	−2.59	−.02	−.02	0.83	0.17	0.37	0.25
1980	−1.93	14.32	−2.63	−.04	.03	0.82	0.18	0.35	0.26
1981	−1.94	14.35	−2.65	−.02	−.02	0.82	0.18	0.35	0.25
1982	−1.96	14.37	−2.70	−.05	−.11	0.80	0.20	0.32	0.23
1983	−1.99	14.39	−2.78	−.09	−.03	0.78	0.22	0.29	0.23
1984	−2.01	14.42	−2.81	−.03	−.01	0.76	0.24	0.28	0.23
1985	−2.04	14.44	−2.84	−.03	.06	0.74	0.26	0.27	0.25
1986	−2.07	14.47	−2.90	−.06	.04	0.71	0.29	0.24	0.26
1987	−2.10	14.50	−2.90	−.01	−.03	0.70	0.30	0.24	0.26
1988	−2.12	14.52	−2.90	.00	−.01	0.68	0.32	0.23	0.26
1989	−2.10	14.55	−2.90	−.00	−.01	0.70	0.30	0.24	0.25
1990	−2.09	14.57	−2.90	.00	−.01	0.70	0.30	0.24	0.25

Sources: Capital stock from Huarachi (1988). Population from International Financial Statistics and census data. Output from Banco Central de Bolivia and Instituto Nacional de Estadísticas.

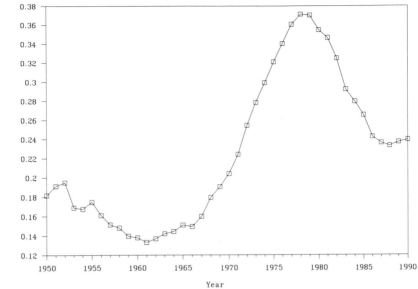

Fig. 8.3   Total factor productivity

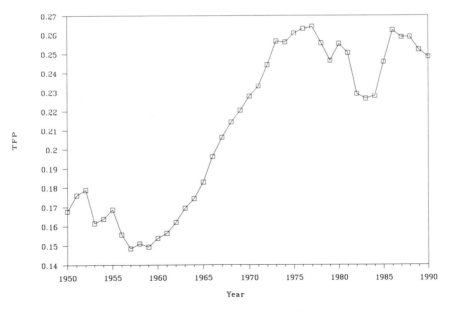

Fig. 8.4   Total factor productivity (informal sector added)

The figure suggests that the 1985 stabilization brought productivity back to the values observed at the beginning of the 1980s.

In trying to understand the sources of productivity, several variables are clearly relevant. Since TFP for Bolivia is a stationary series (an augmented Dickey-Fuller test [three lags] gives a coefficient of -3.35, which clearly rejects the hypothesis of unit root), standard econometric techniques are appropriate in this case. In particular for the period 1954–90 and the official data, the following regression is performed:[9]

$$TFP = 0.1281 - 0.0001\pi + 4.6E - 9\pi^2 + 0.0004Tin +$$
$$\quad (6.83) \quad (-2.23) \quad (2.16) \qquad\qquad (6.92)$$
$$\qquad\quad 0.0002Zinc - 0.0076PI .$$
$$\qquad\quad (0.39) \qquad (-1.19)$$

The first three variables, the inflation rate, the inflation rate squared, and the dollar price of tin, are significant, as indicated by their corresponding serial-correlation robust Newey-West t-statistics. The dollar price of zinc together with political instability (*PI*, understood as the number of changes in executive power during a given year), while of correct sign, have no significant effect on productivity.[10] Inflation has had a negative effect on productivity; increases in the price of tin and zinc have increased productivity. As expected, the coefficient on inflation is negative and that on inflation squared is positive, indicating that the costs of inflation do not increase as quickly once inflation has risen to high levels. R^2 equals 81%, so that a substantial portion of the movements in productivity are accounted for by these few variables.[11]

I do not find the insignificance of the *PI* dummy to be very revealing. First, it is clear that the political turmoil of the early 1950s and 1980s was associated with poor growth performance. Second, most of the effects of the *PI* variable may be colinear with the inflation rate, as both high inflation and political turmoil come together. Finally, it is difficult to capture the notion of political instability with a set of dummies in a time series approach. Cross-section growth models have certainly found important effects of many political variables on growth performance. I therefore conclude that, in spite of the result,

9. The inclusion of a trend variable proved insignificant.

10. Regressions were also performed using a political instability dummy that takes a value of 1 only when the change in executive power leads to a change in policy; that is, the new power is ideologically different than the previous one. The results were similar.

11. The strong effect of the price of Bolivia's main exports on productivity requires an explanation. An example may illustrate the relevant issue. Imagine an economy that produces only an internationally traded export: $X = F(K_t, L_t)$ valued at price p_{x_t} in international markets. Nominal GNP will then equal $Y_t = p_{x_t}X_t$. Consumers in this country purchase, with the proceeds of exports, a commodity basket with a corresponding price index denoted p_{c_t}. Real GNP equals $y_t = y_t/p_{c_t} = p_{x_t}/p_{c_t} F(K_t, L_t)$. Notice that the first term, which denotes a relative price effect, enters exactly like the TFP index in standard growth models. The result generalizes to allow for domestic production of the consumption good. While this measurement problem exists in all estimates of Solow residuals, it appears especially acute for a country like Bolivia, which relies so heavily on a small subset of export products.

it is very difficult to disregard the hypothesis that political instability affects growth performance negatively.

When computing the same regression for the data that include the contribution of the informal sector, I obtain

$$TFP = 0.16 - 0.00004\pi + 3.6E - 9\pi^2 + 0.001Tin$$
$$(8.77) \quad (-2.97) \quad (3.02) \quad \quad (2.60)$$
$$+ 0.001Zinc - 0.0043PI \ .$$
$$(2.92) \quad \quad (-1.07)$$

Again the standard errors are Newey-West corrected for serial correlation. Inference is as above, though the R^2 coefficient falls to 62%.[12]

I have identified two important sources for understanding Bolivia's growth performance: the price of Bolivia's main exports and the inflation rate. In sections 8.3 and 8.4 I discuss each of these in turn. Section 8.3 develops a model that reveals the role played by the export of primary products, specifically of mining, on growth and relative prices. This primary sector, characterized by decreasing returns to scale, is important for growth, as it is the main source of foreign exchange used for the purchase of capital goods. While recently several nontraditional exports have been increasing in importance (soybeans and natural gas among them), it appears that no alternative sector could substitute in the role played by mining in the near future. Coca production is an alternative source of foreign exchange and is discussed below.

Section 8.4 discusses the issue of inflation. Stabilization has been considered a main asset for the Bolivian economy and a warranty of future growth. I analyze in this section how inflation relates to the growth rate of the economy.

8.3   A Model of the Bolivian Economy

A distinguishing characteristic of the Bolivian economy is its reliance on natural resource production for the provision of foreign exchange. Production of tin, zinc, and more recently natural gas has been important in generating the external resources required for capital accumulation (see table 8.3). Morales, Espejo, and Chavez (1992) document the participation of tin, zinc, and natural gas in total exports since 1929 and show this participation has fluctuated between 50 and 70% of total exports. When the prices of mineral products and

---

12. Econometric problems are more serious for this specification. An augmented Dickey-Fuller test for TFP with a coefficient of -1.83 does not enable rejection of the hypothesis of a unit root. Furthermore, when a cointegration test is performed on the residuals of the cointegrating relation, the augmented Dickey-Fuller test equals -2.18, which does not allow rejection of noncointegration when compared to the critical values in Engle and Granger (1987) and Engle and Yoo (1987). In order to compare the results with the previous example and because of the low power of unit root tests, I feel confident of the results of the regression and have decided to show them here. Finally, while a trend was not significant in the TFP equation for official data, this is not the case for the current specification. Including a time trend delivers a coefficient of 0.041 with a Newey-West coefficient of 5.22.

Table 8.3   Income from Mining

Year	% of Government Revenue	Revenue (% of GNP)	Price of Tin	Tin (% Exports)	Mining (% GNP)
1970	na	1.4	166.63	46.9	17.29
1971	na	0.4	159.30	49.0	18.36
1972	na	0.8	169.64	46.5	19.97
1973	7.70	1.7	217.83	38.7	21.68
1974	17.82	2.9	371.23	38.0	20.17
1975	8.41	1.0	311.92	32.9	18.65
1976	12.51	1.5	344.08	34.7	17.85
1977	16.46	1.9	390.08	46.1	17.81
1978	18.09	2.0	584.01	51.6	16.98
1979	15.90	2.3	700.68	46.2	15.62
1980	15.02	1.5	761.03	36.5	15.78
1981	7.60	0.6	642.69	34.5	16.23
1982	9.20	0.4	581.95	31.0	16.45
1983	4.10	0.1	589.11	25.4	16.78
1984	13.30	0.7	554.76	31.7	14.77
1985	2.50	0.2	523.16	27.8	12.93
1986	0.40	0.0	294.31	16.3	11.25
1987	0.50	0.1	315.61	12.1	11.19
1988	na	0.1	330.94	12.8	12.84
1989	na	0.1	394.95	15.4	14.89
1990	na	0.1	281.03	11.2	na

Sources: Columns 1 and 4 from Morales, Espejo, and Chavez (1992). Columns 2 and 3 from Banco Central de Bolivia, Annual Memory (1990, 1980).

particularly of tin collapsed in the early 1980s, the Bolivian economy experienced one of its biggest recessions, a collapse of investment, and acute lack of foreign exchange. Bolivia faced problems with its foreign debt prior to the general onset of the debt crisis; this of course was a product of the collapse of the tin market in 1980.[13]

To understand the growth potential of the Bolivian economy, we need to study the implications of this dependence on mining. In the mining sector decreasing returns to scale are bound to appear. If the sector that sustains capital accumulation has this characteristic, growth eventually disappears. As discussed in the introduction, both a sectorial and geographical transformation of the Bolivian economy have been observed in the last twenty years due to the declining productivity of the mining sector. This process of transformation, or of movement toward the valles and the llanos, was temporarily halted with the mining boom of the late 1970s but has accelerated considerably since then.

In this section I look at the growth dynamics of an economy dependent on

13. There is some evidence that after the collapse of tin markets in late 1985 the fraction of exports accounted for by tin has declined steadily, reaching about 11% in 1990. (The decline in terms of government resources is even more significant.) See Morales, Espejo, and Chavez (1992) and table 8.3.

a tradable, decreasing returns-to-scale sector for the provision of foreign exchange. The model accounts for the effect of the price of minerals on productivity and growth. It traces the dynamics of investment and the real exchange rate and allows us to study the effects of price shocks on the Bolivian economy.

The economy is composed by a representative agent that maximizes the utility function:[14]

$$(8) \qquad U = \int_0^\infty \ln c e^{-\rho t}\, dt,$$

where c denotes consumption.

The economy produces two goods with three factors of production. It produces a "mineral" product (T) that is exchanged in world markets for an investment good at an exogenous international price. It also produces a consumption good that is nontradable. This implies that the equilibrium relative price between the investment (mineral) good and the consumption good measures the real exchange rate. In summary, the possible spending levels of investment are given by

$$(9) \qquad I = p_T T = p_T A'(z(1 - \phi))^\beta M^{1-\beta} = A(z(1 - \phi))^\beta M^{1-\beta},$$

where $A = A' p_T$, with A' an exogenous productivity parameter and p_T the relative price between the investment and mineral goods. This relation introduces a link between export prices of mineral products and productivity. z indicates the stock of capital and ϕ the fraction of the capital stock used for consumption purposes. Finally, M indicates the number of "miners," which we will consider fixed and normalized to one.

Because $\beta < 1$, the model indicates that the marginal product of capital is not bounded above the value of the discount factor, and growth will eventually disappear.

Capital is accumulated with technology:

$$(10) \qquad \dot{z} = I - \delta z,$$

where δ is the depreciation rate. Finally, consumption is produced with production function

$$(11) \qquad C = B(\phi z)^\alpha L^{1-\alpha},$$

where $\alpha < 1$, and L is the number of "workers," which we also consider fixed and equal to one. Maximization of (8) subject to the previous constraints can be reduced to the dynamic system in (ϕ, z). After simplification the solution of this system has first-order conditions

---

14. The assumption of a representative agent basically indicates that distributional issues are not important. This of course is just a first cut; I deal with the issue of distributional conflict below.

(12)
$$\dot{\phi} = \frac{(1 - \phi)^{\beta}\phi\beta A z^{\beta-1}}{(1 - \beta\phi)} - \frac{(\delta + \rho - \beta\delta)(1 - \phi)}{(1 - \beta\phi)}$$

and

(13)
$$\dot{z} = A(z(1 - \phi))^{\beta} - \delta z.$$

These two equations are graphed in figure 8.5, which shows that the steady state is a saddle and therefore the equilibrium is unique. The relation between consumption share and capital is positive: the economy increases consumption as it accumulates capital.

The steady-state solution is given by

(14)
$$\phi = \frac{\delta(1 - \beta) + \rho}{\delta + \rho}$$

and

(15)
$$z = \left(\frac{\beta A}{\delta + \rho}\right)^{\frac{1}{1-\beta}} \frac{\delta + \rho}{\delta\beta}.$$

Notice that the solution for ϕ does not depend on the productivity coefficient A; this is a special characteristic imposed by assuming log preferences but which has no major implication for the issues at hand.

From the first-order conditions for capital investment, we obtain an expression for the real exchange rate or relative price of tradables to nontradables (q). Because capital is perfectly mobile, the return to capital must be equalized across the two sectors; this implies

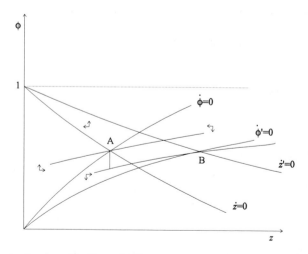

Fig. 8.5   An increase in mineral prices

(16)
$$q = \frac{\alpha B(1 - \phi)^{1-\beta}}{\beta A \phi^{1-\alpha}} z^{\alpha-\beta},$$

so that q decreases with both ϕ and z. The decrease of the real exchange rate as a function of the level of capital accumulation is a reflection of the Balassa-Samuelson hypothesis on real exchange rate. The tradable sector is more capital intensive than the nontradable sector. As development proceeds, real wages increase, pushing up the relative price of nontradables. This is true here, with the caveat that the change in real wages is induced by an endogenous change in relative prices: as relative productivity in the nontradable sector lags behind, the relative price of nontradables increases. The response of the real exchange rate to ϕ reflects the fact that the allocation of capital to the tradable sector increases in its relative price. Along the growing path both (ϕ, z) are increasing, so that the real exchange rate appreciates.

The model can be used to study the effects of shocks to the economy, such as changes in the world price of minerals. Imagine an increase in the price of minerals. This will shift both curves in figure 8.5 to the right, with the intersection remaining at the same level of ϕ (we have seen the steady-state value does not depend on A). As in the new steady state the optimal level of capital and productivity have increased and the value of ϕ remains the same, the real exchange rate appreciates. This corresponds to the notion that equilibrium real exchange rates respond to terms of trade (see Edwards 1989). More interestingly, the model predicts a transition characterized by a fall in ϕ with convergence to the same value at a higher level of the capital stock. While the real exchange rate appreciates in the long run, notice that in the adjustment to higher productivity (or higher prices), the economy shifts resources from consumption in order to allow for capital accumulation, thus the need for a short-run depreciation of the real exchange rate.

Shocks to the nontradable sector can also be studied. If the productivity parameter (B) changes there will be no effect on investment decisions and growth performance (notice that B docs not appear in the dynamic equations). It will nevertheless affect the consumption possibilities of nontradables and the real exchange rate.

8.3.1   Endogenous Growth?

The previous model can easily be extended to include the cases of endogenous growth. For this I assume $\beta = 1$. Equations (12) and (13) become

$$\dot{\phi} = A\delta - \rho$$

and

$$\dot{z} = Az(1 - \phi) - \delta z.$$

The solution is presented in figure 8.6, where there will be steady-state growth as long as $A - \delta - \rho > 0$. Because in steady state $\phi = \rho/A$, the equilib-

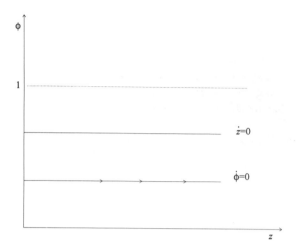

Fig. 8.6   The endogenous growth version

rium growth rate will equal $A - \delta - \rho$. This model has the attractive feature that changes in productivity will affect the growth rate.

8.3.2   Capital Adjustment

Independent of accepting a traditional growth model, or the endogenous version presented in section 8.3.1, it will always be the case that changes in productivity are the leading force in inducing changes in the capital accumulation process which allows for long-run changes in income per capita. Figure 8.7 shows the contribution of capital accumulation to the growth process both for the official data and for data including the informal sector. The value is computed as $\alpha_k \dot{k}/k$, where k is the capital/labor ratio. The graph is interesting because it shows that capital accumulation moves at low frequencies. The economy presents long intervals, in general over ten years, in which the contribution is either positive or negative. The graph shows that capital was a force in economic growth only between 1965 and 1980. During the other years the contribution was negative; that is, there was a decrease of capital.

This sluggish adjustment of capital to productivity shocks (after the 1956 stabilization, capital accumulation finally picked up ten years after productivity started to increase) arises from several factors: the existence of lags in installation, sluggishness in the revision of forecasts about the future economic situation, or irreversibility in investment decisions, which gives value to the option of waiting before committing investment resources.

Another reason capital accumulation adjusts so slowly arises from the movement in tax rates. Table 8.3 shows data on fiscal income accruing from mining taxes. The first column shows the fraction of total government revenue collected from mining taxes. The second column computes the same revenue as

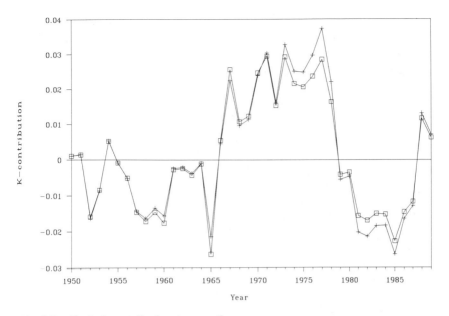

Fig. 8.7   Capital contribution to growth

a percentage of GNP. The last three columns indicate the nominal price of tin (see also figure 8.12), the share of tin in Bolivia's exports, and the participation of mining in GNP.[15]

These taxes have not been stable: while they were high and positive in the 1970s, when prices of mineral products were high, they fell drastically in the early 1980s, and even more after the collapse of tin prices in 1985. In this section I try to explain this variability in the tax rates. Trade taxes in developing countries have been strongly countercyclical with respect to the evolution of international prices. Morales and Sachs (1989) discuss the role of the Bolivian public sector as a "shock absorber" for external shocks, but this relation has been found for other developing countries as well (see Krueger, Schiff, and Valdes [1992] for Argentina and Schiff and Valdes [1992] for a cross section of developing countries). In Bolivia this pattern is clear from the system of *regalias,* in which the tax is computed as a function of the difference between world prices and a "presumed cost" set by the Bolivian Ministry of Mines. When the price increases, so does the implicit tax rate, reducing price variability at the producer level. While the regalias system appears to be providing insurance, it does not reduce price fluctuations for the economy as a whole and

15. Mineral prices fluctuate considerably. Morales, Espejo, and Chavez (1992) propose an intervention mechanism in order to reduce variability in real prices. This variability is considered to have negative effects by imposing strong variability in consumption. Morales et al. estimate this variability to imply a welfare loss for Bolivia of the order of 0.7% of GNP per year.

cannot be considered insurance for producers, who obtain no return when prices are low.[16] In 1991 a new mining tax law was approved that taxes utilities of mining companies at a fixed rate. But nothing in the political structure has changed to suggest that, if mineral prices increase, the government will not once again tax the mining sector with more intensity.

One possibility for explaining the time variation in the level of transfer relies on the political economy structure of the model in section 8.3. The economy has three factors of production: capital (used in both sectors), miners (specific to the mining sector), and workers (specific to the nontradable, consumption sector). While the assumption that miners cannot move is rather extreme, it should be appropriate in the short run. The income for each group can be determined from the production functions in competitive factor markets. The groups vote for taxing either mining or consumption. Under these assumptions it is easy to show that the miners would never vote for taxing the mining sector, as they would suffer from the tax and it would reduce in turn the total level of the capital stock. For workers the choice is ambiguous: A consumption tax reduces their income, but a mining tax reduces the capital stock and through that channel reduces their income. If they side with miners, the mining sector would never get taxed. This is certainly not the case, so we assume the contrary. The remaining group is capital owners, who, having a stake in both sectors of the economy, can be a shifting coalition depending, for example, on the international price of mineral products. If so, the setup works in a way opposite to that of the stylized facts previously described. If the price of the mineral products increases, capitalists will side with miners (because the tax becomes more onerous the higher the price of minerals), and government revenue will be levied through other mechanisms such as inflation. This is contrary to the evidence.

An alternative explanation relies on "optimal" taxation approaches. This approach can give a better account of the intertemporal change in taxes than the political economy explanation. Imagine a policymaker who tries to set up a tax policy to maximize the utility of workers.[17] The solution to this problem implies that, if the productivity of the mining sector increases, the taxes or transfers from that sector increase as well. The trade-off arises because, while the policymaker does not care about miners, he realizes that taxing this sector will jeopardize the process of capital accumulation and therefore reduce the productivity of labor (i.e., his constituency) in the nontradable sector.

16. It could be argued that there is an insurance component to the extent that the mining sector needs the provision of basic infrastructure. If the infrastructure provided is not affected by the fall in taxes when prices are low, then the mechanism may smooth out the payment of such services.

17. Choosing the workers as the target group of the policymaker can be justified in two ways. First, it generates a result that is compatible with the evidence on Bolivia. Second, workers are the biggest group and are therefore an important source of political legitimization. A formal solution is presented in the appendix.

Taxes on mining are important, since this sector is essential in generating the resources for capital accumulation, thus affecting growth. The most comprehensive study of Bolivia's public mining sector concludes, "The origin of the operating rules for COMIBOL, maximizing production in the short run, was based on the needs of the state of maximizing, also in the short run, the availability of income and foreign exchange" (CEMIT, 1989, 40).

In the model in section 8.3, consider a tax on the production of minerals at a rate τ. Solving the optimization problem, the optimal capital stock is now

(17)
$$z = \left(\frac{\beta A(1 - \tau)}{\delta + \rho}\right)^{\frac{1}{1-\beta}} \frac{\delta + \rho}{\delta\beta},$$

so that the tax on mining reduces the capital stock for the economy.

In the presence of price shocks we expect investment to adjust optimally. Fluctuating tax rates may choke the adjustment to shocks. Morales, Espejo, and Chavez (1992) find mixed evidence on the presence of unit roots for prices of major export products. Unit roots may be important because they indicate the existence of permanent shocks. A compensating tax increase may induce a stock of capital that never is at the optimal level.

8.3.3   The Effects of Coca Production

The importance of coca production for the Bolivian economy cannot be dismissed. As discussed before, it represents an alternative source of foreign exchange that is critical for the capital accumulation process. While the discussion here is in terms of coca production, the results of this and section 8.3.4 apply equally to the role of nontraditional exports and foreign indebtedness.

I capture this by adding a term Δ to the investment accumulation equation (13). Δ represents the resources made available by coca production. The dynamic equations that describe the optimization problem now become

$$\dot{\phi} = \frac{(1 - \phi)^\beta \phi \beta A z^{\beta-1}}{(1 - \beta\phi)} - \frac{\delta(1 - \beta)(1 - \phi)}{(1 - \beta\phi)} - \frac{\beta\Delta(1 - \phi)}{z(1 - \beta\phi)}$$

and

$$\dot{z} = \Delta + A[z(1 - \phi)]^\beta - \delta z.$$

The dynamics are depicted in figure 8.8. The difference from the previous models relies on the possibility of sustaining a capital accumulation process with high consumption shares, even in those cases in which the capital stock is very low. Consider an increase in Δ, which may arise because of legalization of drug production, lower enforcement, or positive technological or price shocks for coca production. Figure 8.8 shows the implications of this for capital accumulation and the real exchange rate. The real exchange rate appreciates across steady states on impact. Output increases with the process of capital accumulation, but consumption increases as well, as indicated by a jump in ϕ.

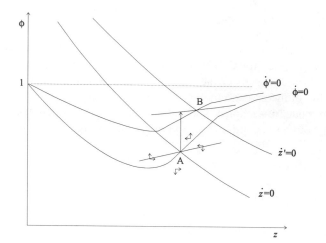

Fig. 8.8   The economy with coca production

The current formalization does not allow for steady-state growth, for the exogenous contribution of coca production to the process of capital accumulation becomes insignificant as capital accumulation takes place.

Notice that the analysis disregards the substitution effect known as "Dutch disease." This nevertheless may be an important issue in the presence of learning or irreversibility of investment projects.

8.3.4   Endogenous Growth Again?

Assume that the contribution of coca production is Δz. In this case it is easy to see from the equation of capital accumulation that the rate of growth of capital will equal $\Delta - \delta$ in steady state. The assumption that the resources of coca production increase linearly in the capital stock is very stringent. How likely is it that it will be satisfied? There are two reasons that suggest that this condition may be possible and three reasons that suggest it is very unlikely to be satisfied. On the positive side we have some evidence that yields may be improving. The NNICC (1989) estimates the coca-leaf yield to have increased from 1.4 metric tons per hectare for the period 1984–88 to about 2.7 metric tons per hectare for the period 1990–91. More important, there has been an upgrade in the production process in Bolivia. While initially Bolivia exported only coca paste, it now has expanded to the production of cocaine hydrochlorate, a much more advanced stage in the production process for cocaine. On the negative side we have, first, that production is constrained by the availability of natural resources (appropriate land) for coca cultivation; therefore it is unlikely that increases in physical yields will persist for a long time. Second, the price of coca has been decreasing substantially in international markets (a reflection of an inelastic demand for cocaine). Godoy and De Franco (1990) show that the wholesale price of cocaine in the United States has fallen from US $6,000 per kilogram in 1980 to less than $2,000 in 1988. More important, the price of coca paste, Bolivia's main export, fell by a half, from $1,500 to $700 between 1987 and 1989. Finally, most of the resources obtained from coca production are not retained in the country. Doria Medina (1986) estimates that about 80% of the value added of cocaine production leaves the country as capital flight. It is true that the return to this capital is a component of Bolivia's GDP as it accrues to residents. With open capital markets it may even be possible to argue that, if invested abroad, this capital will obtain a higher rate of return. Unfortunately, this is not the case; drug capital is not easily "whitened." In this case, some of this capital flight may be incurred at a loss of rate of return.

Overall it seems unlikely that coca and derivatives will become an engine of growth for Bolivia in the future. Other nontraditional exports—cattle, soybeans, and gold—will probably play a more important role than coca production in the near future.

8.4 Inflation and Growth

Table 8.4 shows Bolivia's inflation. The table underscores a major point: Bolivia is not a high-inflation country, with years of extreme inflation in the triple digits, such as Argentina, Brazil, or Peru. In this context the hyperinflation of 1985 seems a rare occurrence and therefore may have different effects and implications than in countries with chronic inflation.

Regarding TFP the inflation rate seems important in explaining the performance of the Bolivian economy. As inflation increases, the productivity of the economy falls. In section 8.2 I estimated the relation between inflation and TFP. Figures 8.9 and 8.10 show the efficiency of the Bolivian economy relative to that of a situation with no inflation, both for the official GNP and for data including the informal sector. The main implication of the graph is the negative impact of the high-inflation (hyperinflationary) experience of the mid-1980s. In both cases the data indicate that the economy during 1984–85 operated at

Table 8.4 **Yearly Inflation Rates**

Year	π	Year	π	Year	π	Year	π
1952		1962	5.80	1972	6.50	1982	123.50
1953		1963	−0.70	1973	31.40	1983	275.60
1954	124.80	1964	10.10	1974	62.80	1984	1,282.40
1955	77.90	1965	2.90	1975	8.00	1985	11,857.10
1956	181.20	1966	6.90	1976	4.40	1986	276.30
1957	115.50	1967	11.10	1977	8.10	1987	14.60
1958	3.00	1968	5.40	1978	10.40	1988	16.00
1959	20.30	1969	2.20	1979	19.70	1989	15.17
1960	11.50	1970	3.80	1980	47.20	1990	17.12
1961	7.50	1971	3.60	1981	32.10	1991	14.52

Sources: Morales and Sachs (1989); Banco Central de Bolivia, Monthly Bulletin.

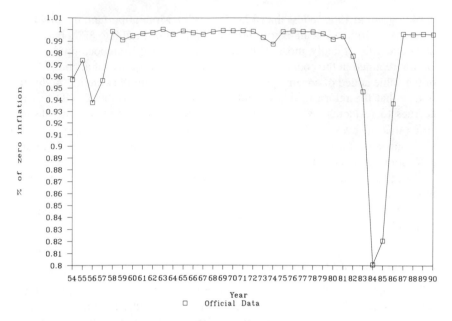

Fig. 8.9   Productivity effects of inflation (official data)

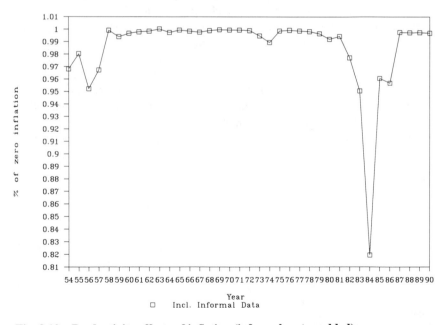

Fig. 8.10   Productivity effects of inflation (informal sector added)

about 80% of its potential productivity (and at about 95% during 1983 and 1986).[18]

The evidence on the effects of inflation on growth or productivity is not entirely new and has been found by many authors for cross-sectional studies. Fischer (1991) and Kormendi and Meguire (1985) find a negative relation between inflation and growth. Barro (1990a) finds that inflation enters insignificantly in the growth equations, but that inflation affects the level of output.

While the exact measure of the effect of inflation remains controversial, the qualitative effect of inflation on economic efficiency is not. Why does inflation affect productivity? First, it reduces the use of an efficient transactions mechanism. This is captured both by Bailey's monetary triangle and in the shoe-leather costs discussed in Fischer and Modigliani (1978). A much more important effect of inflation comes from the disorganization of the production system. Ball and Romer (1992) and Tommasi (1992) have suggested that high inflation has negative effects on economic efficiency because agents decide to gather less information, as inflation reduces the informational content of prices through an increase in the variability of relative prices. In equilibrium the price system is less efficient in allocating resources, and more inefficient producers remain in the market. Another dimension in which inflation affects efficiency is by affecting agents' time allocation. De Pablo and Martinez (1989) comment that "in Argentina, CEOs are so busy that they don't have time to work." In Sturzenegger and Tommasi (1992) in the context of a Schumpeterian model of growth, we discuss how high inflation may use up scarce entrepreneurial time for activities such as information gathering or financial activities rather than for pursuing growth-enhancing activities.[19]

A final and crucial mechanism through which inflation affects productivity is the financial sector. The financial sector allocates savings to investment projects, monitors their execution, and provides working capital for firms. At the same time it is strongly affected by market imperfections arising from adverse selection problems and moral hazard issues. If inflation increases the variability of relative prices, these two problems are aggravated by an increase in the inflation rate.

Table 8.5 shows the amount of financing provided by the banking system as a percentage of GDP, and the percentage of this financing provided by commercial and specialized banks, as opposed to the central bank. The total amount of financing fell drastically with hyperinflation but has recovered since. This is clear reflection of how the moral hazard and adverse selection problems become more acute in the presence of high inflation. This in turn affects productivity adversely. A final reason why the financial sector becomes less efficient in times of high inflation is understood by looking at the third

---

18. This may be an overestimation due to widespread excess capacity induced during the same period.

19. See also De Gregorio (1991, 1992); Roubini and Sala-i-Martin (1992).

Table 8.5   Financial Indicators

Year	Savings/ GNP	Total Financing/ GNP	Commercial Banks/ Total Financing
1980		24.4	56.7
1981	12.5	25.2	59.0
1982	19.3	42.5	42.6
1983	12.0	32.2	41.4
1984	11.2	24.2	48.0
1985	9.2	7.1	200.8
1986	5.4	5.0	214.1
1987	5.1	9.7	140.0
1988	7.0	13.9	108.1
1989	8.0	20.4	87.5
1990	8.8	24.0	87.3

Source: Banco Central de Bolivia, Annual Memory (1990).

column of table 8.5. During hyperinflation the public sector became a net borrower in financial markets. In 1985 commercial banks lent about the same amount to the public sector as they did to the private sector. This is a development not unique to Bolivia; Argentina, for example, experienced a similar process during the late 1980s. More recently the proportion of total lending provided by commercial and specialized banks has increased substantially as compared to the prehyperinflation period. This is a positive development since it ensures better allocation of investment projects.

Inflation has been shown to have important negative effects on productivity. Is it possible to argue that it has a positive effect? I believe there are two important reasons that suggest this may be the case. In particular, hyperinflation has developed the financial sector considerably and has allowed fiscal reform to take place. I discuss each of these developments in turn.

The development of the financial sector has two somewhat related objectives. First, it allocates savings to investment and therefore performs a critical role in the growth process. Second, it becomes a hedge against high inflation. The hyperinflation period was accompanied by strong development of financial institutions, a process that is common to all high-inflation experiences. While some of that development certainly reverses after price stability is achieved, it is possible to argue that in the new equilibrium the total use of financial instruments is greater. In the presence of fixed costs (and low marginal costs) to the use of financial instruments, the high-inflation period may have brought an important fraction of consumers to the financial sector. These do not exit automatically when inflation falls. These hysteresis effects are supported by two basic empirical facts: (1) money demand has not increased to prestabilization levels, and (2) the financial sector exhibits strong dollarization of financial instruments (see Dornbusch, Sturzenegger, and Wolf 1990).

Figure 8.11 shows some of these developments. Total liquidity fell during hyperinflation and has recovered somewhat since. But notice that the recovery is in indexed assets, $M4 - M1$, rather on monetary holdings. Hyperinflation has therefore played a role in changing the relative composition of monetary holdings in favor of indexed assets in the financial sector. The total amount of $M4$ is today higher than at the beginning of the 1980s, and this recovery has been made possible by the development of new financial instruments induced by inflation. These instruments have taken the form of dollarized indexed deposits.

The second positive effect of high inflation is the readjustment of the political scenario. Drazen and Grilli (1990) and Velasco (1992) have stressed that extreme-inflation experiences may be a catalyst for change and induce the political support for reform. They show that, though inflation is costly, the fact that reform is made possible may make inflation, even hyperinflation, desirable. Labán and Sturzenegger (1992a, 1992b) have shown that, in addition to making reform acceptable, inflation may have strong income distribution effects, which should not be disregarded when evaluating the "benefits" of hyperinflation. Because inflation is more painful for the agents who do not have access to the financial sector, these groups eventually lose in the bargaining process that characterizes a stabilization program. The income distribution implications may be long-lasting. In general, it seems difficult to argue that hyperinflation can be desirable, but is undeniable that, once the costs of inflation become overwhelming, reform is implemented.

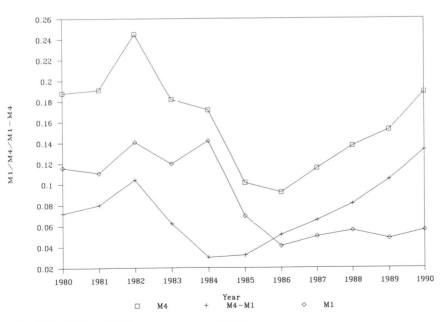

Fig. 8.11   M1 and M4 as percentage of GNP
Source: Data from Banco Central de Bolivia.

These two developments allow the possibility of long-lasting stability. Any deviation from strict fiscal balance, in the presence of a dollarized financial sector (and very low holdings of domestic currency), would immediately trigger hyperinflation. The risk of this outcome is what makes the current program of fiscal austerity sustainable from a political point of view.

8.5   Poststabilization Productivity

8.5.1   Stabilization and Productivity

Stabilization is considered the main asset of the Bolivian economy. The *Estrategia de Desarrollo Económico y Social, 1989–2000* claims: "The permanent control of inflation constitutes a basis for economic growth and for the long-term policies considered in the strategy for economic and social development. Keeping price stability has maximum priority in this strategy, helping in achieving the objectives of improving the international competitiveness of the Bolivian economy, of maintaining consistently an equilibrium in the balance of payments, and using investments efficiently" (Ministerio de Planeamiento y Coordinación 1989, 43).

This statement reflects the current belief in Bolivia. Notwithstanding this, we know that growth has been slow to return, and income per capita has re-

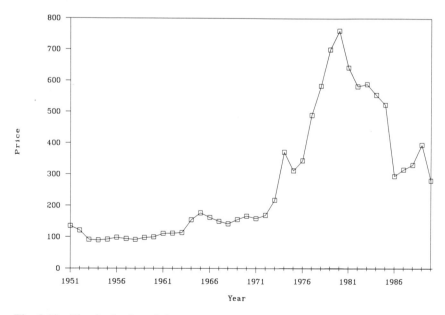

Fig. 8.12   Nominal price of tin
Source: International Financial Statistics.

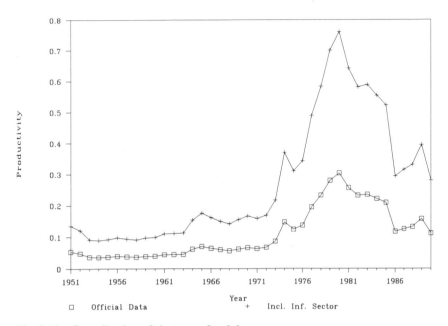

Fig. 8.13   Contribution of tin to productivity

mained at best stagnant (see figs. 8.1 and 8.2). Productivity, as measured by
TFP, has remained stable at a level similar to that of 1985. This seems to contradict the previous result that the reduction in inflation has boosted productivity at 20%; the additional factor to be considered is the price of tin. Prior to
the outset of the debt crisis Bolivia suffered a drastic reduction in the price of
tin, its main export product. The price of tin (dollars per pound) fell in nominal
terms from 7.61 in 1980 to 6.39 in 1981 and 5.78 in 1982, and in 1985 from
5.38 to 2.57. Figure 8.12 shows the nominal price of tin, and figure 8.13 shows
the contribution of tin to TFP. As can be seen, between 1985 and 1986 the
economy experienced a drastic decline in productivity due to this channel. Decreased inflation managed to counteract this decline. The overall effect was to
leave productivity virtually unchanged. (In the case of data for the informal
sector, TFP actually increases after 1985; i.e., stabilization more than compensated the decrease in productivity induced by the fall in tin prices.)

Compare Bolivia's experience in the 1950s. The stabilization program of
1956 was as successful in halting inflation as the 1985 stabilization. But as can
be seen from table 8.2, it was eleven years before productivity again reached
the value achieved in 1956. It did so due to the increase in mineral products,
an event completely exogenous to policy variables. The outlook for the 1990s
appears more favorable. Even though the price of tin plunged after 1985, productivity has remained constant or has slightly increased.

8.5.2   Structural Reform and Productivity

The stabilization program also implemented a sweeping reform in trade and financial markets (see Morales and Sachs 1989). In order to show the effects of these reforms on the economy, an independent measure of productivity was estimated for different industrial sectors.[20] Figure 8.14 shows the average yearly increase or decrease in productivity between 1986 and 1989 for a number of industrial sectors. The sectors are numbered following the Bolivian classification (see appendix). I chose industrial sectors not related to mining in order to discuss the implications beyond the effect of mineral prices on productivity. In addition I have used the period 1986–90 in order to avoid the big fluctuations induced by hyperinflation. The estimates are computed using data on total employment, value added, and investment by industrial sector. The employment data allowed computation of the labor share, while from investment a measure of the capital stock was estimated. Consumption of electricity was used as a proxy, though very imperfect, of capacity utilization. (For a more detailed description of the corresponding sectors and methodology, see the appendix.) Despite the assumptions, no strong productivity increase reveals itself clearly. Figure 8.14 shows that only seven out of seventeen sectors experienced a positive productivity shock during this period. There is no clear pattern of industry type in which sectoral productivity has been particularly boosted. The upper range of manufacturing starting in the 360s (nonmetallic products) and 381 (metallic products) seems to be the most favored. On the other hand productivity in the chemical industry (350s) seems to have uniformly deteriorated, sector 356 (plastic products) exhibiting the largest drop in productivity. It is difficult to infer much from these numbers, except that there is no clear upward trend in productivity arising from the current reforms. This study has the virtue of finally measuring these effects and therefore allowing serious evaluation of the structural reform programs.

The results presented in figure 8.14 are interesting because they suggest that the effects of structural adjustment on productivity (and therefore on capital accumulation) may not be immediate. Taking figure 8.14 literally would suggest that productivity actually deteriorates in the short run, while Edwards (chap. 1 in this volume) shows that structural reform significantly improves productivity in the long run. This is important because many countries implementing structural reform programs expect quick improvements in productivity as a consequence of structural adjustment. Combining these two results suggests the existence of a J-curve to structural adjustment. A J-curve may exist for two reasons.

First, there is a need for industrial reconversion when relative prices are changed. In the presence of irreversible investments this may lead to decreases

---

20. Because industrial sector price indices are used, the relative price measure problem is non-existent in these estimates.

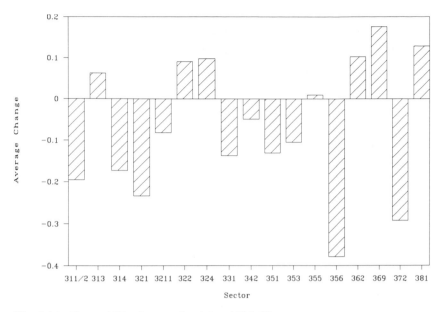

Fig. 8.14   Poststabilization productivity, 1986–89
Source: Based on data provided by Instituto Nacional de Estadísticas.

in productivity as firms use less than optimal production techniques to accommodate their equipment to the new production mix. The striking decrease in tin prices, for example, will induce a significant reconversion of industrial production. Such a reconversion is basically equivalent in the context of irreversible investments to a loss of part of the capital stock. If the price of tin falls to zero, for example, all the investment specific to tin production losses its value. True enough, much of the equipment or the training of the labor force will be substituted into other areas of production. But as the experience of Eastern Europe suggests, this is not a painless process and entails an important decrease in the total level of output.

Second, there is the issue of partial reform. When only some sectors of the economy are deregulated, distortions can be exponentiated. For example, imagine that wood is used both for boxes and for house construction. Say that initially the price of wood is regulated and equal across sectors, but with chronic excess demand. The government, in its attempt to deregulate, decides to free the price of wood used for house construction. Immediately the price of wood for housing purposes will jump, and no more wood will be allocated to production of boxes. Of course this may have very negative effects on the distribution process for other products and a significant negative effect on total productivity. Both mechanisms are at work. The experience of East Germany, which completed its reform quickly and across the board, suggests that the industrial reconversion hypothesis cannot be easily dismissed.

What the numbers indicate from the "model" case of Bolivia is that policymakers should not expect wonders from price liberalization or trade reform. Even less should they expect important effects in the short run.

8.6 Other Important Issues

We turn now to the discussion of additional factors to consider when evaluating the growth possibilities of the Bolivian economy. These include the possibility of development traps, the importance of human capital, the role of the financial sector, the importance of "animal spirits," and income distribution considerations.

8.6.1 Development Traps

The J-curve of structural reform can have long-run detrimental effects on the level of output in the presence of development traps, as it may shift the economy to a completely different equilibrium. Azariadis (1992) has suggested that development traps are very likely to appear once we depart slightly from the traditional assumptions of neoclassical growth models. For development traps to appear, the savings rate must increase very rapidly with the level of income, so that it is possible to sustain a high level of capital accumulation (because then income and savings are high) but also a low level of capital accumulation (where both income and savings are low). This may happen due to externalities (increasing returns to scale) or to saving behavior differing between capital and labor owners (the traditional renditions for the existence of development traps), but also to Leontief technologies (because factor payments change drastically beyond a certain level of the capital stock), subsistence consumption levels, and endogenous population growth. The presence of development traps makes a compelling argument for government intervention. This argument was implicitly behind many development programs like the "big-push" ideas during the postwar period. A consensus on whether these programs work is still to be achieved. I return to this point below.

Figure 8.15 shows the drastic decline in the capital stock per capita during the 1980s. The capital stock, estimated by Huarachi (1988), does not include capital gains and losses implied by changes in relative prices. Therefore it probably underestimates the decline in the level of the capital stock experienced during the 1980s.

The development trap model suggests that a collapse in the capital stock will lead to such impoverishment that savings and capital accumulation will fall even further. The average investment rate for 1972–77 was 16.31% of GDP; the corresponding investment figures for the 1980s are shown in table 8.6. While investment has fallen (a reflection of the collapse of mineral products, the shrinking of the government, and hyperinflation), the collapse has not been massive. Additional evidence is presented in figure 8.7, in which we see that the capital contribution has recovered extremely quickly (at least as compared with the 1956 stabilization). Due to this recent recovery of investment

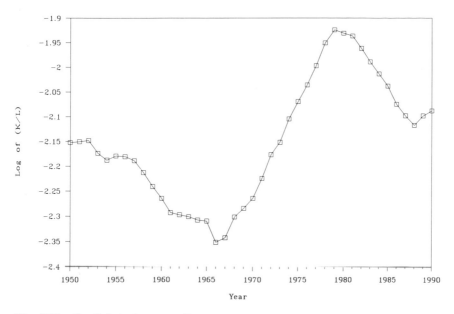

Fig. 8.15   Capital stock per capita
Source: Based on data from Huarachi (1988).

rates, it is safe to argue that there is no serious evidence of a development trap in the case of Bolivia.

8.6.2   Human Capital

The role of human capital has been emphasized in the new growth literature as a potential source of long-run growth. The highly educated labor force in Korea, Mexico, and Brazil has been argued to be an important element in ex plaining those countries' growth performance. Estimates in cross-country growth regressions have reinforced the notion that human capital accumulation is fundamental for growth. Barro (1991) estimates that an increase in 10% of the enrollment ratio in secondary education increases the growth rate by 0.3%. Similarly, for primary education the growth rate increases by 0.25%. These numbers suggest that a strategy of development of human capital resources is necessary and should be recommended.

Table 8.7 shows the evolution of some human capital indicators. The table shows that progress was made even during the 1980s. Still, these improvements seem not to have spurred any substantial growth, so the question remains, why did Bolivia not attain significant growth during the 1980s, when illiteracy rates fell by 50%.[21]

---

21. Human capital indicators were not included in the regression analysis because of the scattered nature of the data. Still, I have shown that the other variables accounted for about 80% of the variability of TFP and that this TFP was a stationary series. Both elements indicate that it is unlikely that human capital has played a very significant role.

Table 8.6   **Investment Rates**

Year	Investment Rate (% of GDP)	Year	Investment Rate (% of GDP)
1980	14.25	1985	9.48
1981	13.77	1986	9.47
1982	10.24	1987	9.72
1983	7.94	1988	9.66
1984	10.43	1989	10.14

Sources: Banco Central de Bolivia and Instituto Nacional de Estadísticas.

Table 8.7   **Human Capital Indicators**

	1965	1980	1988	1989
Primary enrollment				
Total	73			81
Female	60			77
Secondary enrollment				
Total	18			34
Female	15			31
Tertiary enrollment	5			23
Illiteracy		36.8	18.3	
Urban		15.2	7.7	
Rural		53.1	31.1	
Infant mortality		123	102	

Source: World Bank (1990); *World Development Report* (1992).

Most growth models that discuss the role of human capital (in particular Lucas 1988) assume a stock of human capital that is passed on, accumulating forever, from parents to children. But education and knowledge are not similar to physical endowments and do not accumulate automatically, as they are constrained to an individual person and disappear with him or her. In school we spend most of our time studying what our parents, and their parents, had to study: how to learn and write. If this is true, we should not expect human capital to increase significantly through time and become a thriving force of economic development, except for countries experiencing quick progress in literacy and enrollment rates. Even so, it is not clear whether these indicators properly capture progress in human capital development.

The literature has stressed two measures of human capital, average level (because it potentiates interactions and therefore individual productivity) and total level (because one profits from a general externality). Here I claim that the distribution of the human capital is important as well. Figure 8.16 shows the distribution of basic services and some human capital indicators by language spoken. I divide the population into Spanish, bilingual, and native (Aymara and Quechua) speakers. The first four categories represent basic services, the last five education indicators. As can be observed, there is a major difference among language groups. If one group lags behind in its human capital skills, then the economy will have to adjust to the human capital of that group to interact at all with those agents. Imagine two agents who want to communicate in writing. If one does not know how to read and write, there is no point for the other to improve his literary skills. Distribution matters, and the production function in human capital models should perhaps have a term that resembles a Leontief production function ($F(K, L, H)$ where $H = \min(h_1, h_2)$). If this is correct, a basic implication is that more effort should be made to homogenize the provision of human capital across different social groups.

8.6.3   Financial Markets

Growth performance cannot be independent of financial markets. The process of capital accumulation cannot be supported if there are no mechanisms that allow savings to be allocated into investment projects. If savings are not intermediated through the financial sector, the chain between savings and capital accumulation underscored in the neoclassical growth theory is broken, and there is no possibility of growth. The distinction that is relevant here is that between a "storage" and an "investment" economy. If people save by storing goods, this does not allow buildup of the capital stock, and growth will not happen; it is necessary then to transfer the savings from storage to the financial sector. In this sense the long-run effects of hyperinflation may be very positive.

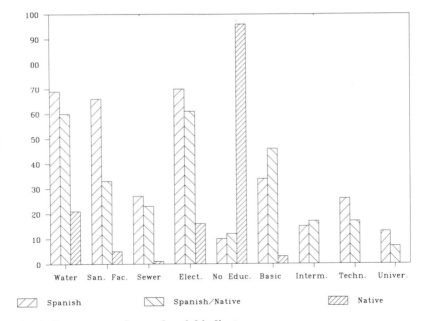

Fig. 8.16   Language spoken and social indicators
Source: World Bank (1990).

By developing the financial sector, ever-increasing savings are intermediated to productive activities.[22]

Both interest rates, that is the incentive to save, and the characteristics of the institutional system are fundamental for this transmission process. High reserve requirements will reduce the amount of credit; regulated interest rates will reduce the incentive to save. Savings have fallen since the collapse of tin prices and the stabilization program (see table 8.5), and while there is a steady recovery, the level of savings remains well below historical averages. Low savings may be a reflection of expectations of transitory low levels of income.

Other institutional arrangements also contribute to low savings. The Aymara communities, for example, have implicit (informal) arrangements by which those individuals with unexpectedly high income (unexpected good harvest) have to transfer some of their income to the less fortunate. These schemes are possibly welfare enhancing, as they permit avoiding very low consumption levels, but they also induce a lower degree of overall savings.[23]

8.6.4   Multiplicity and Animal Spirits

Animal spirits have been emphasized since Keynes and Schumpeter as important driving forces of growth and business cycles. Korea, Brazil, and Chile are usually portrayed as countries in which the "excitement" of entrepreneurs is sufficient to keep the country growing. Recently, the big-push ideas have been formalized in the context of imperfect competition models by Murphy, Shleifer, and Vishny (1989a, 1989b). The idea is simple: in the presence of imperfect competition, pecuniary externalities matter. If the level of activity is believed to be low, then it does not pay to finance high levels of fixed investment, which in turn contributes to keeping output low. An alternative equilibrium is one in which everybody believes output will be high, investments look ex ante profitable, and entrepreneurs finance high investment levels. This in turn sustains the high output level. In addition to development issues there is some evidence on the relation between animal spirits and business cycles. Farmer and Guo (1992) have shown that fluctuations in consumer confidence permits replication of most of the characteristics of business fluctuations for the United States.

What assessment can be made of this mechanism? The multiplicity story is true in the presence of effective lack of demand, and therefore may be true only for closed economies. A small open economy cannot face an effective lack of demand. But for primary products, such as Bolivia's mineral exports, the argument does not hold (even taking into account that the Tin International

22. In addition, it has recently been argued that financial development allows better information revelation and therefore better decisions (see Greenwood and Jovanovic 1991).

23. Those individuals who are successful and do not abide by these social rules are in general discriminated against and rejected from the community.

agreements and the bilateral negotiations with Argentina regarding gas exports provide some imperfect competition characteristics even to these markets.)

In one dimension the model may, nevertheless, be relevant. This dimension includes the issue of capital repatriation. Dornbusch (1990) develops a model in which there is multiplicity in the rate of returns on capital, depending on the degree of capital repatriation.

The issue is polemic because it leads to recommendation of extensive government support for investment projects, while extensive evidence in Latin America indicates that these policies are very negative in the long run. Long periods of high subsidies have allowed the existence of a protected and inefficient industrial sector. The reason is that protective policies are time inconsistent (Tornell 1991) and affect the incentives of firms. If the subsidy will always be there, no incentive exists for becoming efficient.

8.6.5   Development Paths

Ed Leamer (1987) has coined the expression "paths of development" to characterize the evolution of output and factor prices as factor accumulation takes place. In standard neoclassical growth models there is only one path of development, and that is with capital accumulation and increasing real wages. If the model allows for more than two factors of production and more than one good, then the evolution of real wages and the return to real factors of production may not be monotonic.

For Bolivia, figure 8.17 shows a triangle of factor endowments. It represents all possible combinations of land, labor, and capital the economy may have. The endowment of factors of production will change as development takes place.

The economy can produce two industrial commodities (which do not use land): a labor-intensive and a capital intensive good. The economy can also produce a good called "cattle," which uses only land and labor, or a good called "coca" or soybeans, which uses the three factors of production. The exact location of the corners depends on technology, and the partition of the triangle depends on final goods prices (see Leamer 1987). In the upper-left triangle capital is very scarce and both cattle and coca are produced; the return to capital is very high. In the lower-right triangle capital is very abundant, and only coca and the capital-intensive industrial products are produced; the return to capital is relatively low. A path of development following the arrow indicates an increase in capital and in land/labor ratio. Real wages in general increase along this development path but fall in the transition from the upper-left triangle to the next. The composition of the production mix now supports a lower real wage. It is not unlikely that this development path will find strong political opposition. For Bolivia this is a critical issue because the development of the economy has been characterized by an increase in the importance of the lowlands, and therefore by an important change in relative factor endowments, with an increase in the endowment of arable land.

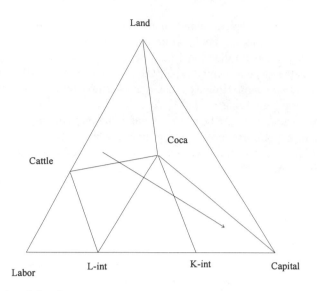

Fig. 8.17   Paths of development

8.6.6   Income Distribution

It has been argued in our discussion of human capital that Bolivia presents sectorial and ethnic segmentation. In addition income distribution is very regressive. Lorenz curves have been computed for 1982, 1985, and 1988. The distribution of income seems to look rather constant across time, especially between 1982 and 1988. In both cases the poorest 30% of the population earns about 10% of income and the poorest 50% of the population earns 20% of income. In 1985 the richest 5% had doubled its income relative to 1982, but this increase seems to have faded as stability consolidated. This strong effect of inflation on income distribution is consistent with the findings in Cardoso, Paes de Barros, and Urani (chap. 5 of this volume) for Brazil.[24]

Perotti (1990) stresses the relation between income distribution and human capital formation. In poor societies a very regressive income distribution may make the accumulation of human capital impossible for wide sectors of the population. The economy then finds it impossible to take off. Inequality also feeds into the political process by calling for radicalization and transfers. If this leads to higher capital taxes, it may reduce equilibrium growth, as suggested in Alesina and Rodrik (1991) and Persson and Tabellini (1991). The argument is that very unequal societies will tend to have higher taxation of capital; this in turn will translate into less growth.

24. Extreme inflation tends to deteriorate income distribution because some agents in the economy do not have access to financial adaptation technologies. See Sturzenegger (1992a, 1992b).

Recently Bolivia has followed the trend in Latin America toward more moderate economic policy, and political polarization is not a major threat at the moment. This has also been helped by the changes in the world and in other Latin American countries, which tend to suggest the possibility of successful reform programs. But countries also experience inverted-U Kuznets curves of income distribution; how long political moderation will last is an open question.

Income distribution has certainly been a major concern in Bolivia's policy making. Land reform was a major political event that still accounts for most of the support received by the MNR. Unfortunately, land reform did not improve income distribution significantly. When in power, the MNR implemented a promised land reform by which estates in the altiplano were divided and allocated to individual families. Landowners were compensated with large estates in the (at that time) underdeveloped area of Santa Cruz. Unfortunately, this meant that peasants were constrained to remain at a single location in the altiplano, which cannot support a family all year long. Indians used to move during the winter to the valley, or *yungas,* which is better for winter agriculture. Anthropologists point to the discontinuous space conception of Aymara Indians, who were used to this migration process. Land reform prevented this migration from taking place, and poverty therefore increased significantly in the altiplano.

8.7 Conclusion

Given the facts discussed in section 8.6, can something be done to stimulate the sluggish growth performance of the Bolivian economy?

Godoy and De Franco (1991) argue that Bolivia has to rediscover itself. But what does that mean? Does it mean extensive government intervention, strong laissez-faire, or a balance of both? Latin America and the world in general have recently undergone a major transformation in terms of acceptable economic policies. A shift toward free markets and international integration, pioneered by Chile and Mexico, followed by Bolivia, Argentina, and to a lesser extent other Latin American countries, is generally attributed to three main causes: (1) exhaustion of a given economic model as represented by the import-substitution, inward-orientation, high-deficit strategies of the past (see Vial 1992); (2) ideological change induced by exogenous factors, such as the relative success of the economic policies of the Reagan and Thatcher administrations and the collapse of communism (see Cardoso's chapter in Vial 1992); (3) implementation of International Monetary Fund and World Bank reform programs.

These three factors are relevant in the real world, and Bolivia has not been immune to any of them. Therefore the prevailing mood is one of minimal government control and regulation. This mood has been reflected in many countries through widespread programs of privatization and deregulation. While Bolivia was a pioneer in macroeconomic reform, it has so far been unable to launch a significant privatization program. This can be an important drawback if partial reforms are important but has given Bolivia time to learn from the hasty privatization attempts of its neighbors. In Argentina privatization seems a desperate attempt to signal a change of policy rather than an effort to increase the efficiency of the economy; that is, privatization is taking place without any regulatory framework and with extensive monopoly concessions granted to the new owners. It is likely that there will be efficiency gains as principal-agent problems and the level of corruption decline significantly. But the current situation will lead to major departures from optimal pricing which Bolivia should try to avoid.

Barro (1990b) has emphasized the relation between government infrastructure and growth. He claims a nonlinear relation between the two variables. If infrastructure is very low, there is a positive association between infrastructure and growth, while beyond a certain threshold the relation runs in the opposite direction because the tax burden on the private sector more than outweighs the benefits of a larger infrastructure. Government spending has been historically allocated to subsidies, inefficient projects with no clear public service component, and administrative bureaucracy. The challenge of the new leadership is to allocate the properly financed (i.e., not with monetary creation) government resources to badly needed public goods and infrastructure.[25] The government should continue its program of structural reform, but not allow the current tide of minimalist government to interfere with the realization that it has, through the building of infrastructure, a significant role to play in increasing Bolivia's productivity. To some extent this message seems to be taken into account. Table 8.8 shows the percentage of GDP allocated by the nonfinancial public sector to capital spending. The recovery is healthy, bringing capital spending back to the levels of the early 1980s, though not yet making up for years of low capital spending.

A development policy might possibly use alternative models of development such as the Japanese and Korean. Contrary to mainstream thought, I believe that the main factor behind the strong growth performance of these economies is not industrial targeting and R&D but the existence of tight links between firms and the banking sector. In Japan the *keiretsu* is an industrial conglomerate that, headed by a financial institution, owns and controls a wide variety of vertically and horizontally integrated firms. This system (similar to the Korean *jaebuls*) may provide implicit insurance and allow a reduction in the strong level of asymmetric information present in credit markets, thereby deblocking and allowing implementation of profitable projects, which a completely decentralized market cannot achieve. Of course, this institutional framework cannot arbitrarily be put in place. There is not even a compelling argument for think-

25. For example, it takes, even today, two days to travel from La Paz to Santa Cruz.

Table 8.8   **Capital Expenditures as a Percentage of GDP**

Year	Capital Spending	Year	Capital Spending
1980	7.39	1985	3.34
1981	6.10	1986	4.58
1982	5.93	1987	5.34
1983	4.24	1988	6.84
1984	3.73	1989	5.81

Source: Unidad de Análisis de Política Económica.

ing that it may be appropriate to Bolivia. In Japan it appeared as a historical derivation of the *zaibatsu,* and there may be important thresholds both in size and in endowment of human capital that may make the system work. Whether these institutions would spring up from decentralized markets is yet to be seen and is an important topic for further research, as are the mechanisms by which the government could help in its implementation.

I have stressed the importance of financial institutions and of financial sector development in transforming a stagnant storage economy into a growing capital accumulation economy. Much of the work has been done by the high-inflation experience of the mid-1980s. It is the task of the government not to mingle with the financial sector to the point where some of these gains are lost. I have also stressed the important negative effects of inflation. Maintenence of stabilization should also be considered a priority for the government, even more so in the presence of a very dollarized financial sector. Finally, I have stressed the need to homogenize the provision of human capital across agents, and have pointed to possible income distribution problems along the current development path; the government should be active in neutralizing and compensating some of these changes. Bolivia can spare some active redistribution; it cannot afford to have its development path blocked.

Appendix

Proof of Tax Policy

For the model of section 8.3 the policymaker maximizes workers income,

(A1) $$I^w = (1 - \alpha)B(1 - \psi)(\phi z)^\alpha + g,$$

subject to the budget constraint of the government that includes taxes either on consumption (ψ) and on mining production (τ),

(A2) $$g = \psi B(\phi z)^\alpha + \tau A((1 - \phi)z)^\beta.$$

The first-order conditions of this problem, assuming an interior solution, can be reduced to the equation

(A3) $\phi^\alpha \alpha z^{\alpha-1} \dfrac{\partial z}{\partial \tau} + \dfrac{A}{B}((1 - \phi)z)^\beta + \dfrac{A}{B} \tau \beta (1 - \phi)^\beta z^{\beta-1} \dfrac{\partial z}{\partial \tau} = 0,$

plus the budget constraint. Implicit differentiation of the system of equations (A2) and (A3) gives the result

(A4) $\dfrac{d\tau}{d\frac{A}{B}} > 0.$

Total Factor Productivity

The computation of TFP for industrial sectors implied the following steps. First a measure of real output was obtained by deflating nominal sectoral value added by the industrial sector price index. Employment in number of hours of labor was provided as data. Total income accrued to that labor was also given as data and used to compute the labor share. Computation of capital was by the inventory accrual method based on the investment figures provided for the corresponding years. Adjustments were made to account for the change in number of firms surveyed each year. Once both capital and labor shares are computed, TFP computation is straightforward. The numbers presented are the average for the periods and sectors considered.

The sectors are

311/2	Food products	351	Chemical industry
313	Beverages	353	Oil refineries
314	Tobacco	355	Rubber products
321	Textiles	356	Plastics
3211	Apparel	362	Glass and derivatives
322	Clothing	369	Nonmetallic products
324	Shoes	372	Nonferric metals
331	Wood products	381	Metallic products
342	Printing		

References

Alesina, Alberto, and Dani Rodrik. 1991. Distributive Politics and Economic Growth. NBER Working Paper no. 3668. Cambridge, MA: National Bureau of Economic Research.

Azariadis, Costas. 1992. Poverty Traps in Convex Economies. University of California, Los Angeles. Mimeo.

Ball, Laurence, and David Romer. 1992. Inflation and the Informativeness of Prices. University of California, Berkeley. Mimeo.

Barro, Robert. 1990a. Comment on "Extreme Inflation, Dynamics, and Stabilization" by Rudiger Dornbusch, Federico Sturzenegger, and Holger Wolf. *Brookings Papers on Economic Activity* 2:68–75.

———. 1990b. Government Spending in a Simple Model of Endogeneous Growth *Journal of Political Economy* 98 (5), pt. 2: S103–25.

———. 1991. Economic Growth in a Cross Section of Countries. *Quarterly Journal of Economics* 106(2): 407–44.

Centro de Estudios de Mineria y Desarrollo (CEMYD). 1989. *Desempeno y Colapso de la Mineria Nacionalizada en Bolivia.* La Paz: CEMYD.

De Gregorio, José. 1991. Inflation, Taxation, and Long-Run Growth. International Monetary Fund. Mimeo.

———. 1992. Economic Growth in Latin America. *Journal of Development Economics* 39 (1): 59–84.

de Pablo, Juan Carlos, and Alfonso Martinez. 1989. *Argentina: A Successful Case of Underdevelopment Process.* Buenos Aires. Mimeo.

Dollar, David. 1988. The Factor Price Equalization Model and Industry Labor Productivity: An Empirical Test across Countries. In R. Feenstra, ed., *Empirical Methods for International Trade.* Cambridge: MIT Press.

Doria Medina, Samuel. 1986. *La Economia Informal en Bolivia.* La Paz: Unidad de Análisis de Política Económica.

Dornbusch, Rudiger. 1990. Short Term Macroeconomic Policies for Stabilization and Growth. Mimeo.

Dornbusch, Rudiger, Federico Sturzenegger, and Holger Wolf. 1990. Extreme Inflation: Stabilization and Dynamics. *Brookings Papers on Economic Activity* 2:1–84.

Drazen, Allan, and Vittorio Grilli. 1990. The Benefits of Crises for Economic Reform. NBER Working Paper no. 3668. Cambridge, MA: National Bureau of Economic Research.

Eder, G. 1968. *Inflation and Development in Latin America: A Case History of Inflation and Stabilization in Bolivia.* Michigan International Business Studies no. 8. Ann Arbor: University of Michigan Press.

Edwards, Sebastian. 1989. *Real Exchange Rates, Devaluation, and Adjustment.* Cambridge: MIT Press.

Engle, Robert, and Clive Granger. 1987. Cointegration and Error Correction: Representation, Estimation, and Testing. *Econometrica* 55 (2): 251–76.

Engle, Robert, and Byung Sam Yoo. 1987. Forecasting and Testing in Co-integrated Systems. *Journal of Econometrics* 35:143–59.

Farmer, Roger, and Jang-Tin Guo. 1992. Real Business Cycles and the Animal Spirits Hypothesis. University of California, Los Angeles. Mimeo.

Fischer, Stanley. 1991. Growth, Macroeconomics, and Development. In O. Blanchard and S. Fischer, eds., *NBER Macroeconomics Annual.* Cambridge, MA: MIT Press.

Fischer, Stanley, and Franco Modigliani. 1978. Towards Understanding the Real Effects and Costs of Inflation. In *The Collected Papers of Franco Modigliani,* 5:280–303. Cambridge: MIT Press, 1989.

Godoy, Ricardo, and Mario De Franco. 1990. The Economic Consequences of Cocaine Production in Bolivia: Historical, Local, and Macroeconomic Perspectives. Harvard Institute for International Development. Mimeo.

———. 1991. The Untraveled Road: Non-economic Barriers to Growth in Bolivia. Harvard Institute for International Development. Mimeo.

Greenwood, Jeremy, and Boyce Jovanovic. 1991. Financial Development, Growth, and the Distribution of Income. *Journal of Political Economy* 98 (5), pt. 1: 1076–1107.

Griliches, Zvi, and Vidar Ringstad. 1971. *Economies of Scale and the Form of the Production Function.* Amsterdam: North-Holland.

Gutierrez and Pando. 1989. *La Problematic de la Coca y su Relación con la Producción de la Cocaina.* La Paz: Ministerio de Asuntos Campesinos y Agropecuarios.

Huarachi, Guarachi. 1988. Estimación del Stock de Capital Fisico Total de la Economia Boliviana. Unidad de Análisis de Política Económica. La Paz. Mimeo.

Jones, Larry, and Rodi Manuelli. 1990. A Convex Model of Equilibrium Growth: Theory and Policy Implications. *Journal of Political Economy* 98 (5), pt. 1: 1008–38.

Kormendi, Roger, and Philip Meguire. 1985. Macroeconomic Determinants of Growth, Cross-Country Evidence. *Journal of Monetary Economics* 16:141–63.

Krueger, Anne, Maurice Schiff, and Alberto Valdes, eds. 1992. *The Political Economy of Agricultural Price Policy.* Baltimore: Johns Hopkins University Press.

Labán, Raúl, and Federico Sturzenegger. 1992a. Distributional Conflict, Financial Adaptation, and Delayed Stabilizations. University of California, Los Angeles. Mimeo.

———. 1992b. Fiscal Conservatism as a Response to the Debt Crises. University of California, Los Angeles. Mimeo.

Leamer, Edward. 1987. Paths of Development in the Three-Factor, *n*-Good General Equilibrium Model. *Journal of Political Economy* 95 (5): 961–99.

Lucas, Robert. 1988. On the Mechanics of Economic Development. *Journal of Monetary Economics* 22:3–42.

Ministerio de Planeamiento y Coordinación. 1989. *Estrategia de Desarrollo Económico y Social, 1989–2000.* La Paz: Republica de Bolivia.

Morales, Juan Antonio. 1988. La Inflación y la Estabilización en Bolivia. In M. Bruno, G. DiTella, R. Dornbusch, and S. Fischer, eds., *Inflación y Estabilización la Experiencia de Israel, Argentina, Brasil, Bolivia, y Mexico.* Mexico: El Trimestre Económico.

———. 1991. The Transition from Stabilization to Sustained Growth in Bolivia. In M. Bruno, S. Fischer, E. Helpman, N. Liviatan, and L. Meridor, eds., *Lessons of Economic Stabilization and Its Aftermath.* Cambridge: MIT Press.

———. 1992. Bolivia's Tin and Natural Gas Crises of 1985–1989. Documento de Trabajo 4/92. Instituto de Investigaciones Socioeconomicas, Unviersidad Católica Boliviana.

Morales, Juan Antonio, Justo Espejo, and Gonzalo Chavez. 1992. Shocks Externos Transitorios y Politicas de Estabilización para Bolivia. Documento de Trabajo 2/92, Instituto de Investigaciones Socioeconomicas, Universidad Católica Boliviana.

Morales, Juan Antonio, and Jeffrey Sachs. 1989. Bolivia's Economic Crises. In J. Sachs, ed., *Developing Country Debt and Economic Performance.* Chicago: University of Chicago Press.

Murphy, Kevin, Andrei Shleifer, and Robert Vishny. 1989a. Income Distribution, Market Size, and Industrialization. *Quarterly Journal of Economics* 104 (3): 357–64.

———. 1989b. Industrialization and the Big Push. *Journal of Political Economy* 97 (5): 1003–26.

National Narcotics Intelligence Consumer Committee (NNICC). 1989. *Narcotics Intelligence Estimate.* Washington, DC: Drug Enforcement Agency.

Pereira, Rene, Jaime Montano, and Moises Calle. 1991. Bolivia: Movimientos Migratorios, Estrategia de la Población, y Efectos de las Politicas de Ajuste Estructural. La Paz, July.

Perotti, Roberto. 1990. Political Equilibrium, Income Distribution, and Growth. MIT. Mimeo.

Persson, Torsten, and Guido Tabellini. 1991. Is Inequality Harmful for Growth? Theory and Evidence. University of California Berkeley Working Paper no. 91-155.

Rebelo, Sergio. 1991. Long-Run Policy Analysis and Long-Run Growth. *Journal of Political Economy* 99 (3): 500–521.

Romer, Paul. 1986. Increasing Returns and Long-Run Growth. *Journal of Political Economy* 94:1002–37.

Roubini, Nouriel, and Xavier Sala-i-Martin. 1992. A Growth Model of Inflation, Tax Evasion, and Financial Repression. NBER Working Paper no. 4062. Cambridge, MA: National Bureau of Economic Research.

Sala-i-Martin, Xavier. 1990a. Lectures on Economic Growth I. NBER Working Paper no. 3564. Cambridge, MA: National Bureau of Economic Research.

———. 1990b. Lectures on Economic Growth II. NBER Working Paper no. 3565. Cambridge, MA. National Bureau of Economic Research.

Schiff, Maurice, and Alberto Valdes. 1992. "Effects of Intervention on Price Variability." In Anne Krueger, Maurice Schiff, and Alberto Valdes, eds., *The Political Economy of Agricultural Pricing Policies,* vol. 4, *A Synthesis of the Economies in Developing Countries,* chap. 13. Balitmore: Johns Hopkins University Press.

Sturzenegger, Federico. 1992a. Currency Substitution and the Regressivity of Inflationary Taxation. *Revista de Analisis Económico* 7, (1): 177–92.

———. 1992b. Inflation and Social Welfare in a Model with Endogenous Financial Adaptation. NBER Working Paper no. 4103. Cambridge, MA: National Bureau of Economic Research.

Sturzenegger, Federico, and Mariano Tommasi. 1992. Deadlock Societies, the Allocation of Time, and Growth Performance. UCLA Working Paper no. 660.

Tommasi, Mariano. 1992. The Welfare Effects of Inflation: The Consequences of Price Instability on Search Markets. University of California, Los Angeles. Mimeo.

Tornell, Aaron. 1991. Time Inconsistency of Protectionist Programs. *Quarterly Journal of Economics* 106 (August): 963–74.

Velasco, Andrés. 1992. A Model of Fiscal Deficits and Delayed Fiscal Reforms. CV Starr Center for Applied Economics no. 92/06. New York University.

Vial, Juan. 1992. *Adonde va America Latina? Balance de las Reformas Económicas.* Santiago: Corporación de Investigaciones Economicas para Latinoamerica.

Wang, Fang-Yi. 1990. Reconsidering the "East Asian Model of Development": The Link between Exports and Productivity Enhancement Evidence from Taiwan. University of California, Los Angeles. Mimeo.

World Bank. 1990. *Bolivia: Poverty Report.* Washington, DC: World Bank.

World Bank. 1992. *World Development Report.* Washington, DC: World Bank.

Comment on Chapters 7 and 8   Jacques Trigo-Loubière

Comment on Chapter 7

One of the paper's main virtues is its recognition of the need for the reform process to be steadily pursued for years to come if the cumulative structural distortions of the Argentine economy of the last few decades are to be corrected.

However, while I agree that the reform process will continue for a prolonged period, I wonder whether this does not clash somewhat with the conclusion

Jacques Trigo-Loubière is chief of the Country Economics Division at the Inter-American Development Bank and former president of the Central Bank of Bolivia.

reached at the end of the paper, that "another devaluation would . . . risk an outbreak of another inflation wave." The reasons for avoiding devaluation would appear to be rather seductive in the short term; but in the longer-term context, which, I repeat, the paper rightly recognizes, currency appreciation may become untenable. All the more so if wage pressures cannot be contained.

At the same time, the 1992 deterioration in the balance of trade suggests that if this situation persists for several financial periods it could become untenable and will call for corrective measures. Moreover, in the current context of globalization of markets, the need to maintain external competitiveness simply cannot be ignored; otherwise it could compromise the industrial reconversion program.

The paper recognizes the need to continue increasing fiscal savings. It would entail an enormous additional effort, since the already approved reform of the social security system would involve a 20% increase in budgetary expenditure. Nor does the paper mention the need to find a solution to the fiscal deficit problems that still persist in some provinces.

I agree that the strong inflation evident in the service sector is surprising and deserves more thorough analysis. Perhaps the reason is that the economic agents and consumers, long accustomed to existing in a climate of chronic inflation, are making no aggressive attempts to bring down prices. I understand that Minister Cavallo is constantly inciting the population to negotiate prices when they make a purchase or pay for a service, and I am convinced that this is essential for promoting consumer awareness.

Comment on Chapter 8

Federico Sturzenegger has prepared an interesting study in which he analyzes the performance of the Bolivian economy from a historical perspective, its sources of growth, and particularly the role of the mining and coca-producing sectors. I agree with many of his arguments and conclusions, but would like to touch on a few points where I consider his assertions to be erroneous. I will also touch on some aspects—not dealt with in the analysis, but which I feel need to be highlighted in the case of Bolivia—that address the legitimate concern reflected in the title of the paper.

The study concludes that political instability has had no significant impact on economic growth. I consider this assessment to be incorrect. The sharp decline in the gross domestic product and the high rate of inflation from the early to mid-1950s were preceded by a period of great political instability. More recently, the hyperinflation that peaked in 1985 was also largely due to political, social, and labor conflicts, which led Siles Zuazo, the president elected by an absolute majority of the votes, to demit office a year before his constitutional term was up.

The paper mentions at several points the impact of coca production on the Bolivian economy. It specifically states that the magnitude of the coca economy is equivalent to the gross national product. Reference is also made to a study that put cocaine production at $2 billion in 1985. Had this been the case, Bolivia would never have had a balance-of-payments problem, for at that time $2 billion represented four times the amount of exports.

I believe that the author is confusing the value of coca production with the value of cocaine on the streets of New York, which is certainly $2 billion. A paper prepared by the Analysis and Economic Policies Department of the Bolivian Ministry of Planning suggests that the inflow of foreign exchange generated by the coca economy amounted to $350 million, which would appear to be a more realistic figure.

While the mining industry's current and future importance for the Bolivian economy is indisputable, I do not share the view that there is no alternative sector that could compare to the role played by mining as a generator of foreign exchange. The outlook is good for natural gas and for agriculture, such as cultivation of soybeans, sorghum, and cotton in the eastern plains, especially in the Department of Santa Cruz, and all the more so if the highway projects and the waterway project are implemented.

Section 8.5, which deals with stabilization, reforms, and productivity, notes that, despite reforms in the financial and foreign-trade sectors, the industrial sector has not gained in productivity. On the basis of this finding, the author suggests that the structural reforms have had little impact on economic development. This assertion is certainly polemic, since the industrial sector has been growing at rates of over 5% since 1987, and because any estimate of capital stock must be viewed with great caution. In this regard, there is no explanation as to how the capital stock was measured.

I shall now deal with some of the problems that, to me, partly explain why the Bolivian economy, which has been achieving price stability, has still not attained high levels of economic growth and why the balance of payments is extremely fragile.

The Bolivian model presupposes that reduction of the role of the state would go hand in hand with the strengthening of the private sector, but this has not been the case. Private investment has displayed little momentum. Fixed private capital formation represented 5% of GDP in the last five years, whereas it accounted for 9% in the 1970s. What is the explanation for the attitude of the Bolivian entrepreneur and the foreign investor? I shall try to answer this.

With the change in government, private business stood back and waited, since one of the political parties that acceded to power had advocated throughout the electoral campaign a complete overhaul of the economic model.

With the new government's renewal of the ESAF (extended fund facility) agreement with the International Monetary Fund and the World Bank, the authorities sent out the important signal that the reform process would continue and that the economic model installed by the previous government was the one to follow. The reform process has been slow, however, and some of the ground rules that were thought to be permanent have changed over the years.

For instance, the Law on Tax Reform was altered with supreme decree

22555, which granted tax exemption to a substantial segment of the country's economy (small business) and constituted a clear infringement of the principle of universality of the tax system. Subsequently, tax on the net worth of businesses doubled from 1 to 2%, value-added tax rose from 10 to 13%, fuel taxes were raised with an increase in the price of gasoline from 30 cents to nearly 50 cents a liter, and the tax on beer was also increased. At the same time, public spending began to mount in order to finance excessive current expenditure.

The rational course would have been to cut down on state bureaucracy and refrain from sending out such a damaging signal that the fiscal balance was highly precarious. The precariousness of public finance was confirmed last year when the country failed to meet the fiscal targets agreed upon with the International Monetary Fund. According to preliminary information, it appears that those targets will not be met this year either. Consequently, the conclusion is that the fiscal balance has not been consolidated in the case of Bolivia, which is a sine qua non for maintaining internal stability.

Another change was eliminating the system of export incentives, with the promise that they would be replaced with a more rational system. So far this has not been done.

The Bolivian model also accorded great importance to foreign private investment as a means of boosting the economy. In this connection, a law on investments was promulgated, which meted out equal treatment to national and foreign investment. However, apart from one foreign investment to expand a gold deposit of a firm already in existence, there have been few foreign investments of any significance. This is explained by deplorable experiences such as failure to enter into a concrete agreement with a foreign firm to exploit the Lithium Corporation (LITCO), and the annulment of risk-sharing contracts between the state and local and foreign mining companies for working the Bolívar, Tasna, and Catavi mines. These have sent negative signals to foreign and local private investors alike.

At the same time, structural reforms have continued at a very slow pace.

There have been delays in bringing in thorough financial reform that would help mobilize savings for financing investment funding and credit democratization. The Bank Law has been "on the verge of approval" for over two years, although the government has a parliamentary majority. Also, the lending rate for both local and foreign currency has remained at very high levels, discouraging private investment. The local currency lending rate was 54% in October 1992, while inflation was 13% in the same month. The dollar lending rate was 19%.

Social security reform has been "under discussion for three years," and a proposal to introduce new instruments and mechanisms that would speed up the functioning of the stock market has yet to be studied by the financial authorities.

Early in 1992 the Reform of the Customs System was approved with much difficulty, and the privatization process was launched in the middle of the year.

Comment on Chapters 7 and 8   John Williamson

Rudiger Dornbusch's paper gives a graphic description of the sixty years of Argentina's economic decline, from its position as the seventh member of the contemporary version of the Group of Seven in the early 1930s to its reputation as a case study in economic failure by 1990. The causes of this dismal record were defiance of the rules of good economic management in both the micro- and macrodimensions: extreme import substitution, excessive regulation, and irrational subsidization on the one hand, and eternal fiscal deficits comple- mented by repeated overvaluations on the other hand. The question that Dorn- busch poses in his paper is whether the policy changes introduced by Domingo Cavallo in the last eighteen months, which have brought such hope to the Ar- gentine people, have finally broken the cycle of decline initiated by Peron's populism.

So far as microeconomics is concerned, the omens look propitious. The opening of the economy to both trade and foreign direct investment, deregula- tion, privatization, and now the reform of the social security system, look to be as irreversible as they were profound.

The macro-omens are less reassuring. Dornbusch enthuses that the tax yield in terms of dollars doubled between 1989 and 1991, but since table 7.4 shows a recovery in the tax yield of only 2.8% of GDP, to a level only 0.5% of GDP higher than in 1985, one has to worry that the doubling of the dollar yield is primarily a consequence of the increased dollar value of GDP resulting from real appreciation. One must then ask whether the improvement in tax perfor- mance is large enough—and permanent enough—to have eliminated all need for the inflation tax, understanding that the cornerstone of the current macro- strategy, the convertibility law that supposedly guarantees a fixed exchange rate against the U.S. dollar, excludes any significant future resort to the infla- tion tax.

Dornbusch argues that real appreciation has already—as so often in the past—led to a serious overvaluation of the peso. His evidence for this proposi- tion is hardly conclusive, even though he mentions no less than five measures based on two different concepts, four different price indices, and two different base periods, which one gathers are supposed to demonstrate overvaluation.[1]

John Williamson is a senior fellow of the Institute for International Economics.

1. One can trace changes in the ratio of the price of services to the price of goods—a proxy for the Chicago concept of the real exchange rate, the price of nontradables in terms of tradables— from table 7.9. CPI and WPI inflation are presented in figure 7.5; they suggest that Argentina has lost a lot of competitiveness, as measured by the more traditional concept of the real exchange rate as the relative price of two national outputs, in terms of the former—though not the latter— measure since March 1991. Table 7.10 shows two measures of the real effective exchange rate calculated by the Central Bank of Argentina, one import-weighted and one export-weighted (with- out any statement of the price index utilized, which is apparently a fifty-fifty mix of CPI and WPI), both based on the traditional concept of the real exchange rate, and both of which show a large real appreciation since the late 1980s.

An assertion that a currency is overvalued in comparison to its fundamental equilibrium exchange rate, or some analogous concept, needs to face squarely the difficulties of identifying the equilibrium rate. This is not to argue that the task of diagnosing overvaluation is impossible, but to urge that it needs to be treated seriously rather than dismissed with a few casual statistical comparisons, without even taking the trouble to argue that a particular base period has some claim to be considered an equilibrium.

In fact, Dornbusch's concern about overvaluation probably *is* merited. The next question that arises is what should be done about it. He offers us five alternatives: do not devalue but tough it out by following the gold standard rules of the game irrespective of cost; reinforce the first strategy of not devaluing by tightening fiscal policy, thus reducing the danger of a further accentuation of the overvaluation with its concomitant danger of undermining credibility; devalue one last time (as usual); start a crawling devaluation; and complete the process of dollarization. He advocates the second or fifth strategy, citing in support of his rejection of the devaluation options a *modelzinho* drawn from his earlier work that makes the point that Kiguel and Liviatan have emphasized, that an exchange rate–based stabilization brings an initial boom followed by the need for a prolonged recession in order to deflate prices back to equilibrium.

I endorse Dornbusch's rejection of the option of "one last devaluation." A promise of no subsequent devaluations would have zero credibility, and the whole stabilization program would probably collapse if its linchpin were removed by yet another surprise abrogation of the fixed-rate promise. It is good to see Dornbusch fulfilling the professional duty that often falls on practitioners of the dismal science to warn of the need for blood, sweat, and tears rather than nurturing populist hopes that instant activism can be guaranteed to get growth going again without painful delays.

Nevertheless, we also have a duty to minimize pain, something that nowadays we all believe can be promoted by maximizing credibility. There is in my view a strong presumption that pain could be reduced, inter alia because credibility could be increased, by complementing further fiscal tightening with the initiation of a crawling depreciation. I think it is quite wrong to suggest that the psychology of moving to a crawl would be similar to that of a step devaluation: the change could be debated in parliament prior to its implementation, rather than having to take the form of a surprise renunciation of previous promises. Adoption of a crawl would mark Argentina's passage from the unconvincing posture of promising undying fidelity to a noncredible promise into the ranks of the well-managed Latin American countries like Chile, Colombia, and Mexico that recognize that controlling inflation requires more than an intention to stick with an unchanged nominal anchor.

Federico Sturzenegger's paper deals with the country whose experience of a successful stabilization that failed to crowd in growth originally provoked Dornbusch's concern with this issue (Dornbusch 1989). The paper notes that the stabilization of August 1985 was followed by a second collapse in the price of Bolivia's principal tradition export, tin, and that recovery has been hampered by the illegality of the main nontraditional export, coca (80% of whose foreign exchange earnings are reported never to reach the country). The process of developing alternative nontraditional exports, on the success of which future Bolivian growth surely depends, merited more systematic treatment than it receives in the paper, although there are some indications of hopeful developments.

I have comments on two of the conclusions of the paper.

I doubt whether we should conclude from the econometric finding that Bolivian productivity varied with the price of minerals, that Bolivia's future growth depends on a recovery of mineral prices. Sturzenegger does not offer a theoretical explanation for his empirical finding. I would conjecture that it reflects the fact that in the past the Bolivian economy was dominated by mineral production, and high prices for major exports permit an economy to operate at full capacity which brings a cyclical increase in productivity. If that is indeed the explanation, it follows that Bolivia will still have growth possibilities even if the mineral sector remains as minor as it has now become (table 8.3 reveals that since 1976 tax revenue on the sector has amounted to only 0.1% of GDP, while both legal exports and formal GNP accounted for by minerals have fallen below 15%). Successful development of nontraditional exports could provide a perfectly satisfactory substitute.

The most interesting and useful result in the paper seems to me to be the estimate of the impact of hyperinflation on productivity. Until I find a superior source of evidence, my stylized fact will henceforth be that hyperinflation reduces productivity, and hence output, by around 20%. This interpretation suggests that output first fell around 20% because hyperinflation was allowed to develop, and then failed to recover because the removal of that shock was accompanied by another negative shock—the collapse in the terms of trade—of similar size. It is an interpretation that permits Bolivians some hope that the future will be brighter than the recent past.

Reference

Dornbusch, Rudiger. 1989. From Stabilization to Growth. Paper presented to a conference, The Economic Reconstruction of Latin America, at the Getulio Vargas Foundation, Rio de Janeiro, 7–8 August.

IV Deregulation and Tax Reform

Tax Lore for Budding Reformers

Arnold C. Harberger

9.1 Introduction

When I was first invited to this conference, I was told that part of my task was to convey some of the insights and knowledge that came from long experience with both the theory and practice of public finance. This helps explain the title of this paper, and to motivate my serving up such a bouillabaisse. I like that analogy because I include some items that are very fundamental though familiar (hoping to make the soup rich and nourishing), but also some more exotic ingredients (hoping to give it a special flavor and maybe even signal the identity of the cook).

9.2 On Fairness, Compliance, and Corruption

More and more as I grow older, issues of tax administration and of "fairness" intrude on an economic vision that was for quite a long time dominated by considerations of allocative efficiency. I am impressed by the fact that we live in societies that are composed of many different kinds of people (I almost said "many different groups," but thought the better of it), with widely differing objectives, values, and tastes, struggling against different constraints and obstacles to make their respective ways in life. They are all members of the broader polities that carry out the taxing and spending roles of government. They all receive benefits from the various governments that serve them, and they all recognize that somehow the bill for these services must be paid. Yet we know that governments would not get very far trying to finance themselves (as do churches, colleges and universities, and independent charitable organi-

Arnold C. Harberger is professor of economics at the University of California, Los Angeles.

zations) by voluntary contributions. Thus we come to fees, rates, and taxes—all to a greater or lesser degree involuntary contributions.

Looking around the world, one sees various kinds of patterns in the design and administration of taxes. I would distinguish four main types of relationship between taxpayers and their government: (1) those dominated by mockery and mischief, (2) those dominated by arbitrariness and fear, (3) those dominated by corruption, and (4) those dominated by a sense of fairness and voluntary compliance.

Type 1 is well represented by the relationship between taxpayers and government that prevailed until quite recently in Argentina and a number of other Latin American countries. It can be caricatured as almost a game between taxpayers and the tax authorities. The authorities raise rates, and evasion increases; they lower rates, and evasion decreases. We will see later that this sort of process occurs everywhere, but I would define type 1 as covering cases where it dominates the relations between taxpayers and government.

I recall working on a tax project in Argentina in the early 1960s, in which it fell to me to study what had happened to taxpayer compliance with the income tax during the decade of the 1950s. I did so by performing an exercise that is quite simple—one that I recommend to anybody who has access to the relevant figures (for any country, in any period). I took the official statistics on income tax receipts for 1951, classified by tax bracket. Obviously evasion was already going on in that year, and we have no easy way of knowing its extent. But we pass over that problem and simply take the level of 1951 compliance as a base. We then move to 1955 (or some other year with the relevant data) and *assume* that the relative distribution of income in the taxpaying brackets did not change between these two years. Implementing this assumption, we let L_1^0 and U_1^0 be the lower and upper bounds of the first tax bracket (B_1^0) in year zero (1951) and let N_1^0 be the number of taxpayers declaring income in the first bracket on that year. If prices grew by $\dot{p}$ and real per capita income by $\dot{y}$ between 1951 and 1955, we expect the counterpart of B_1^0 in 1955 (time t) to have a lower bound of $L_1^0(1 + \dot{p} + \dot{y})$ and an upper bound of $U_1^0(1 + \dot{p} + \dot{y})$. Similarly, if the relevant population had grown by $\dot{n}$ between 1951 and 1955, we would expect the number of people in this bracket to have grown to $N_1^0(1 + \dot{n})$. We now look in the 1955 tax table to find how much tax a typical family with income of $L_1^0(1 + \dot{p} + \dot{y})$ would have to pay (or alternatively look at the 1951 data to find out how much a typical family declaring that income actually paid in 1951). We do the same for the income of $U_1^0(1 + \dot{p} + \dot{y})$. Interpolating sensibly, we assign a tax between these limits to the $N_1^0(1 + \dot{n})$ taxpayers whose incomes are calculated to be between $L_1^0(1 + \dot{p} + \dot{y})$ and $U_1^0(1 + \dot{p} + \dot{y})$. Obviously, the top of the first bracket U_1^0 is the bottom of the second, so we can similarly assign to $N_2^0(1 + \dot{n})$ taxpayers a tax that is derived from period t incomes lying between $U_1^0(1 + \dot{p} + \dot{y})$ and $U_2^0(1 + \dot{p} + \dot{y})$.

Projecting 1955 tax revenues in this way, we see what we would collect if

(1) the distribution of taxpayers by income bracket had remained unchanged from 1951 and (2) their degree of compliance had remained unchanged. This projected tax revenue can then be compared with actual revenue for 1955. As I recall the experiment, they found that actual 1955 revenue was barely two-thirds of the projected amount. More astounding still was that, when the same exercise was repeated for the time span 1955 to 1959, the same thing occurred. Thus, by 1959 taxpayers were paying only about four-ninths of the taxes they would have paid on the basis of the level of compliance that prevailed in 1951![1]

One interpretation looks upon what happened in Argentina in this period as a sort of game between the taxpayers and the tax authorities. The taxpayers reduce their compliance; the authorities raise the rates; taxpayers respond by reducing compliance still further; the authorities raise rates again, and so on. Another interpretation simply views the reduction in compliance as the predictable result of increases in rates (see section 9.8).

It is interesting that cases of type 2, tax administration dominated by arbitrariness and fear, tend to come more from the history books than from the annals of recent years. To the best of my knowledge, one finds people in jail for tax evasion most often in the advanced industrial democracies, and least often in countries at the lowest income levels. But the advanced industrial democracies are examples of type 4. They make great efforts to instill in their citizens a sense of the underlying fairness of the tax system and its administration, and impose significant restrictions on their tax administrators, for the precise purpose of avoiding persecution and harassment of taxpayers by tax collectors. These safeguards were instituted as much to keep the tax collectors honest as to ensure compliance by taxpayers. Otherwise, the system can easily deteriorate into one of type 3, dominated by corruption, where taxpayers are content to buy off the collectors but in the process are subject to all sorts of capricious threats.

Modern tax administration is characterized by randomized audits and checks, with computers doing most of the selecting and with the probability of audit increasing with the potential for evasion, as well as with the likelihood that the audit will produce additional revenue. Cases are shifted from one inspector to another with some frequency, and the duties of inspectors are also changed more frequently than would be justified on strict efficiency grounds. All this is done to minimize the temptation to corruption and at the same time to standardize and routinize administrative and audit procedures.

9.3   On Uniform Tariffs

Uniformity of rates of import duties can be looked upon as an administrative device to help guard against corruption, and as a compliance measure to help

---

1. This assumes no major change in income distribution. I believe it is correct to make this assumption because (1) income distributions tend to change relatively slowly over time, (2) exter-

instill in taxpayers a sense that they are being fairly treated, and (compared with most points of departure of trade liberalization programs) as a measure for economic efficiency. I feel that the efficiency motive would likely be dominant if one started from a tariff system that is highly protective, highly distorting, and far from uniform to begin with. But once one has corrected the most blatant disparities in rates, and once one has moved the average rate down to, say, the range between 20% and 40%, then the other two arguments take on greater weight. I doubt that there is any surer temptation to corruption than the power that a customs inspector has to classify a given import good into two or more categories, with substantially different rates. The offense need not be blatant; indeed, a careful inspector could so arrange things (by threatening to put an item in a higher-rate category and accepting a "tip" for putting it in the correct one) that the Treasury loses no money because of his misdeeds. In any case, it is easy in such circumstances for inspectors to make sure that some duty is being collected in every case in which they succumb to a bribe. Contrast this with a uniform tariff; if it is truly uniform and across the board, there is no room at all for corruption that works through classifications. Outright flouting of the law, by letting items pass without paying any duty at all, or by falsifying the documents dealing with customs valuation, becomes a virtually necessary precondition to corruption, once a uniform rate is in place.

In a sense it is obvious how tariff uniformity conduces to a sense of fair treatment on the part of taxpayers: nobody can feel he is being singled out; nobody can sense himself the victim of misunderstanding or prejudice. Everybody, simply everybody, is treated in the same way.

But the usefulness of uniformity goes beyond a simple recognition that the law, on paper, treats every importer and every import good alike. It also carries the implication that the rate of effective protection facing all actual and potential import-competing industries is the same. This in turn (so long as the policy has credibility for the future) seems to reassure potential investors in such industries that they will not be singled out for capricious or arbitrary treatment in the future. Investors may still have to worry about the rate of a general and uniform tariff being raised or lowered, but that is a different thing from a sudden withdrawal of protection from their product (and perhaps a few more) or a sudden increase in the tariffs they (and perhaps a few others) have to pay on inputs. The generality and uniformity of the tariff by themselves convey (so long as they are expected to continue) vast amounts of information and vast amounts of reassurance to economic agents. The risks that a 20% rate will move to 50% or to zero can be quite large when each tariff is treated separately; these same risks are virtually nil if they refer to moving the entire uniform structure up to a general rate of 50% or down to a general rate of zero. Eco-

---

nal evidence from Argentina in the 1950s suggests no dramatic distributional shift, and (3) even simulations based on extreme assumptions of distributional changes result in revenue reductions that are tiny in comparison with the four-ninths factor that we calculated.

nomic agents can move with more assurance, and can think in terms of longer horizons, when all they have to worry about are up and down movements of the general tariff, than when they can be placed in difficulty by all sorts of specific moves concerning their own products and their own inputs, or concerning the products of actual and potential rivals.

So uniformity of tariff rates ends up (compared with typical prereform tariff structures and with most others) by promoting a greater sense of fairness on the part of taxpayers, making tariff administration easier, making corruption much more difficult, providing an unequivocal pattern of uniform effective protection to import-competing activities, and giving clearer, potentially more reliable signals to investors (of real resources) and other economic agents. By the nature of the case, uniformity encompasses the whole range of different rates, so assertions of superiority (to preexisting tariff structures) should be conditioned on the average rate being at worst the same as, and hopefully significantly lower than, the preexisting average. And, of course, the fact remains that world welfare can generally be enhanced by lowering a uniform tariff rate all the way to zero.[2]

9.4   Radial Reductions versus the Accordion Principle versus Sectoral Sequencing in Trade Liberalization Programs

Having proposed uniformity of rates as a plausible and worthy goal of tariff reform, I think it reasonable to insert at this point a discussion of a technical point that is not widely appreciated. Consider a developing country that is about to embark on a major program of trade liberalization. Suppose, for sim-

---

2. Textbooks treat the cases of "optimum" tariffs and export taxes, often in the context of models with one import and one export good. This turns these optimum taxes into general import tariffs and general export taxes, practically by definition. The right way to apply the theory of optimum trade taxes is to recognize that optimum import tariffs are justified solely to the degree they help exploit a national monopsony position, vis-à-vis the rest of the world, while optimum export taxes are justified solely to the degree they help exploit a national monopoly position. I am prepared to concede that some countries have artificially restricted exports of particular goods so as to exploit actual and imagined monopoly positions. But I know of no country that has employed tariffs for the principal purpose of exploiting a monopsony position. Few trading entities possess enough market power on the buying side to be able to act as monopsonists. And those who do (like the United States and the European Economic Community [EEC]) never use trade policy with the aim of exploiting monopsony power. If they did, these economic giants would have high tariffs on copper, lead, zinc, tin, and other metals; and on bananas, coffee, tea, and other food items with rather inelastic total world supply, in which they account for enough of world demand so that their tariffs would significantly lower the world prices of the items in question. It is my contention that the United States and the EEC have never adopted tariffs for the purpose of pushing down world prices. They have, in a few cases, imposed trade restrictions having this effect, but in these cases (sugar in the United States, wheat and meat in the EEC are examples), the motive was patently an old-fashioned protectionist one, not a technocratic exploitation of monopsony power. Given their admirable self-restraint in this regard it is reasonable for economists to ignore monopsonistic motives where the economic giants are concerned. With respect to smaller countries, the facts themselves proclaim the absence of monopsony power.

plicity, that its end objective is a uniform 20% tariff on all imports. How should it proceed? Most analysts and observers agree that a useful starting point is (1) to convert quotas, licensing schemes, and other quantitative restrictions into their rough "tariff equivalents"; and (2) to take the "water" out of tariffs that are at present prohibitive (i.e., bring them close to the point where trade in fact would occur). It is from here on that schemes differ.

Those whose instincts and training lead them to think in terms of industrial groupings are likely to think of a priority ordering in those terms, liberalizing imports first in one group, then another, then another. Those who in observing actual tariff structures have tended to focus most strongly on the highest rates tend to gravitate to the "accordion principle." This principle squeezes the rate structure from above, first reducing, say, to 100% all rates above that figure, then moving the top rate from 100% to 80%, then moving it from 80% to 60%, and so on, until the target level has been reached. (This principle may run into a sort of logical box when the target level is other than zero, but let me simply append to it the notion that, while the maximum rate goes 100% to 80%, the minimum goes from 0% to 5%, that at the next step the minimum moves up to 10%, then to 15%, and finally, say, to 20%.)

The third candidate for our scrutiny is the principle of radial reductions. This works as follows. Let the target tariff in item i be τ_i^*. We start out with a vector of actual tariffs τ_1^0, τ_2^0, and so forth, which we intend by the end of the process to bring to the levels τ_1^*, τ_2^*, and so forth. The principle of radial reductions simply says that at each step we close each gap $(\tau_i^0 - \tau_i^*)$ by a given percentage. Thus at every step of the tariff adjustment, every single tariff moves in the correct direction by a specified fraction of the gap $(\tau_i^0 - \tau_i^*)$. If we are headed for an across-the-board tariff of 20% in four equal steps, then the 100% tariff goes 100, 80, 60, 40, 20; the 40% tariff goes 40, 35, 30, 25, 20; the 12% tariff goes 12, 14, 16, 18, 20; and the 0% tariff goes 0, 5, 10, 15, 20.

The radial reduction method is to be preferred because it never consciously sends a wrong-direction signal to any activity or sector. The other two methods unfortunately have such perverse signalling built in. The problem is that at every step in the process the price signals go in the wrong direction for "most" of the activities in question. This is easiest to show with sectoral sequencing. If we are moving in four steps, we will presumably have four "sectors." When we liberalize imports in sector A, resources are being expelled from that sector. But liberalization in A causes the real exchange rate (defined as the real price of foreign currency, e.g., the real peso price of the dollar) to rise. This partially offsets the effect of tariff reductions on the activities included in A, but it gives an unequivocal signal to draw resources into the activities of sectors B, C, and D. Unfortunately, the likely end result of all the steps will be to expel resources from all four protected sectors. If this is the case, then each of the four will be given the "right" signal at only one of the steps—that step in which its particular tariffs are being adjusted. In all the other steps, it will be given the "wrong" signals, stemming from the real exchange rate effects of the liberalizations taking place in the other sectors.[3]

Under the accordion principle, the effects are essentially the same. To make the exposition easy, let me suppose that all imports are initially subject to tariffs, and that the tariffs lie in the four bands: (1) 80% to 100%, (2) 60% to 80%, (3) 40% to 60%, and (4) 20% to 40%. It is easy to see that when all tariffs in band 1 are lowered to 80%, imports in categories 2–4 receive (through the real exchange rate effect of the tariff reduction in 1) a perverse price signal. Similarly when at the second step all tariffs in 1 and 2 are lowered to 60%, all imports in categories 3 and 4 receive perverse price signals. And finally, when all tariffs in 1–3 are lowered to 40%, activities in category 4 receive yet another perverse signal.

Why should we choose liberalization schemes that have the attribute of sending conflicting price signals to all or nearly all activities as the liberalization process passes from stage to stage? In particular, why should we do so when it is so easy to avoid sending conflicting signals? The obvious answer is simply to choose the radial reduction method of achieving the liberalization targets. This approach guarantees that each activity will receive a signal in the correct direction at each step of the liberalization process. This will be true for activities that in the end will be called upon to release resources, and also for activities that in the end will be called upon to increase their level of resource use. It will hold for normal cases and for anomalous ones, too.

Obviously, there are political pressures and debts, marriages of convenience, sacred cows, and taboos within most real-world settings in which liberalization actually occurs, and real-world governments must make their own judgments as to how genuine and how forceful are these considerations in any given setting. My position is as follows. Most governments will cede something to the above considerations, but those considerations should influence economists only after they bring to the bargaining table the most sensible, most natural solution that economics has to offer. So far as I can see, the principle of radial reduction wins hands down over its two principal rivals and should be the "prescription of choice" for economists as they are called upon for advice and counsel on liberalization programs.

9.5   On Setting the "Boundaries" of Tax and Other Policies

One of the most tricky aspects of economic policy making is the setting of the "boundaries" to be covered by a given policy. If we are to stimulate small

---

3. Real life is usually more complicated than simple examples, so let me mention a couple of complications, neither of which affects the essential point being made. In the first place, within any of the sectors there may be activities whose tariffs are being raised (i.e., for which $\tau_i^* > \tau_i^0$). Such sectors will get signals in the correct direction at each of the four steps, assuming the net effect of each step is an increase in imports. Second, there exist anomalous or perverse cases in

businesses, how do we define "small"? If in a developing country we are to favor nontraditional exports, how do we draw that line? If we have a value-added tax (VAT) that purports to be more or less general, how should we set the limits to its coverage?

For all of these decisions and a myriad of others, technical economic analysis has a lot to contribute, but so do considerations of administrative costs, of fairness, of controlling corruption and evasion, and so forth.[4]

This section really has two purposes. The first is to assert that almost never is an "industry" as we know it a sensible criterion on which to define the limits of a law. The exceptions of this statement are clear: pure food and drug legislation naturally encompasses the pharmaceutical and food-producing industries. Safety on railroads, buses, and airlines is appropriately dealt with by legislation specifically oriented to these activities. Protecting the public against irresponsible (as well as fraudulent) behavior by banks and insurance companies motivates legislation focusing on those industries.

Having said that, I must add that I have never been able to find anybody who could give me a single good reason motivating a tax (or subsidy) on the activities or products of the textile industry (which covers canvas tents, denim jeans, lace panties, nurses' uniforms, and designer clothes, among many others) or of the shoe industry (which covers a range from baby booties to hunting boots to evening slippers), or of the electrical generating industry (whose alleged externalities are like mirages in the desert; they vanish before one gets close enough to touch them).

In this vein, it is easy for me to motivate a tax on noxious emissions, regardless of their source, and then end up exempting some sources because it would be too costly to try to administer a tax striking them. Likewise, it is easy to motivate a general VAT and then end up accepting one of less than full generality for a variety of administrative and pragmatic reasons. But it is very difficult

---

which a rise in the real exchange rate leads to an increase in imports of certain goods. Suppose woolen suits are both imported and made at home; assume, too, that the wool used in the domestically made suits is also imported, and that this is the principal purpose for which imported wool is used. Now let the real exchange rate rise. Less suits are imported and more made at home; because of this, imports of wool for use in making suits will also increase.

4. Note that these additional goals are quite different from "political pressures and debts, marriages of convenience, sacred cows, and taboos," precisely because they can claim a certain generality across time and space, and a purpose of sufficient merit to justify their inclusion in our professional literature and curricula. I for one find it absurd to think of teaching young economists how to help Ferdinand Marcos raid the Philippine treasury, or to aid Anastasio Somoza as he used economic policy to distribute largesse to his friends. By the same token, but to a lesser degree, I do not feel we are at the stage where it is appropriate to teach in economics courses, or to debate in our literature, how we can join with a political candidate as he makes rash promises during a campaign, or with an incumbent as he rewards his friends and neglects (if he does not outright punish) his enemies. I am old-fashioned enough to feel that what we should write about, and teach students about, is how to assess, measure, and articulate the economic costs that such actions typically entail.

to find reasons for taxation that lead to tax boundaries that are coterminous with those of one or of a few standard industrial classifications.

A good rule to follow is that, where public safety or the protection of the public is concerned, it is reasonable to key in those motives in defining the boundaries of legislation. Where externalities are thought to exist, it is reasonable to try to measure or approximate those externalities and to implement legislation that seeks to recognize and reflect the relevant magnitudes (e.g., pollution). Where subsidies or tax incentives are justified in terms of externalities that are deemed to promote economic development, it is particularly important to try to pinpoint the assets or activities involved. I have never seen an argument that would justify subsidizing, say, the purchase or rental of buildings or vehicles on grounds of some supposed externality in, say, the drug or computer-chip industry. It behooves those who propose subsidies of this kind to demonstrate carefully and convincing the approximate size and approximate location of the externalities in question. In brief, an "industry" label is no better at defining the appropriate boundaries of a subsidy or incentive scheme based on externalities than it is for most other policy purposes.

What is involved in the tax area is, quite generally, the weighing of the goal of efficiency against other objectives with some reasonable claim to legitimacy. For example, a VAT at a uniform rate will rarely be progressive, in the sense of falling with a higher average rate on the more well-to-do. A VAT can be made somewhat progressive, however, by applying higher rates to certain commodities bought principally by middle- and upper-income groups. Here one faces a very interesting and challenging problem—of creating, say, three large composite goods, A, B, and C, where A represents basic commodities taxed at the rate of 10%, and C represents "luxury" goods taxed at 30%, while B contains the rest of eligible commodities and is taxed at 20%. Ideally we would like these three composite goods to have relatively low elasticities of demand, so as to keep the corresponding triangles of efficiency cost relatively small. But it would be absurd to approach this problem with only that aim in view, because it would dictate lumping together, say, all refrigerators, all automobiles, all jewelry into category C, and all clothing and food into category A, so as to minimize intragroup substitution. A more suitable grouping, given the objective at hand, would be to put expensive cars, refrigerators, TV sets, suits, dresses, jewelry, and restaurant meals into category C, and to put cheap items of the same types of goods in category A, with the rest going into category B. The trick is to try to see to it that most of the relevant substitutes for items in each group are also in the same group, and that between-group substitution mainly takes place between neighboring groups.

The result of this process does not mathematically minimize efficiency cost, but certainly gives important weight to efficiency as an objective, while striving for a degree of progressivity in the indirect tax structure.

9.6   Arguments against Ramsey Taxation

There has been an enormous revival in the last two decades of interest in Frank Ramsey's famous problem: minimizing the efficiency cost of raising a given amount of revenue via proportional excise taxes on a subset of, say, k out of a total number n of goods and services. In the field of tax analysis the Ramsey problem is something of a bombshell because it decisively demolishes any claim that a uniform tax on the k commodities in the subset is likely to be the efficiency-cost-minimizing solution.

If we assume a reduced form system, with taxes T as policy variables and equilibrium quantities being X, we can describe the system as

$$(1) \qquad X_j = X_j^0 + \sum_{j=1}^{n} R_{ij}T_j \qquad (j = 1, 2, \ldots, n).$$

The welfare or efficiency cost of the system of taxes can be written as

$$(2) \qquad WC = -\frac{1}{2}\sum_i \sum_j R_{ij}T_iT_j = -\frac{1}{2}\sum_i T_i\Delta X_i,$$

where ΔX_i is equal to $(X_i - X_i^0)$. This assumes the reaction coefficients R_{ij} are constant over the relevant range. The Ramsey problem can be stated as

$$(3) \qquad \text{Minimize } [-\frac{1}{2}\sum_i \sum_j R_{ij}T_iT_j],$$

subject to $\sum_{i=1}^{k} T_i X_i = Y$, a constant, and with $T_i = 0$ for $i > k$. This works out as follows:

$$(4) \qquad \frac{\delta}{\delta T_1}\left\{\left[-\frac{1}{2}\sum_i\sum_j R_{ij}T_iT_j\right] - \lambda\left[\sum_{j=1}^{k} T_j X_j - Y\right]\right\} = 0;$$

$$(5) \qquad -\sum_{j=1}^{k} R_{1j}\hat{T}_j - \lambda\sum_{j=1}^{k} \hat{T}_j R_{j1} = \lambda X_1.$$

Here the $\hat{T}$ denote the efficiency-cost-minimizing values of T_j. From (5) we get, using the symmetry property $R_{ij} = R_{ji}$,

$$(6) \qquad \lambda X_1 = -(1 + \lambda)\sum_j R_{1j}\hat{T}_j;$$

$$X_1 = -\Delta X_1 (1 + \lambda)/\lambda.$$

In general, the Ramsey result is

$$(7) \qquad \Delta X_i/X_i = -\mu \quad \text{for} \quad i = 1, 2, \ldots, k.$$

If the system is linear in the relevant range, the criterion for minimum efficiency cost is that the quantities of all goods and services in the taxed subset $(\tau_i = 1, 2, \ldots, k)$ should all shrink by the same proportion. If the goods in the subset are neither substitutes or complements to each other (in the general-equilibrium sense), so that $R_{ij} = 0$ for i and j within the subset, then we have the familiar textbook result that efficiency-cost minimization is achieved when the taxes on goods 1 through k are set at rates that are inversely proportional to their elasticities of response R_{ij}/X_i. This is not the Ramsey solution in the general linear case, however. For that case, the best summary characterization is the one already given—that the quantities of all goods and services in the subset should shrink by the same amount.

I have always been troubled by this attribute of the Ramsey solution. Obviously, I am not implying that it might be wrong in an analytical sense, but rather that it could be troubling to those who would thrust it upon a society on the grounds that it was the best achievable result.

I feel that the most decisive revelation concerning the Ramsey solution is that it puts the state in the role of a sort of discriminating monopolist vis-à-vis its own citizens. This can be seen by recognizing that the problem of minimizing the efficiency cost of raising a given amount of revenue from goods 1, 2, . . . , k is essentially the same as the problem of maximizing the revenue that can be raised from this subset of goods, while limiting the efficiency cost to a given amount. Obviously a different vector of taxes will be associated with each given amount of efficiency cost. But each of these tax vectors will have the characteristic that (for the range in which the R_{ij} are constant) the resulting reduction of the equilibrium quantities of the affected X_i will all be the same.

Now we already know that for the case of linear demand curves, constant costs, and independent markets, a discriminating monopolist will find his profit-maximizing equilibrium at the point where the quantity in each such market is just half the undistorted equilibrium quantity. The monopoly markup will be greater in the markets with more inelastic demand, and lower in those with more elastic demand. Indeed, the markup will end up being inversely proportional to the elasticity of demand in each such market—exactly the result for the tax rates in the corresponding Ramsey problem.

To see the relationship most clearly, consider the fact that the discriminating monopolist does not care (presumably) about the efficiency cost that he imposes. Thus, his solution is the unconstrained revenue maximum. It is one member of the family of solutions to the problem of maximizing revenue from a subset of goods, but subject to an efficiency cost constraint.

The final answer to the relationship between the Ramsey tax solution and the discriminating monopoly solution is as follows (for the linear case): the two solutions are identical in the case where the government is asked to raise (from goods 1 through k) the maximum maximorum of revenue. Where the government is asked to keep efficiency cost below a target level that is less than the one corresponding to the maximum maximorum of revenue, then the government gets less revenue than the discriminating monopolist would. Correspondingly, instead of shrinking all affected quantities $(X_1, X_2, \ldots, X_k)$ by one half, the government shrinks them by some smaller uniform fraction. It acts just "like" a discriminating monopolist, but exercises only a specific fraction of its monopoly power. The fraction is, however, the same for all affected markets. As the efficiency cost constraint facing the government is loosened, the Ramsey solution moves pari passu in all affected commodities toward the discriminating monopoly solution.

In my view, this connection helps take some of the magic, some of the attractiveness, out of the Ramsey solution. It is quite fair to ask whether governments (or "societies") would or should feel at ease in so ordering their taxes as in effect to "exploit" the tastes (or supply constraints) of their citizens. The inequality of rates that emerges from the Ramsey problem turns out to derive precisely from such exploitation. When I ask, "Is this what we want?" I am not trying to demean the quest for lower efficiency costs. But at least in my view, the link to monopolistic exploitation takes some of the sheen off the Ramsey solution and once again (by indirection) brings us back to issues of fairness and nondiscrimination.

9.7   Ramsey Analysis Does Not "Justify" a System of Progressive Commodity Taxes

Writing this section is a somewhat delicate task for me, since it is so easy to be misunderstood. Let me begin by setting out three beliefs that I have held for a long time: (1) a very strong case can be made for value-added taxation over a broad base at a uniform rate; (2) if we deviate from uniformity, we should not do so just to add a last touch of polish or elegance to the tax system, but only to fulfill a serious "need" for nonuniformity in order to reflect the particular society's own sense of values or of fairness; and (3) one pattern of deviation that in some cases will meet the criterion set out in 2 is indeed the sort of moderately progressive tax system discussed in section 9.5.

So I come here not as an advocate, peremptorily arguing against the idea of a progressive system of indirect taxes, but rather as a teacher, pleading with my readers not to try to defend such a system with the wrong line of argument.

That is what I feel has been widely done; even more, it is a conclusion to which economists might quite naturally jump, after a moderate exposure to the idea of Ramsey taxation. Let me take you down what I see as the primrose path that leads to error, and then identify the source of the error. The starting point is the vision of a completely general tax that in principle would have zero efficiency costs. A very simple model reflecting this vision would have labor as the only factor of production, and would go on to postulate a zero-elastic supply of labor.[5]

5. Such a model is not in principle as far from reality as it may at first look. If the scheme used to implement the resulting tax or taxes is a VAT system, one can design the scheme so as effectively to exempt the capital factor from taxation. This can be done by employing a VAT of consumption type, which can be accomplished most easily through the credit method of administration. Under this method each firm pays tax (at the requisite rate or rates) on its total sales, then deducts the VATs that it paid on all its purchases. The consumption type of tax entails allowing such deductions

In such a system there are two equivalent taxes that are completely neutral (i.e., have zero efficiency cost). One is a flat-rate tax on all labor (which strikes the income of people as they earn it), the other a flat-rate tax on all purchases of consumption goods and services (which strikes the income of people as they spend it). The latter tax can be implemented via a VAT of the consumption type.

Now we modify the original problem by releasing the assumption of zero-elastic labor supply. Our uniform tax now covers only $n - 1$ goods and services, the nth (and untaxed) one being leisure. We also know that this uniform tax will not typically be neutral, since it distorts the choice between labor and leisure and, more generally, the choices between leisure on the one hand and each of the remaining $n - 1$ goods and services on the other.

If we are precluded from taxing leisure, the Ramsey solution (for a linear system) entails imposing a set of $\hat{T}_i$ such that the quantities of the $n - 1$ goods and services other than leisure all contract by the same proportion. This entails placing higher taxes on goods that are complementary to leisure, or that are less-than-average substitutes for leisure, and placing lower taxes on those that are better-than-average substitutes for leisure.

This result can be seen intuitively. Suppose there existed one good, say X_4, which was used only in fixed proportions with leisure. Then the fact that we are precluded from taxing leisure would be no constraint at all. The pair of goods (X_4 and leisure) would be like left and right shoes, and we could work on the principle that a tax of $2 per pair of shoes can be replicated either by a tax of $2 per right shoe or by a tax of $2 per left shoe. Applied to our case, leisure would be like the right shoe, X_4 like the left one. We know that a uniform tax on all goods including leisure would be neutral. We hypothetically create such a tax, but then, being precluded from directly taxing leisure, we load the total tax on the pair (X_4 plus X_n) onto X_4 alone. Because of the rigidity of proportions between X_4 and X_n, this modified tax system is equivalent to the uniform one, and hence is also neutral.

If we can't find a target with completely fixed proportions to leisure, then things with close-to-fixed proportions can serve as surrogates. The Ramsey

---

for capital as well as current outlays, so that no distinction need be made between the two; for this reason it is easier to administer than a VAT of the income type (in which capital assets purchases are not immediately deductible but must be capitalized and then depreciated over time, for tax purposes) or one of the product type (in which capital assets are neither expensed nor depreciated, but in which they nonetheless must be distinguished from current inputs, which *are* expensed). When capital assets are expensed (as occurs with the consumption type of tax), one can say that the capital factor is thus freed of tax. This is self-evident for a constant rate (t) of VAT. The firm pays t on the service yield (S) of capital assets as it accrues over time, but pays $-t$ on the acquisition cost (C). Considering that at the firm's own rate of discount the present value of the service yield (PVS) will tend to equal the present value of acquisition cost (PVC), it becomes clear that no net tax payment is involved. The government in effect "invests" tC and takes a return of tS; it thus ends up as a $t\%$ partner in each capital asset so treated, rather than as a taxing agent.

solution says that goods whose quantities increase least when the price of leisure rises should be taxed at the highest rates, and vice versa. This is the source of the notion that the Ramsey solution tells us to tax more heavily those goods that are complements to, or less-than-average substitutes for, leisure.

So far we have traveled a considerable distance without getting into trouble. The trouble appears right at this point, as we face the question of which goods are complementary to leisure, which are good substitutes, and which are poor substitutes. For something close to twenty years now, I have performed an experiment with my public finance classes and with occasional seminar audiences. Let us make a list, I suggest, of goods that are complements to leisure, and I then receive suggestions from the floor. "Television sets," says one. "Movies," says another. "Vacation trips," says a third. Then comes a whole barrage: sporting goods, restaurant meals, concerts, night clubs, summer houses, leisure-time clothes, and so forth.

When the list gets long enough, I tell my students that they really should do better than that—they are not really thinking like economists. To think like an economist about this problem one should pose a scenario that will automatically reveal the answer.

I have two such scenarios. They both start with a full equilibrium, where everybody is working his or her desired number of hours at the going wage. In the first scenario, this equilibrium is disturbed by a government decree, requiring each of them to work one or two hours less, at the same wage as before. This move entails no first-order income effect. Each person has less money income, counterbalanced by more leisure. Their money income may go down from $500 to $475, and we have to ask, which goods will see an increase in demand (these will be complements to leisure), which goods will see a small decrease (these will be poor substitutes), and which goods will see a big decrease (these will be good substitutes for leisure).

The best course at this point is to follow the advice of the Austrian school, and simply look inside ourselves for the answer (introspection, they call it). My answer is that if I were faced with such an arbitrary cut in my working hours and in my money income, I would react much the same as if I had the same cut in income (say from an increase in taxes), without the drop in working hours. The result is not exactly the same because the "time constraint" behaves differently in the two cases. But I certainly would allow my behavior to be guided more by a 5% cut in money income than by two extra hours of leisure. Following this line of reasoning I conclude that the cross-elasticities of demand for different goods and services with respect to changes in the price of leisure (η_{in}) are not exactly proportional but are close to proportional to the income elasticities of demand (σ_i) of those items. Exact proportionality prevails if people pay no attention at all to the change in the time constraint.

Once this example has been presented, my audiences over the years have overwhelmingly agreed with me that the real complements to leisure are likely to be the inferior goods (those with $\sigma_i < 0$), that the strong substitutes for leisure are strong luxury goods (those with $\sigma_i > 1$), and that the weak substitutes for leisure are probably "ordinary necessities" (with $1 > \sigma_i > 0$). These audiences have certainly recognized the absurdity of their original line of thinking about the problem, which departs from the premise that anything you use in your leisure time is a complement to leisure. That premise, taken seriously, leads to the conclusion that everything is a complement to leisure except for overalls and lunch pails (the things you actually use while at work).

The second scenario leads to the same conclusion. In that scenario everybody starts in equilibrium at the prevailing wage, and is now offered the opportunity to work overtime at a premium wage. Everybody will respond by working more (or at worst the same), because, once again, no first-order income effect is involved. Do you think they will take *fewer* vacation trips, go to *fewer* movies, buy *fewer* restaurant meals, own *fewer* summer houses, and so forth, as a consequence of working a few more hours at overtime rates? Much more plausible is the result that they spend the extra income in much the same way as they would spend the proceeds of a reduction in taxes or of an annuity received as an inheritance.

One final shot on the point being made here. I am asserting that the η_{in} (cross-elasticities of demand for goods with respect to the price of leisure) are approximately proportional to the σ_i (income elasticities of demand for the respective goods). My parting shot is that we had better all hope it is that way, because the things we measure and label as income elasticities are in reality complex jumbles in which the σ_i and the η_{in} are inextricably mixed. Consider a typical time series demand analysis. Most of the changes in real income recorded over, say, a twenty- or thirty-year period will stem from changes in real wages; another part will come from changes in income from capital. Well, the part coming from wage rate changes affects consumption of good i by both an income effect (σ_i) and a substitution effect (η_{in}) with respect to the price of leisure. Only the part coming from changes in capital income gives us a pure income effect.

Consider now a typical cross-section analysis of demand. Once again the main differences in income among the people (or households) represented in the analysis are likely to stem from differences in their hourly wage rates. Once again the response of demand for good i with respect to these income differences incorporates effects from both σ_i and η_{in}. Only the response of demand to differences in the capital income of the different households reflects a pure income effect.

So, if we want to *really* measure income elasticity of different goods and services, we have to treat as separate variables in our demand functions the real income stemming from labor on the one hand and the real income stemming from nonlabor income in the other. Only the coefficient of the latter gives us a pure income effect. But if the two coefficients are close together, if we cannot distinguish very clearly between the ways small increments of the two types of income (starting from a given base) would be spent, then the data would be corroborating the point that I am making here.

The end of this long lesson is that the Ramsey analysis would lead us to tax most highly the inferior goods, next most highly the ordinary necessities, and least highly of all, the luxuries. As I survey my students and colleagues, looking for supporters of this package as serious, real-world legislation, I find an empty set. Moral of the story: please do not propose a progressive structure of excise taxes, and invoke the Ramsey rule as your reason!

9.8   More on Drawing Boundaries and on Evasion

The theme of this section is welfare triangles. The general-equilibrium version of the textbook triangle ($-1/2T_1\Delta X_1$) is the "generalized triangle" $-1/2$ $\sum_i T_i\Delta X_i$, where ΔX_i is measured from the undistorted equilibrium $(X_1^0, X_2^0, \ldots, X_n^0)$ to the full equilibrium (X_i) with all the T_i in place. As indicated in section 9.5, the trick in setting boundaries is to put close substitutes together within a classification, so as to tax them all at a single rate. By treating packages of close substitutes as composite commodities, we eliminate tax-induced substitution among them; that is, we eliminate what we can call within-group substitution. What we are left with, if we have several different groupings of commodities, is between-group substitution.

Consider that we have a tax T_3 on four-door sedans, X_3 only. The welfare triangle $-1/2T_3\Delta X_3$ will have an enormous base, compared with what is feasible through good boundary drawing. The base ΔX_3 would include substitution between four-door sedans and two-door sedans, between four-door sedans and coupes, convertibles, station wagons, and so forth, as well as between four-door sedans and motorcycles, between four-door sedans and panel trucks, between four-door sedans and other trucks, and finally between four-door sedans and everything else.

The tax T_3 thus defined qualifies soundly as an utterly stupid tax. It is slightly improved by setting T_4 on two-door sedans at the same rate, and putting T_5, T_6, and T_7 on coupes, convertibles, and station wagons, also at the same rate. At the end of this process we have a tax T_a on all automobiles, which if at the same rate raises much more money than did T_3, and which if set to raise the same amount of money as T_3 can do so at a much lower efficiency cost (because of a greatly lower rate and because the elasticity of demand for automobiles is very much less than for sedans).

But that is not the whole story by any means. I mentioned panel trucks and motorcycles for a reason, for we know from experience that very interesting, very curious things can happen to these vehicles if automobiles are very heavily taxed. I recall some decades ago when Chile had very heavy taxes (they were actually tariffs) on cars, but much lower ones on panel trucks. The result was a vast increase in the importation of panel trucks, which was spawned by an entirely new Chilean industry—that of "converting" panel trucks into something that looked like and served as a car. The panels were invariably knocked out and replaced by glass windows. Upholstered seats were installed in the back. Sometimes new doors were added, sometimes not.

In the case of motorcycles, my example comes from Indonesia. Again the story starts with a heavy tax on imports of cars, with a much lower (maybe even zero) tax on motorcycles. But here it was the motorcycles that underwent conversion. Three-wheel cycles were converted, by artful additions, into virtual buses, or at least taxis. Sometimes a single bench was added, with the passenger looking backward. Other times the cycle was stretched at the back, with two benches going down each side, and maybe even with an extra little running board cutting laterally across the rear (where the rear bumper of a car would be). I must say I was truly astounded when I saw my first eight-passenger motorcycle, but I came to relish the experience.

I hope that readers can see the close analogy between these newly spawned conversion industries and what we have come to regard as rent-seeking activity. The difference between the tax rates on cars and trucks, or between those on cars and motorcycles, generates the use of real resources (1) to take advantage of a potential economic rent generated by a misguided law, (2) to avoid paying the tax on cars, and (3) to reflect the same kind of tax-induced substitution that always takes place when given items are taxed and actual or potential substitutes are taxed either at lower rates or not at all. If the above were a multiple-choice question, my answer would be "all of the above." Answers 1, 2, and 3 are different descriptions of the same phenomenon. The curious behavior of the panel-truck converters in Chile and of the motorcycle converters in Indonesia is in principle just as natural an economic consequence of taxation as it is for people to drink more beer when the tax on wine is raised. But surely resources were in some sense wasted in the process; efficiency costs would be dramatically reduced if the boundaries of the automobile tax had been so drawn as to include converted panel trucks and converted motorcycles, if not all trucks and all motorcycles as well.

This brings me to the topic of tax evasion. This is just another way in which the bases ΔX_i of the generalized triangle $-1/2 \sum_i T_i \Delta X_i$ end up being made bigger. And it is quite analogous to the reconversion activities referred to above. They would be called *tax-evasion activities* if they were illegal; as it is they can be fairly labeled *tax-avoidance activities*. But is there any real difference between converting a motorcycle into a "taxi" using real resources so as to *avoid* the tax on cars, compared with using real resources to smuggle TV sets or whiskey into a country so as to *evade* its tax on these items? And, going one step further, is there any real difference between using real resources to smuggle whiskey on the one hand, and using real resources to hide certain receipts from the income tax collector? I for one think that in none of these cases is there any real difference.

Just as the welfare triangle associated with the tariff on cars is made bigger by the existence of the "conversion" activities (whether of the Chilean or of the Indonesian type), so too is the welfare triangle for imported whiskey made larger by the fact of smuggling. If in the base of the whiskey triangle we have substitution toward gin, toward rum, toward wine, toward beer, and toward all other things, we also have to insert substitution away from taxed whiskey and toward untaxed (i.e., smuggled) whiskey. ΔX_{13} (if that is whiskey) is *not* the difference between whiskey consumption in the undistorted equilibrium and whiskey consumption in the presence of the tax. No, it is instead the difference between whiskey consumption in the undistorted equilibrium and "taxed-whiskey consumption" in the presence of the tax.

Out of this comes an insight that I think of as reasonably penetrating: when we are analyzing taxes, the definition of a commodity is what the tax law itself, *plus its administration,* determines it to be. Just as the size of the triangle's base can be greatly affected via bad or good drawing of boundaries (i.e., definition of what is being taxed), so too it can be greatly affected by the ease of administration and by its effectiveness. Ease of administration largely depends on how the law is written; effectiveness of administration depends on how much effort and ingenuity the administrators put in and, of course, on how honest they are.

One final point: once we recognize that evasion is "just another substitute commodity," we can see that it is absolutely natural and normal that it should increase with every notch by which the tax rate itself is raised. It is just the same as people drinking more beer as the tax in whiskey goes from 40% to 60%, and drinking still more beer when it goes from 60% to 80%. At the margin, evasion efforts will be pursued until the extra cost of evading the tax on another unit of the commodity is itself just equal to the tax rate.

This helps explain the behavior of Argentine taxpayers described in section 9.2—how with every increase of the tax rate imposed by the authorities there was a new burst of additional evasion. That is something that is perfectly natural, perfectly predictable, perfectly understandable in economic terms.

How then can tax authorities cope with this type of natural phenomenon? I think the answer is overkill. If the penalties for evasion are high enough, most people will be "honest" even if the tax does go up from 40% to 60% to 80%. By raising the costs of evasion high enough, we may be able to drive people into that corner solution called "honesty." This is an important and serious message, and one that lies at the heart of needed tax and administrative reforms in many developing countries.

References

Atkinson, Anthony B., and Joseph E. Stiglitz. 1980. *Lectures on public economics.* New York: McGraw-Hill.

Boskin, Michael J., and Charles McLure, eds. 1990. *World tax reform: Case studies of developed and developing countries.* San Francisco: Institute for Contemporary Studies.

Due, John F. 1990. Some unresolved issues in design and implementation of value-added taxes. *National Tax Journal* 42 (December).

Gillis, Malcolm, ed. 1989. *Tax reform in developing countries.* Durham, NC: Duke University Press.

Ito, Takatoshi, and Anne O. Krueger. 1992. *The political economy of tax reform.* Chicago: University of Chicago Press.

Newbery, D., and Nicholas Stern, eds. 1989. *The theory of taxation for developing countries.* London: Oxford University Press.

Tait, Alan A. 1988. *Value-added tax.* Washington, DC: International Monetary Fund.

Tanzi, Vito, ed. 1990. *Public finance, trade, and development.* Detroit: Wayne State University Press.

World Bank. 1988. *World development report, 1988.* Washington, DC: World Bank.

10   Deregulation as a Source of Growth in Mexico

Arturo M. Fernández

10.1   Economic Institutions

Economic institutions, like technology, constitute key factors in determining the level of output society may attain with a given amount of resources.

Economic institutions provide the environment in which transactions take place and therefore play a key role in the development of markets and specialization. In fact, one of the main functions of economic institutions is to reduce transaction costs. One fundamental factor in the definition of economic institutions is the legal framework. Legal considerations range from constitutional provisions, which establish the right of private ownership over goods and assets, to the freedom of employment and industry, and of course the definition of the regulatory power of Congress and other branches of government.

The legal framework affects the efficiency of production factors in that (1) they define the certainty by which economic agents are able to appropriate net flows from their economic activity, (2) they help determine the conditions for entry and competition in the various industries, and (3) they contribute to the development, or at times even to the existence, of some markets.

In developing countries, institutional problems can take on great importance or may even become obstacles to development.

One very clear task of development policy is to improve the quality of institutions under their responsibility, as well as the legal framework governing economic activity.

Many regulations have arisen in response to real or perceived problems. Often regulations are introduced for consistency with other regulations (an extension of the second-best argument). On other occasions, they are the result of

Arturo M. Fernández is professor of economics and rector at the Instituto Tecnológico Autónomo de México (ITAM), and advisor of the Free Trade Agreement.

pressure exerted by interest groups or mere copies of the regulations adopted by other nations. It must also be recognized that the interests of the bureaucracies or publicly run enterprises have often been the moving force behind regulations that have openly sought to protect these entities from competition.

In many countries, economic reforms have led to evaluations and reviews of existing regulations. In Mexico, this process, together with macroeconomic stabilization, privatization, and other institutional reforms, has been a pillar of the economic program aimed at modernizing the country. The Mexican privatization process has been linked to the process of deregulation, and in fact has served as a balance against the mere goal of maximizing revenues from privatization.

Several specific cases show that the nationalization of industries or the government acquisition of private businesses has been associated with the failure of private industries—a failure closely linked to undue or excessively onerous regulations. Among the reasons for the failure of the Mexican sugar industry were price controls and restrictions on land tenure; the telephone industry was also burdened by discretionary tariff controls and other types of restrictions and obligations.

The privatization process must be linked to the revision of all regulatory aspects, so that the resulting privatized industries can develop in an appropriate and competitive environment.

The economic deregulation program in Mexico was conceived as a means of improving the quality of regulations. Involved in the process was the elimination of those that inhibited competition, created monopolies or oligopolies, impeded the participation of the private sector, or simply generated unnecessary costs. To improve the quality of regulations, it has also been necessary to introduce rules that, for example, create conditions under which private parties could participate in the construction and operation of both infrastructure and some public services that have traditionally been the responsibility of the government. The purpose of this paper is to show with specific evidence that improvement in the quality of regulation is a factor of growth.

10.2   A Brief Diagnosis of the Regulatory Framework

This section contains a brief summary of the most important characteristics of the regulatory framework in Mexico. The sources listed as references at the end of this chapter provided the information on which this section is based.

A large part of Mexico's regulations are obsolescent or inconsistent viz-à-vis trade liberalization and new technologies. Many regulations were introduced to face, at a cost, economic issues linked specifically to a small economy relatively isolated from foreign competition. Under these conditions, the size of certain markets may only allow one or two firms to operate, or companies may not be able to take full advantage of economies of scale.[1] That is, the technology available and the relatively small size of the market generate problems typical of a natural monopoly (as happened in Mexico in automobiles, steel, petrochemicals, glass, etc.). In addition, these circumstances can lead to actual or potential conflicts involved in bilateral and exclusive economic relationships that discourage investment or that have to be avoided through vertical integration. The hypothesis is that small closed economies face substantially higher transaction costs than open economies. For example, what happens in the exclusive and unavoidable relationships among five automobile manufacturers, one glass producer, and two steel producers? In fact, the complex structure of regulations applied in Mexico to the automobile industry was designed to cope with these coordination and bilateral monopoly problems. Therefore, it can be argued that small closed economies, facing high transaction costs, have a higher demand for institutions and regulations to cope with their inherent "market failures." In the case of Mexico, the opening of the economy demanded less regulations.

Government intervention to try to solve these problems has ended up introducing other distortions ("regulation failures"), such as entry barriers, which will be commented on in section 10.3, price controls, market segmentation, controls on technology transfers, and others.

By the way, more regulations also mean better opportunities for rent-seeking activities. The Mexican experience also shows cases where, even though the initial regulation was acceptable, it eventually became the booty of interest groups.

In this context, the traditional treatment used to evaluate the advantages of opening an economy to foreign competition does not measure all the gains in efficiency. It provides only a very abstract analysis of the gains stemming from the better allocation of resources; it fails to penetrate into the details that actually give rise to the high costs and distortions linked to the accompanying regulations. These gains can be more fully understood from some of the Mexican experiences described in this paper.

Substantial barriers to entry and generalized barriers to competition have been introduced under the rationale of industrial policy or public service regulation. In the case of industrial policy, controls have been on entry and competition in order to administer industries with the assumed or real kinds of natural monopoly problems described above. Such control was easily enforced through import permits for inputs and capital goods, through explicit entry regulations, or through legal recourse on behalf of the public interest.

Regarding the legal Mexican doctrine of public service, the laws establish the existence of this condition and provide regulatory power over these activi-

---

1. These industries were not able to exploit economies of scale through exports, since the inefficiencies caused by a closed economy did not allow them to be competitive.

ties. Under this doctrine, the basic responsibility for rendering public services lies with the government. It may, however, use its discretion in granting concessions to third parties to render these services, ensuring their reliability, regularity, and obligatory availability, all at equitable rates. This legal doctrine was developed to regulate natural monopolies, but unfortunately it has been used to regulate industries that hardly bear up to this criterion—since neither the doctrine nor the legislation imposes objective conditions for defining the concept of public service. Under this guise, regulations have been imposed on trucking, interstate busing, airlines, ports, longshoremen's services, and even the production and distribution of tortillas.

The regulatory framework has not promoted an efficient division of labor between the public and the private sectors. The absence of rules to guide the decisions of government and private parties has kept the latter from participating in some important infrastructure sectors, for example, ports and highways, and certain public services, such as the distribution of drinking water. The size of the public sector and its financing requirements are intimately linked to the regulatory framework. In the process of stabilization, it was found that the sources of public expenditures had to be reviewed very carefully. In doing so, it was discovered that an important share of the public sector budget and government programs and regulations responded to regulations that in one way or another impeded the participation of the private sector or that were simply established for the purpose of administering those programs and regulations. Public sector spending is only the tip of the iceberg; sustaining it is the regulatory structure.

The phenomenon of an underground economy can be explained by several factors, but in many cases it is the direct result of the regulatory framework governing a sector.

This brief characterization summarizes many of the regulatory problems existing in Mexico up to 1988. It is also worth mentioning that many of the regulations, as well as their costs, were not openly pointed out or even recognized as causes of problems of efficiency or productivity. They were considered normal. However, foreign investors had always pointed to the high cost of doing business in Mexico, and when the veil of protection was lifted, Mexican producers discovered that their structures and levels of certain costs became obstacles to their productivity and competitiveness.

In reviewing the existing regulations, emphasis was put on the nontradables sectors, since they have repercussions on the productivity of the economy as a whole and trade liberalization did not substantially change their conditions for competitiveness.

Lack of space imposes a trade-off between the extent of my analysis of the deregulation program in Mexico and the number of cases presented. It is more interesting to have more examples and discover the major possibilities for enhancing growth in many specific sectors. It is not possible to talk even briefly about all cases. In three years, more than forty-five legal instruments (including laws and regulations) were changed. Neither is it possible to go into other factors that have played important roles in increasing the efficiency of the Mexican economy. Among these were the policy to eliminate price controls that had affected 198 generic products including 260,000 presentations, the in-depth reforms on land tenure that allow more than 60% of all land in Mexico to change from a communal system to private property; the regulatory changes accompanying the privatization of TELMEX—the national telephone company—that increased its market value from $3 billion dollars in 1988 to $25 billion in 1992; or the deregulation of the automobile industries, which fostered an increase in production from 277,000 to 720,000 units between 1987 and 1991.

10.3   Some Examples of Regulatory Changes

10.3.1   Trucking

The accident of geography that made Mexico a primarily mountainous country, lacking in internal navigational waterways and having in general high transportation costs, has created throughout the country's history an obstacle to the economic integration and development of the country.

Trucking is the most important means of merchandise transport in Mexico. Trucks move 75% of all cargo, adding up to approximately 100 billion tons-kilometer. In contrast, railroads move only 15% of the total.

The regulatory framework for trucking in effect until 1988 was introduced fifty-two years ago under the legal doctrine of public service, and under the rationale that this service must make use of general communications networks, specifically the federal highways. The purpose of the regulations was to ensure that the service would be regular and reliable, would encourage investment, and would be rendered at reasonable rates.

At that time, the highways were very unsafe and in bad condition. Scarce and deficient service of transportation had prevented economic integration among cities that were not already served by the railroads. Furthermore, Mexican industry was insisting on the need to count on regular highway transport services.

The trucking industry generated direct and evident costs to the economy, since tariffs were higher than those that would exist under competition. But other, less obvious costs were also generated through underutilized capacity and effects on inventories and productive processes.

Diagnosis

In Mexico prior to 1988, it was almost impossible to become a trucker. The law considered trucking a public service, meaning that it should be available to any user that asks for it, and identified two ways of providing public trucking services: regular and specialized cargo.

Regular cargo was available from franchises that allowed a trucker to transport any type of product, but only on certain routes. There were nine main routes in the country. Established concessionaires had, by law, preference if any new concessions were to be granted.

Although the law established that a person could not hold franchises for more than five trucks, in practice some concessionaires controlled large fleets of 300–500 trucks through name lenders.

The law also established that all truckers on the same route providing the same type of service should form a company. This meant that, if a trucker was lucky enough to get a concession, he still had to be accepted in one of the established companies. This was enforced through the *carta de porte,* the official transportation contract, which had to be perforated by the Ministry of Transportation (SCT). The SCT would give perforated cartas de porte only to the established companies.

Regular cargo was handled by 1,495 companies with 72,000 vehicles.

The law also allowed a second way of providing trucking services: specialized cargo, through permits. These permits allowed a trucker to transport only one type of good, on any federal highway. There were sixteen specific categories of permits, the main one being for agricultural products, which represented 40% of all loads in Mexico.

Permits were not easy to obtain, either. Established interest groups for each category controlled the granting of permits.

Specialized cargo was transported by 1,355 companies, with 78,000 vehicles. Figure 10.1 summarizes the main characteristics of these regulations.

In practice, trucking fleets were allowed to grow through the issuance of "temporary permits," which eventually would be regarded as permanent.

Furthermore, there were restrictions for loading and unloading in certain cities. This meant that if you had a concession for the route Mexico-Monterrey-Laredo, probably you were allowed to unload in Laredo but not to reload.

In the midseventies, cargo centers were created. In some cities, especially at ports and borders, cargo centers evolved as controllers of the cargo and as a means of sustaining the power of the concessionaires. Use of the cargo centers was mandatory. These were owned by the established concessionaires, who charged a fee for their services. The fee ranged from 5% to 25%, depending on whether you were a member. Some cargo centers applied a queuing system for both shippers and truckers that did not allow for direct negotiation between the two parties. In other cities, such as Monterrey, if you were not affiliated with the cargo center, you simply could not load.

This was enforced by the highway patrol, who was in charge of checking whether the carta de porte, was sealed. If it was not, you had to go back.

In summary, the legal framework structured a sector characterized by two segmented oligopolies: one organized by routes for regular cargo and the other organized by products for specialized cargo on any route.

The entry restrictions were:

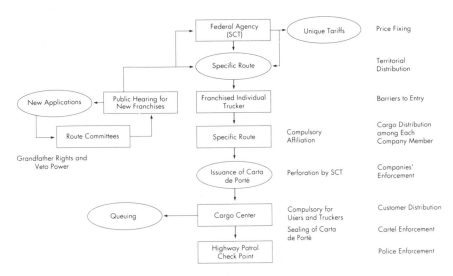

Fig. 10.1   Trucking regulation in Mexico: A textbook case for a cartel

1. Obtaining a permit for a concession from SCT. The process included consulting the route committees, made up of the established concessionaires. The process was slow and, in general, biased against those not already belonging to the established group. There was a well-organized black market for license plates, and their price was well above the official cost of obtaining them.

2. Affiliation with a company. The costs of affiliation were equivalent to 10% of gross revenue.

3. Restrictions on loading and unloading.

4. Mandatory use of the cargo centers.

Barriers to mobility among markets included:

1. Division of routes and the distinction between regular cargo and specialized cargo. This limited competition by dividing the market by territory and by product.

2. Fixed routes. This generated underutilized capacity from the usual directional cargo unbalances (point A does not have the same amount of cargo as point B). Also, for certain goods, especially agricultural products, demand changes by season. Fixed routes do not allow trucking to respond to regional changes in demand, which often translates into a lack of service.

3. Prohibiting private carriers from transporting third parties' cargo. This generated costs through empty back haulages and underutilized capacity, as private companies usually have one-way transportation needs.

There were also barriers to competition in each market (route).

1. The franchises specified the restrictions for loading and unloading in a route. Therefore, although some truckers did have franchises on high-priced routes, they had loading restrictions in certain cities on the route.

2. Allocation of cargo by queuing (a kind of random allocation) did not permit the user to negotiate directly with the trucker. This did not provide incentives for higher-quality service and made it impossible to establish long-term relationships between users and truckers.

Effects on the Economy

This structure affected the economy in a number of ways.

Trucking services were unreliable, inflexible, insufficient, and of low quality.

Trucking services rates were 10–50% higher (depending on the route) than they would have been in a competitive market. Although official rate schedules were established for the entire country, truckers had many opportunities to charge above these tariffs, for example, by charging for a full truckload when only half the truck was filled, or by delaying arrival. In practice, rates were higher than the official rates. There was also evidence of price discrimination by charging different rates for different commodities.

As an example of the high rates, to move something thirty kilometers from the city to the port of Tampico, you paid US$4.50 to $6 per ton. In the United States, from Long Beach to Los Angeles (the same distance) the cost is US$3.00 to $3.50 per ton.

Companies were forced to keep "just in case" inventories—because they could not count on reliable shipping schedules—instead of the inventories required for "just in time" processes. Some companies even had to close whole production lines because the inputs had not arrived on schedule.

Private companies had incentives to get their own trucks, with the consequent empty back haulage and underutilized capacity.

The *maquiladora* industry preferred to rely on inputs from just across the border and to locate close to them, because if located farther south, they could not maintain zero inventories.

As trucking demand increased, a large informal sector grew; some speak of forty to sixty thousand truckers. The informal sector included those who, having one type of permit, were supplying a different service, renting out plates, and so forth.

The regulatory framework generated a monopolistic sector that imposed huge welfare costs to the economy, not only because of the constrained supply of services but also because of arrangements to enforce the cartel.

The established concessionaires who controlled companies and cargo centers obtained an average annual rate of return on investment of 37%, plus charges to small truckers for affiliation with the company and with the cargo centers. These truckers used to say that they were able to recover the full value of the truck in two to three years.

Regular cargo concessionaires had annual monopoly rents of $450 million, specialized cargo permit holders, $82 million, amounting to a total of $532 million in annual monopoly rents.

The Economics of Deregulation

There is no evidence that a system of cross-subsidies existed in Mexico. Concessionaires were not obliged to service a low-traffic route in exchange for the right to exploit a high-traffic route.

In fact, low-traffic routes applied higher effective tariffs and provided less frequent service. Truckers in high-traffic routes were not obliged to service low-traffic routes.

On the cost side, the trucking industry has a structure that allows it to function perfectly well in a competitive environment. Variable costs represent 70% of total cost, and capital (the vehicles) is flexible enough to be reallocated in different markets and places. Therefore, the main objective of trucking deregulation was to promote a more competitive structure that would allow greater diversity of tariffs, consistent with the quality of the service. The challenge was to establish a legal framework that set clear rules for a competitive structure.

After long negotiations, on July 6, 1989, the new regulations were issued. The main points were

1. Freedom of transit through all federal highways.

2. Freedom to transport any load (except highly toxic and explosive products).

3. Elimination of all restrictions on loading and unloading, including ports, borders, and railway stations.

4. Maximum tariffs instead of fixed tariffs, which allowed free negotiation between users and truckers. In January 1990, tariffs were liberalized.

5. Elimination of the queuing system in cargo centers, and freedom for both users and truckers to use the cargo center.

6. Permission to private carriers to transport other parties' cargo under predetermined contracts, acting as contract carriers.

7. Opening, simplification, and decentralization of the process of granting permits.

8. Elimination of the compulsory 25% surcharge on empty back haulage, except in the case of exclusive hiring, and elimination of the 15% surcharge for imports.

9. Regularization of all the informal truckers, called the "pirates."

10. Elimination of the perforation of cartas de porte. Instead, the Ministry of Finance issued rules on the format of the carta de porte.

Results

The results of the new regulations included transference to the rest of the economy on the order of $1 billion a year, resulting from lower rates and increased supply due to increased competition; a decrease in underutilized capacity; and the elimination of monopolistic rents.

The total number of permits issued in the six months after deregulation was

32,000, representing a 21% increase in the total formal trucking power. As of March 1992, more than 95,000 new permits had been issued.

The average effective tariffs fell 25%. On some routes rates have fallen up to 50%, in real terms, over the last two years. In a very few places rates have increased by 10%, mainly in the southern part of the country.

Other effects were elimination of monopolistic rents, net efficiency gains for the economy of $600 million annually, and higher quality of service. Private companies now subcontract trucking services instead of transporting their own cargo.

Domestic production of trucks soared as a result of deregulation: the rate of growth of domestic production was 32.7% in 1989, in 1990 it was 13.8%, and in 1991 it was 22.8%.

Before I end this section on trucking deregulation, I would like to say a few words about the political economy context.

The political clout of the trucking industry had been significant since the late fifties. The truckers managed to avoid paying income and value-added taxes, and for many years, they paid only 40% of the international price of diesel. Trucking and passenger companies joined the Mexican Chamber of Federal Transportation Services. They were also very well represented in Congress, having one senator and four congressmen.

In the case of trucking, about fifteen families controlled the whole industry, even when there were a few thousand individual truckers. Most drivers could not join unions. Some of the most prominent truckers did not even own a truck, as their power came from the control and ownership of cargo centers. These families were able to organize a textbook-case cartel enforced by law and government officials.

Such unity and consensus were attained by the system's maintenance of territorial and cargo distribution of the market. This peaceful and profitable cartel was disturbed by the consequences of the government decision to open the economy to foreign trade and enter the General Agreement on Tariffs and Trade (GATT). In the past, the distribution of markets responded to the transportation flows generated under the import substitution strategies followed during thirty-five years. Opening the economy to trade induced a severe change in trade flows (exports tripled in five years) and brought substantial changes in the structure of cargo movements. Cargo increased substantially in the routes connected with international trade, that is, Mexico-Monterrey-Laredo, Mexico-Veracruz, and Manzanillo-Guadalajara, but decreased relatively in internal routes like Mexico-Guadalajara and Guadalajara-Monterrey.

These changes introduced conflict among the members of the trucking chamber. Deregulation came at the right time: truckers who were losing traffic, individual truckers who were being exploited by cargo centers, all users and truckers who were constrained to move agricultural products, supported the new regulations.

10.3.2   Multimodel Transport and Package Delivery Services

Multimodel transport (when merchandise requires more than one means of transportation—a situation primarily affecting freight packaged in containers) has been standardized across borders through international accords. Multimodal transport firms coordinate the different modes of transport to be used.

This service was regulated by government granting of public service concessions, assuming that the size of the market was too small to exploit economies of scale. The concessions were given only to two firms, one of which controlled all but one port.

The virtual monopoly existing for these services caused practically all users to bypass this service. Arrangements would usually be made whereby the monopoly would issue a waiver after receiving a payment of $5 per container.

In July 1989, these activities were also deregulated. Under the new rules it was established, first of all, that there would be freedom to contract the services either through a multimodal firm or individually with each mode of transport. Thus the obligatory intermediary was eliminated, and those who did not provide a service would not survive in the business. In a short time, more than twenty new companies sprang up to compete with each other without restriction. For example, they would be free to use either Mexican or foreign ports.

While the cost of freight transport has gone down, even more important, the firms arising from this new environment are offering quality services that basically concentrate on serving the foreign trade sector. Between 1989 and 1990, the use of freight containers in Mexican ports increased from 269,000 to 325,000.

Because of these regulations and those of cargo transport (where cargo weighing less than three tons was liberated) and the jealous enforcement of the postal service monopoly, there were practically no package delivery services operating in Mexico. The government stopped impeding access to specialized companies, allowing the development of a new and aggressive industry that includes various Mexican consortia (associations between interstate busing companies and airlines) and international companies such as DHL, UPS, and so forth.

Such a regulatory change may appear trivial, but the benefits to the economy are incalculable. Previously, nearly all firms and even the government itself had to rely on armies of their own private messengers. Furthermore, these services are beginning to transform the way many goods are marketed. For example, many retailers (such as hardware, shoes, etc.) had to maintain large inventories to satisfy their clientele. Little by little they are developing central warehouses that maintain collective minor inventories and distribute through UPS or similar firms.

Cargo transport regulation, as well as that of multimodel transport, was having grave effects on the economy. Most serious was the impact on foreign trade: in-bond assembly operations and exporters had to incur excessive costs in terms of transport and logistics. Curiously enough, the oligopolistic structure of the transport system had a greater impact on exports than imports. What is strange here is that production structures resulted in higher volumes of imports than exports flowing in and out of Mexico.

10.3.3   Ports

With the government takeover of the port of Veracruz and the release of new regulations on port maneuvers, May 31, 1991, marked the beginning of a new era of substantial improvements in the efficiency and productivity of the national port system.

There had been three basic problems with the Mexican port system. (1) The port of Veracruz was dominated by four unions that maintained high degrees of inefficiency, crime, and corruption in the port. (2) Most ports were administered by state-run firms that suffered serious efficiency problems. (3) The private sector could not invest in infrastructure to render public port and handling services.

The port of Veracruz is the largest, oldest, and most important port in the country. Four unions had physically divided the port: one handled loading and movements on board the ships, one handled the registry of cargo and unloading movement to the side of the ships, one controlled the movement of merchandise from the docks to the warehouses, and the fourth handled merchandise within the warehouse. To add insult to injury, the four unions had also formed a firm to carry out coordination services, and each entity charged individually for the same service.

Export companies from the cities of Puebla, Cordoba, and Orizaba, all located relatively close to Veracruz, preferred to take their merchandise 300 kilometers farther to the port of Tampico, or even 700 kilometers away to Brownsville, Texas.

Most union members did not do the work themselves, but rather subcontracted other workers. In a typical movement of containers, the longshoremen's union would charge $2,000, but only $100 went to the workers. Furthermore, charges would be added for the use of equipment. That is, union fees would add up to $1,900, while direct payment to workers was only 7%. Part of the fee eventually reached the pocket of the worker, but most of it was diverted in the process.

In many parts of the world, port service operations are a big headache. Three fundamental economic problems are involved. The first is the variability of the demand for labor and the preference of most firms to hire temporary employees for the services. Such a situation often generates labor unrest and political mobilization. The second is the bilateral and almost exclusive relationship of workers with one firm (which in many cases is the major employer in a port), a situation favoring opportunistic behavior on both sides. The third is that port operations are extremely capital-intensive and the long period of depreciation favors the monopolistic actions of the workers.

The government took over the port of Veracruz and issued two sets of regulations in June 1991. One is applicable to the entire country, and the other pertains specifically to Veracruz.

The Regulations on Stevedoring in Federal Port Zones established the free entry of commercial service firms; the elimination of arbitrary zones and services segmentation; facilities for subcontracting services between companies; and free determination of service rates.

Free entry was necessary to prevent the resurgence of monopolistic control over the ports, as well as to inhibit unduly onerous labor contracts. The requirement that the companies be organized as commercial entities was necessary to keep the unions from rendering the services directly. The possibility of subcontracting is important in reducing the variability of labor demand in every company. Of course, workers kept the right to unionize in terms of the federal labor law, and they unionized to negotiate with the new stevedoring firms (a different union for each firm).

After the takeover, three new companies began to operate, each with a union. All are in competition with the others as well as with other potential entrants. The cost of service went down 30% on average, but more important, the quality and efficiency of service improved remarkably. From June 1991 to June 1992, the number of containers handled in the port increased by 47%.

As for private sector participation in port activity, the Law of Navigation and Maritime Trade was reformed to allow private parties to build and operate port installations and carry out maneuvers for public service. Prior to the reform, the law allowed private firms to operate their own installations only for their own merchandise. The main objectives of this constraint had been to keep state-run firms from having competition and to protect the interests of the unions. Public firms needed this protection because they were very inefficient and had excess capacity.

Some mining, cement, and petrochemical companies established their own costly installations, but even these were underutilized. For example, in the port of Altamira, a consortium of four petrochemical companies had a $20 million chemical terminal that was extremely underutilized. After the legislative change, this company began to offer services to other companies that had been importing chemical products by truck from Houston at very high cost.

In summary, the reforms on port services have resulted in cost reductions and improved port installations. Now the government is proposing that port infrastructure be privatized. Such a move would imply serious challenges to regulators. Measures would have to be taken to avoid monopolization of certain ports where competition is not economically viable, even in the medium term.

10.3.4   Interstate Busing and Tourist Transport

Interstate busing and tourism transport were regulated by the same legislation as the trucking industry. For interstate busing, the country was divided among the companies. Entry was practically impossible for anyone who had to subject himself to the route committees. The control of busing rates and the approval of only first- and second-class service kept more exclusive services from competing with the airlines.

In May 1990, new regulations were issued for interstate passenger services, which move 90% of all interstate passenger traffic. The new regulations eliminate territorial divisions and allow free entry into the industry without being subject to rate schedules. They establish only entry and exit rules. Any company can choose its routes, but once it does so, it has to remain committed to those predetermined routes with their predetermined chosen schedules and frequencies. To change or leave these routes, the company has to give thirty-days' notice. These entry and exit rules provide greater stability and reliability to the service, while contestability is maintained.

The regulations also control creation of and adherence to service classification standards.

Deregulation brought about new services, greater competition, and an investment boom. Real bus fares went up because they had been subject to exaggerated controls. For example, the fare for the eighty-kilometer trip between Mexico City and Cuernavaca was only $2.

As a result of deregulation, 8,345 new permits were issued.

Tourist transport was also subject to concessions. One company managed to acquire all of the permits, and the government refused to issue more. But this company did not actually render transportation services. Rather, it rented permits to independent bus companies, who would pay between 15% and 25% of gross revenues for the privilege. Service was expensive and of low quality, and there was little investment. The companies providing the services never knew when they would fall out of the good graces of the monopoly.

In March 1990, new regulations eliminated entry barriers into the activity and liberated fares. In only a few months, many new companies sprung up, with 4,225 buses. Fares went down between 10% and 20%, and service improved substantially.

10.3.5   Airlines

Until 1987, there had been two large Mexican trunk airlines whose stock was held mostly by the government. These companies had divided the market into exclusive routes, charter services were greatly restricted, and the competition for international flights was highly regulated with strict divisions of passengers.

These two airlines were privatized, and a gradual deregulation process was initiated. These efforts resulted in the rise of various commuter carriers, the liberalization of international charter flights, and open competition for international flights, as long as there was reciprocity for Mexico.

The most important step, however, took place in July 1991, when airfares were liberated and entry restrictions were lifted for trunk carriers. This measure has resulted in lowered fares on those routes, in some cases, such as the Mexico-Tijuana route, as much as 50%; enormous growth of a third Mexican airline; and a significant reduction in the market share of the largest airline. The number of passengers on domestic flights has increased dramatically—making a 12.7% jump in 1991 and a 7.5% increase during 1992, in the middle of a recession.

Government control of the hubs has been a decisive factor for contestability and therefore competition. Now the government is planning to sell the airports, but there is still a great deal of debate about how to do it so that the control of the hubs does not lead to the control of the airway market. There has also been a merger wave in the airline market. This wave began before deregulation.

10.3.6   Controls on Technology Transfers

In 1973, the Mexican Congress passed a law on the control of technology transfers and acquisition of patents and trademarks. The regulations contained in the law had been promoted by the nonaligned countries movement and recommended by the Andean Pact.

The objectives behind the law were to prevent outflows of foreign exchange for technology transfer contracts, patents, or trademarks; to promote the development of domestic technology; to improve the country's terms of trade by reducing royalties; to prevent some monopolistic practices; and to protect national identity.

Some businessmen welcomed these regulations as an opportunity to improve contracting conditions, since each contract had to be approved by the Ministry of Trade. The cost of red tape and lawyers' fees per single contract often went up to $10,000. Some five hundred basically unqualified bureaucrats were in charge of issuing opinions on complex technology or cybernetics contracts. In practice, these regulations were used to selectively reduce competition and prevent "overproduction" or the displacement of established firms. These arguments must be analyzed in the context of a small closed economy, where the complex regulatory scheme had achieved, for example, the peaceful coexistence of two steel companies. A new patent for one would mean that the other would be at a disadvantage, and might even have to close. These regulations were also used to create monopolies. For example, only one company was making "tetra-pack" paper milk bottles, and the government didn't allow any other company to acquire the patent, reasoning that the country should not pay twice for the same patent.

There is no question that these regulations both impeded the development of franchises, an effective mechanism for modernizing trade and services, and inhibited technological advancement. In the long run, they were also responsible for increasing royalties.

In June 1991, the 1973 law was repealed and the bureaucracy disbanded. In only a few months, the country experienced a boom in terms of franchise contracts (more than two hundred), patents, and technology transfers. Some evidence shows that the average percentage of royalties also decreased. This last result should not be surprising. Fierce competition among franchisers of different companies and patent and technology salesmen has led to a drop in the royalties that were previously protected by effective entry barriers.

10.3.7   Electrical Energy

The Mexican government holds the monopoly on the production and distribution of electricity to the public. The regulations in this area were designed to impede almost any deviation from the rule. With very few exceptions, self- or cogeneration was permitted only for one's own use. Some studies have shown the annual flow of electricity can be increased by 25% just by taking advantage of cogeneration technology.

In May 1991, the regulations were modified to permit industries to collectively self-generate their own electricity, setting forth clear rules for the sale of any surplus to the state-run electricity company.

Congress passed a bill to reform the current law, in order to permit the private production of electricity for its bulk sale to the state firm or for direct export.

The purpose behind all these reforms is to increase efficiency, reduce energy requirements, reduce government investment requirements, and take advantage of opportunities for energy export, especially to California.

As a result of the reforms, some sugar mills are generating their own electricity and selling any surplus. Some industrial parks are investing in self-generation schemes, and cogeneration projects are being developed at a very fast pace.

The privatization of the electricity company is not being considered at this time. Putting the electricity industry, mainly the distribution network, into private hands has so many regulatory complexities that the possibility has not stirred up much enthusiasm. How would network externalities be handled? How would demand be allocated? In addition to the constitutional change that would be required, there would be a large number of coordination and rate problems.

10.3.8   The Petrochemical Industry

The Mexican constitution reserves basic petrochemical activity to the government. The definition of petrochemicals, however, remains rather arbitrary. Apart from the continuous changes in technology, there are no chemical formulas that can be used to strictly define the activity.

The government has controlled the petroleum industry and a large part of the petrochemical industry since 1938. In the case of petrochemicals, the private sector was allowed to produce commodities only in the "secondary petrochemical sector," as well as "downstream products." In 1986, the production of fifty petrochemical inputs had been explicitly reserved for the state, including ethylene, propylene up to polyethylene, and other products that represented 78% of total production.

This regulatory scheme gave rise to two basic problems. First, the government had to finance costly petrochemical projects, and second, the scheme prevented the private sector from developing according to world standards. The arbitrary distinction between basic and secondary petrochemicals caused the artificial fragmentation of the productive processes. Private petrochemical firms had to buy inputs from Pemex that did not exist on the international market, where production is highly vertically integrated.

Such a situation gives rise to monopoly-bilateral problems, involving Pemex vis-à-vis its clients, not to mention those of a natural monopoly, since the private plants could not operate at optimal scales[2] and were designed to serve only the domestic market. To deal with these and related problems, the Mexican Petrochemical Commission was created and empowered to issue secondary chemical production permits, distribute the production volumes between Pemex and private firms, regulate installed capacity, and regulate the sale prices of Pemex's inputs, as well as those charged by private firms.

In 1988, Pemex's petrochemical investment demands amounted to $3 billion. In August 1989 and August 1992, it was decided to liberate the petrochemical industry, eliminating permits and controls on production and capacity. Furthermore, import permits were eliminated on all products and inputs except natural gas. The government has even decided to sell off some of its petrochemical installations.

The industry is in a rapid restructuring process. Some plants will have to be relocated, while others will have to be closed. It will take some time to see all the benefits of petrochemical deregulation.

10.3.9 Customs Brokers

The Mexican customs law establishes that customs transactions must be undertaken by a custom broker. It is a regulated profession, established long ago, that aids the tax authorities in the task of enforcement. The entry restrictions generated rents, so that the agent would be discouraged from committing tax fraud. The weak surveillance and enforcement of the scheme and the large amount of contraband and corruption in customs transactions converted the scheme into one of feudal rents. A would-be broker had to take an examination to secure a customs patent (operating license). Only a few influential persons

---

2. For example, some polyethylene plants in Mexico have a scale of 100,000 tons annually, while the international scale is 250,000 tons.

managed to pass. There was no transparency to the process, and the selection was entirely arbitrary.

Until 1989, there were only 689 agents in the entire country, and each was allowed to service only one federal customs office. Agents' rates were fixed by law: 0.5% of the cost insurance and freight (CIF) value of imports and 0.25% of the value of exports. If any agent were to give a discount, his patent would be taken away. That is, they had a potential gross annual income of $235 million dollars. Their responsibility was to fill out a tax form and hand it in at custom office. It was like an import-export tax, but collected privately.

The law also authorized customs representatives; a firm could solicit that one of its own employees act as a customs broker. Only 325 of these posts were authorized for two hundred firms, most of which were state-owned.

Reforms were implemented in December 1989 and in 1990 to deregulate the activity. The previous access scheme was replaced with a bonding mechanism. Firms are allowed to name customs representatives. The official rate was eliminated, and agents can work with more than one federal customs office.

The effects could be seen immediately. In less than a year, the number of agents doubled, a considerable number of firms appointed customs representatives, and fees plummeted. For example, Kimberly Clark de México had been spending close to $350,000 per year in customs agent fees, and it was able to get its agent to reduce his charges to $100,000.

10.3.10   Fishing

Socialist policies in the late thirties favored the protection and promotion of the cooperative movement. The system was promoted by reserving economic areas, especially areas such as public services and public infrastructure. One of the areas reserved during the seventies was fishing exploitation and farm fishing for certain high-priced marine species such as shrimp, lobster, abalone, oysters, and clams.

For example, the entire commercial shrimp fleet was expropriated and transferred to the cooperatives in 1981. By 1989, the ships were unserviceable, and the production and export of shrimp plummeted as the capital stock was being consumed. While in 1980 34,170 tons of shrimp were exported, in 1991 this amount went down to 21,076 tons. The government transferred enormous quantities of credit through Banpesca, a government bank that went bankrupt when it was unable to obtain repayment on loans.

In the case of farm fishing, Mexico has an enviable potential: thousands of miles of tidelands, ponds and lagoons, and 450,000 hectares of prime waterfront that has no alternative use. This activity requires a great deal of capital and technology. The cooperatives had neither the interest nor the resources to exploit it. By 1989, there were no more than ten fishing farms in the entire country.

The cooperatives could not issue stock or secure bank credit, since it was illegal to mortgage the fishing concessions. Furthermore, the government had purchased a private consortia, Ocean Garden, from the ex-owners of the shrimp industry based in San Diego, which distributed shrimp, lobster, and other products in the United States. Its growing inefficiency forced the company to pay the fishermen less than international market prices. Thus the cooperatives, to avoid paying back their loans and to receive higher prices, used to sell their catches on the high sea.

Another problem not yet solved with the cooperative legislation is that it provides disincentives for capital accumulation; as employees cannot be hired, each new collaborator becomes a partner without having to make any initial capital contribution. Any contribution required is taken out of his dividends.

In December 1989 and December 1991, the fishing law was reformed so that cooperatives would no longer have exclusivity. The private sector is investing and repairing the fishing fleet from scratch. It will be some years before the industry again becomes the source of wealth it was in the past.

10.3.11   Regulation of the Textile Industry

The textile industry was heavily regulated. Natural and petrochemical fibers, fabrics, and apparel were subject to import licenses.

From 1937 to 1953, several regulations were issued for the purpose of avoiding "destructive competition and undesired overproduction" (Decree to Regulate and Rationalize the Industry and Trade of Silk and Other Derivations, 1937 and 1938). These regulations were enacted to enable the industry to face some of the consequences of the Great Depression.

These regulations allowed the Ministry of Trade and Industry to control the installation of new factories, changes in installed capacity, and the imports of textile machinery and equipment. Also, exchange among fiber and fabric producers was regulated by establishing permits to buy and sell.

The whole structure of regulation tried to deal with the natural monopoly and bilateral monopoly issues affecting fibers and fabrics industries that can be typical of small closed economies, and with coordination problems that arise as a result of other distortions from price supports to agriculture.

The textile industry grew fast for several decades. With the passing of time, however, complex and well-organized cartels became more and more inefficient. Regulations allowed industries with inferior technologies (from the 1930s and 1940s) to survive and to profit by being protected from new companies. In fact, the market was distributed to allow modern plants to service the market growth.

The opening of the economy since 1985 has disturbed this peaceful setting. Many companies have had to close, and the survivors asked the government to dismantle the entire regulatory structure. In January 1991, all regulations were eliminated.

10.3.12   Two Anachronist Regulations

To complete this review of selected cases, I would like to mention two humorous cases of anachronistic regulations.

Incorporating a company in Mexico used to take about six months. A public notary wrote the deed that was signed by the parties involved. A federal judge had to review the deed and write an evaluation authorizing the incorporation. Finally, the entire set of papers was sent to the attorney general's office for further evaluation and authorization to include the deed in the Public Property Registry.

It seems absurd, but this legal procedure may still prevail in countries that follow the Napoleonic Code. Its origin appears to be kings' and states' fears that a limited-liability company might be able to grow and become more powerful than they were, by issuing stock indefinitely.

In Mexico this cumbersome legal procedure was eliminated in December 1991.

Another amusing regulation was the definition of beaches and waterfronts as state property (La Ley de Bienes Nacionales); twenty meters of the waterfront was the inalienable property of the state.

This regulation impeded investments and introduced risk to investment in tourist facilities like hotels and marinas. If a private investor built a marina on his own land, as soon as the water flooded in, the land, water, and twenty meters around became government property. Investors had to get a concession for the exploitation of government resources for a maximum of twenty years and pay rent for it.

This anachronistic regulation came from colonial legislation that required such property to be maintained to defend the country from foreign enemies. Twenty meters was the distance required for the maneuvers of a horse pulling a cannon. This regulation was changed in August 1991.

10.4   Conclusions

Examples of some of the most representative deregulation experiences have been presented. From them several lessons can be learned.

Small closed economies face higher transaction costs than open economies. So they develop costly institutions and regulations to deal with issues that arise from small markets and unexploited economies of scale, bilateral monopoly conflicts, indivisibilities, exclusive and bilateral contracts in key industries, and inconsistencies within the regulatory framework as a whole. Such regulations sooner or later become the booty of rent seekers who are able to organize and enforce expensive and inefficient cartels. They go from being solutions for "market failures" to being "regulation failures."

In Mexico, trade liberalization became the economic and political driving force to eliminate distortions and costly regulations and to foster competition. Trade liberalization demands as a complement a deep review of the regulatory framework.

Stabilization programs can be more successful if accompanied by trade liberalization that allows less regulation and as a consequence less government spending.

Privatization efforts should be linked to prior adjustments to the regulatory framework. This ensures that privatized companies are able to develop in a competitive environment without regulations that impede their productivity and growth.

Trade liberalization efforts should be linked to deregulation or better regulation of nontradable sectors (like transportation, telecommunications, etc.), since they have a considerable effect on the productivity of the whole economy.

Deregulation efforts require considerable research about the nature of such regulations, in order to provide viable and efficient policy options.

In some cases, the benefits from deregulation arise in the very short run, mainly in industries where fixed costs are not considerable. In others, they arise in a longer period after a painful adjustment in which capital is reallocated.

Deregulation can enhance growth, as shown in this paper. (1) New opportunities are open for private investment that allows the most efficient exploitation and allocation of resources. (2) Costly regulations are no longer necessary to cope with "market failures" inherent to small closed economies. (3) Cartels are destroyed, output expanded, and costly arrangements necessary for their enforcement are eliminated. (4) Better rules allow for a better division of labor between the private and the public sector and therefore better economic performance. (5) The underground economy induced by regulations becomes open and formal, and its entrepreneurial drive can take advantage of market and legal institutions. (6) Regulation risks, arising from bureaucratic discretionality, are either reduced or eliminated, bringing higher expected rates of return to investment and access to capital markets that are not willing to bear unforeseeable risk. (7) Less government intervention means that fewer resources are required to manage regulations, and more resources are freed for investment.

References

The regulations listed here are all found in the *Diario Oficial de la Federación* (official federal gazette).

Reglamento para el Autotransporte de Carga, Secretaría de Comunicaciones y Transporte (SCT) (Trucking regulations). July 6, 1989.

Reglamento para el Transporte Multimodal Internacional, SCT (Multimodal transport regulations). July 7, 1989.

Acuerdo que Establece las Reglas de Administración y Operación del Puerto de Veracruz, SCT (Agreement establishing administration and operation rules for the port of Veracruz). June 1, 1991.

Reglamento para el Servicio de Maniobras en Zonas Federales de los Puertos, SCT (Regulation for maneuvers in federal port zones). June 1, 1991.

Reglamento para el Servicio Público de Autotransporte Federal de Pasajeros, SCT (Interstate busing regulation). May 30, 1990.

Reglamento para el Autotransporte Federal Exclusivo de Turismo, SCT (Tourism transport regulation). July 11, 1991.

Rutas y Tarifas del Transporte Aéreo Nacional (Decreto en trámite), SCT (Routes and tariffs of the national transport airlines). July 11, 1991.

Se Abroga la Ley Sobre el Control y Registro de la Transferencia de Tecnología, Secretaría de Comercio y Fomento Industrial (SECOFI) (Abrogation of the law regarding control on technology transfers). June 27, 1991.

Reglamentos de la Ley de Servicios Públicos de Energía Eléctrica en Materia de Autoabastecimiento, Secretaría de Energía, Minas, e Industria Paraestatal (SEMIP) (Regulations on the law of the self-supply of the public service of electrical energy). May 31, 1991.

Resolución que Clasifica los Productos Petroquímicos dentro de la Petroquímica Básica o Secundaria, SEMIP (Resolution of petrochemical classification into the categories of basic and secondary petrochemicals). August 15, 1989, and August 17, 1992.

Ley que Establece, Reforma, Adiciona y Deroga Diversas Disposiciones Fiscales (Ley Aduanera), Secretaría de Hacienda y Crédito Público (SHCP) (Law to amend and derogate various fiscal provisions [customs law]). December 28, 1989.

Decreto que Reforma, Adiciona y Deroga Diversas Disposiciones de la Ley Federal de Pesca. (Law to amend and derogate various provisions of the federal fishing law). December 30, 1989. Decreto que Modifica el Reglamento de la Ley Federal de Pesca, Secretaría de Pesca (SEPESCA) (Resolution that amends the administrative regulations of the federal fishing law). February 7, 1991.

Decreto por el que se Abrogan Ordenamientos que Regulan la Industria y el Comercio de la Seda y Artisela y sus Derivados, SECOFI (Decree that abrogates regulations of the commerce and industry of silk and its derivates). January 7, 1991.

Decreto que Reforma, Adiciona, y Deroga Diversas Disposiciones de la Ley de Sociedades Mercantiles, SECOFI (Decree that changes and derogates various provisions of the Mercantiles Society Law). June 11, 1992.

Reglamento para el Uso y Aprovechamiento del Mar Territorial, Vías Navegables, Playas, Zona Federal Marítimo Terrestre y Terrenos Ganados al Mar, Secretarí de Desarrollo Urbano y Ecología (SEDUE). (Regulation for the use of the territorial sea, navigation routes, beaches, federal sea zone, and land won to the sea). August 21, 1991.

Comment on Chapters 9 and 10   Jonathan Gruber

Arnold Harberger and Arturo Fernández have both written very interesting papers on the government's role in developing economies. Reflecting my relative expertise, I will spend most of my time discussing the Harberger paper on taxation. At the end, I will offer a few thoughts on the Fernández paper as well.

I found Harberger's paper to be an impressive survey of issues in taxation for developing countries. I will highlight three key points made by the author, then suggest one direction for future empirical research in this area.

The first section of the paper discusses tax evasion, and the author offers some evidence suggesting that compliance fell in Argentina in the 1950s as tax rates rose. I found this one of the most interesting points of the paper, given the debate over tax rates and revenues that has dominated the United States

Jonathan Gruber is assistant professor of economics at the Massachusetts Institute of Technology and a faculty research fellow of the National Bureau of Economic Research.

for the last fifteen years. If we think about it, there is one clear reason why rising tax rates would lead to higher revenues, which is the direct intention, but at least two reasons why rising rates lead to lower revenues. The first is compliance: higher rates lead to lower compliance, which leads to lower revenues. The second one has been the focus of the most attention in the United States, and is commonly called the "Laffer-curve effect": higher rates lead to lower effort by earners, which leads to lower income and tax revenues.

Unfortunately, it is very difficult to separate these two effects with the type of data used by Harberger. What we would like to know is, if revenues are falling as rates rise, how much is due to evasion and how much is due to reduced effort? In the United States, data from taxpayer audits are currently being used to address the first part of this question. To the extent that such data can be collected by tax authorities in developing countries, it would be interesting to investigate this question further as well.

The fact that most attention in the United States has focused on the Laffer-curve effect is indicative of the difference in the magnitude of evasion that goes on in the United States and in developing countries. In the United States, the "tax gap," the difference between what would be expected in revenues with no evasion and what is collected, was estimated at 13% of revenues in the mid-1980s. On the other hand, in Brazil, only about one in ten individuals with earnings actually pays income tax at all.

What can account for the massive difference in the propensity to evade taxes? One problem is very high tax rates, as discussed above. However, the top income tax rates in developing countries today are not very much higher than the 70% rate that prevailed in the United States as recently as 1980. Thus, while there may be some increased evasion from higher rates, my hunch is this is a second-order problem, and that lowering rates will not massively increase compliance.

The more important problem appears to be lack of enforcement. There are two instruments at the government's disposal for increasing enforcement: higher penalties for noncompliance, and expenditures on enforcement personnel and technologies. Harberger appears to favor the former strategy. However, at least two important reasons explain why there may be a "penalty Laffer curve," whereby less severe penalties are enforced more often and raise more revenues on net. First, when penalties are very steep, enforcement officials are hesitant to enforce them at all. Second, as penalties grow, the incentive to bribe the enforcers to avoid the penalty grows as well. It therefore may be more efficient to devote increased resources to enforcement, rather than just raising the penalties, even if those resources have some shadow value in the government's budget constraint.

Another important contribution of this paper is its discussion of how policymakers should think about setting boundaries for nonuniform commodity taxes. The author suggests two rules for setting these boundaries. First, we should minimize the extent of *intergroup substitutability*. The more homogeneous commodities are within tax groups, and the more distinct they are across tax groups, the less deadweight loss there will be from substitution between groups. For example, in section 9.5 the author points out that we should not blindly group goods by their industry type, that is, calling refrigerators a necessity and jewelry a luxury. Rather, we should think harder about substitutability, and group expensive refrigerators and expensive jewelry together and cheap refrigerators and cheap jewelry together. That is, if commodity taxes are to be nonlinear, a more sensible basis for the nonlinearity may be price rather than industry of production.

Second, we should minimize the extent of *substitution in conversion,* which arises from making highly taxed goods look like lower taxed goods. For example, a tax on cars but not on motorcycles in Indonesia led to the advent of the eight-person motorcycle. In this case, the possibility of making a taxed good look like a nontaxed one allows for more substitution and thus more deadweight loss. The rule here would seem to be to choose immutable properties of goods as boundaries for setting tax differences.

These are both very important and sensible rules, but there may be cases where they contradict each other. Take, for example, the case of taxing boats. The first rule would imply that we should not tax all boats equally just because they are produced by the boat industry, but we should tax yachts at the rate that we tax other luxuries, and dinghies at a lower rate. Yet when the United States tried to implement a yacht tax, which was levied on all boats that cost more than $100,000, firms responded by selling individuals dinghies for $95,000, and then selling them the mast for another $50,000 and the motor for $10,000 more.

This, of course, is just an example of the type of substitution in conversion discussed by the author. However, this sort of transfer pricing problem is unavoidable once you tie a nonlinear tax to the price of a good. Thus, while using price as a group definition may minimize substitution across groups, it may also allow excessive opportunities for substitution in conversion to avoid the nonlinearities in the tax schedule. These two goals may therefore contradict each other, and we need to trade off these two considerations in designing the optimal boundaries.

My third point relates to the paper's focus on the optimality of uniform commodity taxes and tariffs. A well-known result from the optimal commodity tax literature is that uniform commodity taxes are optimal only under quite stringent theoretical conditions. However, the author presents some interesting arguments for uniformity in developing countries, which may counteract the theoretical presumption against it. He notes that uniformity may limit the possibilities for corruption by customs officials, since such corruption would now involve not just reclassification of goods, but "outright flouting of the law" such as letting goods pass through untaxed. Furthermore, uniformity of protection of industries can lead to increased investment in the country, due to a lack of fear of future capricious government policies.

These both strike me as very important points, and worthy of empirical analysis. For example, one could ask what happens to the level of revenues collected by tariffs and taxes as their *variance* is reduced, for a given overall level of tariffs or taxes. What does reduced variance of tariffs do to investment in the country, holding other features of the investment climate constant? For this latter point, it would also be interesting to investigate the time series pattern of tariffs and investment: is it uniform tariffs that reassure investors, or the stability of tariffs over a number of years, regardless of their level?

The other argument for uniform taxation, which is made in section 9.7, is the author's refutation of the common argument that the Ramsey optimal tax model suggests the use of progressive consumption taxation. The traditional motivation for this argument is that, in the Ramsey model, our goal is to achieve an equal compensated reduction in demand for all goods. However, leisure is an untaxed good. Thus, the efficient policy will be to tax goods that are complements to leisure. Since we normally presume that luxuries are complements to leisure, then it will be optimal to tax luxuries.

The author claims, in response, that it is wrong to think of luxuries as complements to leisure. He reaches this conclusion by considering the example of a forced work reduction, which leaves the individual with less money income but no lower utility (since the increased leisure is valued at her wage). He then assumes that the extra leisure will not lead to higher demand for luxury goods, but that the lower money income will lead to reduced demand for luxuries. Thus, he concludes that luxury goods are substitutes for, not complements to, leisure.

This conclusion, however, may derive from the structure of the example. Since this is a discussion about optimal taxation, I will change the example somewhat, to one where the government increases the tax on the individual's wage by a small amount, rather than simply forcing her to work less. In that case, she will choose more leisure, but have lower money income, as in the author's example. However, we also have to consider what is done with the money that is raised by the tax. Normally, public finance economists consider Musgravian "differential incidence," and assume that the money is returned to the individual as a lump sum. In that case, there *is no money income effect* of the type pointed out by the author, so that consumption of luxuries does not fall as leisure rises.

The key point is that, since the author does not consider a tax, but rather a work rule, no revenues are raised, so he can ignore what is done with the revenues. In reality, revenues are almost always raised by a tax, and the income effect will depend on what is done with that money. We therefore cannot say, in general, that luxuries will be substitutes for leisure.

I now turn briefly to Arturo Fernández's paper on deregulation in Mexico. This paper provides a very interesting catalog of the regulatory restrictions that were, in the author's opinion, choking the Mexican economy until the late 1980s. His basic point is an important one: regulations that are necessary in a small closed economy, due to monopoly power in certain sectors, are no longer necessary once international trade has introduced an element of competition. Thus, in Mexico, trade liberalization became the driving force to eliminate these costly regulations. And he documents the impressive gains to the Mexican economy from their elimination.

I have a hard time arguing with the efficiency arguments made by the author. Mexican reform during the Salinas regime should be a model for other developing nations as they attempt to rid themselves of government impediments to the functioning of their economies. However, it is worthwhile to pause and consider the distributional consequences of deregulatory policies. The regulated sectors, as the author discusses, gave rise to large monopolistic rents. Presumably, these accrued to relatively few wealthy individuals, so that deregulation could be justified not only on efficiency but on equity grounds also. However, much recent research in the context of the United States has suggested that monopolistic and oligopolistic rents may accrue to other groups as well.

For example, work by Larry Summers and Larry Katz of Harvard has demonstrated that the excess rents earned by many industries in the United States appear to accrue, to some extent, to the workers in those industries, rather than purely to capital.[1] Similarly, much of the work studying airline deregulation has focused on safety considerations. If the airlines were spending some of their excess rents on safety before deregulation, then the advent of competition may have been associated with an increase in fatalities. This can lower the estimated welfare gains from deregulation, which are generally measured in terms of price alone. Finally, in my own work, I have focused on the effects of competition among U.S. hospitals on their provision of charity care to the poor. Hospitals are a highly regulated sector in some states, and large rents were being earned until the late 1980s. Since then, however, private insurers have begun to shop more diligently among hospitals on the basis of price, putting pressure on these excess rents. However, the reduced rents are not simply a transfer from the hospitals to the private payers. Some of these funds were used to provide charity care to the uninsured poor, for whom the hospital is the only source of care, and who do not pay much of their bills. In fact, I find that for every dollar in reduced private revenues received by hospitals, they reduced their care to the uninsured by over 50 cents.

Returning to the Mexican context, my point is that a complete analysis of deregulation requires not only an assessment of what happened to prices and quantities, but also the consequences of reduced monopoly rents. For example, what has happened to trucking and airline safety? The author claims that trucking firms did not use their excess revenues from high-volume routes to subsi-

---

1. Of course, as Sebastian Edwards correctly notes, workers in the regulated sector in Mexico are also a group away from which we may want to distribute, toward the "lower class" of workers in other sectors.

dize low-volume ones. One way to assess whether this is true is to ask what effect competition has had on the services received by low-volume trucking routes. Are there now regions of the country that are not receiving service? Similar questions could be asked about low-density bus routes after deregulation.

Of course, in a world of costless transfers, many of these points would be moot. The efficiency gains from deregulation could simply be spent to compensate any losers in a distributional sense; for example, the government could subsidize the new private bus companies to serve the low-density routes. However, thinking about this in the U.S. hospital context for a moment points out the difficulty with this proposition. That is, the government would somehow have to define the price gains to private payers, and then tax away part of those gains to provide increased care to the poor. Even under a Democratic administration, such a policy seems unlikely. Is it any more likely in Mexico that the increased rents that accrue to bus travelers along crowded routes will be taxed away to fund bus service along very low density routes?

I should conclude by noting that this point is essentially a very minor one that should not be construed as decrying the drastic reduction in regulatory barriers to economic activity in Mexico. Rather, I am simply noting that deregulation may create some losers among disadvantaged groups as well as the wealthy, and it may be important for the government to use a portion of the rise in social surplus to compensate those groups.

Comment on Chapter 10   Andrés Velasco

The tales told by Arturo Fernández are a splendid example of how and where economists can do good in the course of economic development. Free of the disagreements over models and sequencing that trouble macroeconomic reforms, microeconomic deregulation is an area where efficiency gains, as Fernández documents, are readily identifiable, substantial, and fairly easily achieved. Moreover, many of the reforms are Pareto improving; when they are not, it is hard to sympathize with the losers: former monopoly rent holders who collected fat fees for performing activities whose social value was zero or negative.

My brief comments focus on some of the problems that may arise in the process of deregulation and on some tasks still ahead for Mexico—drawing to some extent on the experience of Chile, the other country in the hemisphere to have pursued wide-ranging microeconomic reform.

One problem, mentioned by Fernández but which may well deserve additional emphasis, is the potential conflict between the requirements of privatiza-

Andrés Velasco is assistant professor of economics at New York University.

tion and those of successful deregulation. Financially strapped governments, whether in Latin America or eastern Europe, face strong incentives to maximize the revenues associated with privatization; they are also compelled to carry out privatization as quickly as possible, in order to send a strong signal about the depth and irreversibility of the announced reforms. But both of these pressures conspire against a successful deregulation drive. The need to maximize sale prices may induce regulators to assure buyers of a privileged regulatory situation, at least transitorily. The need to sell quickly may leave insufficient time to ensure that the business environment in which the newly private firms will operate is competitive and transparent. Both points have great practical relevance, as suggested by the recent experience of countries throughout the region. State-owned unnatural monopolies are socially undesirable; privately owned ones are no less so.

A second problem is that, in the drive to eliminate the gross distortions created by government meddling, reformers may overlook other kinds of market failure that become painfully evident once deregulation sets in. An example should help drive the point home. In the 1960s and early 1970s, the transport system in Chile's large cities was either state-owned or heavily regulated by the state. Many of the inefficiencies chronicled by Fernández were present; bus services suffered from short supply and low quality. The military government went for wholesale privatization and deregulation. Practically anyone who wanted to become a bus owner/driver could do so. The policy may have at first seemed sound, but the results were disastrous. The effects of two obvious yet neglected externalities—congestion and pollution—were soon felt. The number of buses operating in Santiago went from two thousand to over twelve thousand in less than a decade. Congestion and air pollution levels today rival those of Mexico City, and several studies blame the phenomenon on the excess number and poor maintenance of buses. To make matters worse, bus owners have become cartelized, and the increase in supply has not manifested itself in higher quality or lower real prices. Until recently, the existing anticollusion agencies have been unwilling and unable to tackle the problem.

The moral of the story is simple. Governments in countries such as Chile and Mexico have gone far in dismantling the obvious, government-created distortions. Now the really hard task begins for the regulators. The emerging market-based economies of the region must be supported by modern, technically minded, and agile state agencies, which, with honorable exceptions, are nowhere to be seen. A privatized electricity sector, as Fernández points out and the experience of Chile confirms, is filled with regulatory riddles, which existing bureaucracies are ill-equipped to deal with. The same is true of other fast-growing and newly private sectors. Privatized social security systems can soon have assets that account for a large share of GDP; the potential consequences of mismanagement of this large pool of savings are not trivial, and the activities of pension funds must be adequately watched. Elsewhere in banking and finance, long-dormant government agencies are suddenly being asked to supervise complex transactions in foreign exchange and derivatives. OECD country regulators have a hard time keeping track of and regulating such transactions, many of which are off balance sheet; the same and worse is bound to be true of their counterparts in Latin America or eastern Europe. In telecommunications, new markets in cable television, data transmission, cellular phones, and other innovative products urgently demand appropriate regulatory frameworks.

With the retrenchment of the state and the rapid disappearance of price and interest rate controls, marketing boards, planning apparatuses, and other devices typical of the 1950s and 1960s, whole bureaucracies (and sometimes ministers themselves) have been left without much of a job to do. The most obvious response has been to send them back to the labor market, where they may perhaps find employment with a positive marginal product. Some of them, however, may have to be retained and retrained. The need to develop a modern and deeply reformed state apparatus is still the biggest challenge facing countries such as Mexico and Chile.

Finally, a comment of a more technical nature. The title of the paper stresses that deregulation may be a source of growth in Mexico and elsewhere. Yet one must be careful to delimit the scope of this claim. In the language of recent growth theory, we must distinguish between level and rate effects. The policies described by Fernández are certainly efficiency-enhancing. But not all of them may permanently increase the private return to capital and therefore the growth rate, as required by the models of Romer, Lucas, Rebelo, and others. The removal of a de facto export tax (to the extent that it acted as a tax on the income of exporters) should raise the rate of return on that sector and therefore stimulate investment and growth. Other policies, such as removing artificial barriers to the supply of trucking services, should only have a once-and-for-all upward effect on that sector's supply.

But whether of the level or rate-of-growth variety, it is likely that many of the positive effects have not yet materialized in Mexico. Some observers have recently been puzzled by Mexico's apparent inability to grow at rates above 3–3.5% per annum on a sustained basis. One possible answer is that many of the microeconomic reforms are only a couple of years old—a fact that is bound to strike any reader of the paper. By contrast, many of Chile's microreforms have been in place for a decade or more. If this hypothesis is right, we may expect even further benefits from the remarkable string of policy changes chronicled by Arturo Fernández.

V How to Stabilize

11   Partial Adjustment and Growth in the 1980s in Turkey

Anne O. Krueger

11.1 Introduction

Until 1980, Turkish economic policies were broadly typical of those of most developing countries. A policy of import substitution had been consistently followed at least since the 1950s, with prohibition of imports of commodities for which domestic production was deemed adequate. In part to foster import substitution, but more importantly because foreign exchange was always scarce, those policies were buttressed by quantitative restrictions on imports and tight exchange control, which increased the inner orientation of the economy even beyond that which would have resulted from those policies undertaken to encourage import substitution. State economic enterprises (SEEs) had been established and expanded to process and market agricultural commodities, to extract and export minerals, and to produce a wide variety of manufactured goods. Negative real interest rates enabled the government to direct resources through allocation of rationed credit, as well as through import licensing.

In the course of economic growth in the postwar period, the Turkish authorities had already twice been confronted with mounting balance of payments difficulties and rising inflation. In both instances, there had been fairly typical stabilization programs, which succeeded in improving the foreign exchange situation and, in the earlier crisis in 1958, drastically reducing inflation.

By the late 1970s, Turkey was confronting yet another crisis. Inflation had accelerated throughout the 1970s, and reached an annual rate of over 100% by

Anne O. Krueger is Arts and Sciences Professor of Economics at Duke University and a research associate of the National Bureau of Economic Research.

The author is indebted to Ömer Gokcekus and Ahmet Kipici for valuable research assistance in gathering recent data and analyzing time series behavior of inflation, and to Tercan Baysan for valuable comments on the penultimate draft of this paper.

late 1979 in a country with relatively few indexation mechanisms and strong sensitivity to it on the part of influential groups (including the civil service and the military).

While the political reaction to inflation would probably in itself have forced policy changes, foreign exchange shortages at an increasingly overvalued exchange rate were also resulting in major difficulties and dislocations. Some economists even estimated that there were negative *gross* foreign exchange reserves by late 1979! Whether true or not, there were certainly long delays in obtaining import licenses and foreign exchange, embassy employees overseas went months without being paid, there was no coffee, and the short supplies of petroleum and other imports resulted in severe dislocations and hardships during the severe Anatolian winter. According to the official statistics, real GNP fell only 5% over the 1977–79 period, but contemporary accounts and observations of those who lived through it suggest a far steeper drop, especially starting in the second half of 1979.

Throughout the latter part of the 1970s, successive coalition governments had attempted unsuccessfully to grapple with economic difficulties. Several IMF-supported programs had been started, only to be abandoned when it proved infeasible to implement them. Governments had changed frequently, in large part in response to dissatisfaction with economic performance. By the beginning of the 1980s, it seemed clear that Turkey was in for yet another round of stabilization following the pattern of 1958 and 1970.

Instead, when policy changes came in early 1980, they were far different both in announcement and in action from the two earlier episodes. Instead of addressing primarily the macroeconomic issues driving inflation and the immediate balance-of-payments difficulties, the authorities announced a program that had two fundamental objectives: to alter underlying economic policies aimed toward growth and to reduce the rate of inflation. While this second objective had been included in both earlier programs (although the Turks were singularly unsuccessful in achieving it in the second), the enunciation and pursuit of the first objective constituted a major departure from past economic policies.

From its initiation, the sectoral reform program was articulated and designed to shift Turkey's entire growth strategy away from import substitution and toward greater integration with the international market. Moreover, it was explicitly stated that the role of the government in the economy was to be greatly diminished and that private enterprise would be relied upon to generate economic growth. From a historical perspective, this was revolutionary indeed! For purposes of this analysis, I shall refer to the entire set of policies designed to achieve this result as being "sectoral" reforms, contrasted with the policies entailed in stabilization that will be termed "macro" reforms.[1]

---

1. There is, however, at least one important and visible link between macro and sectoral reforms, as defined here. That is, the SEEs were incurring large deficits, financed by Central Bank credits.

After 1980, policy reforms continued. Although macro reforms were initially successful, with the rate of inflation falling from over 100% to a low of about 35% in 1982, the rate of inflation thereafter rose again, and inflation continued as a problem throughout the 1980s. By contrast, the sectoral reforms geared to shifting reliance toward the private sector and integrating the Turkish economy with that of the rest of the world gathered momentum as the decade proceeded. By the early 1990s, it could fairly be said that Turkey's sectoral reforms had been—at least to 1991—successful, while Turkey's macro reforms had largely failed. Important questions focused on the sustainability of the sectoral reforms in light of continuing inflation and macroeconomic difficulties.

It is the purpose of this paper to analyze the Turkish reforms of the 1980s and their relationship to growth. A natural starting point is a brief review of the earlier stabilization programs, the topic of section 11.2. Section 11.3 then covers the economic difficulties and policies immediately preceding the January 1980 reforms. Section 11.4 reviews the initial reform program and the response to it. Section 11.5 covers the second phase of reforms, starting in the fall of 1983. Section 11.6 analyzes the real growth of the economy starting in 1983, while section 11.7 covers the macro reforms and their consequences. Section 11.8 addresses the reasons why the macro reforms were so unsuccessful while the sectoral reforms appear to have delivered such satisfactory growth. Section 11.9 concludes by providing a tentative assessment of the sustainability of the altered policies toward the various sectors of the Turkish economy in light of the overall macroeconomic difficulties.

11.2   Two Preceding Cycles

Turkey became an independent state after the First World War, as the Ottoman Empire disintegrated. With Atatürk as a national charismatic leader, economic policy for raising living standards was already an important national issue in the 1920s and 1930s. After a brief effort to develop through laissez-faire in the 1920s, Atatürk switched to etatism[2] as a philosophy in the 1930s, and the first large SEEs were founded, producing textiles, footwear, and a variety of other manufactured goods.

Atatürk died in 1938 but remained the revered founding father of the nation. In the post war period, economic growth resumed, with SEEs expanding rap-

---

Those deficits alone exceeded 5% of GNP by the late 1970s. Reforms restructuring the SEEs in ways that prevented the expansion of Central Bank credit were both sectoral insofar as they increased the efficiency of SEEs (or reduced the resources allocated to inefficient activities) and macro insofar as they reduced inflationary pressures.

2. See Okyar (1965) for an analysis. For present purposes, it suffices to say that etatism was articulated as a rationale for state economic activities through SEEs. These activities were supposed to coexist, however, with private economic activity. Etatism clearly grew out of the distrust of markets that was worldwide in the 1930s.

idly into new import substitution activities. The underlying policy of etatism remained the guiding principle of development efforts until 1980. Starting in the late 1940s, Turkey's economy grew rapidly, as the opportunities afforded by postwar recovery, receipt of Point IV and Marshall Plan aid, and a buoyant world economy all conduced to economic growth. Simultaneously, there was a rapid increase in government expenditures, especially on investment projects designed to accelerate economic growth.

Starting in 1953, however, export growth ceased,[3] both because of the end of the Korean War commodity boom and because of the shift of resources to the buoyant domestic market. Simultaneously the rate of inflation accelerated. As in many other countries at that time, the Turkish authorities were committed to maintaining a fixed nominal exchange rate. By 1954, the government introduced import licensing in an effort to restrain the demand for imports in line with the availability of foreign exchange. Over the next several years, inflationary pressures intensified[4] while foreign exchange earnings continued to drop.

By 1957, the situation was by any measure serious. Surcharges had been imposed on imports; even those who received import licenses waited eight to twelve months for foreign exchange permits. Export earnings were dropping rapidly, and the black market premium was more than 100% above the nominal exchange rate. At that time, as in many other countries, the top political leadership (Adnan Menderes) was adamantly opposed to any change in the nominal exchange rate. By then, Turks were financing imports with suppliers' credits and other short-term, high-interest-bearing notes. As the harvest approached in 1958, however, even that source of financing was disappearing, and it became evident that little if any gasoline would be available to enable the trucks to move the harvest to ports, without a change in policies.

Reluctantly, the government of Turkey agreed with the International Monetary Fund (IMF) to a stabilization program, the key elements of which were a major devaluation (from TL2.8 to TL9 per U.S. dollar); immediate import liberalization and rationalization of import licensing schemes;[5] ceilings on

---

3. Turkey had expanded the area under cultivation for wheat through introduction of tractors and mechanization in the late 1940s and was even the world's largest wheat exporter in the early 1950s. The evidence suggests that this large effort was in fact uneconomic in the long run, and wheat exports peaked in 1953. See Krueger (1974) for a discussion.

4. It is difficult to provide a good estimate of the rate of inflation. The Turkish authorities imposed price controls on most basic consumer goods in an effort to restrain inflation, and it was the official prices of those goods that entered into the official price statistics. According to those statistics, the rate of inflation reached an annual rate of almost 25% by 1958, having exceeded 10% annually since 1954.

5. Until 1958, import licenses had been dealt with on an ad hoc basis. The 1958 program included provisions so that there would be some imports (on a "liberalized list") for which the granting of foreign exchange was more or less automatic, some imports (the "quota list") for which quantitative limits were set and whose allocation was subject to detailed bureaucratic negotiation, and some imports whose origin could only be Turkey's bilateral trading partners. Any commodity not listed was ineligible for importation. This basic system lasted until the early 1980s, with new lists published every six months. See Krueger (1974, chap. 6) for a detailed description of how the system worked.

government expenditures, credit, and the money supply; and an increase in prices of commodities produced by SEEs, with the removal of price controls over most items for the private economy.[6] Import liberalization was financed by IMF and other official credits; official creditors also sponsored and supported debt rescheduling for Turkey's outstanding debt.[7]

Most of the components of this package are fairly standard in IMF-supported programs, and require little comment. A possible exception is the increases in prices of SEEs, which featured prominently in the 1970 and 1980 reforms as well. As already mentioned, efforts to control inflation in the years prior to 1958 consisted largely of the imposition of price controls. Private sector firms responded either by shutting down or by selling in the black market. SEEs, however, sold at official prices and incurred losses. As inflation accelerated, these losses mounted. The losses, in turn, were covered by credits automatically extended by the Central Bank to the various loss-making SEEs. The result was growth in the money supply fueled in significant measure by SEE deficits. Raising the prices of goods produced by SEEs in 1958 naturally resulted in an immediate once-and-for-all increase in the various price indices; after that, however, the reduced rate of expansion of Central Bank credits resulted in a reduced rate of inflation. Indeed, the 1958 Turkish stabilization program was unusual in that real GDP, which had been declining, started growing immediately in response to greater availability of imports, while the rate of inflation dropped dramatically: from 25% (at the understated official measure) in 1958 to less than 5% in 1959.

After the initial stabilization plan in the summer of 1958, export earnings rose, other foreign exchange receipts increased, and the flow of imports returned to more normal levels relative to the level of economic activity. Although there was a temporary setback in 1959 as the expenditure and other ceilings negotiated with the IMF were violated, a military coup in May 1960 was accompanied by a recommitment to the major provisions of the stabilization program. The rate of growth of real GDP accelerated, and Turkey was among the more rapidly growing developing countries for most of the 1960s.

However, Turkey's annual inflation rate in the 1960s was in the 5–10% range, and the nominal exchange rate was held constant after the 1958 devaluation. Public and private investment expenditures had increased rapidly in the early 1960s, financed largely by foreign aid. When, in the later part of the 1960s, foreign aid did not increase, the government nonetheless attempted to maintain the rate of investment. The increased demand for imports, therefore, resulted in lengthening queues at the Central Bank. Delays in obtaining imports needed for spare parts and intermediate goods of a year to eighteen months were common. The resulting excess capacity in newly established im-

6. For an analysis of the program, see Sturc (1968).

7. In order to ascertain the level of indebtedness, the Turkish authorities had to advertise in western European and other newspapers and magazines, asking creditors to notify them as to the amount they were owed: there was no systematic record of debt in Turkey, a situation that did not change until the 1980s. See Krueger (1974, chap. 2) for an account.

port substitution industries, combined with the slowdown in investment projects resulting from delays in obtaining imports, was a visible restraint on economic activity and growth.

Although inflation was accelerating, the chief impetus to the 1970 devaluation was clearly the foreign exchange situation. Although circumstances were by no means as extreme as they had been in 1958, the import substitution activities that had been carried out during the 1960s had left the economy more dependent on imports of intermediate goods and raw materials to continue factory operations than had earlier been the case; inflation was not widely perceived to be a major problem.

The 1970 devaluation had many of the same components as the earlier one, although emphasis was much more on the foreign trade regime and the exchange rate than in 1958. The nominal exchange rate was adjusted from TL9 per U.S. dollar to TL15; the government again received extensive foreign credits, and imports were liberalized, although the "lists" (see note 5) continued to be used in much the same manner as when they were started in 1958.

In contrast to the 1958 devaluation, however, the economy's response to the 1970 devaluation was much more rapid. In particular, export earnings rose sharply, and, at the same time, Turkish workers in Germany and other western European countries remitted sizable amounts of foreign exchange. There was no mechanism readily at hand for the Central Bank to sterilize these inflows, and as a consequence workers' remittances expanded the Turkish money supply sharply. Inflation therefore accelerated, although foreign exchange was plentiful. During the first half of the 1970s, however, real economic growth was rapid, spurred in part by expansionary monetary and fiscal policies, and in part by the increases in investment that the comfortable foreign exchange position permitted.

As of 1975, Turks regarded their real growth rate of around 7% annually almost as an immutable constant: Turkey had been growing rapidly and per capita incomes had been rising steadily since the early 1950s despite population growth well in excess of 2.5% annually.

11.3   Run-up to the Third Crisis

Inflation had already reached an annual rate of 25% by 1973 when the first increase in the world price of oil was effected. Although the nominal exchange rate had been held constant since 1970, foreign exchange receipts from exports and from workers' remittances continued rising sharply, so that there was no immediate foreign exchange problem. Indeed, the Turkish authorities were in the unaccustomed situation of accumulating foreign exchange reserves in 1971 and 1972.

The result was that, when the terms of trade deteriorated sharply because of oil, the authorities failed initially to alter the internal prices of petroleum and its products, letting the SEE handling petroleum instead incur losses and financing the increased cost of imports out of foreign exchange reserves. Fiscal deficits therefore increased in 1974 and 1975, as the overvaluation of the exchange rate associated with accelerating inflation increased, while the fiscal deficit itself and the failure to change the internal price of oil and its derivatives made the situation worse.[8]

Table 11.1 gives data on the economic deterioration between 1975 and 1980. Annual data understate the extent of the difficulties as they mounted late in 1979 and early 1980, as imports increased sharply in 1980 after the January policy changes and the rapid downward spiral in real GDP was reversed. Even by these annual figures, however, it is evident that real GDP grew only 15% between 1975 and 1980, while population increased by almost the same amount. For a country accustomed to rapid growth in per capita incomes, the slowdown was abrupt. Moreover, acceleration of inflation resulted in economic discomfort for the many influential groups—military, civil servants, academics, pensioners—whose incomes were fixed without indexation.[9] In 1976 and 1977, as can be seen in table 11.1, imports continued to grow, albeit slowly. By 1978, however, sources of financing were disappearing, and imports were reduced with consequent dislocations of economic activity.[10]

Several aspects of economic policy had gone badly wrong in the early 1970s. All measures of the price level reflected sharp increases. By 1975, prices are estimated to have been 134% above their 1970 level, yet the nominal exchange rate was still TL 15.15 in 1975—virtually the same as it had been in 1970. Although the nominal exchange rate was altered more frequently after 1975 as inflation accelerated, the GDP deflator increased 258% from 1975 to 1979, while the official price of foreign exchange was increased 165%. The real exchange rate, therefore, had appreciated massively in a situation in which, given the deterioration in Turkey's terms of trade, it should have depreciated.[11]

SEE deficits were large and increasing in the late 1970s. By 1979, transfers to SEEs to cover their deficits accounted for 13.6% of general government expenditures, and the fiscal deficit was equal to more than 4% of GDP (and 16% of government revenues). Meanwhile, nominal interest rates were kept

8. Dervis, De Melo, and Robinson (1982, 346) estimated the separate contributions of each factor to the buildup of the crisis. As of 1977, they estimated that the economic costs of the crisis were equal to about 9.7% of GDP, of which 1.1% was the result of the negative swing in Turkey's terms of trade (primarily but not entirely oil), 5.1% was attributable to reduced foreign resources, 0.9% was due to increased trade distortions, and 2.6% was attributable to the reduction in domestic production necessitated by reduced imports.

9. Despite periodic adjustments, real incomes of persons in these groups fell, as nominal changes were systematically less than the preceding change in the price level, while inflation was accelerating.

10. To be sure, there was considerable smuggling during this period, so that the official statistics may overstate the reduction in imports. Nonetheless, supplies of commodities that are difficult to smuggle, such as oil, were dropping, resulting in severe dislocation.

11. As imperfect as it is, the percentage by which the black market exchange rate exceeds the official rate gives some idea of the extent of distortion in the nominal exchange rate. In 1975, the black market premium is estimated to have been about 10%; by 1978 it was 51.6%; and by early 1979 it reached a level 91.4% above the official exchange rate. See Krueger and Aktan (1992, 27).

Table 11.1   Indicators of Turkish Economic Deterioration, 1975–80

	1975	1976	1977	1978	1979	1980
Real GDP per capita (1975 = 100)	100	109	113	118	116	115
Wholesale prices (1975 = 100)	100	116	142	213	353	761
Current account deficit (millions of US$)	1,648	2,029	3,140	1,265	1,413	3,408
Imports (millions of US$)	4,502	4,872	5,506	4,369	4,815	7,513
Total debt (billions of US$)	3.6	4.3	11.4	14.8	15.9	19.0

Source: Krueger and Aktan (1992), appendix tables for the first four rows; table 6, p. 28, for debt.

low (in part to facilitate financing public debt). The real interest rate, calculated as the difference between the inflation rate and the general nominal interest rate for medium-term credits, was minus 38.5% in April 1978, minus 51.3% in May 1979, and reached minus 100.5% in March 1980.

One other phenomenon of the late 1970s deserves mention. It has already been pointed out that there were weak coalition governments during that period. In part, those weak coalitions reflected underlying divisions within society and societal unrest. This was reflected, inter alia, in the radicalization of labor unions and of student groups, with attendant violence and civil unrest.[12] It is estimated that 8 million man-days were lost to strikes in 1980, compared to 1 million for all of 1979 (Baysan and Blitzer 1991, 359). The impact on the economy of the unions was substantial. On one hand, they demanded, and most got, large wage increases. On the other, once wage increases were granted, unions were frequently reorganized under new leadership and went on strike once again to demand even more. By the late summer of 1979, real wages of factory workers had increased rapidly over the preceding decade, even during the period when real output was declining. From the viewpoint of Turkish industry, however, the strikes and work stoppages were highly disruptive and were at least as damaging as the delays and shortages of imports.

Thus, by any standard, the Turkish economy was in severe disequilibrium by 1980. Inflation had reached triple digits and was still accelerating; imports were more and more constrained, and the premiums on import licenses and on black market foreign exchange were high and rising rapidly; and real output and incomes were falling. The reasons for this are clear in the policy indicators: a highly overvalued and unrealistic nominal exchange rate and interest rate; a large and growing fiscal deficit and rapid expansion of the money supply; and severe restrictions on foreign trade and domestic investment (because of foreign exchange difficulties).

In 1978 and 1979, two stabilization programs were negotiated with the IMF.[13] Both of these were abandoned when the agreed-upon policies were not

12. See Krueger and Turan (1993) for an account.
13. For an excellent account, see Okyar (1983).

enacted, as the coalition governments were simply unable to restrain government expenditures, reduce SEE deficits, or raise taxes.

When Suleyman Demirel became prime minister of yet another coalition government in the fall of 1979, therefore, he inherited an extremely difficult economic situation. He had no more parliamentary support than had the predecessor governments under Bülent Ecevit, but the fact that economic deterioration had been so prolonged perhaps gave him some room for maneuvering. In a sense, the usual political coalitions that had prevented action earlier were rendered ineffective by the severity of the crisis.

11.4   The 1980 Reform Program and Initial Response

By late 1979, there was universal agreement that the economy was once again in crisis. Unlike the earlier episodes, however, there were significant groups (including most prominently the association of Turkish industrialists) that had concluded that the earlier policies of import substitution had failed and would not generate future growth, even if the crisis was overcome. There was active advocacy of an alternative strategy by the Turkish industrialists and others.[14]

When Suleyman Demirel became prime minister, he appointed Turgut Özal to be deputy prime minister in charge of economic policy. Özal and a very small team of bureaucrats (estimated to have been less than ten persons altogether) then drew up a program for reform, which was announced by the prime minister late in January 1980. Even key ministers had been unaware of the scope of the plan outside their own domain; they were asked to sign a variety of decrees on a piecemeal basis and had no advance information as to what other components of the program would be.

There were several key initial measures: (1) devaluation of the Turkish lira from 35 to 70 per U.S. dollar, with an announcement that henceforth the Turkish lira exchange rate would be changed frequently to reflect the differential between domestic and foreign inflation;[15] (2) increases in the prices of almost all goods produced by SEEs, with an announcement that SEEs would in future be free to set their own prices and would not be permitted to borrow from the Central Bank; and (3) a variety of changes in the organization of the various ministries and bureaus that were responsible for economic policy, with the general purpose of reducing the power of some traditional groups and strengthening the hand of the deputy prime minister.

Thereafter, a number of other economic problems were addressed, and additional policy changes were announced at frequent intervals. Turkish debt was rescheduled under the auspices of the London and Paris Clubs, with financial

---

14. See Krueger and Turan (1993) for an extended discussion.

15. In fact, the Turkish lira was depreciated somewhat more rapidly than the differential in inflation between Turkey and her trading partners; see table 11.2.

support from the European Communities as well as the multilateral institutions. After the January devaluation, the nominal exchange rate was altered frequently, until daily changes became routine starting in mid-1981. In June 1980, ceilings on bank deposit rates were lifted. Throughout the year, conditions under which Turks could hold and use foreign exchange were liberalized, as banks and exporters were authorized to retain sizable fractions of their receipts. Trade in gold had been legalized in January.

It should be noted that the initial January 1980 program was announced and implemented with no IMF program. Although there had been contact between Özal's team and IMF staff prior to January, it was undertaken without waiting for IMF approval and support. An IMF agreement came into effect in June,[16] although its main provisions had already been met ahead of schedule. Throughout the 1980s, the IMF and World Bank[17] continued to provide support for Turkey.

These measures were all initiated under the government of Prime Minister Demirel, as already mentioned. However, civil unrest had been a major problem prior to the outset of the program, and the Demirel government ruled only by coalition. Indeed, it may be said that only the crisis proportions of the economic problem permitted Demirel and Özal to act in January. As they presented tax and other measures to Parliament in the summer of 1980, it became evident that Parliament was unlikely to approve them.

In that atmosphere and with violence increasing, the military intervened in September 1980, ousting the Demirel government. Turgut Özal, however, was retained as deputy prime minister in charge of economic policy. Thereafter, a number of additional measures were undertaken. Perhaps most controversial within Turkey, union activity was forbidden, although the same decree prohibited firms from laying off workers.[18] Other measures included relaxation of restrictions governing direct foreign investment, and liberalization of capital markets as regulations governing bank behavior and trade in securities and other financial instruments were modified.

---

16. For particulars, see Okyar (1983).

17. There were five World Bank structural adjustment loans in support of Turkish reforms. Turkey was the first country to receive such support. For an account of World Bank lending, see Kirkpatrick and Onis (1991).

18. Not only was this measure controversial politically, but it makes interpretation of the subsequent behavior of employment and real wages difficult. While output was growing fairly rapidly in the years following 1983, industrial employment and real wages did not begin to show any significant increases until about three years later. Whether this was because union power in the late 1970s had driven industrial wages and employment to such levels that a retrenchment was avoided through these measures, or whether instead of freezing of employment encouraged employers to adopt capital-intensive methods of production while the absence of union activity permitted wages to languish remains an open issue. Clearly, some of each occurred. At any event, by the late 1980s, employment and wages were growing more rapidly, and any analysis of the relationship of the macroeconomic failures and sectoral successes of the Turkish reforms does not hinge on resolution of that issue. See Krueger and Aktan (1992) for data on employment and real wage behavior and a more extended discussion. See also Celasun (1986) for a much more critical interpretation of the role of labor repression in the 1980s.

Initially, the foreign trade regime was not overhauled, although increased availability of funds for imports necessarily meant liberalization of the regime. In the next several years, however, quantitative restrictions on imports were almost completely abolished, and reliance instead shifted to the exchange rate and aggregate demand management as a mechanism for maintaining external balance.[19] Removal of quantitative restrictions was in itself a major change in Turkish economic policy and in the structure of incentives confronting Turkish producers. Starting in 1984, tariffs were also lowered. By the mid-1980s, Turkey's protection would have been described as moderate, as contrasted with the earlier extremely protective regime.

The net effect of these measures on some key policy variables can be seen in table 11.2. The rate of inflation, as measured by the GDP deflator, fell from over 100% in 1980 to 42% in 1981 and 28% in 1982. Simultaneously, frequent adjustments of the exchange rate led to a depreciation of the real exchange rate from a level of 327 at the end of 1979 to 432 at the end of 1980 and 488 at the end of 1982, altogether an increase in incentives to exporters of 32%.[20]

As can also be seen in table 11.2, government expenditures and the fiscal deficit fell sharply. SEE financing from the Central Bank virtually ended, while the reduction in central government expenditures also reduced the fiscal deficit.

However, at the same time as that happened, the financial liberalization had induced many new entrants into Turkish credit markets. These financiers were borrowing and lending in the newly liberalized markets on relatively thin margins, and in the summer of 1982, one of the large ones (Bankcr Kastclli) appeared in imminent danger of bankruptcy. The military government apparently feared a major financial crisis, and reacted by discharging Turgut Özal and replacing him with a politician believed to be much more sympathetic to expansionary monetary and fiscal policy. Shortly thereafter, the military announced that elections would be held in the autumn of 1983.

There followed a year of relaxation of fiscal and monetary policy. In the 1983 elections, Turgut Özal organized a political party, the Motherland Party, which ran against the party supported by the military. The Motherland Party won, and Özal became prime minister. Thereafter, the second stage of reforms began.

Before turning to those reforms, however, it is instructive to assess the reactions of the Turkish economy to the policy changes over the 1980–83 period. Table 11.3 gives some data. As can be seen, real GDP declined for 1980 as a

19. See Baysan and Blitzer (1991) and Krueger and Aktan (1992) for more detailed accounts.

20. In addition to the exchange rate, a number of other measures were adopted to encourage exports. Many, however, had been in place prior to 1980. They certainly contributed to the overall incentive to export, but protection remained sufficient so that at best the export incentives offset a significant proportion of the bias that still remained toward import substitution through the trade regime. That bias began falling significantly after 1984, and the special export incentives were reduced, starting at that time. See Krueger and Aktan (1992, chap. 4) for a detailed discussion. In terms of the *change* in incentives for exporting, the depreciation of the real exchange rate was clearly crucial, and far outweighed the changes in other export incentives.

Table 11.2   Economic Policy Indicators for the 1980s

	1980	1981	1982	1983	1984	1985	1986	1987	1988	1989	1990[a]
Nominal exchange rate (TL/US$)	76	111	163	225	367	522	674	857	1,422	2,121	4,168
GDP deflator (% change)	104	42	28	29	51	41	30	39	66	65	59
Real exchange rate[b]	432	432	488	509	527	522	505	499	512	473	473
Nominal interest rate	30	36	36	36	55	62	62	66	87	85	65
Real interest rate	−89	−5	4	1	2	9	18	13	−14	−16	7
Real government expenditures (% of GDP)	25	23	18	23	21	19	21	22	21	23	24
Fiscal deficit (% of GDP)	4.0	2.6	1.7	2.6	5.3	2.8	3.6	4.4	3.8	4.4	4.1

Sources: Krueger and Aktan (1992), rows 1 and 3 from table 9; row 2 from table 12; row 4 from table 16; and row 5 from data appendix, table 10. Rows 6 and 7 from Central Bank of Turkey, *Annual Reports* (1987, 1989, 1991).

[a]Data for 1990 are not always comparable to those for earlier years. Most are derived from International Monetary Fund, *International Financial Statistics,* and the percentage changes from 1989 to 1990 were linked to the data for earlier years.

[b]The real exchange rate was calculated as the nominal exchange rate deflated by the Turkish wholesale price index and adjusted for the price level of Turkey's Group of 7 trading partners.

Table 11.3   Turkish Economic Indicators, 1979–83

	1979	1980	1981	1982	1983
Real GDP (billions of 1968 TL)	208	206	215	224	232
Growth rate	−0.6	−1.1	4.2	4.5	3.3
Real investment (billions of 1988 TL)					
Private	7.6	6.7	6.2	6.5	6.7
Public	9.9	9.5	10.3	10.6	10.2
Index of industrial output (1986 = 100)	N.A.	N.A.	65.1	70.3	76.2
Exports (billions of US$)	2.3	2.9	4.7	5.7	5.7
Imports (billions of US$)	5.1	7.9	8.9	8.8	9.2
Current account deficit	−3.2	−5.6	−4.5	−3.2	−3.7

Source: Krueger and Aktan (1992), appendix tables.

whole, although there is little doubt that quarterly data, if they were available, would show the upturn starting in the second half of the year. Growth was moderate the following three years. Real private investment continued declining in 1981, and did not begin to increase again until 1982; even in 1983 it did not reach its 1980 level, much less the levels of the late 1970s. These data were reflected in the mood of the times: there was considerable anxiety about the policy changes, and uncertainty as to whether reforms would persist. While removal of bottlenecks and disruptions associated with strikes enabled real GNP to begin increasing, the increases were moderate.

The bright spot in the economy during the first three years after the reforms was the behavior of exports. As is evident from table 11.3, exports of goods and services recorded in official statistics were only $2.3 billion in 1979, less than half the level of imports. Imports would, of course, have been greater had foreign exchange been available.[21]

External financing permitted a 50% increase in imports in 1980, so that the current account deficit increased sharply to $5.6 billion in that year, despite an increase in recorded exports of $600 million, or almost 25%. Growth of exports accelerated over the next three years, however, so that export earnings by 1982 were double their 1980 level, and the current account deficit was back to its 1979 level due to the sustained increase in imports.

By 1983, therefore, it could have been claimed that the 1980 program had met its immediate goals: incentives for exports had increased markedly and exports had responded; the program had induced financial support from the international community, which permitted resumption of an enlarged flow of imports necessary to sustain a higher level of real GDP; and the inflation rate had fallen from over 100% to less than 25%.

11.5   The Second Stage of Reforms

Once Prime Minister Özal assumed office in December 1983, an economics team was assembled with the assignment to carry reforms further. There was a flurry of initial measures, including a major realignment of interest rates (which had been recontrolled in the wake of the Banker Kastelli affair), liberalizations of foreign exchange regulations with removal of virtually all restrictions on tourist travel allowances, permission for commercial banks to retain 80% initially and then 100% of their foreign currency receipts, and even permission for capital exports by Turkish residents (with Central Bank approval). Import licensing procedures were greatly liberalized, and the highest tariff rates were reduced in 1984. In the next several years, import licensing was abandoned, and tariffs were further reduced.

The initial moves were followed by a series of major reforms that shifted the Turkish economy still further away from its earlier centralized-control mode. A value-added tax was introduced in 1985. Reopening of the Istanbul stock exchange (in 1986) and a variety of other measures further liberalized the capital market. A foreign exchange market was established, and treasury bonds began to be sold by weekly auction. Efforts were begun to privatize some of the SEEs.

---

21. There is no doubt that smuggling of imports into the country and means of getting exports out without surrendering foreign exchange meant that actual imports and exports were greater than the officially reported numbers. Nonetheless, there is also no doubt that import shortages were real, and that exports had dropped substantially in the late 1970s.

Meanwhile, earlier controls on SEEs' borrowing had their intended results. Whereas SEEs had required financing from the government budget equivalent to about 14% of total government expenditures in the late 1970s and early 1980s, that percentage fell to 7% in 1984, and then stood in the 2–3% range for several years until it jumped back to 9% in 1991.[22] Meanwhile, a second factor also contributed to reducing recurring government expenditures. That is, expenditures on government personnel dropped, both because government employment was frozen as part of the policy reform package, and because wage adjustments in the public sector lagged significantly behind inflation.

One might have anticipated that these reduced claims on government expenditures would have permitted rapid restoration of fiscal balance. Three factors contributed to offsetting the reductions. First, the Özal government increased expenditures on infrastructure and public works sharply. To a degree, some of these increases reflected deferred maintenance and investment from the 1970s. Roads were widened and extended so that traffic delays and damage to vehicles were reduced; overseas telephone line capacity was greatly increased and domestic service enhanced; decades-long neglect of the city of Istanbul was reversed as public works expenditures changed many aspects of that city; and so on. A second factor was that with increases in the nominal interest rate the costs of servicing the public debt increased, rising from 3% of budgetary expenditures in 1980 to 21% in 1991.

The third factor contributing to increased government expenditures was the "political business cycle." Government expenditures rose markedly prior to each electoral cycle. Table 11.4 gives data on the money supply, its components, and its growth rate from 1979 to 1991. As can be seen, monetary expansion slowed dramatically after 1980, reaching its low point between 1982 and 1983. Thereafter, Central Bank lending accelerated prior to each election in response to the government's borrowing requirements. Those requirements, in turn, were driven in large part by increases in expenditures in the months prior to each election. Toward the end of the decade, as the Motherland Party's percentage of popular votes in the polls fell, these accelerations of expenditures increased. As the data in table 11.2 indicate, government expenditures (which do not include SEE expenditures) increased from their low of 18% of GNP in 1982 to 21% in 1986–88 and to 24% by 1990.

Combined with the increases in overall expenditures, some other practices were instituted that tended to undermine some of the gains that had been achieved. Starting in the mid-1980s, off-budget "special funds" were established for purposes such as "workers' housing," financed largely by import charges that were largely, although not entirely, across the board.[23] In the mid-

22. The SEEs' borrowing requirement rose sharply in 1991, equaling 3.2% of GDP despite a larger transfer from the central government. This latter rose from TL1,265 billion in 1990 to TL12,200 billion in 1991. After allowing for 65% inflation, that constitutes a real increase of 480%!

23. See Krueger and Aktan (1992) for details and estimates of the rates. The rate of tax for the special funds reached 10% in 1990.

Table 11.4   Money Supply and Credit, 1979–91 (end of year; billions of TL)

	1979	1980	1981	1982	1983	1984	1985	1986	1987	1988	1989	1990	1991
Money supply (M4)	610	1,074	2,143	3,178	3,984	5,941	9,209	13,152	19,132	29,736	50,054	76,782	123,694
Currency and sight deposits	468	739	1,019	1,407	2,084	2,448	3,420	5,357	8,682	11,312	19,560	31,399	46,793
Time deposits	88	186	690	1,272	1,393	3,045	5,120	6,919	9,020	15,884	27,582	40,173	70,326
Total (M2)	556	924	1,710	2,679	3,477	5,493	8,540	12,276	17,702	27,195	47,142	71,571	117,120
Central bank deposit	144	267	673	866	993	1,279	1,630	1,760	2,371	5,343	8,653	9,947	15,031
Foreign liabilities	199	646	829	1,194	2,129	4,062	6,930	11,955	23,044	38,621	48,564	65,051	113,300
Foreign exchange deposits									1,884	2,926	4,398	5,429	8,034
Central bank lending	382	655	926	911	1,234	880	1,300	1,828	3,439	5,142	6,699	8,294	19,888
Treasury	92	189	262	266	339	528	795	1,052	1,407	2,082	2,565	2,901	13,589
Public enterprise	123	178	233	257	251	37	122	213	763	1,082	1,322	1,565	5,420
Banks	121	240	377	321	569	278	333	479	1,124	1,500	2,200	2,436	3,395
Commercial bank deposits	434	767	1,545	2,384	3,109	5,007	8,038	11,750	17,109	26,209	43,244	66,155	93,219
Commercial bank lending													
Industry	156	283	459	557	526	861	1,722	2,517	3,651	4,233	5,292	8,369	12,815
Agriculture	83	146	266	335	512	530	956	1,782	2,956	4,521	7,404	13,150	18,436
Foreign trade and tourism	28	61	127	440	596	702	985	1,798	2,315	3,432	6,409	10,965	20,748
Housing and construction	17	19	42	71	130	250	594	1,330	2,693	4,127	5,571	8,658	10,255
Domestic trade	47	75	148	284	482	560	910	2,049	3,450	4,961	9,634	19,612	30,759
Unclassified	92	170	213	21	38	64	127	118	240	397	555	1,749	3,308
Total	446	790	1,319	1,806	2,418	3,149	5,568	10,053	16,034	22,771	37,050	65,648	102,240
Annual growth rates													
Money supply (M3)		76	100	48	25	49	55	43	45	55	68	53	61
Total (M2)		66	85	57	30	58	55	44	44	54	73	52	64
Central bank deposit		85	152	29	15	29	27	8	35	125	62	15	51
Central bank lending		71	41	-2	35	-29	48	41	88	50	30	24	140
SEE borrowing													
Commercial bank borrowing		98	57	-15	77	-51	20	44	135	33	47	11	39

Source: Central Bank of turkey, Quarterly Bulletin, 1992–1.

Table 11.5   Economic Performance after 1984

	1984	1985	1986	1987	1988	1989	1990	1991
Real GNP (trillions of 1985 TL)	26.4	27.8	30.0	32.3	33.5	34.1	37.3	38.0
Change from preceding year (%)	6.0	5.3	7.9	7.7	3.7	1.8	9.4	1.9
Investment (trillions of TL)	4.8	5.8	7.3	8.7	8.4	8.1	10.3	11.1
Exports of goods and services (billions of US$)	7.4	8.3	7.6	10.3	11.9	11.8	13.0	13.7
Imports of goods and services (billions of US$)	10.3	11.2	10.7	13.6	13.7	16.0	22.6	21.0
Current account balance (billions of US$)	−1.4	−1.0	−1.5	−0.8	1.6	0.9	−2.6	0.3

Sources: Krueger and Aktan (1992), appendix tables; International Monetary Fund, *International Financial Statistics Yearbook 1992;* OECD, *Economic Outlook* (June 1992).

1980s as well, the government undertook a foreign exchange risk insurance scheme (FERIS), under which it lent in domestic currency to investors who financed their activities with loans and assumed the foreign exchange risk. In the 1970s, a similar scheme, the convertible Turkish lira deposit scheme, had resulted in large increases in the money supply when depositors had been insured against foreign exchange risk in the context of rising inflation.[24]

11.6   Real Growth after 1983

After about 1984, the results of the sectoral reforms in the Turkish economy began to show. They were reflected in rising private investment, accelerated growth of real GNP, and continued growth of exports of goods and services. The data in table 11.5 provide an indication of the degree of success.

As can be seen, real GNP growth averaged over 7% annually in the five years starting in 1984. The OECD (1991, 91) estimates that total factor productivity, which had grown at an average annual rate of 1.1% in 1979–85 with output growth of 3.8% and negative growth of capital productivity, grew at an average annual rate of 4.5% in 1987–89, with an 8% rate of growth of output in nongovernment economic activities.

Rapid export growth also continued: exports had constituted only around 5% of GNP in the late 1970s and were 20% of GNP by 1987. This attests to

24. See Celasun and Rodrik (1989) for an account. The 1980 scheme was not as explosive as the 1970 scheme because interest rates were significantly higher relative to the inflation rate, and all interest rates were adjusted every six months. In the 1970s, fixed nominal interest rates, well below the rate of inflation, had persisted for the life of the loan.

the enormous structural changes that were taking place in the Turkish economy in response to the sectoral reforms.

Although imports of goods and services were also growing, the Turkish current account balance, which had been around $5 billion in 1980 and in the range of $3–4 billion in 1981–85 (see table 11.3), fell to less than $1 billion by 1987 and even turned positive in 1988 and 1989, and again in 1991.

11.7   Failure with Macro Reforms

Thus, in real terms, there was every reason to believe that the Turkish policy changes of the 1980s had been successful. Whereas in 1980 it was believed that further growth possibilities through import substitution had probably been exhausted, by the late 1980s, it was evident that Turkey's potential for growth through integrating with the world economy was substantial. Moreover, the earlier suspicion of private business that had accompanied etatism had been replaced by recognition that Turkish industry could perform when provided with appropriate incentives and adequate infrastructure.

Despite these successes, however, the macro reforms were in difficulty. As already indicated, the major problem was that government expenditures increased beyond the ability of the government to increase tax collections. Government expenditures were growing more rapidly than GNP, despite its rapid growth. This is reflected in the rising share of government expenditures in GNP shown in table 11.6. This increase in expenditures took place despite the repression of civil servant salaries and the virtual elimination of SEE deficits as a budgetary drain (at least until the 1990s). The major increases in expenditures were on infrastructure and interest on the debt, on a fairly sustained basis, and on transfer payments prior to each round of elections. This is reflected in table 11.6, which gives data on government expenditures and their composition. As can be seen, interest payments constituted only 4% of government expenditures in 1981 and had risen to more than 20% by the late 1980s. Investment expenditures rose absolutely and as a share of total expenditures until 1987, and fell thereafter, while transfers fluctuated with the proximity to elections. Simultaneously, tax revenues were growing more slowly than income.[25]

There is no mystery as to why inflation persisted. Throughout the 1980s, monetary expansion continued and by all estimates was the crucial determining factor in the inflation rate. To be sure, financial liberalization, and in particular the moves toward full convertibility of the Turkish lira, led to some currency substitution: whereas the ratio of M2 to GNP fell from .224 to .203 over the

---

25. The imposition of the value-added tax in 1985 was judged a great success and yielded more revenue initially than had been anticipated. However, in order to improve incentives, the Özal government had reduced very high marginal tax rates and corporate tax rates. The net result was that tax revenues did not rise even proportionately with income. Gokcekus and Kipici (1992) ran a logarithmic regression of tax revenues on GNP for the period from 1980 to 1991. Their estimated elasticity of tax revenues with respect to real GNP growth for the entire period is .84.

Table 11.6 Consolidated Budget, 1979–91 (billions of TL)

	1979	1980	1981	1982	1983	1984	1985	1986	1987	1988	1989	1990	1991[a]
Expenditures	613	1,110	1,503	1,575	2,613	3,785	5,263	8,160	13,043	21,447	38,871	68,527	129,345
Current	262	497	645	720	1,069	1,488	2,086	3,051	4,538	7,460	16,660	33,452	60,900
Investment	95	170	310	344	503	677	989	1,619	2,642	3,564	5,818	10,055	16,600
Transfers	256	443	481	434	831	1,179	1,514	2,159	3,598	5,445	8,134	11,054	27,723
SEEs	83	153	214	233	292	275	181	138	446	1,025	1,223	1,257	11,200
Interest	N.A.	N.A.	67	87	210	441	674	1,330	2,266	4,978	8,259	13,966	24,122
Revenues	526	933	1,330	1,424	2,314	2,806	4,476	6,754	10,445	17,587	31,369	56,753	97,000
Taxes	406	750	1,191	1,305	1,934	2,372	3,829	5,972	9,051	14,232	25,550	45,399	78,650
Nontaxes	120	183	139	119	380	434	647	782	1,394	3,355	5,819	11,354	18,350
Deficits	87	177	173	151	299	979	787	1,406	2,598	3,860	7,502	11,774	32,345
Net domestic borrowing	31	17	50	28	167	137	498	476	896	2,433	5,982	7,942	1,812
GNP	2,200	4,435	6,555	8,722	11,552	18,375	27,789	39,310	58,565	100,582	170,412	287,254	454,838
% of total expenditures													
Current	43	45	43	46	41	39	40	37	35	35	43	49	47
Investment	15	15	21	22	19	18	19	20	20	17	15	15	13
Transfers	42	40	32	28	32	31	29	26	28	25	21	16	21
SEEs	14	14	14	15	11	7	3	2	3	5	3	2	9
Interest	N.A.	N.A.	4	6	8	12	13	16	17	23	21	20	19
% of total revenues													
Taxes	77	80	90	92	84	85	86	88	87	81	81	80	81
Nontaxes	23	20	10	8	16	15	14	12	13	19	19	20	19
Ratios													
Government expenditures/GNP	28	25	23	18	23	21	19	21	22	21	23	24	28
Deficit/revenue	17	19	13	11	13	35	18	21	25	22	24	21	33
Deficit/GNP	4.0	4.0	2.6	1.7	2.6	5.3	2.8	3.6	4.4	3.8	4.4	4.1	7.1

Sources: for 1979–80, State Planning Organization, *The Developments before the 5th Development Plan;* for 1981–82, Central Bank of Turkey Annual Report, 1985; for 1983, Central Bank of Turkey Annual Report, 1987; for 1984–86, Central Bank of Turkey Annual Report, 1989; for 1987–91, Central Bank of Turkey Annual Report, 1991. The numbers in Central Bank of Turkey annual reports are based on Undersecretariat of Treasury and Foreign Trade provisional numbers.

[a]Provisional numbers.

1984–90 period, the ratio of M2 plus foreign exchange holdings of Turkish nationals rose from .231 to .253 (having been as high as .275 in 1986) over that period.[26] The Central Bank tried to use a variety of instruments to curb inflation, but was essentially powerless to do so in the face of the financing needs of the government budget.[27] In 1991, the OECD provided reduced form econometric estimates of the inflation rate and the difference between the government deficit and the effect of output growth on base-money demand. According to those estimates, over 70% of the variability in underlying inflation in Turkey could be explained by the monetization of public sector deficits.[28]

Until the late 1980s, the association of prospective elections with successive bouts of inflation (which are much more evident in quarterly data than in annual) was evident to all, and there was some credibility to the notion that government expenditures would be contained "after the election." By the late 1980s, however, it was apparent to all that the support for Prime Minister Özal and the Motherland Party was weakening, and that there was little prospect that government budgetary discipline could be relied upon to bring about a significant reduction in the rate of inflation.

When in 1991 new elections returned Suleyman Demirel to the prime minister's office leading a coalition government, the earlier problems intensified. As can be seen from table 11.6, the fiscal deficit increased sharply, as, among other things, the SEE drain on the government budget increased sharply.

11.8   Reasons for Successful Sectoral and Failed Macro Reforms

There is little mystery remaining in why there was Turkish inflation. The interesting questions center on how the sectoral reforms could have succeeded, at least initially, while the macro reforms were unable to stabilize the economy, and how macroeconomic instability has affected and will affect the sustainability of the sectoral reforms. The first question is tackled here. The second question must await analysis of the first.

Three major factors probably account for the success and durability of the sectoral reforms during the 1980s. First, there was the evident failure of earlier economic policies. Second, there was the personality, determination, and con-

26. From the background paper by Gokcekus and Kipici (1992), based on data presented in Atiyas and Ersel (1992).

27. In 1983–84, there was an effort to curb inflationary expectations by setting the short-term interest rate above the long-term interest rate. When the inflation rate did not decline, however, people shifted to holding short-term accounts, and the policy was abandoned. The Central Bank began auctioning treasury bills in 1985, which drove up the cost of borrowing. Politically, however, there seems to have been no way to curb government expenditures.

In order to investigate whether inflation caused money creation or conversely, Gokcekus and Kipici (1992, 3) used quarterly data for first quarter 1983 through fourth quarter 1991. They used the Schwartz criterion and used a two-quarter lag structure. They found very strong causality between the quarterly inflation rate and changes in reserve money, in both directions, but with stronger causation from money to inflation and the price level than conversely.

28. See also Rodrik (1990), who provides a rationale for such an estimation procedure.

trol of Prime Minister Özal. Third, there was the initial success of the sectoral reforms in bringing about evident changes.

Before addressing these three factors individually, however, one other feature of the Turkish experience must be noted. That is, at least until 1988, the rate of inflation *had* come down, and the argument put forward by Prime Minister Özal and the Motherland Party—that inflation would be reduced after the election—had some credibility. Equally, in the early 1980s, stabilization had initially succeeded, and provided scope for the sectoral reforms within a macroeconomic framework that appeared to offer promise of stability. The gains for the economy that resulted from both the early sectoral reforms and from stabilization provided a momentum that permitted accelerating economic growth at least through the 1986–88 period.

The first factor that permitted the reforms, especially the sectoral reforms, to continue was the evident failure of earlier policies. The fact that the economy had been in crisis, and that the government of Bülent Ecevit had tried the old remedies with little success, had convinced many Turks that there was no alternative to change. In effect, opposition to change had been defeated by the failure of the earlier policies.

The second factor, the personality and commitment of Prime Minister Özal, cannot be doubted. Not only did he believe in changing the role of the government in the economy, he believed it was the achievement for which history would remember him. In that sense, it was at the top of his agenda, and received his personal attention. After the military takeover in September 1980, he had the support of the military for the continuation of the reform program. That gave him, and the technocrats who worked with him, considerable latitude in the short run. Although he lost that authority in 1983, he regained it with the election late in that year, and was again able to appoint and support technocrats who shared his vision of a changed Turkish economy.

During the 1980–83 period, it may be noted, Turkish economic growth was modest, albeit considerably more satisfactory than it had been in the late 1970s.[29] Considerable opposition to the reforms emerged in 1984–85, as military rule had ended and opposition became more vocal. However, by that time, economic growth was accelerating, and that helped to mute it. It is arguable that if growth had not accelerated when it did, the opposition would have been able to reverse some of the sectoral reforms, especially in the import regime.

If those factors account for the sustainability of the sectoral reforms, at least through the late 1980s, why were the macro reforms less successful? Proximately, of course, the reason is that the government was unable to increase revenues or reduce expenditures in ways that would permit the Central Bank

---

29. Most countries during 1980–83 were in deep recession, and it may be argued that Turkish economic growth was sluggish for that reason. The fact that Turkey was doing so much better than other countries, however, was little noted in the domestic policy debate.

to brake the growth of the money supply more than it in fact did. The question, then, is why the government fiscal posture remained so expansionary.

That answer, too, has several parts. First, there is the personality of Özal. Second, there were some genuine infrastructural problems that needed to be addressed if the private sector was to be able to expand in accordance with Özal's blueprint. Third, and most important, however, were the political constraints imposed on the Motherland Party in its attempt to maintain power.

There seems to be little doubt that, committed as Özal was to shifting toward more reliance on the private sector for economic growth, he was also an engineer and, perhaps because of that, a builder. He believed that better telephones, roads, port facilities, and other infrastructure would pay for themselves in accelerated growth. In that sense, he attached less weight to the goal of combatting inflation than he did to the goal of resuming and accelerating growth with more efficient allocation of resources and reliance on the private sector. Belief in the role of incentives led him to support reductions in the earlier very high marginal rates of corporate and income taxation. Despite the success of the value-added tax, tax revenues simply did not rise as rapidly as real income, which contributed to the difficulties. Özal also almost certainly underestimated the risk of inflation, and the ease with which monetary expansion before various elections could be reversed afterward.

The need for improved infrastructure clearly fed into Özal's perceptions. There is little doubt that Turkish exports could not have expanded as much as they did if telephone connections had not been improved, if port and domestic carrying capacity had not been expanded, and if power facilities had not been greatly increased.

But the third factor, the political imperatives of remaining in office, was clearly compelling. In fact, if one observes the explosion in government expenditures attendant upon the shift in power in 1991, one might conclude that Özal had been remarkably successful in containing demands from various political constituencies for greater expenditures. The fact is that Özal's support was weakening, and in an effort to retain power, he apparently perceived little option but to increase expenditures in the hope of gaining support. In the end, he was unsuccessful, but the coalition government that followed found the imperative to increase government expenditures even more compelling, and inflationary pressures intensified.

11.9   Can Sectoral Reforms Succeed while Macro Reforms Fail?

The more difficult question is the impact that failed macro reforms will ultimately have on Turkish economic growth and the sustainability of the sectoral reforms. To date, the evidence is mixed. By the late 1980s, when the inflation rate was remaining stubbornly in the 60–70% range, there was an interval when changes in the nominal exchange rate lagged far behind those in the rate

Table 11.7   **Inflation Rates and the Real Exchange Rate, late 1986–92**

	1986	1987	1988	1989	1990	1991
Rate of inflation (%)[a]	30	32	68	70	53	55
Nominal exchange rate	674	857	1422	2121	2608	5079
Real exchange rate (1985 = 100)[b]	99	95	94	82	59	74

[a]Rate of inflation is percentage change in the wholesale price index, from SIS, *Statistical Yearbook of Turkey* for 1988 and earlier; from Central Bank of Turkey, *Annual Report* (1991) for later years.
[b]Real exchange rate is the nominal exchange rate deflated by the Turkish wholesale price index. An increase in the index indicates a depreciation in the real exchange rate.

of inflation. The result was a major real appreciation of the Turkish lira. Table 11.7 gives the relevant data.

As can be seen, the nominal exchange rate increased by less than the Turkish rate of inflation in each year after 1985. At first, the real appreciation was modest, and arguably was within the range that may well have been appropriate, given rates of inflation in Turkey's major trading partners (at most 4% annually), and the decline in the price of oil in 1986. By 1989, however, the real appreciation was much larger, and in 1990, the nominal exchange rate changed by less than two-thirds the rate of inflation.

By late 1989, the real appreciation of the Turkish lira was already having a visible effect on export earnings and the demand for imports (see table 11.5). By 1991, however, the Turkish lira was depreciating in nominal terms by more than the rate of inflation. Clearly, had the real appreciation of the Turkish lira continued, it would not have been possible to maintain the open trade regime: import licensing would have had to be reimposed, which in itself would have represented a major setback for the credibility of the entire set of sector reforms.[30]

Since 1988, however, the rate of economic growth has fluctuated sharply (see table 11.5). Much of the fluctuation may be attributed to alternative tightening and easing of monetary policy and credit in response to the fluctuations in aggregate demand resulting from expansionary fiscal policies, especially prior to elections.

Those fluctuations in themselves would appear to constitute something of a damper on the potential for economic growth. Real rates of interest have been as high as 50% in periods when the authorities were attempting to reduce aggregate demand. Those rates in themselves, as well as uncertainty as to their future levels, must also be somewhat growth retarding.

Even more problematic, however, is the fact that there is little prospect for

30. There was some concern in the late 1980s that real private investment in manufacturing, necessary to support a continued increase in exports, might not be increasing. Data for the early 1990s, however, indicate that this phenomenon was reversed in 1990. See OECD (1992).

significantly reduced fiscal expansion in the near future. The present government, a coalition, does not appear to have the political ability to withstand expansionary measures. The public borrowing requirement, equal to 12.5% of GNP in 1991, was forecast at 8.8% of GNP for 1992, but by August it seemed evident that that target would not likely be achieved (*Financial Times,* August 3, 1992, 3).

However, if the authorities maintain an open trade and payments regime, it would appear that prospects are for inflation itself to become the "crisis" problem that must somehow be resolved. Given past political sensitivities to inflation, it is perhaps surprising that there has not already been more political protest against it. Yet given a weak coalition government, accelerating inflation and macroeconomic difficulties seem very likely.

The important question is probably not whether there will need to be a period of tight fiscal and monetary policy. The question is how inflation rates of at least 60–70%, if not more, culminating in a period of austerity, will affect the sectoral reforms which so far have succeeded in the Turkish economy.

It is not possible to provide a definitive answer. On one hand, it is possible that the present coalition government, in response to increasing political discontent over inflation, may respond with reimposition of controls over various sectors of the economy, including price controls, credit rationing, import licensing, fixation of the nominal exchange rate to attempt to contain inflation, and other measures. If this should happen, it would of course imply that failure to have achieved macroeconomic stability would have undermined the sectoral economic reforms. Turkey would then presumably undergo a period of stabilization followed by another period of sectoral reform at some time in the future, with poor growth prospect in the interim.

On the other hand, there are some grounds for being somewhat more optimistic. First, the performance of private producers, both in bringing better-quality items to the Turkish market and in competing abroad, has greatly reduced the suspicion with which private economic activity was viewed by the majority of Turks. Because of the greater confidence of the public in the business community, its political positions and influence on the political process are more important than they were prior to 1980.

Second, the earlier import substitution policies seem to have been greatly discredited in the crisis of the late 1970s. While it is imaginable that import restrictions might be reimposed in reaction to accelerating triple-digit inflation, it is not imaginable that Turks would believe that these controls were supporting economic growth as they earlier did. As such, the basis for removing them would be greater.

Third, and perhaps most important, however, is that Turks, especially the middle- and upper-income groups whose desire for modernization and whose views on economic development strategy were so important in support of etatism and government intervention, have benefited enormously from the reforms. Restrictions on currency have been largely removed, and Turks can travel freely. Imported goods are available in the shops, including items such as pharmaceuticals and books that earlier had been more readily obtainable in the black market. And the quality of goods produced domestically has improved, in many cases dramatically. The likelihood that the intellectuals who exercise leadership roles in shaping public opinion could be persuaded of the virtues of the ancien régime seems fairly remote.

The questions then are probably two. The first is whether the Turkish economy can continue to function moderately satisfactorily in the context of rapid inflation. If it can, the next question, and probably the most important one, is whether a macroeconomic stabilization program can be adopted and implemented at some future date in ways that do not seriously distort private sector incentives. If so, the sectoral reforms of the 1980s will have been an important stepping stone toward further growth of the Turkish economy. Even if not, Turkish economic performance and productivity improved significantly in the 1980s. While there would be considerable waste in having to repeat the sectoral reform process, there has been a great deal of learning, and future Turkish efforts would start from a considerably higher base because of the experience of the 1980s.

References

Atiyas, I., and Ersel, H. 1992. The Impact of Financial Reform: The Turkish Experience. World Bank, Washington, DC. Manuscript.

Baysan, Tercan, and Charles Blitzer. 1991. Turkey. In Demetris Papageorgiou, Michael Michaely, and Armeane M. Choksi, eds., *Liberalizing Foreign Trade*, vol. 6, *The Experience of New Zealand, Spain, and Turkey*, 263–405. Oxford: Basil Blackwell.

Celasun, Merih. 1986. Income Distribution and Employment Aspects of Turkey's Post-1980 Adjustment. *METU Studies in Development* 16 (3–4).

Celasun, Merih, and Rodrik, Dani. 1989. Debt, Adjustment, and Growth: Turkey. In Jeffrey D. Sachs and Susan M. Collins, eds., *Developing Country Debt and Economic Performance*, vol. 3, *Country Studies: Indonesia, Korea, Philippines, Turkey*, 615–808. Chicago: University of Chicago Press.

Dervis, Kemal, Jaime De Melo, and Sherman Robinson. 1982. *General Equilibrium Models for Development Policy.* Cambridge: Cambridge University Press.

Gokcekus, Ömer, and Ahmet Kipici. 1992. Background Paper on Turkish Inflation. Duke University Manuscript.

Kirkpatrick, Colin, and Ziya Onis. 1991. Turkey. In Paul Mosley, Jane Harrigan, and John Toye, eds., *Aid and Power: The World Bank and Policy-Based Lending*, vol. 2, *Case Studies*, 9–38. London: Routledge.

Krueger, Anne O. 1974. *Foreign Trade Regimes and Economic Development: Turkey.* New York: Columbia University Press.

Krueger, Anne O., and Okan Aktan. 1992. *Swimming against the Tide: Turkish Trade Reforms in the 1980s.* San Francisco: International Center for Economic Growth.

Krueger, Anne O., and Ilter Turan. 1993. The Politics and Economics of Turkish Policy Reform in the 1980s. In Robert H. Bates and Anne O. Krueger, eds., *Political and*

Economic Interactions in Economic Policy Reform: Experience from Eight Countries, 333–86. Oxford: Basil Blackwell.

Okyar, Osman. 1965. The Concept of Etatism in Turkey. *Economic Journal* 75 (March): 98–111.

———. 1983. Turkey and the IMF: A Review of Relations, 1978–1982. In John Williamson, ed., *IMF Conditionality,* 533–62. Washington, DC: Institute for International Economics.

OECD. 1991. *OECD Economic Surveys: Turkey, 1990/1991.* Paris: OECD.

———. 1992. *OECD Economic Surveys: Turkey, 1991/1992.* Paris: OECD.

Rodrik, Dani. 1990. Premature Liberalization, Incomplete Stabilization: The Özal Decade in Turkey. In Michael Bruno, Stanley Fischer, Elhanan Helpman, and Nissan Liviatan, eds., *Lessons of Economic Stabilization and Its Aftermath,* 323–53. Cambridge: MIT Press.

Sturc, Ernest. 1968. Stabilization Policies: Experience of Some European Countries in the 1950s. *International Monetary Fund Staff Papers* (July): 197–219.

12 Stopping Three Big Inflations: Argentina, Brazil, and Peru

Miguel A. Kiguel and Nissan Liviatan

12.1 Introduction

The recent hyperinflations in Argentina, Brazil, and Peru defy much of the widely accepted views regarding the origins and ends of hyperinflations. These "classical" views essentially state that hyperinflations have clear causes, exceptionally large budget deficits financed by money creation, and are brought to a sudden end, through a comprehensive stabilization program. In addition, the stabilization is achieved without much cost in terms of growth and unemployment. Sargent (1982) provides convincing empirical evidence for these propositions based on the European hyperinflations in the midtwenties. The more recent hyperinflation and stabilization in Bolivia by and large conforms with this view.[1]

In contrast, in two of the more recent hyperinflations, Argentina and Brazil, the origins are less clear. Prior to the hyperinflation, deficits, while large, did not reach enormous proportions while seigniorage levels were not higher than in the previous two decades. The fiscal situation did not reach the crisis proportions of the classical hyperinflations. Instead, these hyperinflations appear to have been the final stage of a long process of high and increasing rates of inflation, in which a final explosion was all but unavoidable. The origins of the

Miguel A. Kiguel is a principal economist in the office of the vice president and chief economist at the World Bank. Nissan Liviatan is professor of economics at Hebrew University and a consultant with the World Bank.

The views expressed in this paper do not necessarily reflect those of the World Bank or its affiliated institutions. The authors are grateful to James Hanson, Leonardo Leiderman, Michael Michaely, and participants at the conference on Stabilization and the Recovery of Growth, held at the Di Tella Institute in Buenos Aires and at the Development Workshop at the University of Montreal, for helpful comments, and to Francisca Castro for her assistance in preparing this paper. This paper was completed in November 1992 and reflects economic developments until that time.

1. The Bolivian hyperinflation and the ensuing stabilization is described in Sachs (1986) and Morales (1988), among others.

Peruvian hyperinflation, on the other hand, are more similar to the classical episodes.

Another difference is that the origins of the classical hyperinflations were clearly related to external problems: reparation payments after World War I, a significant shift in external transfers in Bolivia. In contrast, in the recent episodes domestic factors played a major role while external ones (the debt crisis of the early eighties) were of secondary importance.

The process of stopping hyperinflation has also been more cumbersome than in the classical cases. While experiences varied from country to country, a quick glance at the episodes suggests that policies that have much in common with those that were successful in stopping hyperinflation in its tracks in Europe and in Bolivia, did not yield the same outcomes in the recent three episodes. Although these countries also adopted orthodox stabilization programs of different intensities, based on fiscal balance and tight money, and some of the programs went a long way in demonstrating a change of regime of the type discussed by Sargent, the results were mixed. They all succeeded in stabilizing the exchange rate and in bringing down inflation drastically from the peak of the hyperinflation; however, inflation did not stop in its tracks. Instead, in the more successful cases it remained stuck for a while at rates that on average ranged from 5 to 10% a month, while there were some bouts of high inflation. The programs did not succeed in stabilizing prices in the same way as in the aftermath of the classical hyperinflations.

This paper examines the main reasons for the differences between the classical and the new hyperinflations regarding their origins, and the characteristics of the stabilization process that brought them to an end. We recognize that the recent hyperinflations do not constitute a perfectly homogeneous group, both regarding the origins (Peru having a classical flavor) and the commitment to stabilize (Brazil being the weakest in this respect). Nevertheless, in broad terms there are distinctive features that are observed to different degrees in the new episodes that stand in sharp contrast with the classical hyperinflations.

A central message of this paper is that the recent episodes were different because they took place in countries that had a relatively long history of high inflation. Once inflation is high, it can be destabilized into a hyperinflationary path even by relatively small shocks. Likewise, the process of bringing down inflation is generally longer, and it is more difficult to sustain in these countries. Previous failed stabilizations undermine the credibility of a new program. In order to convince the public the policymakers need to undertake major structural reforms, such as privatization of large state enterprises, reduction in the size of the public sector, and institutional reforms in the central bank. Short of these reforms, any short-term reduction in the budget deficit would seem fragile and unsustainable.

We also argue that, by and large, in the recent episodes countries had more control over the inflation process, as well as on the damaging effects of inflation. Brazil and Peru, for example, experienced high rates of inflation (between

20 and 49% per month) for prolonged periods without facing a full-blown acceleration. This ability to maintain these extreme inflation rates within bounds is unique to these high-inflation economies. Likewise, the ability to limit the damaging effects of inflation is evidenced by the evolution of tax revenues during hyperinflation. In the classical episodes hyperinflation induced a collapse of tax revenues (as a result of the Olivera-Tanzi effect). In contrast, Argentina and Brazil were able to limit the fiscal damage of hyperinflation.

The paper is organized as follows. Section 12.2 presents some basic facts about the behavior of inflation in the episodes that we study, and show that Brazil and Peru had more control over inflation than the other episodes included in our study. Section 12.3 examines the whole process of hyperinflation and stabilization in the classic hyperinflations, with especial attention to the Bolivian case. Section 12.4 concentrates on the causes of the hyperinflations in Argentina, Brazil, and Peru. It is argued that the new episodes are indeed of a different nature, mainly because they took place in countries with a tradition of high inflation. We of course recognize that there were clear differences within this group. Peru has more similarities with traditional episodes regarding the causes, though it managed to avoid a full acceleration of inflation. In Argentina and Brazil the hyperinflation was triggered by different forces. Section 12.5 investigates in what respects the recent stabilization process in Argentina, Brazil, and Peru can be considered as a departure from previous, less comprehensive stabilization attempts, and to what extent we can consider them as representing a change of regime. We also briefly examine the impact of these programs on inflation, and discuss the differences from the classical hyperinflations. We conclude in section 12.6 with some brief remarks on the costs of the recent hyperinflations.

12.2 Basic Features of Inflation

Table 12.1 illustrates some of the differences between the classical and the new hyperinflations.[2] We used Cagan's criterion for determining the beginning and end of a hyperinflation. In his own words, "I shall define hyperinflations as beginning in the month the rise in prices exceeds 50 percent and ending in the month before the rise in prices drops below that amount and stays below for at least a year" (Cagan 1956, 25). In most cases it is easy to establish the beginning and end of the episodes. Peru is the only gray area in our sample because, although inflation reached 114% in September 1988, the next month it fell below Cagan's 50% benchmark and remained at the lower level for almost two years. Thus, if we use Cagan's definition in a strict sense, Peru experienced two hyperinflations, one in 1988 that lasted just one month, and another

2. The appendix tables at the end of the chapter provide more detailed data of the evolution of inflation.

Table 12.1   Differences between Classical and New Hyperinflations

	(1) Approximate Beginning	(2) Approximate Duration (months)	(3) # of Months Inflation above 50%	(4) Hyperinflation Cycles	(5) # of Months Inflation between 20 and 49%
Austria	1921.10	12	6	3	7
Bolivia	1984.04	18	9	4	10
Germany	1923.08	17	14	3	7
Hungary	1923.03	12	5	3	8
Poland	1923.01	13	9	3	7
Argentina[a]	1989.05	11	6	2	5
Brazil[a]	1989.12	4	4	1	15
Peru[a]	1990.07	2	2	1	25

[a] Includes data until the end of 1991.

in 1990 for two months. However, we do not think that this would be a good representation of what happened. The fact that Peru did not experience a full-blown hyperinflation at that time was mainly a fluke, since it was on the verge of it on several occasions. In this paper we take the view that Peru's hyperinflation started in September 1988 and analyzed it in this fashion.[3]

A comparison of these episodes indicates that the classical hyperinflations were by and large longer and more extreme than those of Brazil and Peru. Argentina is the only recent episode where the pattern of inflation is similar to the classical episodes. The second column of table 12.1 indicates the duration of these episodes. Bolivia is the longest within this group, lasting for eighteen months, while the shortest of the classical hyperinflations were Austria and Hungary (twelve months). Argentina comes close, as it lasted for eleven months. The new hyperinflations in Brazil and Peru were much shorter. In Brazil it lasted only four months; in Peru it was short, although Peru was on the verge for a long time.

There is also a distinction regarding the intensity of the episodes. Germany is unique in our sample for the exorbitantly high inflation rates. But even abstracting from that case, it is clear that the other classical episodes were more extreme than Peru or Brazil, while Argentina is not clear-cut. Three crude indicators are the number of months in which inflation exceeded Cagan's 50% benchmark, the number of extreme inflationary bouts within the whole span of each hyperinflationary episode, and the ability, or lack of it, to maintain inflation below 50% for prolonged periods. According to the first indicator, described in column 3, the classical episodes were more extreme, as inflation exceeded the 50% benchmark for fourteen months in Germany and nine months in Bolivia and Poland. Argentina is similar to Austria and Hungary. At

3. In table 12.3, on the other hand, we follow Cagan's definition strictly, so we show that the hyperinflation was shorter.

the other extreme we find Peru, where inflation exceeded 50% for only two months in 1990 and for one month in 1988.

A second feature is the number of episodes in which inflation started below the 50% per month threshold and later on exceeded it. The reductions in inflation below 50% (after the initial rise) were usually associated with unsuccessful stabilization attempts. This measure indicates the ability of the authorities to keep the process under "limited" control; the larger the number of accelerations, the more difficult it was to avoid a full explosion of inflation. Column 4 shows that there were fewer cycles in the recent episodes, indicating that the authorities were able to contain inflation better than in the classical ones.

Finally, column 5 shows the number of months when inflation remained in the high ranges, but below Cagan's hyperinflation level. Once again, the numbers indicate a clear distinction between the classical episodes and Argentina, on the one hand, and Brazil and Peru on the other. The latter countries were able to exert much better control over high inflation, in the sense that these high rates did not explode into hyperinflation territory.

The overall impression conveyed by table 12.1 is that in the new episodes (as a group), the authorities were able to exert more control over inflation and managed to limit the real negative effects of inflation.

12.3   The Classical Hyperinflations

12.3.1   The Origins of the Hyperinflations

The European hyperinflations of the 1920s (in Austria, Germany, Hungary, Poland, and Russia) and the more recent hyperinflation in Bolivia constitute the sample of what we call classical hyperinflations. The most distinctive feature of these episodes is that they had clear origins (large budget deficits financed by money creation), and that they were stopped suddenly, by an orthodox program that addressed the fiscal imbalance and convinced the public that the central bank would not print money to finance the budget deficit.

The origins of these large deficits were clear and typically resulted from unusual circumstances. In the 1920s they were linked to the costs of reconstruction and to the war reparation payments in the losing countries, while in Bolivia it was directly related to a sudden halt in the availability of external financing in a situation in which the country could not produce a sufficiently large fiscal adjustment to service its external obligations.

The background of the hyperinflations in the 1920s was the end of World War I. The losing countries ended up owing reparations to the Allies, while they underwent major domestic instability, which in many cases included difficulties in establishing and securing the country's borders. Germany had the heaviest burden of reparation payments; Austria inherited the largest part of the bureaucracy from the old Austro-Hungarian Empire and not enough resources to finance it; Hungary underwent dramatic political instability, including a brief communist regime, and wars with Czechoslovakia and Rumania. Poland became a new nation after the war and had to fight Russia to secure its borders.

The hyperinflations of the 1920s thus took place under unusual circumstances, in countries that were devastated by the effects of the war. Domestic factors—namely political instability and large deficits—worked in conjunction with external ones—the burden of reparation payments and unsecured borders—to generate a special environment for the extreme phenomenon of hyperinflation.

The more recent hyperinflation in Bolivia was linked to a severe external shock: a sudden and important reduction in the availability of external financing (see Sachs 1986; Morales 1988). During most of the seventies and early eighties Bolivia received positive external net resource transfers as net new lending exceeded net interest payments. The situation took a drastic turn in 1982, and by 1983 net external resource transfers, which had already turned negative in 1982, reached −5.6% of GDP (see table 12.2). This external transfer (as a share of GDP) was larger than the cash reparation payments required from Germany after World War I!

The unusually adverse circumstances described in all these episodes created conditions that were especially favorable for the emergence of hyperinflation.

There is little dispute that the classical hyperinflations were caused by large budget deficits financed primarily by money creation. Table 12.3 shows some fiscal indicators for the classical hyperinflations. Two features are clear. First, in all cases revenues were only covering a small fraction of total expenditures. In Europe, tax revenues covered less than half of government expenditures, and at the peak of the hyperinflation revenues represented just 12% of expenditures in Germany and 16% in Austria. In Bolivia, government revenues fell from around 85% of revenues in 1980 to around 50% for the period 1983–85. Second, a collapse of government revenues coincided with the rise in inflation (an extreme form of the Olivera-Tanzi effect). At the height of the hyperinflation, revenues in Germany were around one-third of what they were before. Likewise, in Bolivia revenues plummeted from 32% of GDP in 1982 to just 14% in 1985. The collapse in tax revenues was more dramatic; they fell from 8 to 3% of GDP between 1981 and 1983 as inflation increased from 30 to 270%. As we will show in the next section, these features were extreme in the recent hyperinflations.

Seigniorage was extremely large in the classical hyperinflations. Figure 12.1 shows estimates of the revenue from money creation for Germany and Bolivia. What happened in Bolivia is well known. Seigniorage increased fivefold from around 2% of GDP in 1979–81 to over 10% of GDP in 1983–85. In Germany seigniorage[4] increased sixfold at the outbreak of the war and remained high

---

4. Seigniorage in Bolivia is calculated as the change in the money base relative to GDP. In Germany we do not have reliable data on GDP, so we approximated seigniorage by the change in base money deflated by the average price level.

Table 12.2   **Bolivia: Annual Economic Indicators**

Period	Inflation	GDP Growth (%)	Seigniorage (as % GDP)	M1/ GDP	Pub.Exp./ GDP	Pub.Def./ GDP	Curr.Acc./ GDP	Tra.Bal./ GDP	Terms of Trade	Real Exchange Rate	Net Transfers
1970–74	21.68	4.40	2.02	10.92	—	—	1.46	5.75	62.04	113.03	3.17[a]
1975–79	10.14	4.06	1.98	10.50	—	—	-5.78	0.08	82.00	101.39	5.14
1980–82	69.73	-1.47	5.77	9.93	45.53	9.97	-3.27	4.44	94.90	79.70	0.93
1983	269.00	-4.50	9.70	7.24	43.30	18.70	-2.40	3.97	88.80	73.78	-4.26
1984	1,281.40	-0.60	15.80	5.15	46.00	25.10	-2.70	4.90	88.30	68.39	-4.84
1985	11,749.60	-1.00	8.30	3.04	23.90	10.10	-5.50	3.14	84.40	27.67	-5.32
1986	276.30	-2.50	2.50	3.37	22.90	3.40	-9.90	-1.31	61.40	106.08	0.50
1987	14.60	2.60	1.07	4.64	24.10	7.80	-9.90	-2.96	50.50	106.68	4.45
1988	16.00	2.96	3.83	5.20	27.80	6.60	-6.90	-1.09	57.00	116.25	0.44
1989	15.00	2.72	1.95	5.44	27.60	5.00	-5.80	-0.13	59.10	123.17	0.40
1990	17.12	2.71	2.13	5.57	27.80	3.30	-4.50	1.23	N.A.	132.44	-0.00

Sources: Seigniorage: based in monetery base; ANDREX. M1: M1 average, ANDREX. Public expenditure: current + capital expenditure, consolidated nonfinancial public sector deficit; UDAPE for 1980–84; IMF and World Bank after 1985. Public deficit: overall deficit, consolidated nonfinancial public sector deficit; UDAPE for 1980–84; IMF and World Bank after 1985. External sector: percentage of GDP; ANDREX. Exchange rate: nominal exchange rate, period average; IMF, *International Financial Statistics.* Terms of trade: terms of trade index 1980=100; ANDREX. Real exchange rate: real multilateral exchange rate index with respect to the top twenty trading partners; 1980=100. Net transfers: World Debt Tables, short- and long-term net transfers including IMF.
[a]1971–74.

Table 12.3   **Poland, Austria, Germany, and Bolivia: Classical Hyperinflations**

		Expenditure (as % GDP)	Revenue (as % GDP)	Revenue/ Expenditure	Inflation
Poland	1921	880,852	345,311.0	0.39202	126.9
	1922	879,313	530,428.0	0.60323	212.0
	1923	1,119,800	426,000.0	0.38043	15,636.0
	1924	1,629,000	1,703,000.0	1.04543	N.A.
	1925	1,981,593	1,981,884.0	1.00015	6.8[a]
Austria	1919	1,309	632.3	0.48308	N.A.
	1920	1,089	166.0	0.15248	N.A.
	1921	660	197.0	0.29853	842.0
	1922	733	116.0	0.15830	3,132.2
	1923	367	256.6	0.70000	135.6
Germany	1920	11,266	4,223.7	0.37492	257.4
	1921	11,963	5,336.2	0.44604	28.7
	1922	9,965	3,580.5	0.35931	1,688.3
	1923	13,513	1,676.7	0.12408	6.7E+10

		Expenditure	Revenue	Tax Revenue	Revenue/ Expenditure	Inflation
Bolivia[b]	1980	48.30	40.50	9.70	0.83851	47
	1981	38.90	32.00	8.30	0.82262	29
	1982	49.40	34.10	5.00	0.69028	133
	1983	43.30	24.60	3.40	0.56813	269
	1984	46.00	21.00	2.20	0.45652	1281
	1985	23.90	13.90	2.90	0.58159	11,750
	1986	22.90	19.40	4.50	0.84716	276
	1987	24.10	16.20	6.20	0.67220	15

Sources: Poland: Sargent (1982); Austria: Dornbush and Fischer (1986); Germany: Young (1925); Bolivia: Country Economic Memorandum.
[a]December rate of change over the preceding three months.
[b]Total expenditures and revenues as percentage of GDP.

until the end of the hyperinflation. In both episodes the level of seigniorage was too large, in the sense that it lay above the Laffer curve, and hence it could not be financed by any stable (no matter how high) rate of inflation. The result was hyperinflation.[5]

An important feature of these episodes is that the rise in seigniorage preceded the actual emergence of hyperinflation. This evidence is consistent with our view that excessive seigniorage led to an acceleration of inflation. In Bolivia, for instance, the increase in seigniorage occurred in 1982, while the hyperinflation became apparent only in 1984. The picture is less clear in Germany, because the lag was much longer. A protracted period of very high seigniorage eventually led to hyperinflation. Annual data indicate, however,

5. This issue is discussed more extensively in Kiguel and Liviatan (1988).

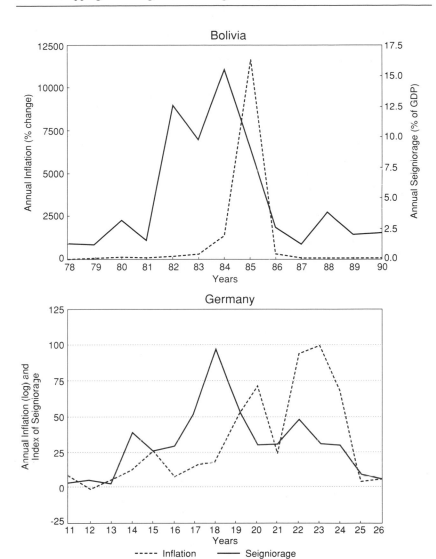

Fig. 12.1   Inflation and seigniorage: Bolivia; Germany (inflation logarithm)

that inflation entered into an accelerating trend around 1917, but became unstoppable only in the second half of 1922.

Finally, it is important to keep in mind that the classical hyperinflations took place in countries where high inflation was the exception rather than the rule. The hyperinflations of the twenties occurred when the world was by and large operating under the gold standard, and in an environment where price deflation was not unusual. The norm was definitely low inflation. Likewise, inflation in Bolivia during the sixties and seventies was moderate by Latin American standards. The worst inflationary episodes occurred in the midfifties when the annual inflation rate remained above 100% for a couple of years. Since then inflation remained fairly low; evidence of this was that the country was on a fixed exchange rate regime since 1959 (with only two devaluations until 1982).

12.3.2   Stopping the Classical Hyperinflations

The classical hyperinflations were abruptly stopped always and everywhere through a comprehensive program that stabilized the exchange rate, reduced the budget deficit sharply, and sent a clear signal that the central bank would end domestic credit to the government. In Germany the exchange rate was stabilized on November 20, and prices stabilized the following week.[6] Likewise, the hyperinflation in Bolivia was stopped in its tracks, the exchange rate was stabilized on August 29, and during the second week of September the economy experienced deflation.

The stabilization programs that brought the European hyperinflations to a sudden end are extensively discussed in existing works such as Sargent (1982), and Dornbusch and Fischer (1986), among others. In all cases the success was based on fixing the exchange rate, balancing the budget, and making a credible commitment to stopping central bank financing of the deficit (this was usually done by creating an independent central bank). External support was critical in these cases, because a large part of the fiscal deficits resulted from the war reparation payments.

The Bolivian hyperinflation was also brought to a quick end, by a stabilization program based on a firm commitment to balance the budget on a cash basis, and a policy of tight money to stabilize the exchange rate and prices. As shown in Sachs (1986), the program succeeded immediately in stabilizing the exchange rate, and as a result hyperinflation very quickly came to an end. In this respect the outcomes were similar to the stabilization programs that ended the European hyperinflations in the midtwenties and after World War II.

The success in stopping hyperinflation did not require balancing the budget on a longer-term basis, though it was necessary to signal unequivocally that the central bank would not issue money to finance the deficit. In fact, after an initial period in which the government ran a balanced budget, deficits remained relatively large without becoming a destabilizing force. Once the government establishes its determination to sustain price stability, it can run budget deficits that are consistent with the availability of noninflationary finance. In Bolivia the deficits were mainly financed externally without resorting to seigniorage (which, as can be seen from table 12.2, fell to prehyperinflation levels of around 2% of GDP). The Austrian stabilization of the 1920s provides another illustration of the complexities of the role of the budget deficit in stopping hyperinflation. In that episode the government continued to run deficits in 1923

---

6. See data in Webb (1986, 788).

(as shown in table 12.3), for a whole year after the end of the hyperinflation. Nevertheless, this was not a source of inflation, mainly because the stabilization package was comprehensive enough to remove uncertainty regarding the commitment to the new regime.

A common feature in all the programs that succeeded in stopping hyperinflation was their ability to signal a change of regime (as argued in Sargent). In the 1920s this typically was done by a stabilization package with external support. This was critical because, in the absence of a resolution of the reparation payments, there was no way to ensure a strong fiscal position. The programs of the 1920s also included the creation of an independent central bank, thus removing the ability to finance deficits through money creation. The creation of the independent central bank would have not been possible (nor credible) in the absence of clear indications that the budget would be balanced. In Bolivia the change of regime was less clear initially (see Sachs 1986 on this issue). On the fiscal side a key action was the creation of a cash committee whose main task was to maintain a balanced budget on a cash basis. This was supported by the reestablishment of external lending, and by far-reaching structural reforms that signalled a departure from past inflationary practices. Nevertheless, Bolivia did not go as far as the European countries in reforming the central bank.

The end of the hyperinflation in Bolivia provides mixed signals of the success of the program in changing long-term expectations. The persistence of high real interest rates and the slow remonetization of the economy are just two indicators of the difficulties in reversing long-term expectations. While real interest rates came down from the extremely high levels that prevailed during the first year (of around 100%), they are still very high by international standards (exceeding 20% per year). Also puzzling is the very small increase in real money balances. By 1989 with an inflation of just 15%, M1 as a share of GDP was slightly larger than at the peak of the hyperinflation. This slow remonetization of the Bolivian economy stands in sharp contrast to the rapid increase in real money balances in the 1920s. Money supply increased dramatically once price stability was achieved. These expansions in the money supply were not inflationary, as they accommodated a rapid increase in money demand.

12.4   Origins of the New Hyperinflations in Argentina, Brazil, and Peru

12.4.1   The Background of High Inflation

The more recent hyperinflations occurred in countries with a long tradition of high inflation (see tables 12.4 to 12.6). Argentina had continuously experienced three-digit annual rates of inflation since the midseventies. In Brazil annual inflation was already at 40% in the midseventies and reached three digits in the early eighties. Peru started to experience high inflation later, in the

Table 12.4   **Argentina: Annual Economic Indicators**

Period	Inflation	GDP Growth (%)	Seigniorage (as % of GDP)	M1/ GDP	Pub.Exp./ GDP[a]	Pub.Rev./ GDP[a]	Pub.Def./ GDP	Curr.Acc./ GDP	Terms of Trade	Real Exchange Rate	Net Transfers (as % of GDP)
1970–74	38.30	1.96	4.60	15.10	40.19	35.26	4.93	−0.35	141.52	135.50	−0.07[b]
1975–79	227.58	−0.10	8.36	8.88	45.53	38.70	6.84	0.44	112.44	187.39	0.38
1980–82	123.34	−4.85	5.37	7.07	50.51	44.97	5.54	−3.47	96.03	140.59	2.42
1983	343.82	1.46	8.61	5.12	55.59	45.09	10.71	−3.77	96.20	228.32	−0.46
1984	626.72	1.06	7.12	4.01	51.86	44.20	7.65	−3.21	97.00	195.86	−4.58
1985	672.15	−5.68	6.51	3.89	52.09	49.91	2.16	−1.46	89.80	220.51	−6.36
1986	90.10	4.20	3.46	5.20	34.80	31.91	2.89	−3.63	85.30	220.91	−6.04
1987	131.33	1.20	4.03	4.43	35.47	30.48	4.99	−5.13	81.80	238.42	−4.99
1988	342.96	−3.73	5.17	3.24	34.01	28.21	5.80	−1.75	86.20	260.55	−2.54
1989	3079.81	−5.65	9.00	3.05	34.95	31.16	3.79	−2.16	89.60	297.57	−5.04
1990	2313.97	−0.79	4.81	2.38	29.93	27.93	2.00	1.80[c]	n.a.	200.32	−3.57
1991	171.67	7.21	2.65	4.41	30.66	29.86	0.80	−1.97[c]	n.a.	147.12	−5.66

Sources: World Bank; International Financial Statistics, IMF; *Indicadores de Coyuntura Economica* (Buenos Aires: FIEL). Seigniorage: based on M1: M1 average; Andrex; 1991 FIEL. Public expenditure: current + capital expenditure, operations of the consolidated public sector; 1970–85 FIEL; 1986–90 Secretaria de Hacienda. Public revenue: current + capital revenues, operations of the consolidated public sector; 1970–85 FIEL; 1986–90 Secretaria de Hacienda. Public deficit: overall deficit, operations of the consolidated public sector; 1970–85 FIEL; 1986–90 Secretaria de Hacienda. External sector: IMF. Terms of trade: terms of trade index 1980 = 100; Andrex. Real exchange rate: real multilateral exchange rate index with respect to the top twenty trading partners; 1980 = 100. Net transfers: World Debt Tables, short- and long-term net transfers including IMF.

[a]Starting in 1986 it excludes provincial governments' revenue and expenditure.

[b]1971–74.

[c]Preliminary.

Table 12.5   Brazil: Annual Economic Indicators

Period	Inflation	GDP Growth (%)	Seigniorage (as % of GDP)	M1/ GDP	Pub.Exp./ GDP[a]	Pub.Rev./ GDP[a]	Pub.Def./ GDP	Curr.Acc./ GDP	Terms of Trade	Real Exchange Rate	Net Transfers (as % of GDP)
1970–74	19.87	7.03	1.53	15.58	35.79	35.40	—	−2.00	167.22	69.99	3.05[b]
1975–79	41.22	3.42	2.38	11.18	47.12	40.36	—	−3.96	135.06	73.90	2.33
1980–82	95.38	−1.37	2.01	6.86	48.26	41.72	5.76	−5.17	94.03	88.39	−0.73
1983	142.14	−5.55	1.30	4.59	45.97	41.91	4.80	−3.30	91.00	134.50	−1.43
1984	196.98	2.99	2.34	3.36	43.83	37.67	2.70	0.02	94.00	134.56	−1.22
1985	226.86	5.64	2.32	4.03	49.11	37.83	4.30	−0.10	89.10	138.64	−2.80
1986	145.24	5.31	3.60	8.69	29.20	27.10	3.60	−2.00	110.00	147.77	−3.46
1987	229.66	1.46	2.73	4.95	31.90	27.00	5.50	−0.50	97.20	147.73	−2.80
1988	682.30	−2.13	3.41	3.07	30.70	28.30	4.80	1.20	116.80	136.90	−2.85
1989	1286.98	1.22	5.02	2.25	34.90	26.20	6.90	0.23	120.10	109.73	−1.72
1990	2937.82	−5.95	4.36	3.75	32.70	31.50	−1.30	−0.80	N.A.	93.52	−0.74
1991	440.84	−0.74	2.76	2.82	N.A.	N.A.	N.A.	N.A.	N.A.	116.49	−3.34
1992[c]	910.41[d]	−1.80[e]	2.16[e]	4.64[c]	N.A.	N.A.	N.A.	N.A.	N.A.	N.A.	N.A.

Sources: World Bank; International Financial Statistics, IMF. Seigniorage: based on monetary base. M1: M1 average, Central Bank. Public expenditure: total expenditures of the operations of the central government + operations of public enterprise, 1980–85: Werneck (1991); 1986–1990: IMF. Public revenue: total revenues of the operations of the central government + operations of public Enterprise, 1980–85: Werneck (1991); 1986–1990: IMF. Public deficit: public sector operational deficit; Brazillian Institute of Geography and Statistics. External sector: Andrex. Terms of trade: Terms of trade index 1980 = 100; Andrex. Real exchange rate: Real multilateral exchange rate index with respect to the top twenty partners, 1980 = 100. Net transfers: World Debt Tables, short- and long-term net transfers including IMF.

[a]After 1985; nonfinancial expenditures (revenues) of the public sector, IMF.

[b]1971–74.

[c]January to June.

[d]Annualized based in the first eight month of the year.

[e]Estimates.

Table 12.6 Peru: Annual Economic Indicators

Period	Inflation	GDP Growth (%)	Seigniorage (as % of GDP)	M1/ GDP	Pub. Exp./ GDP	Pub. Rev./ GDP	Pub. Def./ GDP	Curr. Acc./ GDP	Terms of Trade	Real Exch. Rate	Net Transfers (as % of GDP)
1970–74	9.08	3.69	1.53	14.86	28.79	25.95	2.84	-1.21	—	68.93	0.32[a]
1975–79	43.94	-1.08	2.41	13.45	41.24	34.88	6.38	-3.36	—	87.60	2.85
1980–82	66.34	0.76	2.35	8.34	47.78	41.78	6.00	-4.63	126.83	88.78	-1.68
1983	111.13	-14.62	2.87	6.58	53.78	43.96	9.82	-4.39	110.60	85.31	2.86
1984	110.21	3.44	2.45	5.57	45.75	39.57	6.18	-1.07	101.00	85.32	2.34
1985	163.41	-0.18	9.86	6.09	46.05	43.66	2.39	0.75	90.60	104.60	-0.82
1986	77.92	6.69	4.23	8.69	37.95	32.96	5.00	-4.02	66.40	93.11	-1.39
1987	85.85	6.09	5.74	8.58	33.54	26.81	6.74	-3.37	66.90	82.09	0.29
1988	667.03	-10.07	7.89	5.04	30.27	23.55	6.72	-2.97	74.90	90.39	0.41
1989	3398.58	-13.63	6.10	3.43	25.21	18.58	6.62	0.87	72.50	56.64	0.78
1990	7481.66	-6.30	5.42	3.96	22.59	19.58	3.01	-2.60	65.00	44.87	-0.34
1991	409.53	0.49	n.a.	n.a.	n.a.	n.a.	n.a.	-3.88	n.a.	36.24	-3.39

Sources: GDP Bank of Peru, millions of Intis 1979. CPI: consumer price index for metropolitan Lima, 1979 = 100; INE. Seigniorage: monetary base; currency + bank deposits; Central Bank. M1: M1 average, International Financial Statistics, IMF. Public expenditure: current + capital expenditure, nonfinancial public sector operation; Central Bank. Public deficit: overall deficit, nonfinancial public sector operation; Central Bank. External sector: Central Bank, millions of US$. Terms of trade: terms of trade index 1978 = 100; Central Bank. Real exchange rate: real multilateral exchange rate index with respect to the top twenty trading partners, 1980 = 100. Net transfers: short- and long-term net transfers including IMF.

[a]1971–74.

second half of the seventies, but by the early eighties it was also suffering from inflation rates of three digits.

This long history of inflation had its roots in large budget deficits and the continuous growth of the public sector. As shown in table 12.3, budget deficits were already very large in Argentina and Peru in the early seventies, while in Brazil they became large in the second half of the decade. In addition, the size of the central government and of public sector enterprises mushroomed during the decade. In contrast to the classical episodes, however, these countries were able to maintain limited control over inflation; it did not get out of hand.

The links between seigniorage and inflation were not as sharp as in the classical hyperinflations. Figure 12.2 shows annual seigniorage and inflation for these countries. The contrast with Germany and Bolivia is clear; there was no sixfold increase in seigniorage in any of these countries. Seigniorage in Argentina had been large at least since the early seventies, but except for a few short episodes it never went out of control. The story in Brazil is even more puzzling, where seigniorage has been relatively moderate and stable since the seventies. The increases in inflation in 1975, 1979, and 1982 were not associated with any noticeable increases in seigniorage (which in fact remained at around 2% of GDP). These increases in inflation instead resulted from devaluations that were accommodated through easy money and wage indexation. The Peruvian experience, on the other hand, is much more similar to the classical episodes; the rise in seigniorage *leads* the outbreak of hyperinflation.

The ability of the high-inflation economies to avoid hyperinflation for such a long time was related to the development of mechanisms that allowed them to live with inflation. We already mentioned that in the classical episodes government revenues collapsed, usually before the full hyperinflation set in (e.g., in Bolivia tax revenues more than halved as inflation reached three-digit levels). On the other hand, Argentina and Brazil were able to maintain government revenues at stable levels in spite of the increases of inflation (see table 12.7). There was no noticeable loss of revenues in Brazil in spite of dramatic increases in inflation since 1986. Likewise, in Argentina, for which we have quarterly data, we find that the hyperinflation had a discernable impact on revenues only during the second quarter of 1989. Only in Peru we find some evidence of a fall in revenues, although the most dramatic fall occurred relatively late in the inflation process (between the third quarter of 1989 and second quarter of 1990).

The ability to cope with high inflation, which was absent in the classical episodes, can explain why these economies were able to avoid hyperinflation for a long time. In spite of large budget deficits and short periods of high seigniorage, inflation was high but not exploding. This was possible because revenues did not collapse (as was the case in the classical hyperinflations), and hence the governments were able to take the required fiscal actions to avoid excessive seigniorage and keep inflation within the boundaries of high inflation.

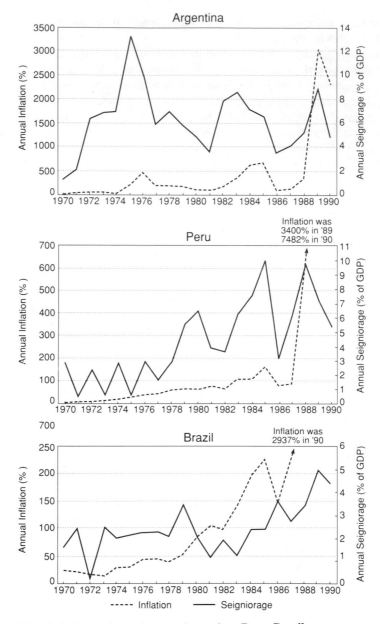

Fig. 12.2 Inflation and seigniorage: Argentina; Peru; Brazil

		Expenditure	Revenue[a]	Tax Revenue	Revenue/ Expenditure	Inflation[b]
Argentina	1985	42.26	38.82	22.04	0.91860	672.2
	1986	39.18	36.96	21.96	0.94334	90.1
	1987	39.28	33.75	20.81	0.85922	131.3
	1988	34.08	28.97	16.21	0.85006	343.0
	I	35.66	28.83	17.39	0.80847	179.9
	II	34.20	30.50	16.64	0.89181	480.0
	III	30.56	27.93	15.97	0.91394	954.8
	IV	36.47	29.19	15.90	0.80038	220.2
	1989	30.85	27.58	16.16	0.89400	3,079.8
	I	37.15	28.86	15.74	0.77685	189.2
	II	38.68	26.76	11.52	0.69183	12,459.0
	III	22.49	24.06	14.71	1.06981	198.171.2
	IV	36.01	30.27	17.80	0.84060	350.9
	1990	26.06	28.07	16.95	1.07713	2,314.0
	I	22.62	21.23	12.35	0.93855	35,399.7
	II	31.28	29.27	17.40	0.93574	1,807.3
	III	30.59	28.88	17.28	0.94410	352.0
	IV	29.52	28.51	17.13	0.96579	192.1
Peru	1985	23.50	14.80	14.30	0.62979	163.4
	1986	21.30	12.60	12.20	0.59155	77.9
	1987	18.20	9.20	9.30	0.50549	85.8
	1988	15.60	9.20	9.10	0.58974	667.0
	I	18.90	10.90	11.20	0.57672	310.4
	II	14.00	9.10	9.50	0.65000	424.2
	III	17.50	7.70	7.90	0.44000	2,615.3
	IV	14.70	9.70	9.30	0.65986	8,501.3
	1989	13.20	6.00	6.50	0.45455	33,398.6
	I	14.40	9.10	9.40	0.63194	6,830.8
	II	12.70	7.70	7.90	0.60630	4,579.9
	III	12.40	5.50	6.00	0.44355	1,362.4
	IV	13.60	5.70	6.20	0.41912	1,527.8
	1990	14.50	7.80	7.90	0.53793	7,481.7
	I	12.70	4.80	5.00	0.37795	2,403.8
	II	21.30	5.40	5.70	0.25352	3,728.5
	III	13.70	6.60	6.70	0.48175	524,510.2
	IV	14.40	8.60	8.70	0.59722	942.4
Brazil	1986	29.20	27.10	20.30	0.92808	145.2
	1987	31.90	27.00	18.10	0.84639	229.7
	1988	30.70	28.30	17.80	0.92182	682.3
	1989	34.90	26.20	18.40	0.75072	1,287.0
	1990	32.70	31.50	23.90	0.96330	2,937.8
	1991[c]	28.30	27.60	20.30	0.97527	440.8

Sources: Argentina: Ministry of Economy; Peru: Central Bank of Peru; Brazil: World Bank, *Brazil: Recent Economic Development.*

Note: Consolidated public sector (Brazil and Argentina, central government (Peru).

[a]Total revenue, except only the current revenue for Peru.

[b]The quarterly data are annualized.

[c]Projected.

Nevertheless, as time went by and high inflation persisted, it became more difficult to avoid hyperinflation. One important development in this respect was the gradual shrinking of money holdings (relative to GDP) over time, which slowly increased the fragility of the financial system. In Argentina M1 dropped from 14% of GDP in 1970 to just 3% in 1990; likewise, in Brazil, it fell from 16% in the early seventies to just over 3% of GDP in the late eighties (the drop in the monetary base was similar). As a result, the central bank diminished its ability to offset shocks, and the economy became more susceptible to being destabilized by adverse developments. For example, if the government needs to rely on seigniorage to finance a temporary shortfall in taxes that amounts to 3% of GDP, this would have amounted to an approximate 20% increase in the monetary base in the early seventies, while in the eighties this would have represented an almost 100% expansion. The size of the shocks are dramatically different, and the inflationary effects are likely to be much larger in the second case. Likewise, shifts in private portfolios are also likely to be more destabilizing the smaller the size of the monetary base relative to domestic liquid assets. This problem is particularly acute in Brazil, where the monetary base is just 2% of GDP while M4 is close to 30% of GDP. In this situation it is almost impossible for the central bank to offset any changes in the demand for domestic assets through open market operations. In particular, a generalized run out of domestic assets will almost certainly result in a significant increase in domestic interest rates or else in a large increase in inflation.

12.4.2 Direct Origins of the Recent Hyperinflations

A distinctive feature of the new hyperinflations is that they were not clearly driven by a single cause; there is no unique simple explanation that can rationalize each of them. This stands in contrast from the classical hyperinflations, where the origins were very clear. Instead, they resulted from a combination of several domestic and external factors. In Argentina and Brazil the hyperinflations were the culmination of a long process of deterioration in the fiscal accounts, increased fragility in the financial system, and a tendency to accept high inflation. As inflation became entrenched at higher plateaus, it was more difficult to avoid a final explosion. Of course, the situation was complicated by limited access to external financing since the beginning of the debt crisis, weak monetary and fiscal control, and very limited availability of noninflationary domestic financing to the government. But each of these elements by themselves need not have caused a hyperinflation.

The story in Peru is somewhat different, because outright populist policies played a big role in starting the hyperinflation. In this respect, the causes were clearer. Nevertheless, after the initial outbreak the Peruvian hyperinflation and the ensuing stabilization process shared many elements with those of Argentina and Brazil. In this respect, it does not look like a classical hyperinflation.

It is useful to take another quick look at the relationship between seigniorage and inflation in these three countries (this time using monthly data) before

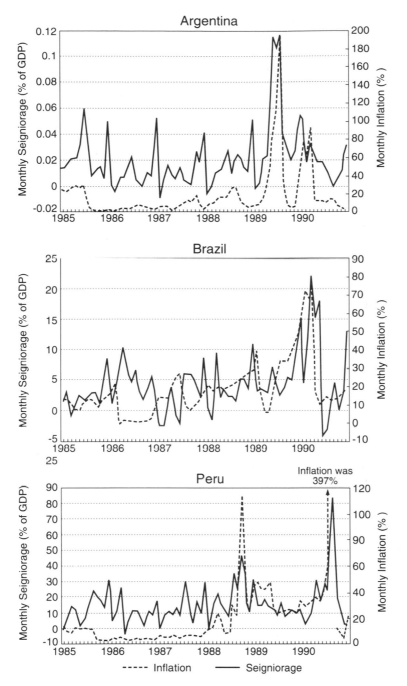

Fig. 12.3   Seigniorage and inflation: Argentina; Brazil; Peru

examining each of these experiences more closely. Figure 12.3 shows the monthly inflation and estimates of the revenue from money creation (or seigniorage) for the three countries.[7] It is clear that in Peru the beginning of the hyperinflation era was linked to excessive money creation in 1985 and 1986, which eventually led to an explosion in inflation starting in 1988. Likewise, the hyperinflation outburst of 1990 was *preceded* by a large increase in seigniorage. This episode resembled the classical hyperinflations. In contrast, the relationship between seigniorage and inflation is less clear in Argentina and Brazil. In both cases, seigniorage appears to have increased in response to the beginning of the hyperinflation rather than the opposite as a result of an extreme Olivera-Tanzi effect. Inflation was pulling up seigniorage in the hyperinflations of 1989.

This evidence indicates that the causes of the recent episodes are not as clear as in the classical cases. In what follows we will examine each experience in more detail and indicate in which respects the new episodes are different.

Peru

The hyperinflation in Peru resulted from the overexpansionary domestic policies of Alan Garcia (annual data for Peru are presented in table 12.6). In August 1985 his administration launched a so-called stabilization program aimed at reducing inflation, which was mainly based on income policies, in the form of price and wage controls, and a fixed exchange rate. This was accompanied by expansionary monetary and fiscal policies. While monthly inflation initially fell from 10 to 3%, the success was short-lived, as could easily have been predicted. The government succeeded in preventing a full-blown increase in inflation by keeping public sector prices and the official exchange rate artificially low, and by financing the expansion in economic activity through losses in international reserves. In the end, however, the government ran out of reserves, and this triggered the beginning of a long hyperinflation.

One unique and intriguing feature of this hyperinflation is that, by and large, inflation did not accelerate in an explosive manner, except at the very end. This stands in contrast with the classical hyperinflations, where once inflation reached hyperinflation levels it very quickly exploded (see figure 12.3c). There was an extreme increase in inflation in September 1988 (when inflation exceeded 100%), but to a large extent this was equivalent to a one-time increase in the price level in noninflationary economies. Inflation then remained at the 40% per month step for around seven months, and then fell to the 30% per month step for around a year. This ability to maintain relatively stable inflation at rates as high as 30 or 40% per month is unique to Peru, since the available evidence from high-inflation economies indicates that inflations in excess of 20% per month are unstable and lead to hyperinflation (that was the case in

7. The revenue from money creation is calculated as the change in the money base divided by the price level.

Argentina and Brazil). This in itself is an indication that Peru is one of the high-inflation economies and hence that its hyperinflation has many features in common with those of Argentina and Brazil.

Figure 12.3c shows that in Peru this period of high but stable inflation was accompanied by decreasing seigniorage, thus suggesting that this was probably an important factor in explaining the limited control that the government was able to exert over inflation. This period is generally seen as one of tight money (e.g., Lago 1991), indicating that tight money could be used to avoid an explosion in inflation even in situations where the fiscal position is out of control.

Argentina and Brazil

The origins of the hyperinflations in Argentina and Brazil were somewhat different. We already argued that they were not directly generated by unusually large increases in seigniorage. Seigniorage levels, while high, were not out of line with historical levels.

In our view, the more immediate origin of the hyperinflations in these two countries was an increase in the instability of inflation in economies that already were facing very high rates of inflation. This instability developed as a result of stop-and-go policies toward inflation, in which most stabilization attempts were based on a large dose of income policies. The Austral plan in Argentina and the Cruzado plan in Brazil represent the beginning of this period of inflation-stabilization cycles.[8] In the end the recurrent failed stabilization attempts destabilized inflation in the longer term, and gave rise to similar hyperinflations in both countries.

Of course, failed stabilization attempts would not have resulted in hyperinflations if the economies were not already experiencing high inflation. Likewise, high inflation could have been avoided by the adoption of policies to bring it down at an earlier stage. The combination of high inflation and the induced nominal instability, caused by unsound stabilization strategies, created the conditions for inflation to explode.

The most relevant features of the period of the cycles in Argentina and Brazil can be readily noticed from figure 12.3. The 1985 Austral plan in Argentina represented a break with previous stabilization efforts, as it was the first comprehensive stabilization program in many years. A heterodox program, it combined orthodox elements—namely, a reduction in the budget deficit and a fixed exchange rate—with the heterodox component—wage and price controls. The initial success was later reversed, and as inflation started to pick up momentum, it was stopped through a new heterodox program (the first Plan Primavera) with less emphasis on fiscal discipline and more on income policies. The failure of this program gave rise to new cycles, which were subsequently stopped by the February Plan, the Austral II Plan, and the better-known Plan Primavera. The failure of this last plan gave rise to a full-blown hyperinflation.

8. These cycles are examined in more detail in Kiguel and Liviatan (1991).

A similar pattern is apparent in Brazil, where the cycles started with another so-called heterodox program, the Cruzado Plan. Like the Austral Plan, it also relied on price and wage controls; unlike the Austral Plan, it did not perform any adjustment on the fiscal side. In the end, however, this difference did not matter much, as inflation in Brazil evolved in a similar manner as in Argentina. The follow-up stabilization programs—the Bresser Plan, the Summer Plan, and so forth—shared a similar stabilization strategy, and the ultimate outcomes were essentially the same.

The cycles set the stage for the outbreak of the hyperinflations. In each new cycle, inflation reached a higher peak, while the periods of low inflation that followed the implementation of each stabilization attempt became shorter. The inflation-stabilization cycles thus became shorter and more pronounced, eventually exploding into hyperinflation in both countries. Hyperinflation was all but unavoidable.

The outbreak of the hyperinflation in Argentina coincided with the collapse of the Plan Primavera. According to most analysts (e.g., Machinea 1990), the situation was complicated by the possibility that the domestic debt would be repudiated, a situation that led to a flight of domestic assets. In Brazil, inflation probably accelerated in anticipation of a new income-policies-based stabilization program to be implemented by the Collor de Melo administration, and the possibility that the government would also repudiate its mushrooming domestic debt (especially once Argentina took those steps in December 1989).

In both cases, however, the specific circumstances that triggered the beginning of the hyperinflation cannot be separated from the overall conditions prevailing at the time. The cycles were explosive, and it is very likely that hyperinflation would have taken place even if there were no expectations that the government would repudiate its domestic debt. Anything short of a major stabilization package capable of changing inflationary expectations in a dramatic way would have been insufficient to avoid hyperinflation.

12.5   Programs to Stop Three Big Inflations

12.5.1   Basic Features of the Programs

In the span of a year Argentina, Brazil, and Peru implemented major stabilization programs aimed at stopping hyperinflation. The launching of these programs coincided with the inauguration of a new administration in each country: July 1989 in Argentina under the Menem administration, March 1990 in Brazil under the Collor de Mello administration, and August 1990 in Peru under the Fujimori administration.

The three stabilization programs represented a break from previous disinflation attempts. There was a clear shift to more emphasis on orthodox measures and only a limited use of income policies, which was done mainly to demonstrate a departure from previous stabilization strategies that were identified with failure. Balancing the budget on a cash basis became an explicit objective of the three programs, and Peru and Brazil were relatively successful in sticking with it. In addition, there was a clear shift in the choice of nominal anchor, relying more on money rather than on the exchange rate (the latter also being associated with failed stabilization attempts). In Peru and Brazil this was done from the outset, while Argentina shifted to a money-based program later on (in December) after a failed attempt to stabilize the exchange rate. Finally, the programs were announced as comprehensive efforts also aimed at changing the long-term prospects for growth, and for this purpose they included major structural reforms, mainly privatization of public sector enterprises and trade liberalization.

The comprehensiveness of these programs indicates that in all cases policymakers were seriously attempting to bring the economies back to a path of continuous price stability. The thoroughness of the stabilization attempts and the adherence to fiscal discipline (especially in Peru) indicate that the basic strategy was comparable to the one that succeeded in stopping hyperinflation in Bolivia.

The effectiveness of these programs was mixed. True, they all succeeded in bringing down inflation quickly from the peaks of the hyperinflation to much lower levels. Nevertheless, inflation was stubborn, and it did not fall quickly to low or moderate levels (unlike the case of Bolivia where it fell to around 20% per year). In Argentina the initial attempt was followed by other deeper stabilization programs, and despite mixed results for a long time, inflation appeared to be finally receding; but this took over two years. In Brazil the results were worse; after the failed stabilization attempt inflation rose, it then stabilized at around 20% per month, and the possibility of a new hyperinflation cannot be ruled out. Finally, Peru in 1992 was still fighting to get inflation down in a sustainable manner. While the worst part of the hyperinflation was over, the authorities were still fighting monthly rates of inflation that remained stubborn at around 4%.

We will now discuss the main features of the programs and examine the reasons for the difficulties that these countries are facing in bringing down inflation in a sustainable manner. In particular, we will argue that it is much more difficult to generate a change of regime after hyperinflation in the high-inflation economies than it was in the classical hyperinflations.

12.5.2   Classic Stabilization Programs with Nonclassic Outcomes

Peru

The stabilization program in Peru, launched in August 1990, was designed along the lines of the very effective Bolivian stabilization program, but did not achieve the same degree of success. There was a clear commitment to balancing the budget, and for this purpose the government created a cash committee that would operate under a strict rule of keeping payments in line with revenues, similar to one that operated in Bolivia. The committee in fact has abided by this rule, although some arrears mounted along the way. On the monetary side, the program aimed at restraining monetary growth, although there were no explicit targets except for domestic credit to the government. While the program did not use the exchange rate as the nominal anchor (on the contrary it allowed it to float freely), the exchange rate was stabilized very quickly, as in the classical hyperinflations.

The fiscal adjustment was primarily effected by increasing revenues, which had all but collapsed during the hyperinflation. Government expenditures were already very low, and reducing them further was not a realistic possibility. The increase in revenues was achieved by levying emergency taxes (on trade, real estate, etc.), by elimination of tax exemptions, and by drastically increasing public sector prices (e.g., the price of gasoline was increased twentyfold).

In addition, the government announced an ambitious program of structural reforms with the objective of reversing the detrimental effects of widespread government intervention. The foreign exchange market was unified, bank deposits denominated in dollars were authorized, and the economic team quickly started to work on reforming labor market legislation, deregulation and trade liberalization, tax reforms, rationalization of public sector expenditures, and privatization of public sector enterprises. This was accompanied by a determined effort to reinsert Peru in the world financial markets, reapproaching the multilateral organizations as well as the commercial banks.

This program was very ambitious, and its scope and depth clearly marked a break with the old regime of populism and widespread government intervention. It had many elements that showed a definite commitment to low inflation. In its design the program did not look very different from the 1985 Bolivian stabilization effort. Both programs combined a commitment to stabilization with structural reforms. While it could be argued that the Peruvian program was fragile, the same could be said about the Bolivian one.

A puzzling aspect of the Peruvian program was that stabilizing the exchange rate was not enough to stabilize prices. Sachs (1986), in discussing the Bolivian experience, argues that in the short run stabilizing the exchange rate was enough to stabilize prices. This, however, was not the case in Peru. So why did Bolivia manage to stop inflation in its tracks while Peru could not? We will address this issue in section 12.5.3.

Brazil

The Brazilian stabilization program of March 1990, the Collor Plan, also started along very orthodox lines and shared many elements with programs that stopped hyperinflation. The program also included the announcement of a comprehensive package of structural reforms, providing a clear indication that the intention was to break with the past. The main objective was to reduce the role of the state in the economy through privatization of public sector enterprises, trade liberalization, and reforms in the labor market. On the fiscal side, there was a firm commitment to eliminate the budget deficit and to generate a surplus in the primary and operational balances in 1990, an objective that was achieved. The available information indicates that the primary surplus between April and December 1990 was around 2.5% of GDP. This was a major achievement, given that the government had been running deficits in previous years.

Income policies played a secondary, temporary role only at the beginning of the program. This represented a clear departure from previous stabilization strategies, which put more weight on fighting the "inertial" forces of the inflation process, and essentially viewed as unnecessary any adjustment in the fundamentals.

A central, though controversial, component of the program was a mandatory freeze of approximately 70% of the financial assets for eighteen months. While depositors lost access to their money during the freeze, the funds were supposed to earn indexation plus 6% per annum, with no servicing till September 1991. Until the freeze was enacted, most public financial assets were in fact domestic government debt, with one day maturity and at a floating interest rate. The financial system acted primarily as an intermediary for the government. The main purpose of the freeze was to improve the fiscal balance (by postponing payment on the service of domestic debt) and to regain control over the monetary aggregates.[9]

As a result of the freeze liquidity fell from around 30% to just 9% of GDP. This drastic reduction in liquidity started to exert severe recessionary pressures early on, prompting the authorities to implement a partial reversal of policies. As a result, by the end of April liquidity increased to around 15% of GDP. In spite of this reversal, money continued to be tight in the sense that monetary aggregates remained well below the levels where they were prior to the Collor Plan.

In contrast to the Argentine and Peruvian programs, the exchange rate continued to be managed as in the past. It was not used as the nominal anchor; in fact, most of the time the exchange rate had a passive role and simply accommodated inflation. Nevertheless, as in the other two programs the parallel exchange rate was stabilized.

As in the other recent experiences, despite a major stabilization effort (at least at the outset) inflation was not eliminated. On the contrary, after an initial fall from 81% in March 1990 to just 9% in May, inflation climbed back to 19% in December and has remained high since then.[10] The final effect of this program was thus not very different from previous ones that did much less in terms of fiscal and monetary adjustment. A frustrating outcome.

A new set of measures, the Collor II Plan, was announced on January 31, 1991, to deal with the resurgence of inflation. One component of the new pro-

---

9. Zini (1992) provides a more detailed description and analysis of the freeze.

10. Monthly data disguise the fact that prices were fully stabilized for around three weeks early on.

gram was an attempt to deepen the fiscal adjustment, by dealing with the finances and the debt overhang of the state and local governments. However, this orthodox message was accompanied with the old practice of price and wage controls (which had proved ineffective in the past), and new attempts to regulate financial markets, this time by eliminating overnight operations.

These mixed signals had a negative effect on the government's image. The initial attitude of the Collor administration of being tough and willing to pay the costs of disinflation, gave way to one where the authorities were concerned about reducing the costs of this process. In addition, the use of old failed policies affected expectations in an adverse way, as they were associated with quick increases in inflation.

Argentina

The Argentine stabilization program of July 1989, the Bunge and Born (BB) Plan, was the first stage of what has been a long-term effort to stop hyperinflation. In contrast to the programs in Brazil and Peru, the BB Plan used the exchange rate as its nominal anchor, though like the others it was solely based on orthodox measures and explicitly avoided the imposition of any type of controls on prices or wages. It also relied on a major fiscal adjustment, and it announced major structural reforms. Among them was the privatization of the national telephone company (ENTEL) and the national airline (Aerolineas Argentinas).

The program evolved through a number of phases, as new waves of increases in inflation forced the introduction of new measures to stabilize in a sustainable manner. The BB Plan was followed by three stabilization efforts, each of them strengthening the prospects for price stability. The Plan Bonex of December 1989 included a forced rescheduling of the domestic debt (similar to the one later implemented in Brazil), aimed at improving control on the money supply and reducing the budget deficit by severing the links between tight money and high interest rates. Liquidity was cut sharply, because short-term time deposits were exchanged for long-term bonds, which were transacted in the secondary market at around 30% of their face value. The Plan Bonex also represented a change in the stabilization strategy, as the exchange rate was allowed to float and money took the role of nominal anchor. This harsh program failed to control inflation, and the government responded with a new stabilization effort in March 1990 (Decree 435). This program essentially supplemented the previous one by deepening the fiscal adjustment (through cuts in subsidies and public employment as well as some revenue-enhancing measures). Once again, there was a reversal on the inflation front with a brief acceleration in January and February 1991. In response to the latest reversal, a new economic team (led by Minister Cavallo) announced a major stabilization effort, the convertibility or Autumn Plan, the most recent and audacious effort to stop inflation. Not only was there a stronger effort on the fiscal side, especially through higher revenues, but the new economic team went further and tied its own hands by adopting full currency convertibility at a fixed exchange and by imposing strict limits on the amount of central bank financing to the nonfinancial public sector. Under the convertibility scheme, the central bank is required to hold enough international reserves to back the monetary base, while any devaluation will need to be approved by Congress.[11] The program is showing signs of success; as of November 1991 inflation was still falling and converging to international levels, though there was a slight setback in January 1992, as inflation reached 3%. While at the time of this writing it is still too early to assess the sustainability of this program, it seems clear that the economy is much closer to securing price stability than it has been in the last four decades.

12.5.3   Why Has Inflation Been So Persistent?

Based on the findings of Sargent (1982) and Dornbusch and Fischer (1986), one would have predicted that, given that the three countries were facing acute hyperinflations, and that the three of them launched orthodox stabilization programs that also included many of the ingredients that could signal a change of regime (of the type suggested by Sargent), the ensuing outcome would have been price stability. However, this did not happen. Nor was stabilizing the exchange rate enough to stabilize prices (as argued in Sachs 1986 for his analysis of Bolivia). Argentina and Peru stabilized the exchange rate temporarily early on, but inflation continued at a higher pace. While in the three countries the initial programs succeeded in bringing inflation down from the heights of hyperinflation, none of them was able to bring about full price stability.

The persistence of inflation in these episodes is linked to the inability of the authorities to convince the public that the programs could sustain low inflation on a long-term basis. In the high-inflation economies stabilization appears to be a long-term process. The numerous failed stabilization attempts of the past—which were the norm in these economies—meant that any new program had to confront adverse expectations from the outset. Policymakers needed to continuously demonstrate their commitment to the stabilization program, and in most cases this task required the adoption of a comprehensive set of policies that went beyond restoring fiscal balance on a short- or medium-term basis. Programs could not be credible unless they frontally attacked the structural features that gave rise to an inflationary economy, namely, addressing the deficits of the public enterprises, reducing the size of the public sector, and introducing institutional reforms to restore control over the money-supply process.

Brazil: Was a Larger Primary Surplus the Answer?

The stubbornness of inflation in Brazil can be explained in different ways. One explanation (e.g., Rodriguez 1992), is that the primary surplus created in the Collor Plan was not large enough to service the domestic debt, and that it eroded very quickly. While the Collor Plan dealt with the domestic debt prob-

---

11. See Canavese (1992) for a more detailed analysis of the convertibility program.

lem in the short run by freezing domestic assets, this was just a transitory solution. Once these assets were defrozen, the burden of servicing this debt would amount to around 4% of GDP. If the government were to service the external debt as well, the required primary surplus was around 6% of GDP. Since the Collor Plan fell short of this target, proponents of this view would argue that expectations of large future budget deficits was the main reason for the persistence of inflation.[12]

While there is no doubt that those who claim that a primary surplus of at least 4% of GDP was essential to make the package credible have a valid point, we still have serious doubts as to whether generating a surplus of that size would have been enough to stop inflation. In our view the answer is no. Since there is usually a strong deep-rooted mistrust of the government in these economies, policymakers need to do more to demonstrate their commitment to stabilization. Without this commitment, which goes much further than a reduction in the budget deficit, there is little chance of bringing down the basic level of inflationary expectations. Disinflation is typically a long-term process in these economies, mainly because it takes time to put in place the reforms that are necessary to build credibility in the program.

The inability of the Collor Plan to achieve price stability primarily lay in the failure to undertake structural changes that would reverse expectations in a more durable manner. In fact, the Collor Plan did not make much progress in three key areas: in privatizing public sector enterprises, in providing a *permanent* solution to the domestic debt problem, and in limiting the power of state banks to get access to central bank credit.

Argentina: Stabilization Has Been a Process

The recent Argentine experience vividly illustrates that there is slow convergence to low inflation after stopping a hyperinflation in a chronic-inflation economy. In Argentina this reduction was possible because the authorities undertook wide and far-reaching structural reforms in key areas. While the economy maintained a small primary surplus since 1990, the size of the fiscal adjustment was not large enough to convey convincing signals about the long-term commitment to stabilization. The reduction in inflation was achieved gradually, as the policymakers undertook and deepened structural reforms.

Figure 12.4 shows that the reversal in the inflation pattern, the period of exploding cycles that preceded the BB Plan, has been followed by another of

12. It should be noted that this criticism of the plan is based on the assumption that the real interest rate on the domestic debt would remain at around 20% per annum, which reflects the high risk premium on holding government securities. Under this approach the closing of the deficit is a difficult, though not impossible, task; an internal debt of about 30% of GDP, which is about its current size, would require revenues of 6% of GDP to service the interest payments. The problem, however, would be less severe if the government were able to reduce real interest rates closer to international levels. In any case, there is no doubt that those who claim that a primary surplus of around 4% of GDP is essential for a credible fiscal policy have a valid point. In this sense the criticism of the Collor Plan is well taken.

Fig. 12.4   Inflation: Argentina

converging cycles. The BB Plan was successful in stopping hyperinflation, though inflation continued at around 5% per month. The initial program was clearly unsuccessful in showing that the new regime was one of price stability. The failure of the initial attempt became apparent when a new inflationary explosion started in December 1989, prompted by a new run toward foreign currency as the government announced the Plan Bonex. This new burst of hyperinflation was milder and shorter than previous ones, and again it was brought down very quickly, this time through a program that succeeded in stabilizing the exchange rate (which was at the time flexible). Inflation, however, continued at rates far above international levels (around 10% per month) for almost a year, and then it experienced a new increase that was even shorter and milder. Since then inflation has been receding, and recently has been hovering around 1.5% per month for eighteen months, a major achievement.

The new pattern of converging cycles has been induced by a continuous stabilization effort, where each setback (or rekindling of inflation) was fought with a new, more drastic program. The basic reforms started already in the early stages of the Menem administration in 1989 with the launching of the BB Plan. The new government passed legislation authorizing the sale of public enterprises, suspension of most subsidies, limitations on central bank credit to the public sector, and a major tax reform that broadened the base of the value-added tax. The Plan Bonex, of December 1989, tried to provide a permanent solution to the domestic debt problem that had undermined so many stabilization efforts in the past, by enacting a forced conversion of time deposits and short-term debt into long-term dollar-indexed bonds. In the course of 1990 the government made great progress with the actual implementation of its privatization program. The Decree 435 stabilization attempt went much further on the fiscal side than any previous program. The government was finally confronting the industrial promotion law, which provided generous subsidies and numerous tax loopholes without clearly motivating industrial activities, and also announced important changes in tax administration and public sector reform. Finally, the convertibility program went further than the others in imposing fiscal discipline, while undertaking numerous measures to improve enforcement in tax payments.

During these three years, in spite of changes in economic teams, the movement has been in just one direction: more fiscal adjustment, through privatization of public sector enterprises; rationalization of public sector expenditures; and better enforcement on tax collection (the latter has recently been accompanied by simplification and rationalization of the tax system). Not once during these years has there been an important reversal in policies. In addition, unlike the period in which the cycles were becoming more explosive, the authorities have refrained from actively using price and wage controls as a way to bring down inflation, and have instead stressed the importance of getting the fundamentals in place.

Although the Menem administration acted relentlessly on all the relevant fronts, the basic level of inflation in 1990 was still around 13–15% per month. There are three basic reasons for the sluggish response of inflation. First, the design and implementation of reforms takes time, especially when they involve privatization. Since the reforms must reach a critical mass before they can bring about a basic change in expectations, the effect on inflation is necessarily delayed. Second, the policymakers themselves do not know at the outset what precisely is required in order to generate the required critical mass. Argentina's experience shows clearly that the evolution of the reforms involved a process of trial and error—whenever there was a resurgence of inflation, the government added another dose of reforms. This learning process is inevitably time-consuming. The process is further complicated by the parallel program of structural reforms, which are intended to move the country quickly toward a market economy.

The third reason for the slow convergence of inflation relates to nominal aspects. In the classical hyperinflations the price level was stabilized by a simultaneous change in the fiscal regime and the exchange rate regime; specifically, all the classical cases were stopped by fixing the exchange rate. This simultaneity cannot be achieved in the new hyperinflations, because the commitments on the fiscal and monetary fronts have to be backed by implementation of fundamental reforms that involve a time-consuming process; an early use of a fixed exchange rate policy, before reforms reach a critical mass, will not be effective. In the meantime money is used as a nominal anchor. However, experience in the high-inflation economies in Latin America shows that, while tight money was effective in blocking hyperinflationary outbursts, it has not been effective in bringing down inflation to single-digit levels.

Peru: Balancing the Budget Was Not Enough

The very slow convergence of inflation in Peru may appear puzzling because of the impressive structural reforms that have been carried out in that country, and especially because of its persistent adherence to a balanced budget on a cash basis. Yet the fiscal position in Peru remains in a fragile state. This is especially the case with regard to taxation, which has not regained the levels of the pre-Garcia years. The restoration of the tax base to levels that are consistent with a long-term fiscal balance requires not only reforms but also the allocation of appropriate manpower for their implementation.

It has been noted that the stabilization program in Peru involved periods in which the nominal exchange rate was stable (even appreciating slightly), as for example in July–September 1991 and December 1991–March 1992, yet inflation did not respond to this development. This is because the path of the exchange rate was variable, with the periods of stability being short. Thus on average the monthly rate of devaluation in 1991 was 6%, with inflation being 7.5%.

A special factor that hinders disinflation in Peru is the high degree of dollarization, which developed over the long inflationary period and which surprisingly has not displayed any signs of reversal during the stabilization period. This led to the paradoxical phenomenon that stopping hyperinflation did not result in an expansion in the real monetary base or M1; in fact, both of them declined as more dollars were introduced into the formal financial sector. The fact that money demand does not recover during the stabilization phase leaves the system vulnerable to a resumption of inflation, and thus slows down the convergence of inflationary expectations.

Why Was It Not Possible to Fix the Exchange Rate after the New Hyperinflations?

In contrast to the programs that stopped the classical hyperinflations, Brazil and Peru did not fix the exchange rate at the outset. Argentina fixed it in the BB Plan but had to abandon it quickly when the program proved unable to bring inflation to a halt.

The ineffectiveness of using a fixed exchange rate early on can be illustrated by the BB Plan. Table 12.8 shows that when the exchange rate was fixed in September 1989 inflation fell from the previous high rates but continued to stay at around 6% per month, with lending rates being in the range of 9–13% per month and real wages rising. While lack of credibility can explain the persistence of inflation, Dornbusch (1987) describes how fixing the exchange rate in the midst of the German hyperinflation (in February 1923) stabilized inflation immediately; there was in fact an actual deflation in March. Later devalua-

Table 12.8   **Argentina: Selected Economic Indicators**

	Monthly Percentage Rates			
	Inflation	Devaluation	Lending Rate	Real Wages (1985 = 100)
BB Plan				
1989.08	38.9	15.4	17.9	69
1989.09	9.4	0.0	11.3	67
1989.10	5.6	0.0	9.0	69
1989.11	6.5	0.0	12.8	89
1989.12	40.1	70.4	32.9	94
Convertability Plan				
1991.01	7.7	28.8	18.5	79
1991.02	27.0	44.6	23.0	71
1991.03	11.0	1.0	19.4	76
1991.04	5.5	3.4	5.1	74
1991.05	2.8	0.8	4.6	73
1991.06	3.1	0.7	5.0	72
1991.07	2.6	0.0	5.0	71
1991.08	1.3	0.0	4.6	70

tion was resumed as a result of large reserve losses. There is no reason to believe that the German program of February 1923 was more credible than the BB Plan, yet inflation stopped temporarily in one case but not in the other.

While fixing the exchange rate in the BB Plan did not work, it was effective when used in the convertibility plan of March 1991. In the latter case, monthly inflation came down to 3% and loan rates to 4.5% within three months, without a rise in real wages (table 12.8). All this took place after an inflation of 8% in January and 27% in February.

While it is true that the convertibility plan was accompanied by further fiscal reforms and a new law that effectively converts the central bank into a currency board, yet it is unthinkable that any announced reform could cause inflation to fall so dramatically without fixing the exchange rate. In fact, success was achieved by combining a critical mass of reforms effected during the stabilization and by fixing the exchange rate.

The success of the Argentine strategy poses a key question for Peru, a country that has been stabilizing and reforming for over two years. Are the conditions now ripe for fixing the exchange rate as a way to bring about full price stability in that country? There is some consensus that the stabilization program in Peru has primarily relied on tight money. Under this strategy inflation fell but displayed significant persistence, recently at around 4% per month.

While an exchange rate–based stabilization program is very likely to succeed in bringing inflation further down in the short term, the longer-term success of such effort is still questionable. The main difficulty is that Peru has not been able to demonstrate that the fiscal situation is sustainable. Tax revenues are still very low, conflicting with demands for basic expenditure in infrastructure and in the social sectors. In addition, the external situation continues to be blurred, without a clear way out of the debt crisis. It seems that fixing the exchange rate continues to be a very risky proposition.

12.6   Hyperinflation, Stabilization, and Growth

12.6.1   The Costs of Hyperinflation

Hyperinflation is a phase in the inflation process where even the most indexed economies cannot avoid output losses. The recessionary effects come from the disruptive effects of hyperinflation itself as well as from the desperate stabilization measures undertaken under conditions of extreme stress. Brazil embraced for many years the philosophy that indexation can enable sustained growth even under conditions of high inflation. Indeed, this strategy worked quite well in the miracle years of the sixties and seventies. Brazil's recovery of growth after the debt crisis of the early eighties was also remarkable. However, as inflation moved from the 200% plateau of 1984–87 to 700% in 1988 and 3,000% in 1990 (in annual terms), the growth of GDP came to a halt (table 12.5). Industrial production in 1991 was lower than in 1987, implying a decline in per capita terms. Since the economy was not facing severe foreign exchange constraints, which could be associated with import compression, it is reasonable to attribute the decline in output growth to the hyperinflation. Thus the classical indexed economy was no longer able to isolate the real economy from inflation. On many occasions in recent years Brazil attempted to get rid of indexation, but these efforts were frustrated by the resurgence of inflation. In a broad historical perspective Brazil traded short-term gains of growth for a possible long-term stagnation.

The fact that the hyperinflation in Brazil did not bring about a collapse of the economy can explain why the required reforms are still postponed. Thus the economy became a captive of its own inflation-mitigation technology.

In the case of Peru the outbreak of hyperinflation led to a much sharper drop in output as well as to a concomitant collapse of public sector revenues, in the classical fashion. This is the main explanation for the extreme form of regime change that took place under the Fujimori administration.

There is little doubt that the significant drop in GDP growth in Argentina with the sharp acceleration of inflation in the 1988–90 period, including the collapse of public sector finances in the second quarter of 1989, contributed to the readiness to implement the radical reforms of the Menem administration and to its success in bringing down inflation. However, the success of dealing with inflation is only one component of the resumption of growth; no less depends on the progress achieved with the structural reforms toward a market economy.

It is tempting to regard the big jump in Argentina's growth in 1991 (7% in per capita terms) as being due entirely to the effect of reforms and liberalization that took place in the past two to three years. Usually the genuine effect of reforms appears gradually over the longer term. However, one has to distinguish in this episode between the cyclical and the sustainable aspects of a stabilization cum reforms package. For example, in the case of Chile the main effects of the massive reforms of the seventies bore fruit only in the second half of the eighties. The growth that Chile experienced in the seventies was largely cyclical, being associated with the exchange rate–based stabilization of that time. It may be recalled that toward the end of the seventies Argentina implemented a similar (Tablita) policy, which was associated with a GDP growth of 7% in 1979, only to be followed by a sharp recession later on. It should be stressed, however, that the fiscal reforms, and especially the trimming of the public sector, under the Menem administration are unprecedented in Argentine history, which may make a difference between the experiences of the seventies and the nineties.

12.6.2   Real Appreciation and the Costs of Stabilization

Experience with disinflation programs shows that they involve not only the cost of a slowdown of GDP growth, which is discussed in section 12.6.1, but also a worsening of conditions in the tradables sector as a result of a tendency for the real exchange rate to appreciate. This is also a standard result in models of flexible exchange rate systems with capital mobility, where disinflation involves tight monetary policies. Similar tendencies are likely to appear in disinflation programs that adopt the fixed exchange rate system as part of the policy package, but in this case the program may generate a temporary boom of the type described in the previous section. In any case, it is hard to avoid the unfavorable effect of disinflation on the tradables sector, and consequently on the resumption of export-led growth.

Since the underlying cause of the real appreciation in any of these regimes results from rigidities in domestic wages or prices, one might expect that the elimination of inflation inertia through hyperinflation will minimize the real appreciation. However, in the new hyperinflations the major cause of wage and price rigidity is expectational rather than inertial. Consequently, the issue of real appreciation may appear in even stronger force than in ordinary tight-money policies.

Figure 12.5 shows the tendency for real appreciation that accompanied the periods of tight-money disinflation in the three countries. Usually this is also reflected in an increase in our measure of real interest rates. In Argentina the tendency for real appreciation was smoothed, but not eliminated, by the transition to the convertibility plan. In Peru the process goes on from the beginning of the stabilization. Since the real appreciation is driven by capital inflows (part of which is repatriation of flight capital), it does not represent currently a balance-of-payments problem, but it creates a "Dutch disease" problem for the sector of tradables. Brazil, which relaxed its tight-money policy after a short

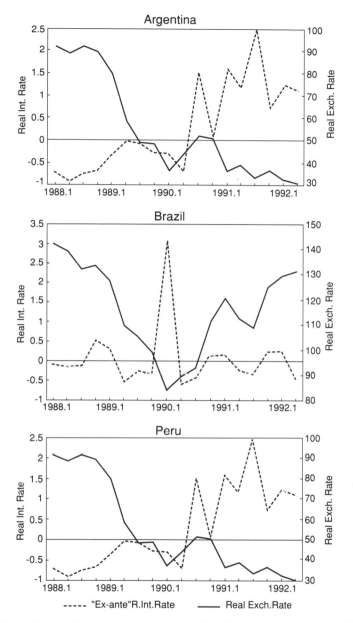

Fig. 12.5 **"Ex ante" rate interest versus real exchange rate: Argentina; Brazil; Peru**

Note: Nominal interest rates were deflated using next quarter's inflation.

while, enabled its real exchange rate to regain its values of ten years ago but at the cost of resumption of inflation. This shows that countries struggling with the pressures of possible renewal of hyperinflation must confront the trade-off between this danger and the damage caused to the tradables sector as a result of real appreciation.

12.7 Summary

Are all hyperinflations alike? Most of the existing wisdom regarding the origins and the ends of hyperinflations is based on Sargent's (1982) influential paper. In his view the origins of hyperinflations are clear, extremely large budget deficits financed by money creation (seigniorage), and so are the policies that are required to stop them, a commitment to a new regime in which the budget is balanced and the central bank is restrained from financing the treasury. Once a decisive stabilization was in place, hyperinflation was stopped in its tracks. Sargent's paper is based on a consistent pattern observed in the European hyperinflations of the 1920s. This pattern was repeated in the Bolivian hyperinflation of the mideighties.

This paper examines the recent hyperinflations in Argentina, Brazil, and Peru. It is argued that, in contrast to the European hyperinflations, the more recent ones were not caused by a sudden, large increase in the budget deficit and seigniorage. Instead, they were the final stage of a long process of high and increasing rates of inflation that lasted for around two decades. For a while it looked as if high inflation could be a stable process. In the end, however, it became clear that hyperinflation was all but unavoidable.

It is also argued that the process of restoring price stability in the new episodes appears to be longer and more costly than suggested by Sargent. Despite decisive stabilization programs, none of these countries was able to stop hyperinflation in its tracks. Instead inflation pulled back to high levels (monthly rates oscillated between 4 and 8%). The reason for the difference is that it is more difficult and costly to demonstrate a regime change in countries that have a tradition of high inflation. Balancing the budget for a year or two is not enough to convince the public that the economy is departing from a long history of high inflation.

An implication of our analysis is that the costs of high inflation might become apparent only at a very late stage of the process. These episodes helped to dispel the myth that it is possible to maintain a high and stable rate of inflation on a long-term basis, without harmful effects on growth.

Appendix

Table 12A.1   **Monthly Inflation**

Month		Austria	Germany	Hungary	Poland	Month		Bolivia
1920	01	N.A.	56.91	N.A.	N.A.	1983	01	−0.87
	02	N.A.	34.13	N.A.	N.A.		02	10.53
	03	N.A.	1.18	N.A.	N.A.		03	11.90
	04	N.A.	−8.19	N.A.	N.A.		04	8.51
	05	N.A.	−3.82	N.A.	N.A.		05	9.80
	06	N.A.	−8.61	N.A.	N.A.		06	3.57
	07	N.A.	−0.72	N.A.	N.A.		07	10.34
	08	N.A.	5.84	N.A.	N.A.		08	25.00
	09	N.A.	3.45	N.A.	N.A.		09	17.50
	10	N.A.	−2.00	N.A.	N.A.		10	11.70
	11	N.A.	2.72	N.A.	N.A.		11	24.76
	12	N.A.	−4.64	N.A.	N.A.		12	25.19
1921	01	N.A.	0.00	N.A.	N.A.	1984	01	9.76
	02	41.00	−4.17	N.A.	26.60		02	22.78
	03	−13.48	−2.90	N.A.	3.31		03	21.27
	04	−4.92	−0.75	N.A.	−3.56		04	**62.69**
	05	4.31	−1.50	N.A.	2.93		05	47.02
	06	23.97	4.58	N.A.	8.43		06	4.06
	07	−4.67	4.38	N.A.	29.00		07	5.25
	08	16.78	34.27	28.57	16.31		08	14.96
	09	28.74	7.81	15.74	13.38		09	37.30
	10	**54.88**	18.84	8.00	8.86		10	**59.21**
	11	**69.97**	39.02	22.96	−10.61		11	31.52
	12	**66.43**	2.05	−0.60	−2.62		12	**60.90**
1922	01	21.23	5.16	−1.82	3.83	1985	01	68.77
	02	25.04	11.72	4.94	7.11		02	**182.76**
	03	2.03	32.44	16.47	15.79		03	24.94
	04	11.12	17.13	8.59	2.23		04	11.78
	05	25.26	1.57	2.33	4.70		05	35.67
	06	**68.69**	8.82	17.27	11.52		06	**78.46**
	07	41.19	44.52	34.88	15.84		07	**66.30**
	08	**128.70**	**88.98**	22.99	33.66		08	**66.46**
	09	**81.88**	**49.48**	24.30	12.21		09	**56.51**
	10	−7.58	**97.21**	23.68	32.16		10	−1.86
	11	−4.77	**103.36**	−0.91	36.89		11	3.20
	12	−1.54	28.13	2.45	25.65		12	16.80
1923	01	0.67	**88.84**	15.27	**57.26**	1986	01	32.96
	02	1.85	**111.31**	8.57	**57.72**		02	7.95
	03	1.98	−16.94	**57.89**	15.06		03	0.07
	04	6.72	6.63	26.52	7.12		04	3.59
	05	5.26	**56.75**	12.57	6.27		05	0.97
	06	0.16	**137.27**	**53.72**	**67.18**		06	4.26
	07	−5.44	**285.80**	**97.92**	**63.17**		07	1.78
	08	−4.42	**1,162.31**	**61.71**	**72.47**		08	0.64
	09	13.20	**2,431.67**	19.78	37.92		09	2.28
	10	1.01	**29,565.27**	5.96	**274.96**		10	0.59

(continued)

Table 12A.1 (continued)

Month		Austria	Germany	Hungary	Poland	Month		Bolivia
	11	1.48	**10,139.77**	8.18	**148.14**		11	−0.11
	12	1.72	**73.55**	12.44	**109.44**		12	0.65
1924	01	5.00	−7.14	43.70	**70.18**	1987	01	2.45
	02	1.72	−0.85	**79.24**	2.59		02	1.23
	03	0.00	3.45	12.93	−1.27		03	0.70
	04	0.11	3.33	2.79	−1.21		04	1.59
	05	1.87	−1.61	6.32	N.A.		05	0.34
	06	1.98	−4.92	−2.72	N.A.		06	−0.22
	07	N.A.	−0.86	3.93	N.A.		07	−0.05
	08	N.A.	4.35	−2.29	N.A.		08	0.99
	09	N.A.	5.83	−0.24	N.A.		09	0.58
	10	N.A.	3.15	2.17	N.A.		10	2.09
	11	N.A.	−1.53	1.06	N.A.		11	−0.28
	12	N.A.	1.55	1.61	N.A.		12	0.80

Table 12.A.2 **Monthly Inflation**

Month		Argentina	Brazil	Peru
1988	01	9.18	21.16	12.76
	02	10.34	17.89	11.84
	03	14.73	18.88	22.59
	04	17.31	19.69	17.90
	05	15.59	18.58	8.51
	06	18.08	20.33	8.86
	07	25.64	20.87	30.88
	08	27.56	21.74	21.71
	09	11.68	25.16	**114.09**
	10	9.03	26.53	40.60
	11	5.73	27.70	24.40
	12	6.83	28.23	41.87
1989	01	8.93	39.07	47.34
	02	9.56	13.10	42.49
	03	17.00	5.79	41.99
	04	33.40	5.36	48.63
	05	**78.48**	13.26	28.61
	06	**114.47**	28.00	23.05
	07	**196.63**	33.87	24.58
	08	37.86	33.39	25.06
	09	9.36	34.08	26.86
	10	5.60	38.65	23.25
	11	6.52	45.48	25.84
	12	40.07	**51.47**	33.75
1990	01	**79.20**	**72.84**	29.73
	02	**61.57**	**67.52**	30.59
	03	**95.53**	**80.75**	32.63
	04	11.37	17.24	37.39

Table 12.A.2   (continued)

Month		Argentina	Brazil	Peru
	05	13.61	9.63	32.80
	06	13.90	12.75	42.52
	07	10.83	14.71	**63.28**
	08	15.34	12.86	**396.96**
	09	15.68	13.12	13.77
	10	7.69	14.04	9.61
	11	6.18	16.74	5.93
	12	4.68	18.87	23.73
1991	01	7.70	19.91	17.83
	02	26.99	21.53	9.42
	03	11.04	6.60	7.70
	04	5.51	8.61	5.84
	05	2.80	7.05	7.64
	06	3.12	11.72	9.26
	07	2.59	13.31	9.06
	08	1.30	15.49	7.24
	09	1.77	16.87	5.56
	10	1.35	23.98	3.95
	11	N.A.	25.36	3.96
	12	N.A.	23.79	3.74

References

Cagan, Phillip. 1956. The Monetary Dynamics of Hyperinflation. In *Studies in the Quantity Theory of Money,* ed. Milton Friedman, 25–117. Chicago: University of Chicago Press.

Canavese, Alfredo. 1992. Hyperinflation and Convertibility-Based Stabilization in Argentina. Instituto Di Tella. Mimeo.

Dornbusch, Rudiger. 1987. Lessons from the German Inflation Experience of the 1970s. In *Essays in Honor of Franco Modigliani,* ed. R. Dornbusch, S. Fischer, and J. Bossous. Cambridge: MIT Press.

Dornbusch, Rudiger, and Stanley Fischer. 1986. Stopping Hyperinflation Past and Present. *Weltwirtschaftliches Archiv* 122 (January): 1–47.

Kiguel, Miguel A., and Nissan Liviatan. 1988. Inflationary Rigidities and Orthodox Stabilization Policies: Lessons from Latin America. *World Bank Economic Review* (3): 273–98.

———. 1991. The Inflation Stabilization Cycles in Argentina and Brazil. In *Lesson of Economic Stabilization and Its Aftermath,* ed. M. Bruno, S. Fischer, E. Helpman, and N. Liviatan. Cambridge: MIT Press.

Lago, Ricardo. 1991. The Illusion of Pursuing Redistribution through Macropolicies: Peru's Heterodox Experience, 1985–1990. In *The Macroeconomics of Populism in Latin America,* ed. R. Dornbusch and S. Edwards. Chicago: University of Chicago Press.

Machinea, José Luis. 1990. Stabilization under the Alfonsin Government: A Frustrated Attempt. World Bank. Mimeo.

Morales, Juan Antonio. 1988. Inflation and Stabilization in Bolivia. In *Inflation Stabilization*, ed. M. Bruno, G. Di Tella, Rudiger Dornbusch, and Stanley Fischer, 307–46. Cambridge: MIT Press.

Rodriguez, Carlos. 1992. Inflation in Brazil. Centro de Estudios Macroeconomicos de Argentina, Buenos Aires. Mimeo.

Sachs, Jeffrey D. 1986. The Bolivian Hyperinflation and Stabilization. NBER Discussion Paper no. 2073. Cambridge, MA: National Bureau of Economic Research.

Sargent, Thomas J. 1982. The End of Four Big Inflation. In *Inflation: Causes and Effects*, ed. R. E. Hall. Chicago: University of Chicago Press.

Webb, Steven. 1986. Fiscal News and Inflationary Expectations in Germany after World War I. *Journal of Economic History* 46 (3): 769–94.

Werneck, Rogério F. 1991. Public Sector Adjustment to External Shocks and Domestic Pressures in Brazil. In *The Public Sector and the Latin American Crisis,* ed. Felipe Larraín and Marcelo Selowsky. San Francisco: ICS Press.

Young, John Parke. 1925. *European Currency and Finance.* Vols. 1 and 2. Washington, DC.

Zini, Alvaro A., Jr. 1992. Monetary Reform, State Interventions, and the Collor Plan. University of São Paulo. Mimeo.

Comment on Chapters 11 and 12   William R. Cline

These two papers concern the case of persistent intermediate inflation (Turkey) and the transition from chronically high inflation to hyperinflation (Argentina, Brazil, Peru, and Bolivia). My comments will focus on the latter, but there are important common themes that warrant an initial statement based on the Turkish case.

I had thought that only the Philippines qualified as an honorary Latin American country, but Anne Krueger's paper shows that Turkey must also be included in this club. All of the familiar Latin American distortions are present: inefficient import-substituting industrialization, fiscal drain from state enterprises, chronic fiscal problems more generally, the eventual frustration of the public with a failed economic model, and economic crisis as the forcing event of model change. Indeed, Turkey turns out to have preceded Latin America in structural adjustment, as it adopted trade liberalization and a slimming of the state sector in 1980, whereas Latin America did so some years later following the debt crisis.

Perhaps the principal differences are that Turkey seems to have been able to achieve faster growth (4 to 7%), avoid inertial inflation despite large devaluations and exchange rate crawl, and keep inflation below three digits despite fiscal deficits averaging some 4% of GDP. Maybe the good neighborhood helped. Overall, the political economy Krueger describes is reassuring with

William R. Cline is a senior fellow of the Institute for International Economics.

respect to the response of trade and growth to exchange rate and trade policy reform, but discouraging with respect to the political sustainability of fiscal adjustment. Her question of whether the "sectoral" (structural) reforms can persist in the face of macroeconomic instability is of great relevance to Latin America today.

Kiguel and Liviatan postulate that the phenomenon of hyperinflation in countries with chronically high inflation (H-CHI) differs from classical hyperinflation of Germany and certain other European countries in the 1920s. Hyperinflation tends to come as a further destabilization from already high inflation rather than as an abrupt break from past stability. Because high inflation reduces the demand to hold money and thus the money base as a share of GDP, the economy becomes subject to larger proportionate monetary destabilization from shocks of identical size relative to GDP. Once ignited, H-CHI is more difficult to stop than in a classical hyperinflation. The thesis has intuitive appeal; after all, it is easier to reform the youth who goes on a single binge than the chronic alcoholic. As I agree with the thesis, I will focus on qualifications and differences of interpretation.

My principal critique of the paper is that it tends to say the classical remedies have failed in situations where the real problem was that the classical remedies have not really been adequately applied. Thus, the authors argue that in Argentina the Bunge-Born program would have worked if the episode had been one of classical hyperinflation, so its failure under H-CHI was attributable to the qualitative differences between these two prototypes. I would disagree. The Bunge-Born Plan never consolidated fiscal adjustment. After an initial megaincrease in public sector prices, there was talk about a value-added tax (VAT), but the tax was not enacted for several months. The real attack on tax evasion did not come until the Cavallo Plan.

Or consider Brazil. The Kiguel-Liviatan data show a reversal of the fiscal deficit from about 5.5% of GDP (operational) in 1987–89 to a surplus of 1.3% of GDP in 1990. They conclude that there was a paradox: classical fiscal correction did not achieve the classical end to hyperinflation. But the 1990 fiscal outcome was misleading. It was attributable to temporary factors, such as a 25% tax on stock market holdings and the sharp reduction in the government's domestic interest burden resulting from the freeze of financial deposits. The public knew the freeze would be reversed in eighteen months and probably sooner, and that structural phenomena such as a utopian constitution meant the fiscal adjustment was not permanently in hand. Moreover, the data in question do not include large quasi-fiscal deficits of the financial system, namely, the expected losses on official sector lending. Thus, Kiguel and Liviatan are on questionable grounds when they call the Collor I Plan "very orthodox." Indeed, at the heart of the plan was an unorthodox asset freeze, what has been called Chicago school economics but of the Al Capone rather than the Milton Friedman variety.

What should be added is that, in the Brazilian case especially, even a convincing fiscal adjustment probably would not have been enough without the definitive end of indexation. Yes, the Collor Plan temporarily eliminated indexation, but it was back within a few months. The combination of only transitory fiscal adjustment, early release of frozen accounts in a context where the freeze itself had caused a downward shock in the demand for money, and the reappearance of indexation meant disaster for the Collor Plan. More generally, the essence of the argument about greater difficulty of stopping inflation after a hyperinflation in a chronic-inflation country must be that expectations and defense mechanisms that perpetuate inflation are much more severe in the chronically high-inflation countries. Thus dealing with indexation and other such mechanisms must be part of the solution. Moreover, as the Collor II Plan showed, the heterodox remedy of a price freeze does not serve this purpose where this instrument has been discredited by previous attempts that did not incorporate fundamental fiscal adjustment. Indeed, the very hint of a new freeze just encouraged the firms to increase prices preemptively.

In contrast to the two Collor Plans and the Bunge-Born Plan, the Cavallo Plan represents a case of successful end to hyperinflation even for a chronically high-inflation country. The reason it was successful was that its fiscal adjustment was much more substantial and permanent. This time fiscal correction was based on the VAT, which rose from about 2% of GDP to about 7%, rather than on such temporary mechanisms as forced saving and an export tax under the Austral Plan. From a high of 10% of GDP in 1983, the primary deficit turned into a surplus of 2% of GDP by 1991. Moreover, Cavallo's law of convertibility achieved the abrupt regime change that is also a required element of the classical remedy. The paper gives short shrift to the plan, perhaps because it has been too successful to fit with the theory of prolonged difficulty of stopping inflation under H-CHI, or perhaps because the authors are afraid the plan is now entering a phase that could lead to collapse.

The Kiguel-Liviatan paper also curiously omits an examination of the key issue of whether use of the exchange rate as a monetary anchor is a good idea or a bad idea in attempts to stop hyperinflation in a chronically high-inflation country. I would submit that the Argentine hyperinflation of early 1989 was exchange rate led. The authors rightly note that seigniorage increase was contemporaneous with rather than prior to hyperinflation. The leading influence was the collapse of the exchange rate under a temporary float in the face of the public's fear about the honoring of domestic government debt. With that experience, it is not surprising that the Cavallo Plan chose to lock in the exchange rate, to minimize the fear of a repetition of exchange rate–led hyperinflation. It would be nice to hear more about the optimal time to use the exchange rate anchor and the optimal time to shift back toward use of the exchange rate to preserve external balance.

The authors propose several lucid suggestions about H-CHI versus classical hyperinflation. As just one example, they note that in the classical case the driving force is a sharp increase in seigniorage, which then causes inflation to feed on itself because of the Olivera-Tanzi effect and its decimation of real tax revenue. In contrast, in H-CHI high seigniorage is at most contemporaneous rather than leading; moreover, the Olivera-Tanzi effect is much smaller. The reason, presumably, is the development of indexed tax revenue mechanisms in a climate of chronic inflation.

Other propositions about the difference between H-CHI and classical hyperinflation are less persuasive. In particular, there was little supporting evidence that hyperinflation has a lower real cost in chronically high-inflation countries. Real GDP fell by 4.5% in Argentina in 1989; what was the comparable figure in the typical European cases?

Other differences warrant further discussion. For example, is seigniorage accelerationist? Does it require a rising rate of inflation to secure a constant amount of seigniorage as a percentage of GDP, as I suspect? If so, then this is one reason why we should expect chronically high inflation eventually to transit to hyperinflation, unless the country takes action. In this regard, it is worth mentioning a growing danger in Brazil: the public simply becomes innured to high inflation, and accepts 20% monthly rates of inflation as "normal." That is surely a recipe for disaster.

I was considerably uneasy about the implication that Bolivia was a classical case of hyperinflation ended by decisive action. In particular, it seems to me that the size of the current account deficit after the correction—10% of GDP in 1986–87 according to table 12.2—was unsustainable and makes the Bolivian case essentially irrelevant for larger countries where such a deficit could not be financed. Similarly, a nominal fiscal deficit of 6.5% of GDP as Bolivia had after adjustment would be explosive in Argentina or Brazil, where an appropriate target for the nominal deficit is on the order of 0 or maybe 1% of GDP.

The Bolivian case also raises a theoretical issue. The authors indicate that hyperinflation started in Bolivia when external finance was cut off. In this regard, incidentally, there seem to be some inconsistencies. The paper says that resource transfers turned to −5.6% of GDP, but table 12.2 states that the current account was not in surplus but was in deficit by about 4% of GDP in 1982–84. The two are inconsistent unless factor payments abroad reached 10% of GDP, which seems highly implausible.

The theoretical issue that warrants a further look, however, is the difference between hyperinflation caused by events that shock the exchange rate and that which could occur even in a closed economy. In particular, if massive seigniorage is used by the government to make domestic purchases, then Keynesian excess demand inflation is no puzzle. However, if the large seigniorage is used to purchase dollars from exporters for the purpose of servicing external debt, then the inflation that results does not stem from increased demand for domestic production, but instead from an expectational price shock in an environment where the public watches the exchange rate as an indication of future inflation.

It would be nice to hear more about the problem of high real interest rates in the posthyperinflation phase for the chronically high-inflation countries. It seems to me that one should be concerned about dynamic instability when real interest rates are 20% or more, because these rates inevitably mean that the domestic debt will balloon as a fraction of GDP, in turn widening the risk premium because of the rational expectation that the government must default on domestic obligations. This is another reason to doubt that Bolivia has consolidated its posthyperinflation adjustment.

Finally, it would have been nice if the authors could have mentioned more about the new problem of large capital inflows, and especially the inflationary consequences in an environment where hyperinflation has reduced the country's monetary base to a small fraction of GDP. It would also have been useful to address the related problem of bimetallism, whereby holdings of dollars should probably be added to the money base to get a clearer picture of monetization.

Overall, nonetheless, the authors are to be commended for an incisive paper.

Comment on Chapters 11 and 12   Holger C. Wolf

Comment on Chapter 11

Anne Krueger's paper provides an excellent overview of the evolution of the Turkish economy during the last decade. Not being an expert on Turkey, let me limit my comments to reemphasizing two political arguments submerged in the paper that not only apply to traditional stabilization episodes but are also highly relevant to the east European transitions.

First, liberalization, like stabilization, is facilitated by major economic crisis placing the competing options in sharp contrast. Indeed, as Aaron Tornell pointed out (chap. 2 in this volume), such upheavals may in some cases be necessary to bring about the political consensus for decisive action.

Second, even if liberalization is ex ante opposed by significant parts of the population, it may very well be ex post politically stable. Part of the explanation might be found in games played between various rent-seeking groups. Krueger suggests a second, less calculating channel: moving from the apparent stability of interventionism to the apparent anarchy of markets requires a leap of faith. Again, economic crisis reducing the appeal of the status quo may facilitate the leap.

Holger C. Wolf is assistant professor of economics and international business at New York University's Stern School of Business and a faculty research fellow of the National Bureau of Economic Research.

Comment on Chapter 12

In their intriguing paper, Miguel Kiguel and Nissan Liviatan argue against the notion of a general model of hyperinflation. Rather, they contend, the recent hyperinflations in Argentina and Brazil significantly differ from the classic interwar episodes in Europe. The difference lies in the origin of the inflation (a one-time increase in the deficit during the 1920s versus a long, drawn-out process in Latin America), in the process itself (extreme instability in Europe, a semblance of government control in Argentina and Brazil), and in the stabilization (instantaneous stability in Europe, lingering inflation in Latin America).

While the dynamics of the two groups of hyperinflations certainly differed, an alternative continuous classification scheme encompassing both groups of inflations as extreme cases may yield insights not captured by the authors' dichotomization. The measuring rod, as identified by Kiguel and Liviatan, is the degree of institutional adjustment to high inflation at the onset of inflation. Four adjustments are of particular relevance here: first, the degree of indexation of prices, determining the pass-through speed of shocks; second, the extent to which wages are automatically indexed to prices, determining the viru- provide hedges against inflation, determining the scope for seigniorage extraction lence of the wage-price spiral; third, the extent to which financial markets tion; fourth, the degree to which taxes are indexed to prices, determining the sensitivity of the deficit to inflation.

Looking in this light at the classical episodes, institutions (formed under the gold standard) were ill-equipped to deal with the emergence of inflation. German courts prohibited price increases on inventory goods as "price-gouging" until the early 1920s. Cost of living indices were only slowly developed as a response to the inflation. Financial institutions offered no more than rudimentary inflation hedges. Taxes remained nonindexed until the summer of 1923, rendering the deficit highly responsive to the inflation process.

In contrast, the latest editions of the Latin American hyperinflations originated in economies already characterized by widespread indexation of prices and wages and—in the case of Brazil—a highly sophisticated financial system. The authors contend that the different starting point suffices to classify the Latin cases as qualitatively different from the European ones. Alternatively, one might endogenize the difference as a function of the inflation history. Altering institutions entails significant costs. As inflation accelerates, these costs are eventually outweighed by the benefits of inflation-proof institutions, prompting wrenching changes in the financial system, in wages, and in price setting. By the end of the German hyperinflation, exchange rate indexing, complete wage indexation, dollarization and tax indexation—features well known from the Latin American inflations—were pervasive. In like vein, the very existence of these institutions in Argentina and Brazil reflects past inflationary excesses.

This dynamic view suggests that equal shocks will have very different consequences depending on the past inflationary history of the country. A second hyperinflation in Germany would have followed a quite different path, a path probably not dissimilar to the recent Latin hyperinflations. The point, incidentally, is not new: in the aftermath of the interwar inflations Ludwig von Mises stressed that any attempt of the government to once more extract seigniorage revenue was doomed to failure, as inflation-proof institutions would immediately spring back into action. This institutional view also suggests that the common focus on the size of the fiscal shock is a misleading indicator of the likely evolution of the inflation. The time integral of monetized deficits, proxying the degree of institutional adjustment, may provide a more reliable measure.

Let me conclude with a factual quibble. The authors present a fashionable yet arguably somewhat streamlined version of the origin and emergence of the classical hyperinflation episodes. In the case of Germany, under an alternative view the period of monetary instability commenced with the abandonment of gold convertibility in 1914, gathered strength throughout the war years during which the inflationary consequences of monetized deficits were held in check by extensive price controls, and exploded as these controls were lifted between 1918 and 1920 and as institutions began to adjust. Viewed in this vein as a drawn-out nine-year process rather than a straight-line explosion caused by a single factor (reparations), the German episode no longer looks that different from the Latin cases. It also bears pointing out that, while the German inflation indeed came to a sudden stop in 1923, several previous stabilization efforts failed after initial signs of success, not unlike the repeated failed stabilizations in Argentina and Brazil.

Contributors

Gil Bufman
12 Hashomron Street
Ramat-Hasharon 47203
Israel

Mauricio Cárdenas
Fedesarrollo
Calle 78 No. 9–91
Apartoda Aereo 75054
Bogotá, Colombia

Eliana Cardoso
Fletcher School of Law and Diplomacy
Tufts University
Medford, MA 02155

William R. Cline
Institute for International Economics
11 DuPont Circle, NW
Washington, DC 20036

José De Gregorio
International Monetary Fund
700 19th Street, NW
Washington, DC 20431

Rudiger Dornbusch
Department of Economics
Room E52–357
MIT
Cambridge, MA 02139

Sebastian Edwards
University of California
405 Hilgard Avenue
Los Angeles, CA 90024

Arturo M. Fernández
Rector, ITAM
Rio Hondo No. 1
Mexico, DF, 01000
Mexico

Kenneth A. Froot
Graduate School of Business
Morgan 391, Harvard University
Soldiers Field
Boston, MA 02163

Jonathan Gruber
Department of Economics
MIT
Cambridge, MA 02139

Arnold C. Harberger
Department of Economics
University of California
405 Hilgard Avenue
Los Angeles, CA 90024–1477

Miguel A. Kiguel
World Bank
Room S9–039
1818 H Street, NW
Washington, DC 20433

Anne O. Krueger
Department of Economics
Stanford University
Stanford, CA 94305

Raúl Labán
Ministry of Finance
Teatinos 120, Piso 12
Santiago, Chile

Felipe Larraín
Instituto de Economia
Pontificia Universidad Católica de Chile
Vincuna Mackenna 4860
Santiago, Chile

Leonardo Leiderman
Department of Economics
Tel Aviv University
Rammat Aviv 69978
Israel

Nissan Liviatan
Economics Department
Hebrew University
Mt. Scopus
Jerusalem, 91905
Israel

Ricardo Paes de Barros
Department of Economics
P.O. Box 1987 Yale Station
Yale University
New Haven, CT 06520–1987

Rubens Ricupero
Ambassador E. and P.
Brazilian Embassy
3006 Massachusetts Avenue, NW
Washington, DC 20008

Miguel A. Savastano
International Monetary Fund
700 19th Street, NW
Washington, DC 20431

Federico A. Sturzenegger
Department of Economics
University of California
405 Hilgard Avenue
Los Angeles, CA 90024–1477

Aaron Tornell
Littauer Center
Department of Economics
Harvard University
Cambridge, MA 02138

Jacques Trigo-Loubière
Interamerican Development Bank
1300 New York Avenue, NW
Washington, DC 20577

Andre Urani
c/o IPEA
Av. Presidente Antonio Carlos 51
20020 Rio de Janeiro
Brazil

Miguel Urrutia
Fedesarrollo
Callo 78 No. 9–91
Apartoda Aereo 75054
Bogotá, Colombia

Andrés Velasco
Department of Economics
New York University
269 Mercer Street, 7th floor
New York, NY 10003

John Williamson
Institute for International Economics
11 Dupont Circle, NW
Washington, DC 20036

Holger C. Wolf
Management Education Center
New York University
44 W. 44th Street, Suite 7–78
New York, NY 10012

Author Index

Subject Index